God and the EU

The current political, economic, and financial crises facing the EU reveal a deeper cultural, indeed spiritual, malaise – a crisis in 'the soul of Europe'. Many observers are concluding that the EU cannot be restored to health without a new appreciation of the contribution of religion to its past and future, and especially that of its hugely important but widely neglected Christian heritage, which is alive today even amidst advancing European secularization.

God and the EU offers a fresh, constructive, and critical understanding of Christian contributions to the origin and development of the EU from a variety of theological, national, and political perspectives. It explains the Christian origins of the EU; documents the various ways in which it has been both affirmed and critiqued from diverse theological perspectives; offers expert, theologically informed assessments of four illustrative policy areas of the EU (religion, finance, environment, science); and also reports on the place of religion in the EU, including how religious freedom is framed and how contemporary religious actors relate to EU institutions and vice versa.

This book fills a major gap in the current debate about the future of the European project and will be of interest to students and scholars of religion, politics, and European studies.

Jonathan Chaplin is Director of the Kirby Laing Institute for Christian Ethics, Cambridge and member of the Divinity faculty, Cambridge University, UK.

Gary Wilton is Programme Director of Faith and International Affairs, Wilton Park-Executive Agency of FCO, and former Archbishop of Canterbury's Representative to the European Union.

Routledge Studies in Religion and Politics
Edited by Jeffrey Haynes, London Metropolitan University, UK

This series aims to publish high quality works on the topic of the resurgence of political forms of religion in both national and international contexts. This trend has been especially noticeable in the post-cold war era (that is, since the late 1980s). It has affected all the 'world religions' (including, Buddhism, Christianity, Hinduism, Islam, and Judaism) in various parts of the world (such as, the Americas, Europe, the Middle East and North Africa, South and Southeast Asia, and sub-Saharan Africa).

The series welcomes books that use a variety of approaches to the subject, drawing on scholarship from political science, international relations, security studies, and contemporary history.

Books in the series explore these religions, regions and topics both within and beyond the conventional domain of 'church-state' relations to include the impact of religion on politics, conflict and development, including the late Samuel Huntington's controversial – yet influential – thesis about 'clashing civilisations'.

In sum, the overall purpose of the book series is to provide a comprehensive survey of what is currently happening in relation to the interaction of religion and politics, both domestically and internationally, in relation to a variety of issues.

Politics and the Religious Imagination
Edited by John Dyck, Paul Rowe and Jens Zimmermann

Christianity and Party Politics
Keeping the faith
Martin H. M. Steven

Religion, Politics and International Relations
Selected essays
Jeffrey Haynes

Religion and Democracy
A worldwide comparison
Carsten Anckar

Religious Actors in the Public Sphere
Means, objects and effects
Edited by Jeffrey Haynes and Anja Hennig

Politics and Religion in the United Kingdom
Steve Bruce

Politics, Religion and Gender
Framing and regulating the veil
Edited by Sigelinde Rosenberger and Birgit Sauer

Representing Religion in the European Union
Does God matter?
Edited by Lucian N. Leustean

An Introduction to Religion and Politics
Theory and practice
Jonathan Fox

Religion in International Relations Theory
Concepts, tools, debates
Johnathan Fox and Nukhet Sandal

Religion in the Context of Globalization
Essays on concept, form, and political implication
Peter Beyer

Religion and the Realist Tradition
From political theology to International Relations theory and back
Jodok Troy

Cosmopolitanism, Religion and the Public Sphere
Maria Rovisco and Sebastian Kim

Religion, Identity and Human Security
Giorgio Shani

Christians and the Middle East Conflict
Edited by John Rowe, John Dyck and Jens Zimmerman

Conservative Religious Politics in Russia and the United States
Dreaming of a Christian nation
John Anderson

European Culture Wars and the Italian Case
Which side are you on?
Luca Ozzano and Alberta Giorgi

God and the EU
Faith in the European project
Jonathan Chaplin and Gary Wilton

Religious NGOs in International Relations
The construction of 'the religious' and 'the secular'
Karsten Lehmann

God and the EU
Faith in the European project

Edited by
Jonathan Chaplin and Gary Wilton

LONDON AND NEW YORK

First published 2016
by Routledge
2 Park Square, Milton Park, Abingdon, Oxon OX14 4RN

and by Routledge
711 Third Avenue, New York, NY 10017

Routledge is an imprint of the Taylor & Francis Group, an informa business

© 2016 selection and editorial material, Jonathan Chaplin and Gary Wilton; individual chapters, the contributors

The right of Jonathan Chaplin and Gary Wilton to be identified as author of the editorial material, and of the individual authors as authors of their contributions, has been asserted by them in accordance with sections 77 and 78 of the Copyright, Designs and Patents Act 1988.

All rights reserved. No part of this book may be reprinted or reproduced or utilised in any form or by any electronic, mechanical, or other means, now known or hereafter invented, including photocopying and recording, or in any information storage or retrieval system, without permission in writing from the publishers.

Trademark notice: Product or corporate names may be trademarks or registered trademarks, and are used only for identification and explanation without intent to infringe.

British Library Cataloguing in Publication Data
A catalogue record for this book is available from the British Library

Library of Congress Cataloging in Publication Data
Names: Chaplin, Jonathan, editor.
  Title: God and the EU : faith in the European project / edited by Jonathan
Chaplin and Gary Wilton.
Other titles: God and the European Union
  Description: 1 [edition]. | New York : Routledge, 2015. | Series: Routledge studies in religion and politics | Includes bibliographical references and index.
  Identifiers: LCCN 2015028350|
  Subjects: LCSH: Christianity–European Union countries.
  Classification: LCC BR735 .G63 2015 | DDC 322/.1094–dc23
  LC record available at http://lccn.loc.gov/2015028350

ISBN: 978-1-138-90863-5 (hbk)
ISBN: 978-1-315-69431-3 (ebk)

Typeset in Times New Roman
by Taylor & Francis Books

Contents

List of tables ix
Acknowledgments x
List of contributors xi
Preface by Rowan Williams xv

Introduction 1
JONATHAN CHAPLIN AND GARY WILTON

PART 1
The EU: Christian inspirations, past and present 11

1 Christianity at the founding: the legacy of Robert Schuman 13
GARY WILTON

2 European integration: a Catholic perspective 33
JOHN LOUGHLIN

3 The EU: Protestant contributions, then and now 50
SANDER LUITWIELER

4 New worlds and new churches: the Orthodox Church(es) and the European Union 70
PETER PETKOFF

5 The German social market economy: its theological justification and role in European integration 89
WERNER LACHMANN

6 Market-state or commonwealth?: Europe's Christian heritage and the future of the European polity 109
ADRIAN PABST

7	European Union, identity, and place JOSHUA HORDERN	129

PART 2
Religion and the policies of the EU 149

8	European religious freedom and the EU THOMAS SCHIRRMACHER AND JONATHAN CHAPLIN	151
9	The representation of religion in the European Union LUCIAN N. LEUSTEAN	175
10	God and the Constitution GUY MILTON	191
11	Christian economic ethics and the euro: which way to go? JOHAN GRAAFLAND	208
12	The greening of the EU? A Christian assessment of the EU's environmental policies for biodiversity and nature JANICE WEATHERLEY-SINGH, TIAGO BRANCO AND MARCIAL FELGUEIRAS	230
13	A soul for European science: exploring the new renaissance in the European Research Area DIANA JANE BEECH	251
14	Conclusion: Christianity and the 'souls' of Europe JONATHAN CHAPLIN	268
	Index	277

List of tables

11.1 Economic developments within the eurozone 212
11.2 OCA criteria for a common currency union 217
11.3 Development unemployment rate: January 2010 – January 2014
   (in per cent) 222

Acknowledgments

Lucas G. Freire, who was Lecturer in International Relations at the University of Exeter and Research Associate of the Kirby Laing Institute for Christian Ethics (KLICE) while this book was being compiled, provided excellent research and editorial assistance on the book. David White, former Director of Trade at the European Commission, offered valuable support and advice for the project since its inception at a seminar for EU professionals held at Holy Trinity Pro-Cathedral, Brussels. We are grateful to The Kirby Laing Foundation for their support of Jonathan Chaplin as Director of KLICE during the preparation of the book.

Contributors

Diana Jane Beech is a Research Associate at the Von Hügel Institute (VHI) and a former Research Associate at the Faraday Institute for Science and Religion, both based at St. Edmund's College, Cambridge. She is an active member of the Euraxess 'Voice of the Researchers' network, representing researchers at the EU level. She is also a co-founder of the UACES-funded collaborative research network dedicated to exploring the governance of the European Research Area.

Tiago Branco is a member of the board of A Rocha Portugal and coordinator of the Alvor Campaign. He has a PhD in photophysics and photochemistry applied to environmental chemistry and previously studied theology at a Baptist Seminary.

Jonathan Chaplin is Director of the Kirby Laing Institute for Christian Ethics based in Cambridge, and a member of the Cambridge Divinity Faculty. He is former Visiting Lecturer, VU Universiteit, Amsterdam and Associate Professor of Political Theory, Institute for Christian Studies, Toronto, where he also held the Dooyeweerd Chair of Social and Political Philosophy. He is author, *Herman Dooyweeerd: Christian Philosopher of State and Civil Society* (University of Notre Dame, 2011) and co-editor, *God and Global Order: the Power of Religion in American Foreign Policy* (Baylor University Press, 2010).

Marcial Felgueiras has served as Operations Director for A Rocha Portugal since 2000. He has a Master's Degree in Agricultural Engineering and lectures in Portuguese churches on theology and environmental issues.

Johan Graafland is Professor of Economics, Business and Ethics, Tilburg University. He specializes in economic ethics, philosophy of economics, corporate social responsibility (CSR) and the relationship between religion and economics and business. During 2010–2013 he was leader of econometric research in the FP7 Impact project of the European Union (www.csr-impact.eu/). He has published many articles in the field of economic ethics and CSR. His books include *Economic Ethics and the Market* (Routledge, 2007) and *The Market, Happiness and Solidarity* (Routledge, xii *List of contributors*

2010). He has served on the advisory boards of several organizations, including The Dutch Council of Churches, Brabants Zeeuwse Werkgeversvereniging (a Dutch employers' organization), Foundation of Christian Philosophy and ChristenUnie (a Dutch political party).

Joshua Hordern is Associate Professor of Christian Ethics, Fellow of Harris Manchester College and Lecturer in Theology, Jesus College, Oxford. He is author, *Political Affections: Civic Participation and Moral Theology* (Oxford University Press, 2013) and *One Nation But Two Cities: Christianity and the Conservative Party* (Bible Society/KLICE, 2010). He has published articles in *Studies in Christian Ethics* and *Clinical Ethics*. In the past he has served as an elected local politician and he now leads the Oxford Healthcare Values Partnership (www.healthcarevalues.ox.ac.uk).

Werner Lachmann was until 2006 Professor of Economic Policy and Development Economics at the Faculty of Economics and the Social Sciences, Friedrich-Alexander-University Erlangen-Nürnberg. He is Chair of the Society for the Promotion of Economics and Ethics (Gesellschaft zur Förderung von Wirtschaftswissenschaften und Ethik) and was until 2014 Vice President of Christliches Jugenddorfwerk Deutschlands e.V. He has held Visiting Professorships at 12 universities around the world. He is author of books on economic ethics, economic policy and Christian economics, and seven economics textbooks, one of which has been translated into Russian. He is editor of the series *Marktwirtschaft und Ethik* (*Market Economy and Ethics*).

Lucian N. Leustean is Reader in Politics and International Relations, Aston University, Birmingham, United Kingdom. He is author of *The Ecumenical Movement and the Making of the European Community* (Oxford University Press, 2014), editor of *Representing Religion in the European Union: Does God Matter?* (Routledge, 2012) and *Eastern Christianity and Politics in the Twenty-first Century* (Routledge, 2014) and co-editor of *Religion, Politics and Law in the European Union* (Routledge, 2010).

John Loughlin is a Fellow of Blackfriars Hall, Oxford. Previously, he was Director of the Von Hügel Institute and is Emeritus Fellow, St. Edmund's College, Cambridge, and Emeritus Professor of Politics, Cardiff University. He has advised the UK government, the Welsh and Northern Ireland Assemblies, the French Senate and the EU's Committee of the Regions, and served as expert for Council of Europe and UN-Habitat. He is author, *Subnational Government: the French Experience* (Palgrave, 2007), co-editor, *The Routledge Handbook of Regionalism and Federalism* (Routledge, 2013), *The Oxford Handbook of Subnational Democracy in Europe* (Oxford University Press, 2010) and *La décentralisation dans les Etats de l'Union Européenne* (Documentation Française, 2003).

List of contributors xiii

Sander Luitwieler is Lecturer in Public Administration, Leiden University and Research Fellow, Evangelical Theological Faculty, Leuven. Formerly he worked for the Research Institute of the Dutch political party Christian Union and for the Christian Political Foundation for Europe. He has a PhD in European Union politics from Erasmus University Rotterdam, the dissertation for which was published as *The Black Box of the Nice Treaty Negotiations: The Influence of the Dutch Cabinet* (Erasmus University Rotterdam, 2009). He is author of *A Community of Peoples: Europe's Values and Public Justice in the EU* (Christian Political Foundation for Europe, 2014).

Guy Milton has worked in the General Secretariat of the Council of the European Union since 1995. He has held a range of posts, specialising in foreign policy and institutional issues. He was a member of the secretariat to the Convention and the Intergovernmental Conferences that drew up the European Constitution and the Lisbon Treaty, and was Head of Unit for relations between the Council and European Parliament for six years. In 2015 he took up the post of Head of Media Relations. Before joining the Council Secretariat, he spent several years as a member of the UK diplomatic service. He is author of *The European Constitution* (John Harper Publishing, 2005).

Adrian Pabst is Senior Lecturer in Politics in the School of Politics and International Relations at the University of Kent and Visiting Professor at the *Institut d'Etudes Politiques de Lille* (Science Po). He is author of *Metaphysics: The Creation of Hierarchy* (Eerdmans, 2012), co-editor of *Blue Labour: Forging a New Politics* (I.B. Tauris, 2015) and editor of *The Crisis of Global Capitalism: Pope Benedict XVI's social encyclical and the future of political economy* (Wipf & Stock, 2011). He is currently co-writing, with John Milbank, *The Politics of Virtue: Post-Liberalism and the Human Future* (Rowman & Littlefield International, 2016).

Peter Petkoff is Lecturer at the Law School, University of Brunel, London and Managing Editor of the *Oxford Journal of Law and Religion*. He is Research Fellow of Regent's Park College, Oxford, where he also serves as Director of the Law, Religion and International Relations Programme of the Centre for Christianity and Culture.

Thomas Schirrmacher is Chair of the Theological Commission of the World Evangelical Alliance (WEA) and Director of WEA's International Institute for Religious Freedom. He is Professor of Sociology of Religion at State University of the West (Timisoara, Romania) and Distinguished Professor of Global Ethics and International Development, William Carey University in Shillong (Meghalaya, India). He also serves as President of the Martin Bucer European Theological Seminary and Research Institutes and as President of the International Council of the International Society for Human Rights.

Janice Weatherley-Singh is former Conservation Policy and Programmes Manager for A Rocha International. She has worked on European Union biodiversity policy for a number of organisations since 2003, including IUCN (International Union for the Conservation of Nature). She has a Master's Degree in Environmental Policy.

Gary Wilton is the incumbent of All Saints, Ecclesall and Programme Director, Faith and International Affairs, Wilton Park-Executive Agency of FCO. From 2008 to 2013 he was the Archbishop of Canterbury's Representative to the European Union and Canon Residentiary of the Pro-Cathedral of Holy Trinity Brussels. He is an Associate Research Fellow of Katholieke Universiteit, Leuven (KUL) and Fellow of the University of Gloucestershire. He is a former Head of Postgraduate Studies in Theology and Religious Studies, University of York St John.

Preface

It hardly needs saying that this book is a timely one: confusion, knee-jerk responses, badly focused resentments, cynicism and boredom – all of these shape far too much of the current discourse in the UK about Europe, and this does not augur well for future decision-making. What these essays do is not only to set out a good deal of history, explaining the diverse models of state and society that shaped the European project, but also to sketch possible futures. It is tempting to say that 'Europe' has been its own worst enemy in the last couple of decades. The Union has failed to articulate a clear moral and political vision for itself (and thus has failed to clarify its role in global politics); it has havered and dithered about its Christian heritage out of misplaced anxieties over religious exclusivism; and it has allowed itself to be defined in the popular imagination by the mobility of working populations and a tunnel-vision legal culture. If 'Europe' means to a lot of British people only a mixture of migrant workforces and incomprehensible bureaucracy (both of these the subject of any amount of paranoid myth), it is no wonder that it commands limited loyalty.

But as so many of these essays make perfectly plain, if the Union did not exist it would have to be invented. The vision behind the EU is the intensely moral conviction that naked national competition, impregnable borders, clashing jurisdictions and mutually suspicious cultures have to be a thing of the past if we are interested in a justice and social well-being that is more than local. And this is not just a means of local problem-solving; it can and should be a challenge to global society and a hopeful proclamation of something beyond violent struggle and self-interest. The Union exists because of a recognition – more deeply grounded in Christian theology than most are comfortable acknowledging – that constructive interdependence is a consequence of certain convictions about human dignity and freedom. And if this is so, a just and sustainable world is one in which both global empires and endlessly quarrelling 'absolute' sovereign units are things of the past. The painful truth is that we are constantly pulled back towards these temptations: we cast our politics in terms of confrontations between global superpowers or at least superstates – East and West in the Cold War, 'the West and the rest' in our current anxieties about 'our' modernity versus Islamist reaction. Or we revert to paranoia about secure borders for our literal territory and our cultural integrity, looking for lastingly valid boundaries that we can defend against strangers.

These various myths and fictions have little to do with actual history and often just as little to do with the real detail of global politics today; but they have a deep influence on our public discourse through media (print and online) and popular perception. What this book affirms, with authority and clarity, is that commitment to 'Europe' does not mean blindness to the administrative tangles and dead-ends of law and regulation; nor does it mean indulging fantasies about a European mega-state; nor does it mean indifference to the density of real cultural difference, local traditions and identities. But for this commitment to mean more, we urgently need a recovery of genuine political theology: a recovery of ways of speaking about human society in relation to that paradigm of human community which is the mutuality of human agents at each other's service in the Body of Christ. These essays deal professionally and insightfully with a range of political, historical and economic issues, and will be valued for that; but in one way or another, they also press the question of what we now do with the foundational metaphysic of European culture. Believed or not, welcomed or not, its presence is still in evidence. For it to be a source of positive and hopeful critique in the face of the resentments and boredoms that we mentioned earlier, it needs sophisticated articulation and serious debate. This is exactly what the present volume offers and demands.

Dr Rowan Williams, Master of Magdalene College,
former Archbishop of Canterbury
Cambridge, October 2015

Introduction

Jonathan Chaplin and Gary Wilton

Aims and parameters

This book explores the historical and contemporary relevance of Christianity to the European Union (EU). Reflecting a variety of confessional, political, and national perspectives, it illustrates some of the ways in which Christian faith has impacted upon the 'European Project' in the past and some of the critical perspectives it might bring to bear upon its present and future. It might be countered immediately that since contemporary Europe, still undergoing 'religious decline', remains the 'exception' to the wider global pattern of resurgent public religion (Davie, 2002), and the EU an essentially secular political entity, such a religious perspective might seem irrelevant. Or it might even be thought that a religiously oriented reading of the EU might breach the hard-won secular canons of modern liberal democracy – running up against "the presumption that the rational secular state is menaced by the public or communal expression of religious loyalty" (Williams, 2012: 37).[1]

Yet if religion has not quite "dramatically reemerged within European politics", as Foret announces (2015: 1), it does at least, as Katzenstein puts it, continue to "lurk underneath the veneer of European secularization" (2006: 33). Much recent research has revealed the extent to which religion has profoundly shaped the origins of the EU, continues to register influence today, and is likely to continue to do so in the future (Philpott and Shah, 2006). Renewed attention has been drawn to the Catholic convictions of many of the founders of what was to become the EU, to the decisive role in European integration played by the largely Catholic postwar Christian Democratic parties (Nelsen and Guth, 2015; Kaiser, 2007) and to the consistent support of the Vatican (Chelini-Pont, 2010; Hehir, 2006). The ambivalent, often reluctant, but nonetheless significant contribution emerging from Protestantism is also being rediscovered (Nelsen and Guth, 2015; Madeley, 2010). The accession of majority-Orthodox east European member states has drawn new attention to how Orthodoxy has construed 'Europe' in the past and how it might relate itself to the EU in the future (Ramet, 2006b). Loughlin, Luitwieler, and Petkoff address these three traditions, respectively, in this volume. Beyond the role of these "confessional cultures" (Nelsen and Guth, 2015), a growing literature is emerging on the multiple avenues through which religious identities and organizations relate to increasingly complex EU institutions and processes (Foret, 2015; Leustean, 2013; Haynes and Hennig, 2011; Leustean and Madeley, 2010). Indeed in Article 17 of the Lisbon Treaty, the EU itself undertook to maintain an "open, transparent and regular dialogue" with churches and religious associations (see Chapter 9).

The distinctive purpose of this book is not, however, to report on the empirical impact of religious actors or organizations on the EU. Several chapters do engage in significant amounts of historical and contemporary description and analysis; Leustean surveys key actors and agencies seeking to influence EU organs, and Milton offers a specific case study of such influence. Most chapters are, however, interpretive essays showing how insights and experiences from diverse traditions of Christian theology and practice can be brought to bear on an assessment of the origins, achievements, pathologies, or possible futures of the EU.

The book is thus a contribution to 'a political theology of the EU'. It thereby stretches the boundaries of what is typically understood as the subfield of 'religion and politics'. 'Political theology' is the longstanding and highly diverse enterprise of reflecting on the many dimensions of human political order in the light of Christian theology and ethics (Chaplin, 2008). There is a wider sense of 'political theology' that would embrace contributions from a plurality of religious traditions, and comparative analyses of such traditions would be highly desirable.[2] This book, however, confines itself to Christian political theology. Although Christianity has historically been the pre-eminent religious tradition in Europe, surprisingly little recent work explores its contemporary potency specifically for the EU.

Political theology is a species of 'normative political thought'. It engages with essentially the same questions of authority, community, power, legitimacy, justice, law, liberty, equality, social change, and so forth that are addressed by other species of the genus, such as the many varieties of secular liberalism, Marxism, feminism, or radical ecologism. Each proceeds from fundamental assumptions about humanity, rationality, sociality, morality, and history, and proposes theories about political orders in the light of those. European political thought was, of course, overwhelmingly 'Christian' in character from at least the eighth to the seventeenth centuries, under the complex religio-political regime known as 'Christendom' (O'Donovan and Lockwood O'Donovan, 1999). Since the eighteenth century, however, political theology as it was classically understood has been almost entirely displaced from the mainstream of European public discourse by theories emanating from secularizing strands of the Enlightenments.[3] Political theology came to be regarded as hopelessly arcane, corrupted by its association with reaction, oppression and intolerance, or simply incapable of satisfying the minimum criteria of modern rational discourse.[4]

In the last two decades, however, the pre-modern genealogy of many fundamental normative principles underlying modern European constitutional democracies has begun to be excavated. Work has been done on notions long thought to have sprung up almost exclusively from the soil of Enlightenment secularism, such as individual liberty, equality, the rule of law, limited government, federalism, judicial impartiality, human rights, association, consent and representation (Siedentop 2014; Witte 2007; Waldron, 2002; O'Donovan, 1996; Hueglin, 1999; Tierney, 1997; Maddox, 1996). Such scholarship suggests that, while these principles were transformed (and in the process secularized) in Enlightenment thought, their origins lie in the Christian political theologies of ancient, medieval and early modern Europe. Williams even ventures that "some aspects of liberal politics would be unthinkable without Christian theology" (2012: 32). This applies even to one of the prized achievements of modern liberalism, namely the very notion of 'the secular' as a public realm over which the jurisdiction of religious institutions does not extend (Casanova, 1996: Ch. 1; Calhoun, Juergensmeyer, and Van Antwerpen, 2011). Historical provenance does not, of course, establish contemporary authority, but it should at least excite curiosity as to how closely our modern accounts of the principles of constitutional democracy resemble their earlier, theologically freighted antecedents and what might have been lost, as well as gained, in their secularization.

Political theology did not disappear as secular political thought assumed European dominance, but only a handful of prominent figures, such as the mid-twentieth century French public intellectual Jacques Maritain, continued to gain a significant hearing.[5] There has, however, been a substantial revival of European political theology since the 1970s (Cavanaugh, Bailey, and Hovey, 2012). While this originated in, and was for a long time only visible within, churches and theology departments, political theology is now beginning to return to the edges of the wider European academic and public stage.[6] This book is a contribution to that return. It is one type of 'minority report' on the current, unsettled condition of the EU – drawing on ideas birthed in what was once Europe's hegemonic religious tradition but which is now only one minority among others within an officially religiously neutral EU.

The book does not presume to represent anything like the full spectrum of current European political theologies. In some chapters the political theology is explicit while in others it is implicit or only described rather than commended. We do not assess the many models of church-state relationship across EU member states or consider the implications of a possible accession of Turkey. Nor does the book convey the full range of political perspectives on the EU: while many chapters present critiques of the EU none argues for either radical euroscepticism or full-blown integrationism.[7] Finally, the book does not attempt to address all the main EU institutions or all the main areas of EU policy. (The book was completed too late to address the refugee crisis appearing in mid-2015.) Its modest goal is to offer a series of illustrative forays into the field designed to show the pertinence of diverse strands of Christian political thought to the EU. Whether or not it is true that "the core of secular Western Europe has preserved Christianity largely as glimmering embers that are no longer able to generate . . . much heat" (Katzenstein, 2006: 2), our hope is that this volume at least casts a few shafts of light.

The chapters

Part One presents diverse theological 'inspirations' that either have been at work in the origins of the EU or might be looked to today as capable of illuminating the structures, values and goals of the EU.

In Chapter 1 Gary Wilton re-examines the legacy of prominent Catholic statesman Robert Schuman, the 'Father of Europe'. Its focus is the epochal Schuman Declaration (Schuman, 1950), a brief statement that nevertheless changed the history of the European continent and was in effect the founding document of the 'European Project'. The Declaration proposed that France and Germany should place their coal and steel industries under a common high authority, thus making "any war between France and Germany not merely unthinkable but materially impossible" (Schuman, 1950). It also set out a much broader framework of values and aspirations about peace, solidarity, and cooperation. Wilton explores the underlying Christian foundations of the Declaration and its relevance to today's EU.

John Loughlin supplies, in Chapter 2, a broader account of the central role of Catholicism in the evolution of the EU. He shows how the history of European integration is profoundly intertwined with the history of the Catholic Church as a body upholding a vision of universal community, describes how from the 1940s Catholic intellectuals animated by such a vision began to promote the cause of European unification and relates how the Vatican also consistently supported it. He enters two important qualifications to the story of Catholic European enthusiasm: first, the Church's support was always framed within a wider vision of world peace – Europe was to take its place within the community of nations; second, the Church has proved critical of aspects of the EU which conflict with Catholic Social Teaching.

In Chapter 3, Sander Luitwieler assesses the distinctive, complex, and more ambivalent stance of Protestantism. Opening with the broader issue of European identity, he argues that Protestantism has substantially contributed to the shaping of this identity. After presenting a framework to analyse specifically the relationship between Protestantism and European integration in terms of ideas and institutions, he applies this framework to the Netherlands, Britain, and the Nordic countries. His account confirms the picture that both ideas and institutions help explain the relatively reserved attitudes toward, and limited involvement in, the European integration process of Protestant leaders, parties, and churches compared with their Catholic counterparts. Yet he notes some important qualifications to this generalization. Finally, he proposes one contemporary Protestant view of the EU based on ideas from a particular strand of Dutch Protestant political thought.

In Chapter 4, Peter Petkoff explores the relationship between Orthodoxy and the EU. He explains how the role of the various national Orthodox churches in the EU is shaped by a complex, often pragmatic interplay of inter-ecclesial relations, relations between local churches and nation-states, and the legacy of the Byzantine Orthodox Commonwealth, and explains why Orthodox social theology has displayed little interest in the structure of secular institutions. Assessing the significance of the role of Orthodox diaspora communities within the EU, the emerging dialogue between Orthodoxy and EU institutions, inter-ecclesial and national government pressures, and new grassroots lay-led initiatives, he reflects on the prospects for a more robust Orthodox political theology able to engage with EU institutions.

In Chapter 5, Werner Lachmann shows how the German Social Market Economy (SME) was one of the two decisive influences, along with the French model of state planning, on the early development of the EU. Lachmann argues that the SME was, in fact, quite strongly rooted in the biblical thinking of key voices within Ordo-liberalism, in which many of the architects of the SME, notably Ludwig Erhard, were schooled. He proposes that the Treaty of Rome can be construed essentially as a compromise between the French state-led model and the German market-led model, that subsequent developments in EU political economy always needed a French-German compromise, and that the creation of the euro again revealed such a compromise. The EU now needs a reassertion of the economic and moral virtues of the SME.

Adrian Pabst argues in Chapter 6 that the EU's contemporary crisis is not first of all the 'democratic deficit' but rather a lack of legitimacy, deriving from its evolution towards a 'market-state' fusing bureaucratic collectivization with commercial commodification. Catholic social thought and cognate traditions, however, reject these as false alternatives. The contemporary EU is undermining Europe's shared cultural identity and hollowing out the universal values derived from the Christian synthesis of ancient and biblical virtues on which vibrant democracies and market economies ultimately depend. His alternative is a 'civic commonwealth', informed by Europe's common Christian heritage – a voluntary association of nations and peoples with a shared 'social imaginary' that can command popular assent and address the legitimacy crisis.

In Chapter 7, Joshua Hordern utilizes a theology of 'place' to explore how EU citizens might think constructively about their political institutions. He considers how Europeans identify with their places and their politics, explores two civic tasks concerning the interrelation of the EU and its member states – "adequate identity" and "sufficient agreement" – and then offers an account of the distinctive contribution of ecclesial identity to European consciousness. He proposes that such theologically informed concepts raise questions for all EU citizens and open up possibilities for conversation with the 'secular' forms of expression proper to political discourse – while claiming that such a notion of the 'secular' itself discloses an originally theological assumption about the nature of government.

The six chapters making up Part Two address four distinct areas of EU policy and practice – the public role of religion, the eurozone, environmental policy, and science policy – in the light of the factor of religion and the insights of political theology.

Chapters 8, 9 and 10 explore the public role of religion within the EU from complementary angles. In Chapter 8, Thomas Schirrmacher and Jonathan Chaplin consider the place of religious freedom within the EU against a larger European canvas. They relate the neglected story of how dissenting Protestant minorities contributed decisively to the arrival of European religious freedom and identify four theological arguments utilized by these dissenters and their successors. After sketching the broader framework of religious freedom established by the European Convention on Human Rights, they assess the engagement of the EU itself in this area. A central concern is the position of vulnerable religious minorities in states dominated either by traditionalist majority religions or by strict public secularism.

In Chapter 9, Lucian N. Leustean examines the political engagement of religious communities in the construction of the EU. He begins with a focus on the historical evolution of religious dialogue between European institutions and 'churches, religions, and communities of conviction' from the Schuman Declaration to the Lisbon Treaty. He then addresses the competing visions of 'Europe' in Catholic, Protestant, and Orthodox communities and the legacy of the Cold War for the ways in which religious communities relate to the EU project. Finally, he explores the framework of religious dialogue in Article 17 of the Lisbon Treaty and the ways in which faith, religion, and politics interact in contemporary European political system.

In Chapter 10, Guy Milton narrates the fraught debate over the place of religion in the proposed EU Constitution. The Convention that drew up the failed Constitution divided over whether the preamble should contain any religious reference, such as a recognition of Europe's Christian heritage or a mention of 'God'. While the final text of the preamble, acknowledging the "cultural, religious and humanist inheritance of Europe", was jettisoned, it was decided to retain the reference to Europe's religious inheritance in the subsequent Lisbon Treaty. Milton argues that, although the churches were disappointed at the lack of an explicit reference to Christianity, the surviving provision that the EU shall maintain an "open, transparent and regular dialogue" with churches and religious associations was of more lasting importance.

The next three chapter address, from different vantage points, the relationship between EU economic policy and the insights of theology and ethics. In Chapter 11, Johan Graafland tackles the current EU financial crisis. At time of writing (May 2015) it remained unclear whether Greece would remain within the eurozone, but whether it has or not the crisis has already posed perhaps the greatest challenge to the credibility of the EU since its founding. Graafland shows how the euro crisis has brought to the surface not only conflicting political interests but also deep economic divides across the EU which make it difficult to meet economic criteria for a common currency union. He explains the background to the euro, assesses the roots of the current crisis, spells out five leading policy options currently being canvassed from a wide variety of quarters across the EU regarding possible futures for the euro, and assesses them against five core Christian values.

In Chapter 11, Janice Weatherley-Singh, Tiago Branco, and Marcial Felgueiras address the EU's policy on biodiversity and nature through an exploration of the role of values in the implementation of EU nature legislation at a Natura 2000 site in Portugal (in which they were involved as environmental practitioners). They argue that EU biodiversity policy is moving away from its earlier commitment to the idea that the natural environment has 'intrinsic value' and towards a utilitarian view of environmental goods moulded to fit an economic growth agenda. They claim, however, that most EU citizens endorse the notion that nature has intrinsic value, and that this standpoint finds robust support within a Christian environmental ethic.

In Chapter 12, Diana Jane Beech assesses EU science and research policy with a focus on 'Horizon 2020', introduced in early 2015 as the EU's largest ever investment in knowledge policies. The programme formalises the European Research Area (ERA) and aims to promote the EU's global competitiveness through "smart, sustainable and inclusive" growth. Beech shows that these measures to create a genuine single market for European research and innovation are not enough to constitute the "new Renaissance" the EU seeks. With special reference to the pioneering history of CERN, she makes the case for formally integrating a values-driven dimension into contemporary ERA policy, in order to find a much-needed 'soul' for European science.

In the Conclusion, Jonathan Chaplin reflects on what the preceding chapters might disclose about how Christianity should comport itself in today's Union. Recalling the ambitious aspirations of Jacques Delors' 'Soul for Europe' initiative, he asks how far it is meaningful to speak of the EU as having, or seeking, a single 'soul' rather than a plurality of partly converging, partly contending 'souls', and what contribution Christian political theology might make to reflecting on the future of an anxiously pluralistic EU.

Notes

1 As Katzenstein notes: "A secular liberalism is deeply ingrained in the self-understanding of most Europeans and in the interpretations of most scholars of European politics" (2006: 7).
2 See, for example, the forthcoming special issues of *The Muslim World* 106.1 (2016) and *Studies in Christian Ethics* 29.2 (2016) on "New Conversations in Islamic and Christian Political Thought".
3 Or, if not displaced, then rendered as a "civil religion" that would serve the interests of the state (Beiner, 2011).
4 For defenses of the 'rationality' of political theology, see Chaplin and Joustra (2010); Habermas and Ratzinger (2006); Milbank (2005); McIntyre (1988).
5 On modern political theology, see Witte and Alexander (eds) (2005).
6 Among English-language contributions, see The Immanent Frame; D'Costa et al. (2013); Williams (2012); McGraw (2010); Witte and Alexander (eds) (2010);

Wolterstorff (2012, 2008); Biggar and Hogan (eds) (2009); Plant (2001); Weithman (1997).
7 On Christianity and euroscepticism, see Minkenbergh (2011).

References

Beiner, R. (2011). *Civil religion: A dialogue in the history of political philosophy.* Cambridge: Cambridge University Press.
Biggar, N., and Hogan, L. (eds) (2009). *Religious voices in public places.* Oxford: Oxford University Press.
Byrnes, T. A., and Katzenstein, P. J. (eds) (2006). *Religion in an expanding Europe.* Cambridge: Cambridge University Press.
Calhoun, C., Juergensmeyer, M., and Van Antwerpen, J. (eds) (2011). *Rethinking secularism.* New York: Oxford University Press.
Casanova, J. (1994). *Public religions in the modern world.* Chicago, IL: University of Chicago Press.
Cavanaugh, W. T., Bailey, J. W., and Hovey, C. (eds) (2012). *An Eerdmans reader in contemporary political theology.* Grand Rapids, MI: Eerdmans.
Chaplin, J. (2008). Political theology. In Vanhoozer, K. J. (ed.), *Dictionary for theological interpretation of scripture* (pp. 597–600). Grand Rapids, MI: Baker Academic.
Chaplin, J., and Joustra, J. (2010). Introduction. In Chaplin, J. and Joustra, R. (eds), *God and global order: The power of religion in American foreign policy* (pp. 1–22). Waco, TX: Baylor University Press.
Chelini-Pont, B. (2010). Papal thought on Europe and the European Union in the twentieth century. In Leustean, L. N. and Madeley, J. T. S. (eds), *Religion, politics and law in the European Union* (pp. 125–140). London: Routledge.
Davie, G. (2002). *Europe, the exceptional case: Parameters of faith in the modern world.* London: Darton, Longman and Todd.
D'Costa, G., Evans, M., Modood, T., and Rivers, J. (eds) (2013). *Religion in a liberal state.* Cambridge: Cambridge University Press.
Foret, F. (2015). *Religion and politics in the European Union.* Cambridge: Cambridge University Press.
Habermas, J., and Ratzinger, J. (2006). *The dialectics of secularization: On reason and religion.* San Francisco, CA: Ignatius Press.
Haynes, J., and Hennig, A. (eds) (2011). *Religious actors in the public sphere: Means, objectives and effects.* London: Routledge.
Hehir, J. B. (2006). The old Church and the new Europe: Charting the changes. In Byrnes, T. A. and Katzenstein, P. J. (eds), *Religion in an expanding Europe* (pp. 93–116). Cambridge: Cambridge University Press.
Heuglin, T. O. (1999). *Early modern concepts for a late modern world: Althusius on community and federalism.* Waterloo, ON: Wilfred Laurier University Press.
Kaiser, W. (2007). *Christian democracy and the origins of European Union.* Cambridge: Cambridge University Press.
Katzenstein, P. J. (2006). Multiple modernities as limits to secular Europeanization? In Byrnes, T. A. and Kastzenstein, P. J. (eds), *Religion in an expanding Europe* (pp. 1–33). Cambridge: Cambridge University Press.
Leustean, L. N. (ed.) (2013). *Representing religion in the European Union: Does God matter?* London: Routledge.

Leustean, L. N., and Madeley, J. T. S. (eds) (2010). *Religion, politics and law in the European Union.* London: Routledge.
Maddox, G. (1996). *Religion and the rise of democracy.* London: Routledge.
Madeley, J. T. S. (2010). E unum pluribus: The role of religion in the project of European integration. In Haynes, J. (ed.), *Religion and politics in Europe, the Middle East and North Africa* (pp. 114–135). London: Routledge.
McGraw, B. T. (2010). *Faith in politics: Religion and liberal democracy.* Cambridge: Cambridge University Press.
McIntyre, A. (1988). *Whose justice? Which rationality?* London: Duckworth.
Milbank, J. (2005). *Theology and social theory* (2nd edn). Oxford: Blackwell.
Minkenberg, M. (2011). Churches in the European integration process: The diminishing confessional divide in Euroskepticism. In Haynes, J. and Hennig, A. (eds), *Religious actors in the public sphere: Means, objectives and effects* (pp. 32–56). London: Routledge.
Nelsen, B. F., and Guth, J. L. (2015). *Religion and the struggle for European Union: Confessional cultures and the limits of integration.* Washington, DC: Georgetown University Press.
O'Donovan, O. M. T. (1996). *The desire of the nations: Rediscovering the roots of political theology.* Cambridge: Cambridge University Press.
O'Donovan, O. M. T., and Lockwood O'Donovan, J. (eds) (1999). *From Irenaeus to Grotius: A sourcebook in Christian political thought.* Grand Rapids, MI: Eerdmans.
Philpott, D., and Shah, T. S. (2006). Faith, freedom and federation: The role of religious ideas and institutions in European political convergence. In Byrnes, T. A. and Katzenstein, P. J. (eds), *Religion in an expanding Europe* (pp. 34–64). Cambridge: Cambridge University Press.
Plant, R. (2001). *Politics, theology and history.* Cambridge: Cambridge University Press.
Ramet, S. P. (2006a). Thy will be done: The Catholic Church and politics in Poland since 1989. In Byrnes, T. A. and Katzenstein, P. J. (eds), *Religion in an expanding Europe* (pp. 117–147). Cambridge: Cambridge University Press.
Ramet, S. P. (2006b). The way we were – and should be again? European Orthodox Churches and the "idyllic past". In Byrnes, T. A. and Katzenstein, P. J. (eds), *Religion in an Expanding Europe* (pp. 148–175). Cambridge: Cambridge University Press.
Schuman, R. (1950). The Schuman declaration. 9 May. Retrieved from http://europa.eu/about-eu/basic-information/symbols/europe-day/schuman-declaration/index_en.htm.
Siedentop, L. (2014). *Inventing the individual: The origins of western liberalism.* London: Allen Lane.
'The immanent frame: Secularism, religion and the public sphere'. Available at http://blogs.ssrc.org/tif/.
Tierney, B. (1997). *The idea of natural rights: Studies on natural rights, natural law, and church law, 1150–1625.* Grand Rapids, MI: Eerdmans.
Waldron, J. (2002). *God, Locke and equality: Christian foundations in Locke's political thought.* Cambridge: Cambridge University Press.
Weithman, P. J. (ed.) (1997). *Religion and contemporary liberalism.* Notre Dame, IN: University of Notre Dame Press.
Williams, R. (2012). *Faith in the public square.* London: Bloomsbury.
Witte, J. (2007). *The reformation of rights: Law, religion and human rights in early modern Calvinism.* Cambridge: Cambridge University Press.

Witte, J., and Alexander, F. (eds) (2005). *The teachings of modern Christianity on law, politics, and human nature* (2 vols.). New York: Columbia University Press.

Wolterstorff, N. (2012). *Understanding liberal democracy: Essays in political philosophy.* Oxford: Oxford University Press.

Wolterstorff, N. (2008). *Justice: Rights and wrongs.* Princeton, NJ: Princeton University Press.

Part 1
The EU
Christian inspirations, past and present

1 Christianity at the founding
The legacy of Robert Schuman

Gary Wilton

Introduction

This chapter offers a reading of the Schuman Declaration informed by the Christian history of Europe. After outlining the historical context of the Declaration, the chapter identifies six of its central themes, illustrates how, contrary to much public perception, these themes continue to animate the contemporary European Union (EU), and commends their relevance for today, both for the EU and the churches.

The European quarter of twenty-first century Brussels is a gleaming pantheon of glass and steel. Yet positioned in front of the Berlaymont Building, the home of the European Commission, is a very simple hewn stone. It is a memorial to Robert Schuman – 'The Father of a United Europe'. Today within the European institutions the name of Robert Schuman has a saint-like quality. On 9th May 1950 at the Quai d'Orsay, Paris, Robert Schuman, the then French Foreign Minister, made the modest public statement that is now recognised as the moment the European Union was born. A number of journalists were present; but there were no photographers, radio microphones, or television cameras to record proceedings. Yet the Schuman 'Declaration' (Schuman, 1950a)[1] changed the history of the continent.

The post-1945 generation of statesmen and politicians dreamed of creating a Europe free from war. Drawing on the work of Jean Monnet and working in collaboration with West Germany, Schuman, a deeply committed Roman Catholic, anticipated a pan-national community that would embed peace in Europe. Central to his proposal was the placing of the primary means of waging war – coal and steel – under a common High Authority thereby making war "materially impossible" (Schuman, 1950a). Although surprisingly brief, the Schuman Declaration thus had at its heart a radical economic proposal as the means of achieving and sustaining peace. It was, for him, the political expression of the Christian values of forgiveness and reconciliation and the precursor to permanent peace. The succeeding 60 years of economic solidarity have indeed contributed not only to peace and reconciliation between historic adversaries but also to unprecedented prosperity and to the creation of the world's only multi-national democracy involving 28 member states with a population of 500 million people (European Union, 2015a). At the same time the High Authority has been transformed into today's European Commission, with competencies far beyond those articulated in the Declaration.

Along with that of De Gasperi, Monnet, and Adenauer, Schuman's Christian faith was the inspiration for a life dedicated to the rebuilding of Europe. Schuman and his peers worked with a profound sense that it was their vocation to restore and re-unite Europe to peace and prosperity. Before attending the Paris conference of 1951 they retreated for meditation and prayer at a Benedictine monastery on the Rhine. As Christian Democrats they shared a common foundation that would underpin the nascent European Community. Although Schuman's initial focus was on coal and steel his underlying concern was to embed democracy in Europe as a bulwark against war and as the authentic expression of Christian political economy. For Schuman, democracy owed its existence to Christianity's commitment to human dignity, freedom, and love (Fountain, 2010: 41). This chapter delineates the key themes of the founding Declaration, and offers analyses of how they have shaped a controversial and increasingly complex institution and how they continue to inform Christian participation in the EU.

Robert Schuman (1886–1963): Christian statesman and father of Europe

Robert Schuman was born in 1886 in Clausen, Luxembourg.[2] His father had been born a Frenchman before being given German nationality after the 1871 annexation of Alsace-Lorraine into Germany. As a student he crossed and re-crossed the French-German border to study law, history, economics, politics, theology, classics, and philosophy at the universities of Berlin, Munich, Bonn, and Strasbourg. From the outset Schuman took his Christian faith most seriously. In 1909 he participated in a pilgrimage to Rome. In 1912 he was joint leader of a German delegation to an International 'Peace through Law' congress at Leuven, Belgium, and in 1913 he attended a Paschal Retreat at Maria Laach with Heinrich Platz, a Catholic pacifist, and Heinrich Bruening, a future German Chancellor.

In 1919, aged 33, Schuman was elected to the French Chamber of Deputies. During the 1920s he led the development of a new legal code which reconciled earlier French and pre-war German legislation for Alsace with mainstream French law. For much of the interwar period he was associated with the Christian peace movement (Fountain, 2010: 31). During the Second World War Schuman was arrested by the Nazis before escaping to work for the resistance. Re-elected to public office in France in 1946 he variously served as Finance Minister, Foreign Secretary and Prime Minister. In 1947 he welcomed Churchill to Metz for his first 'European' speech and was a signatory of the Marshall Plan. In 1948 he was co-author and signatory of the North Atlantic Treaty and a Statute signatory for the Council of Europe. In a speech in 1949 he stated that the Council of Europe laid "the foundations for spiritual and political co-operation from which the European spirit will be born and the principle of a vast and long-lasting supranational union that has neither the objective nor the consequence of weakening our connection to the nation" (Schuman, 1949). In 1958 Schuman was unanimously elected President of the Parliamentary Assembly of the European Assemblies and acclaimed as the 'Father of Europe'.

Schuman wrote widely about the European project. His papers are deposited at the Departmental Archive of the Moselle. In addition, both the European Commission Library and the Robert Schuman Foundation hold extensive material about him. Mayne describes Schuman as "monkish, bookish, almost saintly" (1996: 24). He was a biblical scholar, an expert on medieval philosophy, and a Knight of the Order of Pope Pius IX. Mayne observes that "his faith sustained him", that he was deeply meditative and that he "lived simply like a priest" (Mayne, 1996: 24). It is surprising that educational materials produced by the European Commission make no reference to Schuman's Christian convictions.

The content and continuing significance of the Schuman Declaration

Robert Schuman issued the Declaration at a time of considerable economic and political instability, the Europe of 1950 still economically, socially, and politically scarred by the Second World War. The breakdown of relationships with Soviet Russia raised the possibility of a third world war but nuclear weapons made such a prospect too terrible to contemplate.

Schuman and his colleagues perceived that traditional approaches to economic and political reconstruction were as much a part of the problem as they were of the solution. The way forward had to be communal, international, and possibly federal. Long-standing economic competitors and military foes would need to cede something of their national independence to make a common cause and to build a common future. The Schuman Declaration can be read legitimately as an outline sketch of one such communal way forward – one consciously responding to the particular challenges of the post-Second World War period but underpinned by centuries of Christian public theology, even if the theological underpinnings of its main themes remained assumed and unstated. In what follows I consider six of these themes to illustrate how Schuman's embryonic vision shaped the early development of the European Union and to point to its continuing validity.

World Peace[3]

> World Peace cannot be safeguarded without the making of creative efforts proportionate to the dangers which threaten it. The contribution which an organized and living Europe can bring to civilisation is indispensable to the maintenance of peaceful relations.

> The solidarity in production thus established will make it plain that any war between France and Germany becomes not merely unthinkable but materially impossible.
>
> ... [T]his proposal will lead to the realization of the first concrete foundation of a European federation indispensable to the preservation of peace.

The opening sentences of the Schuman Declaration remind us that peace was its overriding aim. For Schuman, peace and reconciliation were foundational to the rebuilding of Europe. Peace was the first and the last stage in a virtuous circle of nation states coming together, sharing power, creating community, supporting one another, fostering prosperity, and contributing to the wider peace. But the particular genius of Schuman's peace-making proposal was to move away from military solutions to the shared control of economic resources. The removal of the means of making war from France and Germany would make peace not only achievable but sustainable. Whilst NATO inherited the military responsibility for Western European security, the embryonic European Community focused first on coal and steel and subsequently on wider economic, social, and political cooperation as the key means of sustaining peace. The ultimate success of Schuman's approach was only seen much later in the eventual integration of countries from the former Soviet bloc into the EU.[4] Each stage of the enlargement of the European Community extended peace across the continent, making pan-European war increasingly unlikely. This justification for enlargement, however, is not fully owned by contemporary EU citizens. The majority are generally indifferent to enlargement while increasingly troubled by the resulting free movement of labour. This is widely perceived to contribute to competition for scarce jobs and public resources and to fuel various forms of cultural dislocation. Yet the case for further enlargement to consolidate and extend European peace remains compelling – not least in view of the widening threat of terrorism, now striking at the heart of European capitals, and Russian expansionism, already witnessed in Georgia, Crimea, and eastern Ukraine.

The case for the EU as a major contributor to peace beyond its borders is just as compelling. Since 2003, the EU has been involved in conflict prevention and post-conflict reconstruction across the globe, most notably in the Democratic Republic of the Congo. 'Operation Artemis', the EU's first rapid military deployment in support of a UN mission in Africa, specifically answered a request for intervention from the UN Secretary General, Kofi Annan. The operation was a joint EU-UN effort, with 12 member states contributing troops, and, although the EU maintained control of the operation, its actions clearly allowed the UN to strengthen its own mandate. Alexandra Novosseloff observed:

> The EU and the UN worked in close cooperation throughout the planning and deployment phases of Artemis: the deployment of the UN troop reinforcements benefited from EU logistical support, joint planning of the transition period, co-localisation of MONUC and Artemis field

headquarters, implementation of coordination mechanisms such as regular meetings and liaison officers and visit of the Artemis Force Commander in New York.

(2012: 12)

In 2007 the Commission launched its Instrument for Stability to strengthen work in the areas of conflict prevention, crisis management, and peace building. Projects include mediation, confidence building, interim administrations, developing the rule of law, transitional justice, and the role of natural resources in conflict. Under its Peace-Building Partnerships the Commission seeks to develop civilian expertise for peace-building activities. Such international activities are, of course, far beyond even Schuman's prophetic imagination. The EU has gained global respect for its 'soft' activities. In 2012 the EU was awarded the Nobel Peace Prize for its contribution to peace. The award was met with both joy and derision. Those who responded with joy readily acknowledged Schuman's legacy, while those who responded with derision rightly pointed out the lack of peace in Cyprus and the EU's impotence in the face of calamitous civil war in Syria.

Within the Union, the churches have energetically contributed to the 'soft' activities that embed peace. The Commission of Bishops' Conferences of the European Community (COMECE) and the Conference of European Churches (CEC) have worked extensively across the continent to strengthen relationships among churches and across political divides. The International Centre for Reconciliation at Coventry Cathedral is a model of church-based reconciliation ministry, while for a twenty-first century Europe where the integration of minority Muslim communities is a major concern, the work of the St. Ethelburga's Centre for Peace and Reconciliation in London is a model for inter-faith peace initiatives. EU policy-makers might do well to recognise the potential of faith-based organisations to contribute expertise or resources for peace making at diplomatic and even military levels (Coward and Smith, 2004; Johnston, 2003; Thistlethwaite, 2011).

Unity in Europe

In taking upon herself for more than 20 years the role of champion of a united Europe, France …

Europe will not be made all at once, or according to a single plan.

The coming together of the nations of Europe requires the elimination of the age-old opposition of France and Germany. Any action must in the first place concern these two countries.

… a first step in the federation of Europe

The Declaration asserts that the nations and people of Europe should be 'united'. But beyond the specific proposal for coal and steel, Schuman did not delineate what a united Europe might look like, using the word 'federal' without giving it substance. Nonetheless he recognised that the ancient feuding between France and Germany needed to be replaced by a genuine friendship before peace could be secured. The process of European (re)-unification would be evolutionary and voluntary. From the beginning, the project was facilitated by a deliberate vagueness that enabled member states to advance their own interests while finding common cause with others. Not surprisingly in every decade of its history the community has been beset by questions of identity, purpose, and destination.

For much of the second half of the twentieth century Europe was more complexly divided than is popularly recognised. The division of the Soviet-controlled East from the West until 1989 is easily remembered. However, the authoritarian regimes of Southern Europe, Greece, Portugal and Spain also constituted a distinctive bloc, while yet another group – Austria, Finland, Ireland, Sweden, and Switzerland – had declared themselves avowedly neutral. Prior to 1973 the UK stood alone and looked primarily to its transatlantic and Commonwealth relationships. The non-celebration of the fortieth anniversary of the UK's accession to the common market was a clear sign that the UK's unease with 'Europe' remains undiminished. It is easy to forget that the current map of the EU is less than 10 years old. Whilst not all European countries are members of the EU, the creation of a Union of 28 member states is remarkable. Despite a host of complex internal divisions, Europe enjoys a degree of unity of which Schuman and his peers could only dream.

Enlargement of the Union has also provoked concern for 'unity' with non-members of the community. This is particularly apparent in its post-2004 European Neighbourhood Policy designed to "achieve the closest possible political association and the greatest possible degree of economic integration" (European External Action Service, 2015a) with neighbouring states. The Union offers a 'privileged relationship' with neighbouring states on the basis of a mutual commitment to democracy and human rights, rule of law, good governance, market economy principles, and sustainable development. The stronger the commitment to shared values, the more the EU invests in its neighbourhood relationships. Between 2007 and 2013 the EU invested 12 billion euros in European Neighbourhood projects.

Yet serious divisions in Europe still persist. Cyprus remains divided and EU legislation is currently restricted to the south in accordance with Protocol 10 of the Accession Treaty of 2003. While all Turkish Cypriots are recognised as EU citizens and benefit from EU economic and social initiatives designed to bring Turkish Cypriots closer to other European Union citizens, the failure to resolve this conflict is a continuing blemish. While, as noted, the EU's twenty-first century enlargement is a political triumph, the rapid inclusion of 100 million people with fragile democratic traditions only added to the strains within the Union. 'Europe' is increasingly experienced by EU citizens as a distant entity, whether in the UK, France, or Poland. Participation in European Parliamentary elections is on a downward trajectory, and while the EU's complexity is confusing to many citizens this alone does not explain the growing democratic deficit. The continuing decline of political parties and the decay of public trust in political institutions across Europe has created a worrying representative vacuum. The consent of Europe's citizens urgently needs to be regenerated.

The Schuman Declaration, as the founding document of the EU, addresses only nation states. By 1957 the shared experience of the European Coal and Steel Community led the drafters of the Treaty of Rome to speak of "an ever closer union between the peoples of Europe" (European Union, 1957: Preamble). The challenge for the member states and the institutions of the expanded Union of the twenty-first century is to give meaningful expression to the unity of the Union and to nurture the engagement of the citizens. The recent rise of assertively nationalist groups is a clear confirmation that the desire of the European elite for "ever closer union" is actively opposed at grass roots.

EU enlargement only serves to fuel the sense of dislocation for existing citizens. Indeed the enlargement process continues more quickly than the growth of the Union's capacity to deal with this dislocation. Iceland and the former Yugoslav Republic of Macedonia are candidate countries. Albania, Bosnia and Herzegovina, Montenegro, and Serbia are potential candidates. Turkey, home to Istanbul, a European city with a population of 13 million and an extensive Mediterranean coastline, is a possible future member. Its candidature raises profound questions about European identity, human rights, democracy, and the rule of law. Yet to remain healthy, European democracy needs to welcome and engage with "the stranger, including the Muslim stranger in its midst, as a partner in the work of proper liberalism, the continuing argument about common good and just governance" (Williams, 2005).

Given increasing EU-wide concern over the loss of national identity and autonomy, a united Europe needs, as Williams (2005) puts it, to continue to seek "effective partnership with the component communities of the state, including religious bodies." Such partnership, which should include place for dialogue with the churches and other faith groups, could make a significant contribution to reversing the deepening democratic deficit that currently besets the Union.

The sharing of sovereignty

> Franco-German production of coal and steel as a whole be placed under a common High Authority, within the framework of an organisation open to the participation of the other countries in Europe.
>
> By pooling basic production and by instituting a new High Authority, whose decisions will bind France, Germany and other member countries ...
>
> The common High Authority entrusted with the management of the scheme will be composed of independent persons appointed by the governments, giving equal representation. A chairman will be chosen by common agreement. The Authority's decisions will be enforceable in France, Germany and other member countries. Appropriate measures of appeal will be provided for against the decisions of the Authority.

The creation of the common High Authority over the coal and steel industries was at the heart of Schuman's revolutionary proposal. It was the foundation of today's European Commission and European Court of Justice. Schuman was very aware of the revolutionary nature of his proposal: "Never before have states entrusted, nor even envisaged delegating a fraction of their sovereignty to an independent supranational authority" (Schuman, 1950b). Schuman's vision sought to affirm both national self-interest and a wider, evolving sense of transnational interest. Membership of the Community would be open and the Europe envisaged was to be shaped by self-determination. In contrast to the episodes of military occupation and the imposition of rule by one nation over another, the new Europe would be open and voluntary. Smaller nations, demonstrably more vulnerable to military threat, would have the same right to membership as their larger neighbours.

Schuman argued that the creation of a supranational organisation did not undermine the nation state but enabled it to operate on a broader and higher plain. But free membership did not mean that members of the community could opt in and out. The nations of Europe would be bound together by international treaty and would need to negotiate for their own needs always in relationship to their partners. The key to building confidence would be a binding appeals procedure. The ceding of power to an arbiter with binding authority was a requirement on all and vital to the creation of a Common High Authority. If the Common High Authority was the forerunner of the European Commission, the arbiter was the forerunner of the Court of Justice of the European Communities. Although still regularly confused in the popular mind with the European Court of Human Rights based in Strasbourg, the role of the Court of Justice is to uphold Community law. It arbitrates between EU member states, EU institutions, businesses, and individuals. Arbitration means interpreting and adjudicating treaty agreements or Community legislation. The court symbolises and gives substance to the nature of the European Union as a Community based on law. For Schuman, "the rule of law safeguarded a common heritage and argued that every person placed under its jurisdiction should enjoy human rights and fundamental freedoms." This "created the foundations of a spiritual and political cooperation, from which the European spirit will be born, the principle of a vast and enduring supranational union" (Schuman, 1949). I suggest that the sharing of sovereignty between victor and vanquished countries in the creation of common institutions can be seen as a distinctive expression of Christian values of 'forgiveness' and 'reconciliation'. Equally, the creation of the Court of Justice was the political recognition that the nations of Europe are as vulnerable to the 'sin' of narrow self-interest as they ever were.

Solidarity within Europe

> It will be built through concrete achievements which will first create a de facto solidarity.

> The pooling of coal and steel production should immediately provide for the setting up of common foundations for economic development ...
> The setting up of this powerful productive unit, open to all countries willing to take part and bound ultimately to provide all the member countries with the basic elements of industrial production on the same terms, will lay a true foundation for their economic unification.
> In this way, there will be realised simply and speedily that fusion of interest which is indispensable to the establishment of a common economic system;
> The task with which this common High Authority will be charged will be that of securing in the shortest possible time the modernization of production and the improvement of its quality; the supply of coal and steel on identical terms to the French and German markets, as well as to the markets of other member countries; the development in common of exports to other countries; the equalization and improvement of the living conditions of workers in these industries.

The prosaic language of "fusion of economic interest" and "equalization of living conditions" can also be read as a political rendition of the Christian aspiration of 'solidarity' that motivated Schuman. At the end of the Second World War Europe was economically and politically broken. Even the politically strong UK was economically exhausted and near bankrupt. From this shared 'poverty' the declaration sought to facilitate the sharing of the fruits of economic reconstruction. Although France and Germany were identified explicitly, all of Europe was invited to participate, with the more powerful nations encouraged to work mutually and creatively with the less powerful. While the scope of the declaration was broad, its focus was narrow: the shared horizontal and vertical reconstruction of coal and steel industries to ensure equality of supply to France and Germany. Schuman argued that this would lead to a *de facto* solidarity and interdependence, by binding national interest with a shared interest. The successful integration of coal and steel would also create the foundations for further shared and peaceable economic development.

The two key tools for furthering solidarity have been the Common Agricultural Policy (CAP) and regional policy. The CAP, established by the 1957 Treaty of Rome, was designed to support a struggling agricultural sector and to secure food supplies. From the outset the CAP reflected a German recognition of its relative industrial strength and an expression of support for politically powerful but economically vulnerable French farmers. Regional policy gained fresh impetus after the 1992 Maastricht Treaty, which led to a new Structural and Cohesion policy designed to aid the weaker economies within the Union. By 2013 regional policy accounted for more than a third of the total EU budget (European Commission, 2008). In 2010, the 12 members who joined the Union between 2004 and 2007 received more than half of Cohesion and Structural Funds (52 per cent). The same countries received nearly 20 per cent of CAP funding (European Commission, 2009).

Of course, significant inequalities still exist between the East and the South of the Union compared to the West and the North, and these have been exacerbated by the economic and financial crises since 2008. Reforming the EU budget, however, remains mired in controversy. Budget debates tend to reflect the political trade-offs between the competing interests of member governments rather than a new division of resources according to the principle of solidarity. Arguably, however, the EU's response to the crisis in the Eurozone (discussed in detail in Johan Graafand's chapter), while obviously reflecting the persistence of powerful and competing national interests, is at least a partial expression of the principle of solidarity of stronger nations with weaker ones that inspired Schuman at the founding.

At a grassroots level churches across the continent have been working together to support social action projects in countries most affected by the financial crisis. For example, the Church of England has worked particularly closely with the Orthodox Church in Greece providing expertise and financial resources. Since 2009, St. Paul's Anglican Church in Athens has distributed 800 meals a day to immigrants and others made homeless by the turbulence in the Greek economy (The Anglican Church in Greece, 2013).

Solidarity with the wider world

> The production will be offered to the world as a whole without distinction or exception, with the aim of contributing to raising living standards and to promoting peaceful achievements. With increased resources Europe will be able to pursue the achievement of one of its essential tasks, viz the development of the African continent.

Here Schuman's immediate concern extended to Africa, aware as he was of French and other European colonial interests. This was the beginning of the current EU relationship with Africa with its various expressions of solidarity, including substantial development aid, support for civil society, and the promotion of human rights. Inspired by Schuman, solidarity with the wider world was embedded in the construction of Europe (European Commission, 2014a). Articles 131 and 136 of the 1957 Treaty of Rome made provision for the European Development Fund to offer assistance to colonies and other overseas territories. This would place Africa at the heart of the EU Development and Cooperation policy as it evolved. During the 1960s as decolonisation gathered pace, member states agreed to continue supporting the newly independent former colonies. Gradually this was widened to include other developing countries across the globe. Today the European External Action Service (EEAS) describes the relationship between Europe and Africa as:

> [t]wo continents bound together by a common history, culture, geography, and not least by the very close exchanges which they entertain at a human, economic and political level. Cooperation between the EU and

Africa has reflected early on the rich and diverse nature of the relations between both continents while also keeping up to speed with wider economic and political developments.

(European External Action Service, 2015b)

In 2000 the EU entered into the Contonou Agreement with the African, Carribean, and Pacific (ACP) group of countries to promote development, economic, political, and trade cooperation. The ACP currently includes 79 countries, 48 of which are from sub-Saharan Africa. Four out of five of the world's least developed countries are ACP countries, most of them in Africa. Between 2008 and 2013 the European Development Fund granted 22.7 billion euros to projects across Africa. In 2013 this represented 38 per cent of all EU aid allocated to developing countries (European Commission, 2014b: 3). Together the EU and its member states take great pride in being the largest donor of aid in the world. In 2013 they granted more than half of public or official development aid in the world, amounting to 56.5 billion euros (European Union, 2015). 2015 marks the last year in which to achieve the UN Millennium Development Goals. It is also a key year for international agreement on future development frameworks. Resonating deeply with the theological values underpinning the Schuman Declaration, the EU has responded by declaring 2015 as the European Year for Development under the motto 'Our world, our dignity, our future' (European Union, 2015).

While there is much that the EU may properly celebrate here, it must be noted that the post-2008 financial and economic crisis has had a disproportionate impact on Africa. Although the continent has limited linkages with the world's financial systems, reduced demand for African products has led to lower earnings. African economies suffered a $578 billion reduction in export earning between 2009 and 2011, representing 18.4 per cent of GDP and five times the aid expected by the continent during these two years (Maswana, 2010). Such a massive external shock has impacted adversely upon hard-won progress towards the Millennium Development Goals. In addition the unprecedented wave of migration activity from Africa to Europe in the aftermath of the Arab uprisings represents a severe challenge to any notion of solidarity between the two continents. The exponential growth in irregular migration and the repeated humanitarian crises that epitomise failed attempts to reach the shores of Europe means that the EU and member states are under severe pressure to act. Currently member states find it easier to focus on strengthening their borders instead of providing more resources to improve living conditions (and security) in the countries of origin. A cohesive sustainable response will need European and African governments to pursue demanding cooperative action to advance their own interests and to find common cause.

Often linked to European colonial activity, the churches have extensive links with Africa and a longstanding commitment to sustainable development. Two months prior to British accession to the Community, the Church of England's General Synod debated the report 'Britain in Europe' (Board of

Social Responsibility, 1972), which emphasized the need for the European Community to "make a more effective contribution to the improvement of living standards in the developing countries" (Mission and Public Affairs Division, 2004: 41). In 1983, the then Archbishop of Canterbury, Robert Runcie, declared:

> If you picture the world as a great ocean liner, then most of Europe is sitting in the First class dining rooms. Unfortunately, water is pouring into the steerage where the poorer passengers are huddled. The captain and crew must take some time from devising ever more sophisticated menus for the first-class passengers in order to deal with this threat to the whole ship. My hope for the Churches of Europe is that they will not be found saying grace in the first class compartment as the ship sinks, but will be trying to raise the alarm. If we fail with the problems of the steerage we shall not remain insulated from the effects of the incoming water for ever.
>
> (Runcie, 1983: 159)

The ecumenical Churches Commission for Migrants in Europe (CCME) based in Brussels is a respected international think tank on the issue and has substantial expertise and grass roots experience to offer policy makers as they wrestle with the urgent complexities of migration (CCME, n.d.). At the same time there is increasing recognition that the churches, and faith based organisations more generally, are significant actors in a wide range of development contexts (such as health-care provision in sub-Saharan Africa) (Moyo and Ying-Ling Keir, 2014).

Working with the United Nations

> A Representative of the United Nations will be accredited to the Authority, and will be instructed to make a public report to the United Nations twice yearly, giving an account of the working of the new organisation, particularly as concerns the safe-guarding of its objectives.

Perhaps this element of Schuman's Declaration more than any other is a child of its time. It expressed an over-confidence in the embryonic United Nations. Schuman could not have imagined that the proposal for a European Coal and Steel Community might develop into a political union of 500 million. Brussels has become a global capital with the highest concentration of diplomats in the world – higher than in New York, the seat of the United Nations. Rather than needing to account to the United Nations the EU normally acts in UN negotiations as a single body. The EU has a permanent delegation in New York while the UN also has a substantial presence in Brussels. The UN and EU present themselves as partners with numerous joint projects. The UN Brussels office states:

> The United Nations and European Commission are united by common values and principles – by a shared commitment to essential rights and freedoms outlined in the Charter of the United Nations. We pursue common objectives such as the Millennium Developments Goals, and have a shared responsibility for ensuring that we work to reach them in the most effective way.
>
> (Migiro, 2006: 4)

The EU is an unnumbered extra player at G7, G8 or G20 gatherings. The president of the commission and the president of the council sit alongside heads of state or government at such events. As well as being an economy of global significance, the EU brings its commitment to human rights and sustainable development, and belief in a law/rule based approach.

The EU, therefore, cannot without contradicting itself indulge in crude power projection elsewhere in the world at the expense of the virtues of self-limitation, compromise, and submission to the laws that underpin European integration. Rather it must seek to export these virtues. It is no coincidence that the EU's foreign policies have met with their rare successes mostly when European positions expressed values of engagement, respect for the rule of law, and multilateralism (Andréani, 1999: 26). The creation of the EEAS and the appointment of a High Representative for external relations (OJ C115, 2008) were clear signs that the EU was punching below its weight. The current turbulence in global affairs meant that the new service was under pressure to deliver even before its launch. In a world where religion is an implicit as well as explicit element of international relationships, and sometimes key to understanding interactions between different actors, it is therefore important that officials of the EEAS are fully conversant with the complex dimensions of the relationship between religion and foreign policy, and able to recognise that religion can not only mitigate conflict but also absolutise it, thereby exacerbating divisions that might otherwise be resolved by compromise. Here the churches face the demanding task of translating their theological commitments to peace and reconciliation into intelligent and informed support for effective policy-making and practical diplomacy, while policy-makers will need to build upon the as yet optional and embryonic religious literacy training recently introduced by the FCO and shared with the EEAS (UK Parliament, 2014).

Christianity and European democracy

The reading of the Schuman Declaration I have offered obviously invites the question whether such public theology has any place in the contemporary secularised EU. The public expression of Christian faith was part and parcel of the era in which Schuman lived and worked. Politicians would make unembarrassed reference to God or prayer or to the church; such were expected in a Europe so profoundly shaped by Christianity. Even Winston Churchill, who described himself as more a buttress than a pillar of the Church of England, made frequent public reference to the Christian faith (Kemper, 1995: 199). Yet with the exception of those from explicitly Christian political traditions, most contemporary EU politicians are reluctant to accept the legitimacy of overt references to the Christian faith in political settings. As Guy Milton relates in Chapter 10, such tensions were exposed during the debate about the mention of God or Christianity in the preamble to the Constitution of the European Union. Those who championed the secular nature of the European institutions and those who were anxious not to marginalise other faith traditions ensured that explicit reference to Christianity was rejected (Milton, 2005).

The legacy of Schuman might suggest a response along the following lines. Those who supported the mention of God in the Constitution argued that a European polity needed to state its source of values explicitly, while also affirming the rights of all to freedom of belief. As the Bishop of London observed:

> The question of the source of values and principles is profoundly significant and this is why many Europeans are pressing for a recognition of the importance for many citizens of the Union of naming the divine source of values and principles. This should obviously be done in a way that does not marginalise those who would argue that they derived their values and principles from different sources but the Union will be weaker if it excludes faith.
> (Chartres, 2003: 473)

The former Archbishop of Canterbury, Rowan Williams, hardly an apologist for Christendom, has argued that European political actors from all traditions should engage with the root values of our shared democratic culture. In his visit to Brussels in 2005, Williams emphasised, surprisingly to some, the pivotal contribution of the church to the evolution of pluralism, and argued that continued dialogue with the church was important for the future health of democracy in Europe (2012: 75–84). The Christian church (as John Loughlin's chapter points out) is the most extensive and longest enduring institution in Europe. The Roman-based church legislated across the cultural and linguistic boundaries of the continent and beyond. Even after the Reformation, the Roman Catholic Church retained an international reach even while sharing a contested public space with new civil authorities as well as with the new national churches. In the eighteenth century, the reaction against traditional forms of authority, including the church, led to the emergence of the Enlightenment model of universal secular legality. In different parts of Europe, Catholic universalism and the common traditions of custom and mutuality were replaced with a system of legally framed equality and freedom largely separated from religious sanction. Throughout the centuries the churches jostled for space, quarrelling and making deals with the state authorities and each other. In the process they inevitably exercised a substantial and enduring impact on the shared values of the continent (for both good and ill).

Williams argues that the complex and evolving relationships between the churches, common law, canon law, and Romanised law meant that political power in Western Europe was the subject of negotiation and balance (2012: 75–84). The power of the state could be questioned by the church and was restrained by feudal and other obligations to the people. The church was also required to continually reconceptualise its place in society. The Christian history of the continent is thus not solely about the history of the faith but also the history of a political argument, one which was less about debating the appropriateness of church–state relationships and more about the sharing and shaping of public space. In the major strands of political theology informing these debates, the state is construed not, as in popular caricature, as possessing an absolute power conferred directly by God (as the more extreme versions of the 'divine right of kings' had it). Rather, the state was to be held accountable to divine authority via the restraining medium of law (revealed, natural, and positive). The whole political sphere was seen as standing under, and constrained by, a divine mandate. Political actors are ultimately accountable to a power higher than any human assembly. A wide range of positions, some converging, some competing, were claimed as flowing from these debates in political theology. Yet, Williams suggests, notions of pluralism, creative engagement with the state, and recognised limitations on the power of the state that underpin modern European democracy cannot properly be understood apart from these earlier debates in Christian political theology. "Europe is what it is because of its Christian history", he asserts – even if the church often initially resisted liberalising developments (Williams, 2012: 78):

> Reformation and Enlightenment protests upon which much of 'modernity' in Europe rests did not come from nowhere; they were centrally theological disputes, even when they were resolved in ways inimical to the authority and public influence of faith. If we are unaware today of this background, we shall misunderstand where the liberal tradition comes from; and we shall be more than ever vulnerable to a sort of unhistorical optimism.
> (Williams, 2005)

The presence and participation of the church, Williams argues, has served as a persistent reminder that the state does not have ultimate claims on its subjects. Thus if the churches – and other religious communities – were to be excluded from the public realm, liberal democracy would be at risk of sliding into an illiberal pseudo-religion. Williams thus argues, no doubt counterintuitively to many, that Europe shaped by interaction with the church has offered to the world a model in which argument and diversity limit the authority claims of the state. When religious communities are acknowledged as partners in public debate, their creative engagement with secular authorities is likely to lead to authentically European outcomes that benefit the common good. A mature European polity should therefore actively seek partnership with the component faith communities within the state. Doing so knowingly is not any kind of lapse into 'theocracy' but rather the opposite – sustaining a healthy and constructive pluralism. Dialogue with the faith communities and other values-based organizations, Williams holds, enables the Union to engage with its inherited values with integrity and to recognise their contributions to European public space and public policy.

Conclusion

The short history of the European Union is remarkable. A war-torn and economically and politically bankrupt continent has been transformed, peace amongst the EU member states is now taken for granted and the creation of a prosperous multi-national democracy of 500 million people living in 28 member states has far surpassed the dreams of even the most visionary of the post-war generation. The Europe that gave birth to Schuman, De Gasperi, Monnet, and Adenauer had been profoundly shaped by the history of the Christian Church. For the founders of the European Community this was a clear translation of the commitments of Christian public theology into political, social, and economic reality. The presence and persistence of the Christian church within 2000 years of European history not only embedded Christian values within the cultural life of the continent but also contributed to the shaping of the public realm. Notwithstanding its numerous and amply well-documented failings, the churches' extensive engagement with government, including periodic arguments relating to power, authority, independence, and allegiance, has shaped a Europe in which diversity and democratic argument limit the pretensions of the state and safeguard a wide realm of equal public freedom for all citizens. If there is truth in this, we may perhaps look to the Schuman Declaration as more than merely an interesting *pièce d'occasion*.

Appendix: The Schuman Declaration – A transcript

World Peace cannot be safeguarded without the making of creative efforts proportionate to the dangers which threaten it. The contribution which an organized and living Europe can bring to civilization is indispensable to the maintenance of peaceful relations. In taking upon herself for more than 20 years the role of champion of a united Europe, France has always had as her essential aim the service of peace. A united Europe was not achieved and we had war.

Europe will not be made all at once, or according to a single plan. It will be built through concrete achievements which will first create a *de facto* solidarity. The coming together of the nations of Europe requires the elimination of the age-old opposition of France and Germany. Any action must in the first place concern these two countries.

With this aim in view, the French government proposes that action be taken immediately on one limited but decisive point: It proposes that Franco-German production of coal and steel as a whole be placed under a common High Authority, within the framework of an organisation open to the participation of the other countries in Europe.

The pooling of coal and steel production should immediately provide for the setting up of common foundations for economic development as a first step in the federation of Europe and will change the destinies of those regions which have long been devoted to the manufacture of munitions of war, of which they have been the most constant victims.

The solidarity in production thus established will make it plain that any war between France and Germany becomes not merely unthinkable but materially impossible. The setting up of this powerful productive unit, open to all countries willing to take part and bound ultimately to provide all the member countries with the basic elements of industrial production on the same terms, will lay a true foundation for their economic unification.

The production will be offered to the world as a whole without distinction or exception, with the aim of contributing to raising living standards and to promoting peaceful achievements. With increased resources Europe will be able to pursue the achievement of one of its essential tasks, viz the development of the African continent.

In this way, there will be realised simply and speedily that fusion of interests which is indispensable to the establishment of a common economic system; it may be the leaven from which may grow a wider and deeper community between countries long opposed to another by sanguinary divisions.

By pooling basic production and instituting a new High Authority, whose decisions will bind France, Germany and other member countries, this proposal will lead to the realization of the first concrete foundation of a European federation indispensable to the preservation of peace.

To promote the realization of the objectives defined, the French Government is ready to open negotiations on the following bases:

The task with which this common High Authority will be charged will be that of securing in the shortest possible time the modernization of production and the improvement of its quality; the supply of coal and steel on identical terms to the French and German markets, as well as to the markets of other member countries; the development in common of exports to other countries; the equalization and improvement of the living conditions of workers in these industries.

To achieve these objectives, starting from the very different conditions in which the production of member countries is at present situated, it is proposed that certain transitional measures should be instituted, such as the application of a production and investment plan, the establishment of compensating machinery for equating prices, and the creation of a restructuring fund to facilitate the rationalization of production. The movement of coal and steel between member countries will immediately be freed from all customs duty, and will not be affected by differential transport rates. Conditions will gradually be created which will spontaneously provide for the more rational distribution of production at the highest level of productivity.

In contrast to international cartels, which tend to impose restrictive practices on distribution and the exploitation of national markets, and to maintain high profits, the organization will ensure the fusion of markets and the expansion of production.

The essential principles and undertakings defined above will be the subject of a treaty signed between the States and submitted for the ratification of their parliaments. The negotiations required to settle details of applications will be undertaken with the help of an arbitrator appointed by common agreement. He will be entrusted with the task of seeing that the agreements reached conform to the principles laid down, and, in the event of a deadlock, he will decide what solution is to be adopted. The common High Authority entrusted with the management of the scheme will be composed of independent persons appointed by the governments, giving equal representation. A chairman will be chosen by common agreement between the governments. The Authority's decisions will be enforceable in France, Germany and other member countries. Appropriate measures will be provided for means of appeal against the decisions of the Authority.

A representative of the United Nations will be accredited to the Authority, and will be instructed to make a public report to the United Nations twice yearly, giving an account of the working of the new organization, particularly as concerns the safeguarding of its objectives.

The institution of the High Authority will in no way prejudge the methods of ownership of enterprises. In the exercise of its functions, the common High Authority will take into account the powers conferred upon the International Ruhr Authority and the obligations of all kinds imposed upon Germany, so long as these remain in force.

Paris, 9 May 1950

Notes

1 See Transcript in the Appendix.
2 See Lejeune (2000) for biographical details.
3 Subsequent italicized quotations in this section are all from the Schuman Declaration (1950a), as reproduced in the Appendix.
4 These included Bulgaria, the Czech Republic, Hungary, Poland, Romania and Slovakia in 2004, followed by the three Baltic states that had been part of the Soviet Union, Estonia, Latvia and Lithuania, in 2007.

References

Andréani, G. (1999). *Europe's uncertain identity*. CER Essay, 5 February. London: Centre for European Reform. Retrieved from www.cer.org.uk/publications/archive/essay/1999/europes-uncertain-identity

Board for Social Responsibility. (1972). *Britain in Europe: Social responsibility of the Church*. GS 95. London: Church of England.

Chartres, R. (2003). The strange absence of God from the Constitution. Conference of Holy Synod (Church of Greece): Values and Principles for the Building of Europe. 5 May. Athens, Greece.

Churches' Commission for Migrants in Europe (CCME). (n.d.). Thematic priorities areas of work 2009–2015. Retrieved from www.ccme.be/areas-of-work/.
Coward, H., and Smith, G. S. (eds) (2004). *Religion and peacebuilding*. Albany, NY: SUNY.
European Commission. (2014a). *The European Union explained: International cooperation and development*. November. Brussels, Belgium: EC Directorate-General for Communication / Citizens Information.
European Commission. (2014b). *International cooperation and development: Fighting poverty in a changing world*. Luxembourg: Publications Office of the European Union. Retrieved from www.eeas.europa.eu/africa/.
European Commission. (2009). Press release IP/09/655. Retrieved from http://europa.eu/rapid/press-release_IP-09-655_en.htm?locale=en.
European Commission. (2008). Working for the regions: European Union regional policy 2007–2013. Brussels, Belgium: Inforegio. Retrieved from http://ec.europa.eu/regional_policy/sources/docgener/presenta/working2008/work_en.pdf.
European External Action Service. (2015a). 'European neighbourhood policy'. Retrieved from http://eeas.europa.eu/enp/.
European External Action Service. (2015b). The EU's relations with Africa. Retrieved from www.eeas.europa.eu/africa/.
European Union. (2015a). 'Living in the EU.' Retrieved from http://europa.eu/about-eu/facts-figures/living/index_en.htm.
European Union. (2015b). 'European development aid'. Retrieved from https://europa.eu/eyd2015/en/content/eu-development-aid.
European Union. (1957). 'The treaty of Rome'. Retrieved from www.eurotreaties.com/rometreaty.pdf.
Fountain, J. (2010). *Deeply rooted: The forgotten legacy of Robert Schuman*. Amsterdam: The Schuman Centre for European Studies.
Hill, C. (2010). *Church of England House of Bishops Europe Panel*. London: Church of England.
Hume, B. (1994). *Remaking Europe: The gospel in a divided continent*. London: SPCK.
Johnston, D. (ed.) (2003). *Faith-based diplomacy: Trumping realpolitik*. New York: Oxford University Press.
Kemper, R. C. (ed.) (1995). *Winston Churchill: Resolution, defiance, magnanimity, good will*. Columbia, MO: University of Missouri Press.
Lejeune, R. (2000). *Robert Schuman, père de l'Europe 1863–1963: La politique, chemin de sainteté*. Paris: Fayard.
Maswana, J.-C. (2010). The global financial crisis and recession: Impact on and development prospects for Africa. JICA Research Institute Working Paper. 15 April. Tokyo, Japan: International Cooperation Agency Research Institute.
Mayne, R. (1996). Schuman, de Gasperi, Spaak: The European frontiersmen. In Bond, M., Smith, J., and Wallace, M., (eds), *Eminent Europeans* (pp. 24–27). London: Greycoat.
Migiro, A.-R. (2006). Foreword by the United Nations Deputy Secretary-General. In United Nations. *Improving lives: Results from the partnership of the United Nations and the European Commission in 2006*. Brussels, Belgium: United Nations.
Milton, G. (2006). *The European Union: A theological perspective*. Ethics Series, E143. Cambridge: Grove Booklets.
Milton, G. (2005). *The European constitution: Its origins, negotiation and meaning*. London: John Harper.

Mission and Public Affairs Division. (2004). *The Church of England and Europe report*. London: Church of England.

Moyo, P., and Ying-Ling Keir, C. (2014). 'An assessment of the role of faith-based organisations in HIV/AIDS mitigation, treatment and care: The case of Buddhist compassion relief in KwaZulu Natal, South Africa'. *Mediterranean Journal of Social Sciences* 5(2): 345–351. Retrieved from www.mcser.org/journal/index.php/mjss/article/viewFile/1994/1993.

Novosseloff, A. (2012). 'United Nations – European Union cooperation in the field of peacekeeping: Challenges and prospects'. *CGGI Analysis Paper* 4/2012. Brussels, Belgium: Global Governance Institute.

OJ C115. (2008). Consolidated versions of the Treaty on European Union and the Treaty on the Functioning of the European Union. 9 May.

Runcie, R. (1983). *Windows onto God*. London: SPCK.

Schuman, R. (1950a). The Schuman Declaration. 9 May. Retrieved from http://europa.eu/about-eu/basic-information/symbols/europe-day/schuman-declaration/index_en.htm.

Schuman, R. (1950b). Opening speech at the Schuman Plan Conference in Paris, 20 June 1950. Luxembourg: Centre Virtuel de la Connaissance sur l'Europe (CVCE). Retrieved from www.cvce.eu/en/recherche/unit-content/-/unit/5cc6b004-33b7-4e44-b6db-f5f9e6c01023/4d82341b-4d28-4cb5-95d9-41b3c630bdc1/Resources#411d38eb-3475-4a98-b0b3-aecce8ca60a7_en&overlay.

Schuman, R. (1949). The definition of the new Europe. Speech made at the signing of the Statutes of the Council of Europe, 5 May. Retrieved from http://users.belgacombusiness.net/schuman/5May1949.htm.

Sutherland, P. (2008). Europe and its values [Audio recording]. *Hugh Kay Lecture*. Huntingdon: CABE. Retrieved from www.cabe-online.org/2013/01/peter-sutherland-2008-cabe-hugh-kay-lecture/.

The Anglican Church in Greece. (2013). Social and welfare activities of the Anglican congregations in Athens, 29 Dec. Retrieved from www.anglicanchurch.gr/9.html

Thistlethwaite, S. B. (ed.) (2011). *Interfaith just peacemaking: Jewish, Christian, and Muslim perspectives on the new paradigm of peace and war*. New York: Palgrave Macmillan.

UK Parliament. (2014). 'Freedom of religion or belief'. Retrieved fromwww.publications.parliament.uk/pa/cm201415/cmselect/cmfaff/551/55111.htm.

Williams, R. (2012). *Faith in the Public Square*. London: Bloomsbury.

Williams, R. (2005). Religion culture diversity and tolerance: Shaping the new Europe. Retrieved from http://rowanwilliams.archbishopofcanterbury.org/articles.php/1179/religion-culture-diversity-and-tolerance-shaping-the-new-europe-address-at-the-european-policy-centr.

2 European integration
A Catholic perspective

John Loughlin

Introduction

When Pope John Paul II addressed the European Parliament in 1988, the Rev. Ian Paisley MEP, the strident late-Protestant pastor from Northern Ireland, stood up and denounced him as 'the anti-Christ' before being ejected from the chamber by some of his fellow MEPs. Paisley was denouncing not just the Catholic Pope but also what he perceived as the relationship between the European Union and the Catholic Church. Although most Anglican and European Protestant traditions have come to accept the European integration process as a positive development, some of the hard-line 'Free Churches', such as the Free Presbyterians founded by Paisley, continue to regard it as a 'Popish plot' the aim of which was to undermine Protestantism in Europe (Nelsen, Guth, and Fraser, 2001).

At first sight, these staunchly Protestant rejections seem far-fetched. If one looks more closely, however, it might seem that there was in fact, at least in the past, a close connection between Catholicism and the project of European unification. As Gary Wilton observed in the previous chapter, most of the 'founding fathers' were Catholics and, in the cases of Konrad Adenauer, Alcide de Gasperi, and Robert Schuman, were practising and even 'devout.'[1] When reading the biographies of these three men it becomes clear that their Catholic faith was also one of the well-springs underlying their devotion to a unified Europe (Chenaux, 2007: 103–120). René Pleven and Jean Monnet were also Catholics but their faith does not seem to have been as central to their political lives as it was in the other three founders. Not all the founders, however, were Catholic. Paul-Henri Spaak, for example, was a Belgian Socialist rooted in the French secularist tradition of *laïcité,* although he did share some of the political positions of the Christian Democrats (Chenaux, 2007: 123). René Mayer was a Jewish French Radical and André Philip was a Protestant French Socialist (SFIO). Nevertheless, it was probably not accidental that the 1957 Treaty establishing the EEC was signed in Rome nor that the signatories received the public blessing of Pope Pius XII, who was a fervent supporter of the project. To add to the paranoiac anti-Catholic fears of Ian Paisley, the design of the European flag with its 12 stars (and not the number of member states) was allegedly inspired by Revelation 12:1 ("A great sign appeared in heaven, a woman clothed with the sun, and the moon under her feet, and on her head a crown of twelve stars"), which Catholic biblical exegesis from the Middle Ages had interpreted as referring to the Blessed Virgin Mary. Contemporary European officials have sought to play down this reference and have claimed that it is a myth; but the artist who designed the flag, Arsène Heitz, told a newspaper that this was indeed his intention (*Economist*, 2004). Of course, such a symbol would be deeply unattractive to Reformation churches of whatever type. Finally, among academics, there has also often been an assumption (also discussed by Sander Luitwieler in Chapter 3) that Catholicism is broadly supportive of European integration on the grounds that it has always been more 'supranational' while the Anglican and Protestant Churches have been more identified with the modern nation-state (Marks and Wilson, 2000: 438).

The chapter will argue that there is indeed a close connection between Catholicism and European integration and that the official Catholic Church,[2] at the level of the papacy and of many national hierarchies in Europe, has been strongly in favour of it. The chapter will examine the historical context in which this connection has been forged and outline some of the reasons why Rome has been so pro-European. It will also, however, show that the straight one-to-one association between Catholicism and supranationalism and Protestant and the nation-state is over simplified and that a more nuanced interpretation of Catholic approaches to European integration is necessary. Indeed, the Catholic Church has usually been concerned with world rather than simply European affairs and sees the latter from a global perspective. Finally, the chapter will seek to evaluate European integration as it has evolved in practice from the perspective of Catholic theology and social teaching.

The historical context of Rome's relations with 'Europe'

The history of Europe, or at least of the western half of Europe, is also, to a very large extent, the history of the Catholic Church. After surviving serious persecutions in the early years of its existence in the Roman Empire, Christianity found itself in a new situation when the Emperor Constantine converted to the new faith in AD 312. By 380, despite several setbacks, Christianity had progressed sufficiently to supplant Paganism when the eastern Emperor Theodosius and his western counterpart Gratian recognized Christianity as the official religion of the Empire. From this point onwards the Church became intertwined with the political and administrative system of the Empire; its own organization into dioceses closely resembled the imperial structures. Bishops became more or less functionaries of the Emperor, especially in the eastern Empire. It was there that many theological disputes were decided by councils that were summoned by the Emperor and took place under his supervision. At the same time, the Pope, as the Bishop of

Rome and successor of Peter,[3] held the position of *primus inter pares*, which was recognized by the other patriarchal Sees in Jerusalem, Constantinople, Antioch, and Alexandria. East and West shared the same fundamental Christian beliefs but, quite early on, there developed differences in liturgy, spirituality, forms of monastic life, and relationship to the Emperor in each part of the Empire. These differences would eventually lead to the Great Schism of 1054 which split the Latin and Byzantine branches of Christianity, a split that was exacerbated by the Fourth Crusade (1202–04) when crusaders ransacked Constantinople itself rather than achieving their goal of freeing the Holy Land from Muslim occupation.

The two parts of the Empire developed territorial governance and legal systems that were quite different. In the East, the Byzantine Emperor dominated the Church and bishops were more or less functionaries of the state. In the West, there evolved the Papacy and the Holy Roman Empire, feudalism, and later, centralizing states such as France and England, independent cities, and city leagues such as the Hanseatic. This complex system of forms of territorial governance was one in which different orders of sovereignty and law intertwined with each other: customary law, elements of Roman law, ecclesiastical law, and imperial law. Spruyt has described relationships among the different territorial entities as being marked by "competition." He claims that the "winners" in this competition were the territorial states that eventually evolved into the modern nation-states, claiming absolute sovereignty over distinct territories and subordinating all the other entities, including the Church (Spruyt, 1994: 153–181).

The Enlightenment and the nation-state

'Nations' have existed for centuries (for example, the crusaders or universities were organized into national groupings) and, especially in the centralizing monarchies (for example, among the Tudors) there was a sense of national consciousness. But historians such as Linda Colley (2005) and Liah Greenfeld (1992) see the sixteenth-century Reformation as a prime factor in the development of the modern nation, and eventually of the nation-state, as a distinct territorial entity in which territory, sovereignty, and, at first, religion were closely linked. The 1648 Treaty of Westphalia consolidated this consciousness through the creation of state churches and a new system of sovereignty whereby states of different confessional allegiances did not interfere in the affairs of other states on behalf of their co-religionists. This was the confirmation of a principle already enunciated at the 1555 Peace of Ausburg: *cuius regio, eius religio*, which might be paraphrased as: the religion of the ruler will be the religion of the ruled (and the state). This is the origin of the principles of national sovereignty and non-intervention characteristic of modern international relations. Thus, Lutheran states did not intervene to protect Lutherans in Catholic states and vice versa. It is this principle of non-intervention that, in a secularized form, is the basis of modern international relations, even if its religious roots have been largely forgotten.

It is thus during the sixteenth and seventeenth centuries that the modern nation and the modern state were being formed, although they still remained alongside the older forms of political organization such as the Holy Roman Empire and dynastic unions such as that between Scotland and England. 'Religion', in the sense of the different branches of Western Christianity, was an integral part of these developments although not always in a positive sense. This period has been dubbed by historians as that of the 'Wars of Religion' and the memory of these would have profound consequences for future reflections on the relationship between religion (the Christian denominations) and the civil authorities (the new emerging nation-states).

Although recent historical work has tended to play down the explicitly religious or theological dimensions of these European wars (Cavanaugh, 2009), they undoubtedly affected how subsequent philosophers and statesmen thought about religion and the state. At least among the European intellectual elites, throughout the seventeenth and eighteenth (the Enlightenment) centuries, there began a process of questioning of the place of religion in general, and Christianity and the Christian churches in particular, in the modern state. Although most of the philosophers of this period such as Hobbes, Locke, and Rousseau were believers of some kind, they tended towards Deism rather than orthodox Christianity. Some, such as David Hume in Scotland and Laplace in France, were atheists. Voltaire, rather cynically, thought that religion might be useful in keeping the lower classes in check, but the dominant tendency was to try to exclude it from public affairs. The 'Wars of Religion' referred to above provided the rationale for this position. The ground was thus laid for the 'secularization of the European mind' (Chadwick, 1975) and the emergence of the secular state.

This was the intellectual background of a series of revolutions that created the conditions of a new modern political system: the 1688 Glorious Revolution in England that changed the relations between the monarch and parliament (although it severely restricted the rights of Catholics); the American Revolution (1765–83), which rejected the sovereign rule of the English monarch and asserted that of the people and created the first modern federation and, at the same time, separated church and state; and the French Revolution (beginning in 1789) that established the link between nation and state, thus creating the nation-state. In France, after the attempt to create a new religion based on 'Reason', there also emerged a more radical version of secularism compared to the American version based on the notion of *laïcité*, which sought, not simply the removal of religious groups from the running of the state but also from all public life (Burleigh, 2005). Throughout the nineteenth and early twentieth centuries, the secular nation-state would thus become the primary form of political organization and be closely identified with 'modernity' and 'progress'.

Catholic responses to the arrival of 'modernity'

The Catholic Church responded to the rise of modernity in a variety of ways, but largely negatively as the emergence of the new secular nation-state called into question its own political and spiritual authority (Taylor, 2007). Indeed, nation-state nationalism throughout the nineteenth century was closely identified with liberalism and, especially in Catholic countries such as France, Italy and Spain, anti-clericalism. This rejection would reach its apogée in the famous *Syllabus of Errors* promulgated by Pius IX in 1864. At other levels of the Church, however, there was an adaptation to the new forms of political organization. In France, for example, even before the Revolution, the Church adopted Gallicanism, which emphasized the French *national* Church as opposed to *ultramontanism,* which meant loyalty to Rome. Furthermore, in some countries, especially in Ireland and Poland, Catholicism became a key element of nation-state nationalist mobilization and identity. Rome did not always look kindly on these associations, as can be shown in Ireland where the Vatican tended to support the British authorities against some kinds of radical nationalism and especially those that resorted to violence. The point here is that there was not one, single, homogeneous 'Catholic' position on these developments but a series of nuanced positions at different levels of Church life.

The Catholic Church and Europe in the twentieth century

After the election of Leo XIII (1810–1903) as Pope in 1878, the papacy began to come to terms with the modern world, recognizing that the developments it had resisted for so long were irreversible. Leo acknowledged this in his encyclical *Rerum Novarum* promulgated in 1891, a critical and cautious response to modernity that initiated what would become the great corpus of Catholic Social Teaching developed by his successors (Carrier, 1990; McHugh, 2008). Nevertheless, there was still a reluctance on the part of Rome to support nation-state nationalism which the Popes believed to be among the principal causes of war. The first half of the twentieth century was marked by the two world wars and the rise of the totalitarian regimes of Soviet Communism, Italian Fascism and German National Socialism. All of the Popes who reigned during this period believed that these regimes and their underpinning ideologies posed a threat to the very future of humanity itself. During the First World War, the reigning Pope Benedict XV (1854–1922) sought to bring both the Allies and the Axis powers to a peaceful settlement. He was unsuccessful in this and the Catholic Church was excluded from a place in the League of Nations set up after the War. In response to the rise of Fascism in Italy and Nazism in Germany, the Church under Pope Pius XI (1857–1939) adopted a critical but cautious position. On the one hand, it sought to protect the interests of the Church through Concordats. On the other hand, it denounced the ideologies of these movements. Pius promulgated the encyclical *Mit Brennende Sorge* ('with burning anxiety') in 1937 written in German (rather than the usual Latin) as a blistering critique of National Socialism. The encyclical was written with the help of Eugenio Pacelli (1899–1958), Pius XI's Secretary of State and future Pope Pius XII (1939–58).

The Popes, Europe, and the world

During these catastrophic 50 years of European history, the primary concern of the Popes was European and world peace rather than European integration, although of course the latter was also seen positively (Launay, 1999: 11–39). It is true that in the first half of the twentieth century, there was, in some Catholic intellectual circles, especially in France, Belgium, and Italy, a growing European movement that identified the modern nation-state as one of the primary causes of war and thus seeking the end of the nation-state. One important figure was the aristocrat Count Richard von Coudenhove-Kalergi (1894–1972), the founder of the Pan-European Union. Coudenhove-Kalergi published his book *Pan-Europa* in 1923 and the Union held its first congress in Vienna in 1926. Although Coudenhove-Kalergi was a Catholic, his pro-European inspiration came more from his family background, which was multi-ethnic, multicultural, and polyglot. His philosophical beliefs probably owed more to what he himself described as the 'great Europeans', who included figures such as Kant, Napoleon, Nietzsche, Thomas Mann, and Winston Churchill than to Catholicism (Prettenthaler-Ziegerhofer, 2012).

In the inter-war period, however, there was also a movement of mainly, but not exclusively, Catholic intellectuals such as Arnaud Dandieu, Alexandre Marc, and Jacques Maritain, who developed the political philosophy known as 'personalism'. *Personalism* was a philosophical approach that understood the human person in a way different from both individualistic liberalism and totalitarian systems such as Fascism, Nazism, and Marxism, all of which reduced the human person to a cipher in a social class, party, or state. Personalism, to the contrary, viewed the human person as an organic being, rooted in a particular family, community, and society and opening out to other persons. In this perspective, human persons are essentially relational and achieve their full humanity only in society while retaining their inalienable individuality.

Despite these common positions, there were, however, three different schools of personalist thought of which two were explicitly Catholic and one of which was strongly European. The original group, gathered around a journal entitled *Ordre Nouveau,* was founded in 1930 in Paris by a young journalist called Alexandre Marc. Marc was a convert to Catholicism from Judaism and the group Ordre Nouveau grew out of Le Club de Moulin which was founded in 1929 as a centre of religious and ecumenical encounter. Other prominent intellectuals associated with the group were Robert Aron, Claude Chevalley, Arnaud Dandieu, Daniel-Rops, Jean Jardin, Alexandre Marc, and Denis de Rougemont (Roy, 1999a). Although not all the members of the group were Catholic (for example de Rougement was a Swiss Protestant), the majority were, and their version of philosophical personalism, inspired by diverse thinkers from Proudhon to Max Scheler but also Leo XIII's *Rerum Novarum*, was an attempt to relate Catholic social thought to the modern world. Their aim was to bring about a personalist 'revolution' in opposition to those ideologies of the left and right mentioned above that crushed the human person and prevented his full flourishing. What is interesting for this chapter is that they also developed a version of European federalism inspired by personalism, which differed from what they regarded as 'Anglo-Saxon' federalism of the type found the USA. This was based on the understanding of the human person as a being *rooted* in a particular ethnic, cultural, religious, or linguistic group but who *opens out* in an organic way to other similar persons in community. During the War, some members of Ordre Nouveau thought the Pétainist regime fulfilled some of their societal ideals and joined that regime. Many, however, joined the resistance and, after the War, emerged as militants of European federalism and particularly of what became known as *le fédéralisme intégral*. Alexandre Marc was one of the leaders of this movement and Denis de Rougement coined the term 'Europe of the Regions' in the 1960s to designate a certain kind of federalism the basic units of which were 'regions' rather than 'nation-states' (Loughlin, 1988). Given these political choices, Christian Roy designates the stance of the Ordre Nouveau as 'federalist personalism' and its leading light was Alexandre Marc.

The journal *Esprit* was founded in 1932 by Emmanuel Mounier, another committed Catholic who was part of the group of 'non-conformist' intellectuals of the period (Mounier, 1952). Mounier originally adopted the notion of personalism from the Ordre Nouveau group but, by 1934, began to define it in a rather different manner, stressing 'communitarianism'. Mounier emerged during the resistance and after the War as an 'intellectuel de gauche' and was more engaged in an attempted dialogue with Marxism while remaining a fervent Catholic. Mounier was less engaged, however, with European federalism and *Esprit* and *Ordre Nouveau* (both the group and the journal) became increasingly distant from each other. However, his movement did have one important impact: the young Jacques Delors, another Catholic who became a Socialist in the 1950s, described himself as "a personalist, a disciple of Emmanuel Mounier" (Delors, 1999: 82). Delors' personalist 'faith' would become active once again when he took over as President of the European Commission in 1985.

A third group, however, based in Bordeaux, attempted at first to maintain the link between the two groups. Roy has used the term 'ecological personalism' to describe this branch and its two leading lights were Bernard Charbonneau and Jacques Ellul. In contrast to the Catholic-dominated ethos of the first two groups, Charbonneau and Ellul came from the French *laic* tradition, although Ellul converted back to his Protestant (Calvinist) roots and finally became a very well-known Protestant theologian and sociologist. Charbonneau remained an agnostic but was aware of the 'spiritual' dimension of human existence (Roy, 1999b: 35). In the late 1930s, the Charbonneau/

Ellul group grew closer to the Ordre Nouveau movement and became distant from *Esprit*. This is not so surprising as Denis de Rougement, himself a Swiss Calvinist, remained with Ordre Nouveau and Ellul had, therefore, a certain sympathy with his ideas. Both de Rougement and Ellul criticized *Esprit*'s Catholic ethos and, especially the position of Mounier, whom Ellul accused of being a "hard-line Catholic ... and not at all a liberal ... a Jesuit, in the bad sense of the term" (Roy, 1999b: 36). Charbonneau was less interested in the political aspects of personalism and more in the cultural and social aspects, especially the rise of a technological society, which he saw as crushing the human spirit. His project was of a personalist "revolution for an ascetic civilization, against poverty and against wealth" and Roy comments that this "may be seen as the first modern Western proposal for a voluntary limitation of a quantitative economic growth for the sake of a holistic sense of the quality of life" (Roy, 1999b: 35).

The Catholic Church and European integration after 1945

During the inter-war period, the personalist and European movements were followed only by intellectual minorities in the countries in which they were mainly based (France, Belgium, and Italy). During the War, however, the participation of some of their members in active resistance against Nazism and fascism and in discussions about what kind of Europe should emerge after the defeat of these movements, gave them a certain prestige and opened their ideas to a wider group of followers. *Pace* anti-Catholic polemics about the role of the Pope and the Catholic Church during the War that have developed since the mid-1960s, immediately after 1945 the Church was actually highly regarded by the liberated societies. Christian Democracy, the political movement closely linked to the Catholic Church, became one of the key forces that would shape post-war Europe in Italy, France, Germany, and the Benelux countries, in fact in all the countries that would form the nucleus of the European Community.

In a radio allocution given on 9th May 1945, immediately after the armistice, Pope Pius XII welcomed the prospect "of a new and better Europe, of a new and better universe, founded on ... on respect for human dignity, on the sacred principle of equality of the rights of all peoples and all states, large and small, weak and strong." Pius XII's primary concern before, during and after the War was international peace (Launay, 1999: 42–44). He did, however, also recognize that the efforts to create a new and unified Europe were conducive to achieving peace. For this reason, he supported the groups, and especially the Christian Democrats, who were promoting this cause. Three of the Christian Democrat founding fathers of European integration were Catholic: the German Konrad Adenauer, the Frenchman Robert Schuman, and the Italian Alcide De Gasperi. The biographies of the three men are strikingly similar and help to explain their strong commitment to a unified Europe. Not only were they, as noted, practising Catholics but each in his own way saw the

Christian faith as the foundation of European culture, values, and civilization. All three grew up in the cross-cultural and linguistically diverse frontier regions between France, Germany, and Italy. Schuman was born in Lorrain but studied in German universities. De Gasperi, an Italian-speaker, was born in the South Tyrol, a majority German-speaking region that then belonged to the Austria-Hungarian Empire, and pursued his studies in Vienna. Adenauer was born in Cologne, a Catholic bastion near the Belgian frontier, at the time of the *Kulturkamp* between Bismarck and the Catholic Church and became a Catholic militant. All three were imprisoned either by the Nazis or Fascists. All three were influenced by Catholic Social Teaching and, in particular, by the principle of subsidiarity, regarding the nation-state and nationalism as among the primary causes of the Second World War. The principle of subsidiarity, however, emphasized bringing decision making as close to the citizen as possible and saw the commune or the region as also important although this subnational level had been crushed by the centralizing nation-state.

As noted earlier, there were several other important actors in the early years of European integration who were not Catholic. It remains true, however, that the Christian Democrats were the driving force behind the European project in the early 1950s and their efforts were largely supported by the Vatican and Pope Pius XII (Kaiser, 2007). It is this that has given rise to the idea, mentioned in the introduction to this chapter, that European integration is largely a Catholic project and certain evangelical Christian groups in Northern Europe, of whom Ian Paisley is only perhaps the most extreme example have interpreted (and rejected) it in these terms (Nelsen, Guth, and Fraser, 2001). Some secularists also viewed European integration in terms of a Catholic plot. Vincent Auriol, Socialist President of the Fourth Republic (1947–54) commented sarcastically, "L'Eglise a fait triple alliance, Adenauer, Schuman, De Gasperi, trois tonsures sous une même calotte"[4] (quoted in Launay, 1999: 59). This hides, however, a considerable array of positions within Catholicism at this period. We have already mentioned the aim of universal peace that was the preoccupation of the Vatican and the Pope, although they also saw European integration as a step towards achieving this. Further, many Catholics were also sincerely attached to their respective nations and looked askance at some of the wilder ideas (e.g. the proposal to abolish the nation-state made by the *fédéralisme intégral* movement). In fact, the founding fathers were quite moderate with regard to the nation-state and recognized that this could not be abolished overnight but rather should be constrained and 'tamed' by new supranational institutions. In other words, they espoused a moderate federalism.

The Vatican and the Pope, and probably the majority of European Catholics, were also concerned at the menace represented by the USSR and the beginnings of the Cold War. Events such as the suppression of the Hungarian uprising by Soviet tanks in 1956 gave an extra urgency to stopping the spread of communism in Western societies. In the 1950s, however, the Catholic Church in some countries at a grassroots level, that is, at the level of lower clergy and some lay groups, was beginning to adopt positions that were more sympathetic to the Left and even to Marxism than was the Vatican. In France, Emmanuel Mounier's *Esprit* declared itself to be 'de gauche' and sought a dialogue with the secular Left. Some theologians such the Dominicans Marie-Dominique Chenu and Yves Congar and the Jesuit Henri de Lubac were elaborating what became known as *la nouvelle théologie*, revising Catholic theology to take into account contemporary social and cultural realities, including the alienation from the Church of large swathes of the working class in France and Belgium. This led to the founding of the 'worker priest' movement, which prompted many priests, mainly in France, to work in factories, mines, and other places to share more fully the lot of the working classes. This led them to position themselves in greater solidarity with the left and even with the communist and socialist parties but in opposition to the Church hierarchy (Poulat, 1999).

In the 1950s, one of the primary concerns of the Church hierarchy and Rome, however, was the threat of the USSR and this led the Vatican to suppress the worker priest movement, which would re-emerge only after the Second Vatican Council. It was this same fear of the USSR that also led the Vatican to support the embryonic European Community. It was not an accident, therefore, that the 1957 Treaty of Rome was signed in the Eternal City and that the delegates of the Six later had an audience with Pope Pius XII, thus leading to the allegations of European integration as a 'Popish' plot to which we have referred above. With the election of Angelo Roncalli as Pope John XXIII in 1958, however, the mood of the Church began to change. Roncalli is best known for having summoned the Second Vatican Council (1962–65) but, even before this, he was already adopting a more conciliatory attitude towards the Eastern bloc and the USSR. Although he did not neglect the European project, this now came to be construed increasingly in the context of the world peace. In April 1963, during the Second Vatican Council, John XXIII published *Pacem in Terris*, one of his key encyclicals and one of his last acts before his death in June of the same year. The universalism of Pope John XXIII may be seen in this phrase taken from *Pacem in Terris*: "We must remember that, of its very nature, civil authority exists, not to confine its people within the boundaries of their nation, but rather to protect, above all else the common good of that particular civil society, which certainly cannot be divorced from the common good of the entire human family" (John XXIII, 1963: §98).

The Council changed the Church's relationship with the modern world through encyclicals such as *Gaudium et Spes* (*The Pastoral Constitution on the Church in the Modern World*), the final step in the reconfiguring of the Church's reconciliation with modernity that had begun in 1891 with Leo XIII's encyclical *Rerum Novarum*. But the Council gave little attention to the European question preferring, like John XXIII and his successor Paul VI, to adopt the more universal and cosmopolitan approach. Nevertheless, this did not at all mean abandoning the European project. One of the outcomes of the

Vatican II was the formal establishment of Bishops' Conferences. These had existed informally but, in 1966, were now set up on a formal basis. The European Bishops' Conferences established two further groupings of Bishops. COMECE (*Commissio Episcopatuum Communitatis Europaeae* – The Commission of the Bishops' Conferences of the European Community) was founded in 1980 and tasked with following European Union (EU) legislation and providing feedback to the EU institutions. COMECE maintains a secretariat in Brussels with a full-time staff tracking EU developments and analysing them from a Catholic perspective. This is not to be confused with Council of the Bishops' Conferences of Europe or CCEE (*Consilium Conferentiarum Episcoporum Europae*), officially recognized in 1977, which is comprised of the 33 Catholic Bishops' Conferences of Europe and the archbishops of Luxembourg and of the Principality of Monaco, as well as the Bishop of Chişinău (Moldavia).

The Second Vatican Council took place in a period of optimism and economic expansion, at least in Western countries, and the Council, to a large extent and especially in documents such as *Gaudium et Spes*, reflected this optimism. Unlike previous Councils of the Church, the Council Fathers did not issue anathemas but sought rather to find reasons for reconciliation with other Christian bodies and with non-Christian religions as well. From the European perspective the fierce opposition to communism and the Soviet bloc diminished and both John XXIII and Paul VI developed an ecclesiastical *Ostpolitik* similar to the approach being developed by politicians such as the West German Chancellor Willy Brandt. Furthermore, theologians, influenced by the *nouvelle théologie*, many of whose leading exponents had been *periti* (experts) at the Council, engaged in a dialogue with atheists and Marxists seeking some common ground on issues such as social justice. Both Catholic and Protestant theologians began to develop new approaches to theology such as the theology of liberation (Gutiérrez, 1988). These were heady years marked by great optimism but, at least in the view of some commentators, instead of leading to the flourishing of the Catholic Church in Europe, they were on the contrary the beginning of the loss of its position as a social force with a rapid decline in Church practice and in vocations to the priesthood and religious life. Of course, it may be that the timing of the Council was unfortunate, taking place in the midst of the cultural revolution of the 1960s and that the decline would have happened anyway because of the wider changes in society. By the late 1970s and early 1980s, it was even unclear whether the Church would survive, particularly in countries such as the Netherlands and France. At the same time, the traditionally Christian parties such as the Italian DC, the German CDU/CSU and Dutch CDA (which was created through the amalgamation of Catholic and Protestant parties) had 'liberated' themselves from a close connection with their national hierarchies and the Vatican. In practice, though, this meant the CD parties aligning themselves with secularist perspectives on a range of ethical issues such as abortion and homosexuality. In Italy, the DC collapsed in a morass of corruption and finally disappeared.

Popes John Paul II and Benedict XVI

Pope John Paul II was elected in 1978 and brought a new perspective to European affairs. First, he was a Pole who had suffered during the Nazi occupation of his country during the Second World War. Second, he came from a Church which was still fiercely traditional and did not share the rather naïve optimism with regard to the world that had marked much of the Church in Western Europe in the 1960s. As a young priest, he had spent time in Paris and had fallen under the influence of both *la nouvelle théologie* and philosophical personalism. Third, having lived under Nazi occupation, he then experienced life under Communism, which gave him a particular way of regarding the attempts to combine Catholic theology and Marxism typical of the theology of liberation movements. Finally, in 1981, he appointed Josef Ratzinger, then Cardinal Archbishop of Munich, to the key position of Prefect of the Congregation for the Doctrine of the Faith (CDF), which he held until he in turn was elected Pope in 1985. Ratzinger had been a young *peritus* (expert) at Vatican II and, for a time, was associated with the 'progressive' wing of the Church alongside his colleague, the Swiss theologian, Fr Hans Küng with whom he had worked in Tübingen. After the Council, however, their paths diverged. As Küng developed theological positions that were evermore at variance with the Church's magisterium, Ratzinger, like other *periti* such as the Jesuit Henri de Lubac and Hans Urs von Balthasar, swung back to reaffirming fidelity to the magisterium. As Prefect of the CDF, he found himself obliged to rein in what he and John Paul II regarded as excesses, such as some of the more extreme expressions of the theology of liberation or feminist theology and attempts to syncretise Catholic theology with other faiths such as Buddhism or Hinduism. It is worth noting, however, that de Lubac, Wojtyla, and Ratzinger were all fully supportive of the Council and were primarily concerned at the interpretation and direction of some of the reforms particularly in the United States and some European countries such as the Netherlands.

Both John Paul II and Benedict XVI paid close attention to Europe and also to the process of European integration. Their attitude, however, was much less naïve and optimistic than John XXIII or even Paul VI. When John Paul II viewed Europe, he saw a continent divided by the Iron Curtain with the Eastern part under the yoke of Soviet Communism but he was also aware of the even more ancient division between Western Christianity and Orthodoxy. John Paul II combined both these perspectives under the notion that 'Europe', from the Atlantic to the Urals, had a 'soul' which was in danger of being lost to atheistic and materialistic secularism – what he termed the "culture of death" (John Paul II, 1995: §28). The project of European integration was to be supported in so far as it laid the conditions of peace and economic prosperity but it needed to go beyond this to embody a spiritual dimension that would not diminish the human person.[5] Furthermore, European integration should finally aim to include those countries of Eastern and Central Europe that had fallen under Soviet domination. The Polish Pope reached out to the Orthodox Christians in the Soviet Bloc and spoke of the two great branches of Christianity – Catholicism and Orthodoxy – as the 'two lungs' of Europe. Although John Paul II did establish friendlier relations with some of the Orthodox Churches (e.g. in Greece, Romania, and Bulgaria), those linked to the Russian Patriarchate were reluctant to embrace his gestures of friendship.

It is difficult not to detect a close affinity of views on these matters between Cardinal Ratzinger and John Paul II. Indeed, when Ratzinger became Pope Benedict XVI there was a strong continuity between the two pontificates. It might, however, be remarked that Ratzinger was rather less keen than John Paul II on issuing 'apologies' for the alleged misdeeds of the Catholic Church and including leaders of non-Christian faiths in joint celebrations such as the Assisi gathering in 1986. But both leaders were keenly aware of the rapid de-Christianisation of Europe and agreed on the necessity of a 'new evangelisation' of the old continent. But the European political leaders in both the EU and in the Council of Europe, although they issued polite invitations to the Popes to address their respective assemblies, were little inclined to follow their advice on these matters.

The European Constitutional Convention and the Catholic Church

The pace of European integration accelerated from the mid-1980s as a result of European Commission President Jacques Delors' project to complete the Single Market by 1 January 1993. Furthermore, partly thanks to John Paul II's mobilization of Polish civil society in the 1990s, the Iron Curtain came down with the fall of the Berlin Wall in 1989 and the collapse of the other countries of the Soviet bloc soon after (Weigel, 2010). Germany was unified in 1990. It was a period of euphoria and excitement and soon voices were heard advocating the expansion of the Union to the countries in East and Central Europe newly liberated from communist domination. It was in this context that a series of Intergovernmental Conferences (IGC's) in Maastricht (1992) led to changes in the Treaties, both to take account of the institutional and policy changes entailed by the Single Market and to prepare for eventual enlargement to perhaps 30 or more countries: Maastricht (1993), Amsterdam (1999), and Nice (2003). Most interesting and ambitious, however, was the draft Treaty establishing a Constitution for Europe (or Constitutional Treaty) drawn up by a Convention on the Future of Europe (2001–03) presided over by former French President Valéry Giscard d'Estaing and signed by 25 member states in 2004.

Although the Constitutional Treaty was rejected in referendums in France and the Netherlands in 2004 and was later modified and transformed into the Lisbon Treaty (2009), it did, as Milton's chapter documents in detail, produce a revealing debate about the role of religion and, in particular, it showed the place of the Catholic Church in contemporary Europe. The question that emerged during the Convention was whether the Preamble should include a reference to Europe's Christian and religious traditions and even mention 'God' or whether it should maintain an exclusively secular statement. Arguments were advanced from different quarters for and against.[6] In the end, the Preamble included a rather weak reference to 'spiritual traditions' and did not mention either God or Christianity. The Treaty of Lisbon, which replaced the Constitutional Treaty after the latter was defeated in the referendums in France and the Netherlands, retained the same formula. However, Lisbon (Articles 6 and 10) does guarantee respect for the different religious traditions of Europe, religious freedom, and the right of parents to have their children educated in a particular religious tradition. For the first time, there is constitutional recognition (Article 17) of the dialogue between the EU institutions and the churches and religious organisations as well as with 'philosophical and non-confessional organisations' (Bureau of European Policy Advisers, 2010;[7] see Lucian Leustean's chapter).

The refusal to acknowledge Christianity explicitly should be interpreted as a defeat for the Catholic Church and, especially of Pope John Paul II, who, at the time of the European Convention, enjoyed immense prestige as a world spiritual leader. Despite these setbacks, the Catholic Church under John Paul II and Benedict XVI continued to give broad support to the European project and especially to the enlargement of the EU to include the new democracies of East and Central Europe. Although Pope Francis has adopted a different, more informal style than that of his predecessors, he conveyed basically the same message to the European institutions when he addressed them in November 2014. He took the opportunity to reiterate the Church's longstanding if unfashionable positions that human dignity and human rights must be based on the protection both of the family understood as the union of one man and one woman in a fruitful and indissoluble relationship, and of the weakest and most vulnerable members of society including the unborn child and the frail elderly. His message was clearly directed against challenges to the traditional heterosexual family posed by same-sex marriage, abortion and euthanasia.

Pope Francis, like his predecessors, does not separate Catholic teaching on matters of social justice from the Church's pro-life stance but, rather, sees them as integral parts of the same teaching. At the heart of this teaching is the notion of the absolute dignity of every human being from the moment of conception to the moment of natural death. But 'life' here also means the conditions that are necessary to achieve the full flourishing of the human person. This demands attention being paid to adequate health, education, housing, employment, and the like as well as the full participation of the human person in the political, social, and economic affairs of his society (the principle of subsidiarity). On the basis of the 'preferential option for the poor' this also implies paying particular attention to the plight of the marginalized such as immigrants, the homeless, the unemployed and those for whom life has become meaningless (spiritual poverty). When evaluating the EU from these perspectives, although the Pontiffs have been broadly in support, they are also critical of the emphasis on utilitarian economic and market processes that have tended to neglect the human person they are meant to serve. Benedict XVI made this clear in his speech to assembled dignitaries at Westminster Hall, London, in September 2010. Although he was speaking about the 2008 financial crisis, his remarks apply equally to the EU.

Conclusion

This chapter makes clear that the Catholic Church has been a key player throughout the entire history of Europe. The history of particular European nations is also the history of their relationship with Catholicism and, after the Reformation, with Protestantism. It is the Catholic Church, however, which has been the strongest supporter of European unification even if the mainstream Protestant and Anglican Churches have also come to accept this. Catholicism has tended to reject nationalism and, in this sense, it is sympathetic to this aspect of the European idea. At the same time, it is also a global church and this has meant that its perspective has not always been limited to Europe even if the old continent is where it achieved its fullest development and has marked its practices and organization. Nevertheless, one of its concerns throughout the entire twentieth and early twenty-first centuries has been the goal of universal peace and its support of European integration has been seen as a means towards this end rather than an end in itself.

The Catholic Church's support of European integration has also not been absolute when it considers the social and ethical dimensions of the European project. It remains clearly opposed to the secularizing trends within Europe, in some member states but also in EU institutions and policies, and opposed to the use of equality and discrimination norms to promote practices such as same-sex relationships, abortion, and euthanasia, which it continues to regard, counter-culturally, as offenses against the dignity of the human person. But, on a wider level, Catholic Social Teaching also rejects the emphasis on the market and the reduction of the integration project to a giant commercial enterprise rather than one informed by a moral vision of humanity, as was the case with the Catholic founding fathers of Europe. John Paul II, Benedict XVI and Francis have all, each in his own way, drawn attention to these aspects of Europe, which they regard as serious threats to our very humanity. This, however, will not lead the Catholic Church to disengage from Europe. On the contrary, it will further enhance its commitment to it.

Notes

1 There is even a group called the Institut St Benoît that promotes Schuman's canonization by the Catholic Church (Robert-Schuman.com, 2009). The Vatican, however, is reticent about this (Evans-Pritchard, 2004).

2 In this chapter we are primarily concerned with the position of the official Church rather than surveying the entire gamut of attitudes of ordinary Catholics.
3 The patriarchal system of the *Pentarchy* was formulated by the Emperor Justinian I (527–65) who assigned the Bishop of Rome as the Patriarch of the West alongside the patriarchates of Constantinople, Alexandria, Antioch, and Jerusalem. The Pope and the West never fully accepted this system as the Bishop of Rome, even at this early period, tended to see itself as having jurisdiction of the whole Church and not just the West. The title 'Patriarch of the West' was introduced only after the Reformation and was abolished by Pope Benedict XVI.
4 "The Church has made a Triple Alliance. Adenauer, Schuman, De Gasperi, three tonsures under one skullcap [calotte]".
5 Jacques Delors had the same idea and established a group of Benedictine and Cistercian Abbots, later called the Chévetogne Group (the name of the Benedictine Abbey in Belgium where it is based to explore this dimension).
6 For a summary of the different positions, see Robinson (2003).
7 The Bureau is connected to the European Commission.

References

Bureau of European Policy Advisers. (2010). *Dialogue with religions, churches and communities of conviction.* Retrieved from http://ec.europa.eu/dgs/policy_advisers/activities/dialogues_religions/index_en.htm.

Burleigh, M. (2005). *Earthly powers: Religion and politics in Europe from the enlightenment to the great war.* London: HarperCollins.

Carrier, H. (1990). *The social doctrine of the church revisited.* Vatican City: Pontifical Council for Justice and Peace.

Cavanaugh, W. T. (2009). *The myth of religious violence: Secular ideology and the roots of modern conflict.* Oxford: Oxford University Press.

Chadwick, O. (1975). *The secularization of the European mind in the nineteenth century.* Cambridge: Cambridge University Press.

Chenaux, P. (2007). *De la chrétienté à l'Europe: Les Catholiques et l'idée Européenne au XXe siècle.* Tours, France: Éditions CLD.

Colley, L. (2005). *Britons: Forging the nation, 1707–1837.* New Haven, CT: Yale University Press.

Delors, J. (1999). European personalist perspectives: Personalist reflections. *Ethical Perspectives*, 6(1): 82.

Evans-Pritchard, A. (2004). Vatican resists drive to canonise EU founder. *The Telegraph*, 19 Aug. Retrieved from www.telegraph.co.uk/news/worldnews/1469768/Vatican-resists-drive-to-canonise-EU-founder.html.

Greenfeld, L. (1992). *Nationalism.* London: Blackwell.

Gutiérrez, G. (1988). *A theology of liberation: History, politics, and salvation* (Rev. edn). Maryknoll, NY: Orbis. [Originally published in Spanish as *Teología de la liberación: Perspectivas*, 1971].

John XXIII. (1963). *Pacem in terris.* April 11. Retrieved from http://w2.vatican.va/content/john-xxiii/en/encyclicals/documents/hf_j-xxiii_enc_11041963_pacem.html.

John Paul II. (1995). *Evangelium vitae.* 25 March. Retrieved from http://w2.vatican.va/content/john-paul-ii/en/encyclicals/documents/hf_jp-ii_enc_25031995_evangelium-vitae.html.

Kaiser, W. (2007). *Christian democracy and the origins of European Union.* Cambridge: Cambridge University Press.

Launay, M. (1999). *L'Église et les défis Européens au XXe Siècle*. Paris: Les Éditions du Cerf.
Loughlin, J. (1988). Personalism and federalism in inter-war France. In Stirk, P. (ed.), *The context of European unity: The inter-war period* (pp. 188–200). London: Francis Pinter.
McHugh, F. (2008). *Catholic social thought: Renovating the tradition*. Leuven, Belgium: Peeters.
Marks, G., and Wilson, C. J. (2000). The past in the present: A cleavage theory of party response to European integration. *British Journal of Political Science*, 30(3): 433–459.
Mounier, E. (1952). *Personalism*. Notre Dame, IN: University of Notre Dame Press. [Originally published in French as *Le Personnalisme*, 1949].
Nelsen, B. F., Guth, J. L., and Fraser, C. R. (2001). Does religion matter? Christianity and public support for the European Union. *European Union Politics*, 2(2): 191–217.
Poulat, E. (1999). *Les prêtres ouvriers: Naissance et fin*. Paris: Éditions du Cerf.
Prettenthaler-Ziegerhofer, A. (2012). Richard Nicolaus Coudenhove-Kalergi, founder of the Pan-European Union, and the birth of a "new" Europe. In Hewitson, M. and D'Auria, M. (eds), *Europe in crisis: Intellectuals and the European idea, 1917–1957* (pp. 89–108). New York: Berghahn.
Robert-Schuman.com (2009). *L'Institut Saint Benoît*. Retrieved from www.robert-schuman.com/fr/pg-saintete/institut_st_benoit.htm.
Robinson, B. A. (2003). Do "God" and "Christianity" have a place in the European Union constitution? *Ontario Consultants on Religious Tolerance*, 31 May. Retrieved from www.religioustolerance.org/const_eu.htm.
Roy, C. (1999a). *Alexandre Marc et la Jeune Europe (1904–1934): L'Ordre nouveau aux origines du personnalisme*. Nice, France: Presses d'Europe.
Roy, C. (1999b). Ecological personalism. *Ethical Perspectives*, 6(1): 33–44.
Spruyt, H. (1994). *The sovereign state and its competitors: An analysis of systems change*. Princeton, NJ: Princeton University Press.
Taylor, C. (2007). *A secular age*. Cambridge, MA: Belknap Press of Harvard University Press.
The Economist. (2004). Real politics, at last? *The Economist*. 28 October. Retrieved from www.economist.com/node/3332056.
Weigel, G. (2010). *The end and the beginning: Pope John Paul II – The victory of freedom, the last years, the legacy*. New York: Doubleday.

3 The EU
Protestant contributions, then and now

Sander Luitwieler

Introduction[1]

Christian political leaders played a crucial role in the founding of what is now the European Union (EU) in the 1950s and its subsequent development. As the previous two chapters have shown, devout Catholics such as Robert Schuman (France), Konrad Adenauer (Germany), and Alcide De Gasperi (Italy) took the decisive lead in urging Europe towards a peaceful union after the bitter experiences of two world wars. This raises the obvious question: Where were the Protestants? There were indeed some Protestant politicians involved, but in general Protestants adopted a notably more reserved stance towards European integration. Dominantly Protestant countries such as the United Kingdom (UK) and the Nordic states were not part of the founding group. The UK and Denmark joined the then Common Market in 1973, while Sweden and Finland did not accede to the EU until 1995. These late entrants have often shown themselves to be reluctant partners (George, 1998; Gstöhl, 2002). The current position of the UK – poised, at time of writing, to stage a referendum on membership – illustrates this. The differences between Catholic and Protestant political leaders (and nations) are also reflected in the attitudes of Catholic and Protestant followers (Nelsen, Guth, and Fraser, 2001; Nelsen and Guth, 2003; Nelsen, Guth, and Highsmith, 2011; Nelsen and Guth, 2015).

The aim of this chapter is twofold. The first is to shed light on the often neglected and misunderstood question of the relationship between Protestantism and European integration. I pursue this aim both theoretically and empirically, treating the formatives roles of both ideas and institutions. The second aim is to outline a constructive, normative view of the EU drawing on ideas of a particular – and also neglected – strand of Protestant political thought. The first part addresses the question of the broad historical relationship between Protestantism and European identity as such, by means of a critical engagement with the influential account of such identity proposed by French philosopher Rémi Brague. Narrowing the focus, the second part draws on recent research on religion and European integration to propose a framework for analysis of the role of Protestantism. The third part deploys this framework to examine the attitudes of Protestant ecclesial and political elites and their involvement in the European integration process, focussing on the UK, the Netherlands, and the Nordic countries. This part also contains a brief summary of the attitudes of Protestant followers. The fourth part builds on the foregoing and adds a normative dimension, proposing one Protestant view of the EU which, I suggest, could prove fruitful in key debates about the future design of the EU. The chapter closes with some conclusions.

Protestantism and European identity[2]

Europe is a continent lacking a genuine identity of its own. This intriguing proposal comes from the French philosopher Rémi Brague (2002), author of an important book about the historical constitution of European culture. According to Brague, 'Europe' has been constituted during the Middle Ages and relies for its self-understanding on Hellenistic and Jewish sources ('Athens and Jerusalem') that are non-European in origin. The European sense of identity is thus an "eccentric" one (Brague, 2002: Ch. 6). The relation of Europe to itself is indirect or 'secondary', in the sense that what Europe is or intends to be depends on a relationship to sources that are outside itself. There are previous civilizations that are more important, richer, and bearing greater authority than Europe was able to generate of itself. Brague calls the form in which this indirect sense of cultural identity expresses itself "Romanity" (or "Latinity") (2002: 22). It refers in a "Roman way" (2002: 39) to predecessors and does not desire to establish a European identity over and above that. According to Brague, this cultural model typifies the historical relationship of Europe to itself. Europe thus has to find the Roman way to discover what it is. This way is symbolized by the 'Roman Church' and its distinctive understanding of Christianity.

Brague's analysis is insightful and provocative, but it raises a question about the extent to which he presents a specifically Roman Catholic perspective, thus failing to recognise the Protestant contribution to what has become modern European identity. It is true, of course, that the notion that there are important sources (at least biblical ones) of the Christian tradition outside Europe is also alive within Protestantism. Indeed this awareness intensified during the fifteenth and sixteenth centuries when the renaissance of Greek and Hebrew language and literature aided the emergence of new ideas and their integration within wider European culture. It resulted in a significant reconsideration of the 'Roman' model. Yet the Protestant Reformation that took place at that time was in many ways a radical departure from this model: Protestants repudiated the idea that what was handed over by 'tradition' was good in itself. Pursuant to this break, the Reformation broke elite clerical control of traditional religious language (Latin) by translating the Bible into vernacular European languages, thus granting a potentially creative voice to ordinary lay believers. Put more generally, it championed what Charles Taylor calls the "affirmation of ordinary life" (1989: Part III) as the arena where anyone, however lowly, could serve God in 'secular' activities deemed of equal standing to the clerical vocation. This emphasis on the moral responsibility of every individual to contribute to the shaping of culture inaugurated an entirely new sense of identity on the part of both persons and communities.

On the basis of this new, post-traditional model of culture, Protestantism generated a fresh understanding of the European identity.[3] The impact of the Reformation (whether intended or not) was to make room for wholly new forms of political, ecclesiastical, economic, and social life. In time, this secured progressively extended protections of individual, political, economic, and (as Schirrmacher and Chaplin's chapter shows) religious freedoms. New cultural and scientific patterns, more independent communities and nations, and expanding civil societies eventually resulted from this wide-ranging cultural transformation. The Protestant Reformation embedded these innovative and emancipatory dynamics within modern European civilization. Brague's valuable analysis of the central role of Romanity in forging modern European identity thus needs to be supplemented and corrected by a due recognition of this distinctive Protestant legacy.

The analytical framework I now outline draws on recent research that focuses specifically on the relationship between Protestantism (as well as Catholicism) and European integration. In explaining the contrasting stances of religious traditions toward European integration, scholarship has drawn attention to the role of both ideas and institutions. Philpott and Shah (2006) as well as Byrnes (2006) consider both factors when comparing the attitudes of Roman Catholicism, Orthodoxy, and Islam toward European unity. Similarly, Nelsen and Guth (2015) draw a distinction between a Catholic and a Protestant "confessional culture" in explaining their differing attitudes. These confessional cultures provide shared ideas, behaviours and institutions.

Protestantism and European (dis)unity: ideas and institutions

Conceptually and theologically (here focussing on 'ideas'), it is clear that from the outset Christianity sought to present itself as, and was considered, a 'universal' religion. It understood itself as entrusted with a message intended for the whole world transcending all ethnic and national divisions. Central to its self-understanding was Jesus's statement recorded in one of the synoptic gospels commissioning his disciples to "go and make disciples of all nations" (Matthew 28:19). This globally inclusive programme is reaffirmed and indeed radicalized by the apostle Paul who declared that, "there is neither Jew nor Gentile, neither slave nor free, nor is there male and female, for you are all one in Christ Jesus" (Galatians 3:28).[4] Yet while this universal vision has always been proclaimed by both Catholicism and Protestantism, the two traditions have interpreted it in importantly different ways. Whereas Catholicism has emphasised the universality of the *visible* church, Protestantism has emphasised the universality of the *invisible* church (Nelsen and Guth, 2015: 33–77, 88–100; see Philpott and Shah, 2006).

For Catholics, the unity of all believers is made visible in the Roman Catholic Church operating under the universal authority of the Pope. The insistence on universal authority is rooted in medieval notions of universal empire, which were originally developed by the Greeks and the Romans. When Christianity became the official religion of the Roman Empire, spiritual and temporal authority became united in the person of the emperor. After the breakdown of the Western Roman Empire, both the emperors and the Popes claimed and strove for ultimate authority. At first the emperors had the upper hand, but this changed in the course of the eleventh and twelfth centuries. By the beginning of the thirteenth century, the Pope was the preeminent public figure in Latin Christendom. Catholic universalism in the Middle Ages was thus visible spiritually as well as temporally. While the unity of medieval Christendom did not survive the Reformation and the rise of nation-states, the Catholic ideal was still of human unity represented in both a spiritual and political structure at a transnational level. Therefore, Nelsen and Guth state: "All visions of European political unity have their roots in the medieval papal claims of universal temporal authority" (2015: 35).

While Protestants certainly affirmed the universality of the Christian message, they insisted on the invisible rather than visible unity of the church. This originated in the 'doctrine of election' of the Reformers, which led them to make a distinction between the visible and invisible church (a distinction already anticipated by Augustine). The visible church would inevitably contain both saints and hypocrites. "The invisible church is the true universal church because the elect are united, not in a visible institution, but in a spiritual body" (Nelsen and Guth, 2015: 68). In addition to the practical difficulties of unifying a church no longer held together by papal authority, the doctrine of election allowed Protestants to accommodate themselves to the reality of a visible church divided along local or national lines.

According to the Reformers, while Christendom required the cooperation of spiritual and temporal authority in a given community or nation, it did not mandate visible unity under one universal authority, let alone a Pope. The Protestant rejection of universal empire started with a repudiation of the Pope as the universal spiritual and temporal ruler of Christendom. The Pope was even considered by some as 'the Antichrist' graphically depicted in the apocalyptic New Testament book Revelation. The Protestant churches were divided on many points but united in their deep antipathy toward Rome and the papacy. Protestant theology thus provided a powerful (if inadvertent) justification for the religious and political division of Europe. It was, finally, spiritual rather than political union that mattered.

In addition to these (theological) ideas, the role of institutions also helps to explain why Catholics rather than Protestants took the lead in the uniting of Europe. In this connection, a distinction can be made between, on the one hand, ecclesiastical structure and the institutional relationship to the state (Nelsen and Guth, 2015: 77–88; Philpott and Shah, 2006), and, on the other, political parties and transnational church and political networks (Nelsen and Guth, 2015: 122–153, 163–176; Byrnes 2006).

As far as ecclesiastical structure is concerned, certainly by the mid-twentieth century the Catholic Church was still hierarchically organised and dependent on the supreme authority of the Pope, enabling it to speak (officially) with one voice. Catholics viewed the state as a competitor for and hindrance to the realisation of (visible) unity. By virtue of being part of a transnational church structure, the Catholic Church's institutional relationship to the state was necessarily weak. Protestant churches, on the other hand, were organised differently in different countries and on the basis of diverse models (episcopal, consistorial, and congregational). In addition, they were often institutionally dependent on their national states, which provided them with protection and freedom, even forming state churches in Germany, Sweden, Denmark, England, and Scotland. Crucially, this inhibited most Protestant churches from organising and speaking out transnationally.

With regard to political parties, in the late nineteenth and early twentieth centuries, Christian Democratic, i.e. Catholic, parties emerged. They developed a common political agenda and obtained a dominant political position in the six founding member states of the EU. It was either Catholic countries (France, Italy, Belgium, Luxembourg) or countries with a substantial Catholic population (Germany, the Netherlands) that launched the European integration process in the 1950s. Protestant political parties, on the other hand, were rare, small, and lacked a transnational political agenda. In addition, Catholic parties and politicians participated more than their Protestant counterparts in transnational networks that promoted European unity. It was particularly within these networks that they developed a "sense of community" (Nelsen and Guth, 2015: 153) to which the transnational culture of Catholics gave rise more generally. The national orientation and internal divisions of Protestants, on the other hand, prevented them from developing a transnational sense of community among leaders and followers alike.

As far as transnational networks are concerned, at least three of them played an important role in paving the way for European integration: Moral Re-Armament (MRA), the Geneva Circle, and the Nouvelles Equipes Internationales (NEI). Particularly the latter two were dominantly Catholic. MRA, a movement initiated by an American Lutheran evangelist named Frank Buchman, organised meetings for French and German notables from 1946 to 1950 in Caux (Switzerland) to encourage reconciliation between them and thus European unity (Coupland, 2006: 125–127; Fountain, 2010: 63–72; Nelsen and Guth, 2015: 151). Many Christian Democrats visited Caux, among whom Konrad Adenauer and Robert Schuman. Buchman developed close ties with both Adenauer and Schuman and facilitated the relationship between the two founding fathers. MRA thus contributed significantly to promoting French and German agreement over the Schuman plan (1950), which resulted in the European Coal and Steel Community (ECSC) in 1951.

The Geneva Circle consisted of leading politicians from West European Christian Democratic parties that regularly held confidential meetings from 1947 to 1956 (Gehler, 2004; see Kaiser, 2007). It was a German-French initiative mainly aimed at the Franco-German rapprochement, within the framework of European integration. The Geneva Circle provided an important forum for discussions about the Schuman Plan. In addition to the French Mouvement Républicain Populaire (MRP) and the German Christian Democratic Union (CDU)/Christian Social Union (CSU), the other participating parties were the Austrian People's Party (ÖVP), the Belgian Parti Social Chrétien (PSC/CVP), the Italian Democrazia Cristiana (DC), the Dutch Catholic People's Party (KVP), and the Swiss Conservative People's Party (SKVP).

More or less the same parties also participated in the NEI, originally founded in 1947 (Kaiser, 2004; see Kaiser, 2007). Many politicians involved in the Geneva Circle also attended NEI congresses. In 1965, the NEI was transformed into the European Union of Christian Democrats (EUCD) and in 1976 the EUCD parties from the member states of the European Community founded the European People's Party (EPP). Like the other two networks, the NEI played an important role in advocating Franco-German reconciliation and European integration. The NEI promoted the Schuman Plan and played a preparatory role for the negotiations that resulted in the European Economic Community in 1957.

The role of both different ideas and different institutions, then, helps explain why Protestants have been less in favour of and engaged with the European integration process than have Catholics. The next part traces the story of Protestantism and the EU with a focus on three Protestant contexts.

Protestantism and European integration in three contexts

In this part I present some empirical research about the ideas, and institutional involvement, of Protestant churches and church leaders, and Protestant parties and politicians, in the UK, the Netherlands, and (more briefly) the Nordic countries. The rationale for selecting these three countries is as follows: first, these three could be said to represent three different strands of Christian Democracy: the Anglo-Saxon, the Continental, and the Scandinavian (or Nordic) (Fogarty, 1957; Madeley and Sitter, 2003: 3–4); second, the countries represent both 'founders' of the EU (the Netherlands) and consecutive 'latecomers' (the UK and the Nordic countries; Norway is still not a member). This overview offers partial confirmation of the foregoing account of the relationship between Protestantism and European integration and yet also partially qualifies it by showing that a number of Protestant leaders, churches, and parties have actually showed themselves in favour of and engaged with the European integration process.

The Netherlands

In the Netherlands, the KPV, like Christian Democratic parties in other countries, early on declared itself in favour of European integration and participated in transnational networks, such as the Geneva Circle and the NEI. Yet a positive relationship between Protestantism and European integration can be seen in at least two distinct settings.

First, the Dutch Protestant leader Willem Visser 't Hooft played an important role in international church networks that promoted European unity (Greschat, 1994; Leustean, 2014). Visser 't Hooft, with the British leader William Paton, was joint General Secretary of the World Council of Churches (WCC) in Geneva, which was in formation since 1937 and officially established in 1948. During the war years, he "acted as a channel for the thinking of Christians in the resistance in occupied Europe and in organised anti-Nazi opinion in Germany" (Coupland, 2006: 72). He was a key figure in what may be called another 'Geneva Circle', in this case around the WCC. This group advocated a federal Europe. Visser 't Hooft was also involved in the founding of the Conference of European Churches (CEC) in 1959.

Second, Protestant political parties moved, perhaps unexpectedly, towards a more favourable view of and involvement in European integration. The Netherlands is unique in that it is the only founding member state that has Protestant parties represented in parliament. Initially, the Protestant Christian-Historical Union (CHU) and the Anti-Revolutionary Party (ARP) were not in favour of European integration (Vollaard, 2006). This had to do with their attachment to the Netherlands as a Protestant nation, which in their view had been liberated with the help of God from the Catholic-Habsburg yoke by William of Orange (Vollaard, 2006: 280). Giving up again this independence for the 'Catholic project' of European integration did not make sense to them. The ARP and CHU, however, changed their views in the late 1940s and thereafter. This was, among other things, the result of an internal rethinking of their political ideas and the international experience of some of their representatives.

As regards the former, the ARP, for example, presented a distinctive idea of 'public justice', rather than national sovereignty, as the critical norm to assess European integration. Applying this norm created room either to transfer authority to the supranational level or to maintain it at the national level if appropriate. As a result, the CHU and ARP became more internationally oriented than they had been, although they were still not as enthusiastic about European integration as the KVP.

As regards international experience, the foreign affairs spokesman of the CHU, Schmal, was involved in the establishment of the European Parliamentary Union, led by the chairman of the pan-European movement, Coudenhove-Kalerghi. After a failed attempt, together with some like-minded West German and Swiss people, to establish a Protestant alternative for cooperation with the Catholics in 1951 ('Protestantse Vereniging voor Christelijke

Politiek in Europa'), the ARP and CHU joined the Christian Democratic group in the Common Assembly of the ECSC in 1952 (ten Napel, 1996: 233). Both parties moreover joined the NEI in 1954 and, forming with the KVP a common Dutch representation in the NEI, developed more cooperation with the KVP in this context (Kaiser, 2007: 262–263). (This was one factor that facilitated the later fusion of the CHU, ARP, and KVP into the inter-confessional Christian Democratic Appeal (CDA) in 1980).

A similar development, albeit later on, took place in the case of the orthodox Protestant Reformed Political Party (SGP), Reformed Political Union (GPV), and Reformed Political Federation (RPF). Like the CHU and ARP, these parties initially rejected European integration. This had to do, *inter alia*, with an attachment to the identity and sovereignty of the Netherlands as a Protestant nation, which would be threatened by a 'Catholic Europe' as well as by the secularism of the French Revolution (Vollaard, 2006). Another argument was related to a longstanding (and theologically embedded) Protestant reservation about concentration of power, which might be misused by humans due to their 'sinful' nature. On the more conservative fringes of these parties, this was sometimes combined with an 'apocalyptic' element whereby the European Community was considered to be a revived Roman empire in the making, preparing the way for a world empire, both of which would be anti-Christian in nature and heralding the 'end of times' (cf. Herman, 2000).

In the 1990s and thereafter, however, the SGP, GPV, RPF, and – after the fusion of the latter two in 2001 – the Christian Union (CU) transformed their negative attitude into a critical acceptance of European integration. As with the ARP and CHU earlier, this change was related to a renewed critical appropriation by these parties of core themes in Protestant political thought. First, they began to see the EU institutions in biblical terms as a 'government' that, like the national government, is "God's servant" for the good of the citizens (Romans 13:4). Second, and relatedly, they too adopted the notion of 'public justice' rather than national sovereignty as the guiding normative principle to assess European integration. In addition, the experience of representatives from these parties in the European Parliament since 1984 is likely to have contributed to a more positive attitude.

Their degree of theological orthodoxy and their rather limited inter-confessional and transnational links seem to explain why (the forerunners of) the CU and SGP have maintained their eurosceptical position for a longer period and to a greater extent than the CHU, the ARP, and the CDA (Vollaard, 2006).

The UK

In contrast to the Netherlands, there were and are no significant Christian, let alone Protestant, political parties in the UK.[5] Yet at several moments British churches and individual Christians have played an important role in the country's attitude towards European unity and in the European integration process in general (Coupland, 2006).

During the Second World War, the British churches' Peace Aims Group, successively chaired by William Temple (Archbishop of York, becoming Archbishop of Canterbury in 1942) and George Bell (Bishop of Chichester), worked to influence European post-war reconstruction and British participation in promoting European unity. This included an initial flirtation with federalism. As theological justification for their support for European unity, they and other Christian leaders argued that Christians and their churches were part of a universal community (Coupland, 2006: 4–12). While they held that Christians should affirm nations and national differences as expressions of the richness of God's creation, they held that their common Christian identity transcended all others, including national affiliation. In addition and, for some, relatedly, an important argument was the notion of 'Europe as Christendom': Europe needed to be reunited on the basis of a shared Christian foundation as medieval Europe had been (albeit without recourse to the coercive and discriminatory practices of medieval Christendom).

The Peace Aims Group also functioned as a channel for the British government to influence public and elite opinion in the United States (with the intention of involving the USA in the war and the post-war settlement) and to build the Anglo-American 'alliance'. This strengthening of the transatlantic focus implied a shift away from continental Europe on the part of both the government and the churches. In contrast to the Peace Aims Group, the Geneva group around the WCC continued to advocate a federal Europe with full British involvement.

After the war, British churches and Christians were involved both in the ecumenical movement, including the inaugural meeting of the WCC in 1948 and in the movement for European integration, including the inaugural meeting of the European Movement in the same year. The churches supported Churchill's campaign for European unity and the Labour government's proposal for a 'Western Union' (opposed to the Soviet bloc), which was to be a 'spiritual union' rather than a political one. The Catholic Church in England, by contrast, strongly supported political and federal union.

The government initiatives mentioned even stimulated the emergence of a "Christian pro-European movement" (Coupland, 2006: 115) in the late 1940s. In addition to the British Section of the NEI, founded in 1948 and consisting of both Catholics and Protestants, representatives of this movement were Christian Action and the Christian Movement for European Unity. Yet at the decisive moment of the start of the European integration process in the early 1950s, the British churches followed the same line of retreat as the government. MRA, which played an important role in promoting French and German agreement over the Schuman plan (1950), had British roots, but the churches remained largely silent at this moment. In addition to some wider Christian hesitation over European unity in the UK, there were various specifically Protestant misgivings. First, there was still a degree of Protestant suspicion of the 'Roman' flavour of the European integration process. Second, although Christian universalism may be expected to make religious identity primary, British Christians were no less subject to the powerful appeal of national identity than other groups. Elements of this national identity were on the one hand an insular 'Englishness' – of which the Church of England was a central part – and on the other hand a global 'Britishness' – the Church of England was at the head of a worldwide communion that was almost completely extra-European.

The British churches' attitude towards the division of Europe by the 'iron curtain' was ambivalent. On the one hand, they supported the anti-communist 'crusade' of the period and the building of a Western power-bloc, which may have contributed to the division of the Europe that they wanted to unite. On the other hand, the willingness of the ecumenical movement to enter a dialogue with the East may have contributed to creating the conditions for the peaceful removal of this division at the end of the twentieth century (Coupland, 2006: 139–169).

The churches remained largely silent on European integration until the beginning of the 1960s. This changed when the British government announced its intention in 1961 to seek membership of the then Common Market. British churches and individual Christians, particularly Noël Salter, supported the government and played an important role in its campaign for membership, which after two French vetoes (in 1963 and 1968) was eventually achieved in 1973, and in the subsequent referendum campaign over the issue in 1975. In the latter campaign, Christians in the European Movement and particularly the ecumenical group Christians for Europe played an important role. The churches' silence was definitively broken by the report "Christians and the Common Market" of the British Council of Churches issued in 1967 (Coupland, 2006: 172–173). Salter was its main author. In terms of arguments, it was striking that the report propagated a federal Europe from a Christian perspective and that it did not stress 'Europe as Christendom' but rather the ethic of service that Europe and Britain within it could render to the wider world, particularly the 'developing world'. Anti-Catholic sentiment among Protestants was less salient than earlier.

It remains the case, however, that after 1975 and up until the present, most British churches and Christians have generally shown little interest in or active support for the European integration process, in contrast to the Catholic Church and other continental churches (Coupland, 2006: 199). Involvement largely took place through transnational ecumenical channels, with Anglicans, Baptists, Methodists and the other Free Churches working together through the Brussels, Geneva, and Strasbourg-based CEC. The General Synod of the Church England has, however, produced and debated various reports on the Common Market/EU (most notably Church of England 1972; 1990; 2004; 2009). Following on from the 2004 report, the Church of England established its House of Bishops' Europe Panel to engage with European matters. In 2008 it appointed a full-time representative to the EU, based in Brussels (having made a part-time appointment in 1986 [Coupland, 2006: 199]). The Europe panel has participated in various Commission consultations, while each of the last four Archbishops of Canterbury has visited the EU institutions.

Nordic countries

Madeley and Sitter (2003) have examined the relationship between Protestantism and the level of euroscepticism of the Nordic Christian parties: the Christian People's Party in Norway, the Christian Democrats in Finland, the Christian Democrats in Sweden, and the Christian People's Party (now Christian Democrats) in Denmark. They concluded that the Protestantism of these parties has indeed contributed to the Nordic countries being 'reluctant Europeans'. The Protestantism of these parties is, however, the Protestantism of dissident revivalism both within and outside the Lutheran state churches rather than the established Protestantism of the state churches, which have in general supported EU membership. Catholicism has only a marginal presence in the Lutheran Nordic countries and anti-Catholic sentiment seems to be less prevalent here than in the Calvinist Protestant subcultures of the Netherlands, the UK, and North America. Their Protestant identity and attachment to a Protestant-inflected national identity tied up with values such as freedom and localism/nationalism has primarily predisposed the Nordic Christian parties to more eurosceptic positions than their Continental (Catholic) counterparts.

All four parties have over time become less eurosceptic (Norwegian and Finnish parties) or even pro-EU (Danish and Swedish parties). The more positive stance of the Swedish and Danish parties seems to be related to their relative openness, compared to the Finnish and Norwegian parties, to representatives from dissident traditions and, perhaps surprisingly, Pentecostalism. The Swedish and Danish parties have also been more sensitive to shorter-term incentives against euroscepticism related to the pursuit of votes and office.

Protestant followers and European integration

To the extent that Protestant church and political leaders were involved in, and promoted, European integration, it cannot be taken for granted that their positive opinion was shared by their Protestant followers at home, who stood at a greater distance from these developments. Yet as Protestant leaders' involvement in and enthusiasm about European integration was in any case rather limited, it may not come as a surprise that this is reflected in the attitudes of their followers. Nelsen, Guth, and Highsmith (2011) have analysed the impact of religion, compared to economic, political, informational, and identity factors, on public attitudes toward the EU, using Eurobarometer survey data from 25 member states of the EU and some applicant member states in 2006. They distinguish between the *confession* of Catholic, Protestant, Orthodox, or Muslim followers and their *commitment* (frequency of attendance at religious services). Just as in an earlier study (Nelsen, Guth, and Fraser, 2001), they found that religion matters but varies across confessional cultures and different groups of member or applicant states.

In general, Catholics, especially the 'committed', are supportive of the EU. Being Protestant tends to imply weaker support, but commitment has a positive effect. Yet in the earlier study just mentioned, the authors not only found that *orthodox* Protestants are even less supportive of the EU, but also that in their case commitment has a negative effect (for example, they mention "very devout Calvinists in the Netherlands and Northern Ireland"; Nelsen, Guth, and Fraser, 2001: 207–210). Being Orthodox implies more support for the EU, but less so than for devout Catholics or Protestants. Being a Muslim, particularly a committed one, tends to make one less supportive of the EU, but this relationship is the weakest among the various confessional cultures.

Focussing on Sweden, Hagevi (2002), using survey data from 1998, found that religiosity affects opinion on the EU. Members of free churches (most of which are evangelical) tend to oppose Swedish membership. The same applies for evangelicals who are active members of the Church of Sweden. The mainline Protestant majority of the Church of Sweden is positive toward the EU. Members of immigrant churches, who usually have a Roman Catholic or Orthodox background, support the EU more than people of any other religious orientation. Demographic factors (gender, age, national background, degree of urbanisation, level of education, class, and public or private employment sector) do not explain the negative opinion found among members of free churches nor the positive opinion found among members of immigrant churches.

It is important to note, however, that the role of religion in shaping attitudes toward the EU is declining over time. The findings of Nelsen and his colleagues (2011) show that the impact of religion has decreased with each new enlargement of the EU. Besides, in an additional analysis of the first nine member states of the EU, they found that age plays a role in this connection. Catholic and Protestant confessional culture has the greatest impact on older respondents. The confession and commitment of young Catholics and Protestants play only a modest role in their attitudes toward European integration. Interestingly enough, however, the authors indicate that young confessing Protestants might be the only exception; they remain "marginally skeptical" (Nelsen, Guth, and Highsmith, 2011: 20). For Muslims, it is the other way around. Young Muslims, especially the most committed, are more influenced by their confessional culture than their older co-believers.

A contemporary Protestant view of the EU

What might a contemporary, constructive Protestant view of the EU, capable of engaging with the pressing challenges facing the EU today, look like? In this part, I sketch out one possible framing of such a view. As this chapter has made clear, Protestantism has given rise to various, and sometimes opposing, views of the European integration process. It thus obviously cannot be claimed that there is a definitive, or even a privileged, Protestant view of the EU. Yet in light of the foregoing it seems plausible to state that such a view must make clear how it deals with the themes of unity, diversity, and their interrelationship, since these have been central themes in Protestant attitudes towards European integration. In formulating a contemporary Protestant perspective on the EU that addresses these three elements, I propose to draw on a particular strand of Protestant political thought, namely that originating from nineteenth- and twentieth-century Dutch neo-Calvinism. The central idea I deploy is the EU as an instrument of transnational 'public justice' (Luitwieler, 2014).[6]

The notion that the state has a responsibility to realise 'justice' in the public realm – 'public justice' – is widely affirmed in many political theories, including several Christian approaches. The precise meanings attached to the terms 'justice' and 'public' are, however, much contested. Neo-Calvinism has developed a relatively distinctive account of these terms, which derives its content from a robustly pluralistic theory of society. This theory has strong affinities with Catholic social thought (such as that drawn upon in the chapters by John Loughlin, Adrian Pabst, and Johan Graafland) but I will here eschew comparison and simply present a neo-Calvinist account. Building on Mouw and Griffioen (1993), it is possible to make a distinction between three types of societal plurality: (1) 'structural plurality' – the plurality of institutional or associational structures in society, such as church, school, business, trades union, state; (2) 'confessional plurality' – the plurality of faiths, worldviews, or visions of the good life; and (3) 'cultural plurality' – the plurality of cultural (or national or ethnic) contexts. The latter is expressed not only *within* multicultural societies, but in the case of the EU also *between* its member states. The first and third types of plurality can be affirmed as inherently worthwhile expressions of forms of diversity rooted in (a divinely created) human nature. Confessional plurality is not necessarily affirmed as inherently good but must be fully respected by citizens and protected by law, as the public outworking of religious toleration.

As far as structural plurality is concerned, the point is not only that the existence of multiple societal structures is to be valued in itself but also that these structures have a distinct moral *telos*, a particular purpose to fulfil towards the larger goal of human social flourishing. In addition, such structures are seen as engaged in constant interactions of many kinds, each depending on the others and linked via complex networks, including the market. This model argues both for a proper respect for the distinct *tela* pursued by these structures and for a suitable coordination and regulation of these many interactions. The model thus joins with others in championing the importance of the structures of 'civil society' alongside, and as a corrective to, those of the state and the market.

One of the distinct types of societal structure is the state. It is seen as having a decisive role to play in relation to the coordination and regulation of the structures of civil society and the market. This role can be specified thus: the state is responsible for recognising the valid claims of these many structures to just treatment, both by the state itself and by other structures. The content of 'justice' is specified by identifying what is required for each structure to realise and pursue its distinct human purpose, including (as components of what Walzer [1983] has termed each structure's "sphere of justice") the rights it will need in order to safeguard its independence, and the duties it will bear in pursuit of its purpose. These, of course, will frequently be subject to vigorous political contestation. While it is true that what the state is deemed entitled to do will depend to a considerable degree on the outcome of democratic debates, these distinct rights and duties should not be viewed as merely the products of majoritarian decision. In addition to doing justice to structural plurality, the state also needs to do justice to confessional and cultural plurality (see Koyzis, 2003: 202–208; Chaplin, 2006; 2008).

The role of the state does not extend to addressing any and every justice claim that might potentially arise in a complex, plural society. Rather, that role is confined to the coordination and regulation of such claims insofar as they bear public consequences – insofar as they make an entry into the public realm (which, of course, is itself a contested notion, whose meaning is also given concrete shape through democratic debate). This is expressed in qualifying the scope of the justice task of the state as 'public justice'. This involves the coordination and regulation of the many rights and duties of individuals, societal structures, and confessional and cultural communities insofar as they impinge upon the shared public terrain of a society, and doing so according to substantive, and not just procedural, notions of justice. This public and substantive conception of justice also implies that the state needs to contribute through legislation and policy-making to creating the public conditions for human beings to flourish – personally, socially, and ecologically. This both authorises and circumscribes a degree of legitimate state action. The state is not an all-embracing community with managerial oversight of every dimension of human society, but a limited institution whose purpose is the promotion (through the diverse instruments of law and public policy) of public justice.

This model of the purpose of the state was essentially formulated prior to the emergence of the EU as a new political structure. Yet neo-Calvinist thinkers from the 1950s onwards eventually extended the logic of the model, devised for the nation-state, to international organisations such as the United Nations (UN) (Dooyeweerd, 1953–58: III, 599–601; Goudzwaard, 2000; 2001; Chaplin, 2009) and, in time, also to supranational organisations such as the EU (Luitwieler, 2014; 2015). The EU is clearly more than an international organisation, yet while it has a number of state-like features it is evidently less than a state (see, e.g. Keohane and Hoffmann, 1991: 10; Lijphart, 1999: 34). The EU possesses a set of institutions with executive, legislative, and judicial functions that are increasingly functioning as a common 'government' with significant authority in many policy areas (Hix and Høyland, 2011). My own view is that political institutions such as the UN and the EU can properly be viewed as sharing the same mandate to promote public justice as the member states, but now at the transnational level (Chaplin, 2011: 181; Luitwieler, 2014; 2015). Many issues of public justice (such as security, economic fairness, environmental degradation, etc.) clearly arise at the transnational level and necessitate the existence of political authorities equipped to address them effectively. The EU is such an authority. Its rationale and legitimacy ultimately lie in this mandate to promote transnational public justice.

What does public justice at the EU level entail? Focussing on unity, diversity, and their interrelationship, the following suggestions could be made (see Luitwieler, 2014: 123–141). First, the EU institutions should indeed be led by the norm of public justice rather than the logic of economic and financial markets. At the moment, the economic and financial spheres play a predominant role as a result of the EU's focus on internal market integration and, more recently, its dependence on financial markets. The political sphere follows and submits to the logic of the economic and financial spheres. This has resulted in the subordination of other policy areas, such as environmental and social policy, to the economic goal of efficiency and expansion (see Goudzwaard, 2000: 338; Hix and Høyland, 2011: 206–208, 232–233; Luitwieler, 2014: 87–93). Public justice at the EU level implies doing justice to the distinctiveness of various policy areas so as to contribute to creating the public conditions for human beings to flourish – personally, socially, and ecologically. The latter three dimensions may be translated into three specific objectives for the EU: peace, wellbeing, and sustainability. The EU institutions should aim at the 'simultaneous realisation' of these three objectives in policy-making.[7]

Second, public justice in the EU entails doing justice to the distinctiveness of various non-political spheres and structures. The dominance of the economic and financial spheres threatens to breach the distinct identity of other, non-political spheres, such as the family, education, and care (cf. Sandel, 2012). This is not a purely European issue, but the EU has strengthened this tendency through its neo-liberal policy of market integration, which, in turn, has resulted in the liberalisation of most sectors of the European economy (Hix and Høyland, 2011: 216). It is not within the remit of the EU institutions actively to protect the distinctiveness of societal structures within the member states, since this is a task of the member-state governments themselves (also pursuant to the norm of public justice within their own territories). Yet EU policy-making should at least respect the distinctiveness of these structures. The 'simultaneous realisation' of various objectives in EU policy-making contributes to this. The EU institutions should also respect those societal structures that participate at the European level, and they may also encourage the development of a strong European civil society and public sphere.

Third, the promotion of public justice by the EU institutions implies that European integration should be about the political integration of member states rather than the cultural integration of nations. Paradoxically, in following economic and financial logics, the European political sphere is inclined to overstep its own boundaries. The EU institutions have developed common policies in more and more areas, which threaten to undermine the cultural diversity of the member states. As noted, in the EU, cultural plurality is not only found within the member states as multicultural societies but also between them. Member states are primarily responsible for safeguarding cultural plurality within their territories, although one could raise the question whether the EU institutions increasingly have a role to play here, too (for example, via the Committee of the Regions). Public justice in the EU at least means doing justice to the cultural plurality between the member states. The EU's intention to respect cultural diversity is expressed both in the EU Treaties and in Article 22 of the Charter of Fundamental Rights of the European Union, which, according to Article 6 (1) of the Treaty on European Union, has the same legal value as the Treaties.

Fourth, while member-state governments are primarily responsible for protecting confessional plurality, one could again raise the question whether the EU institutions also need to be involved in this. Freedom of religion and belief is laid down as a right in Article 10 of the Charter of Fundamental Rights. The EU institutions should at least respect this freedom in their actions and policies (see Chapter 8 and the Conclusion).

Conclusion

This chapter has examined the relationship between Protestantism and European integration theoretically, empirically, and normatively. Opening with the broader issue of European identity, I argued that Protestantism has substantially contributed to the shaping of this identity. This occurred particularly through the Reformation, an important departure from what Brague terms the 'Roman' model. After presenting a framework to analyse specifically the relationship between Protestantism and European integration in terms of ideas and institutions, I applied this framework to the UK, the Netherlands and the Nordic countries. The account confirmed the picture that both ideas and institutions may explain the relatively reserved attitudes toward, and limited involvement in, the European integration process of Protestant leaders compared with their Catholics counterparts. Yet I noted some important qualifications to this generalisation.

In terms of ideas, Protestantism tends to value particularism and national identity. Yet its representatives have at times also propagated a transnational identity, such as the notion of 'Europe as Christendom', and, increasingly so, a Christian universalism based on ideas such as 'public justice' (the Netherlands) or 'service to the world' (Britain). In terms of institutions, specifically ecclesiastical structure and relationship to the state, it is true that their national, state-dependent organisations and divergent models have not been conducive for most Protestant churches to develop a transnational orientation. This has, however, not prevented at least established Protestant (state) churches to be generally positive about the European integration process (e.g. the Nordic countries; the UK).

As far as political parties are concerned, Protestant parties were and are rare and small indeed. Yet they are increasingly developing a transnational political agenda (the Netherlands; some Nordic countries) and have founded their own European party (European Christian Political Movement [ECPM]), which during the last elections won increased representation within the European Parliament. Finally, Protestants initially largely lacked transnational networks, but Protestant politicians participated to a certain extent in the 'Catholic' political networks (Dutch and British in the NEI) and have recently been increasingly developing their own networks, such as the ECPM. In addition, Protestant churches have developed their own transnational organisations, such as the WCC and the CEC, which to a greater or lesser degree have propagated European unity.

Finally, I presented a contemporary Protestant view of the EU based on ideas from a particular strand of Dutch Protestant political thought. I argued that its central notion of 'public justice' urges the EU institutions to aspire to realise peace, well-being, and sustainability simultaneously in policy-making, while also doing justice to structural, confessional, and cultural plurality in the Union. In this way, a proper balance is struck between unity and diversity in the EU. Thus united in diversity, the EU may look forward to a flourishing and hopeful future.

Notes

1 I would like to thank Hans Vollaard for useful literature suggestions and Jonathan Chaplin and Gary Wilton for their helpful comments.
2 I would like to thank Roel Kuiper for his valuable contribution to this section.
3 The Reformation was most successful in the northern parts of Europe that were most distant from the 'Roman' experience, as Brague sees it, of European history. It would perhaps not go too far to speculate that these more remote areas in northern Europe had an indigenous (more 'heathen' or 'tribal') sense of identity.
4 It perhaps hardly needs observing that subsequent Christian practice has often fallen woefully short of this trans-ethnic and transnational vision.
5 Two very small Christian parties were formed in the 2000s but neither has come anywhere near to winning a parliamentary seat. The first, the Christian Peoples Alliance (CPA), was originally inspired by, and remains officially committed to, European Christian Democratic ideas. It was formed in 2000 by members of the cross-party Movement for Christian Democracy and has won a handful of seats on local councils: www.cpaparty.net/. The second, The Christian Party, was formed in 2004 by disaffected former CPA members and adopts a markedly more conservative 'Christian nation' position: www.ukchristianparty.org/.
6 For analyses of the neo-Calvinist sources of these ideas, see Bratt (2013) and Chaplin (2011).
7 Goudzwaard (1979) applies the idea of the 'simultaneous realisation of norms' to economic policy-making, but one could also apply it to (EU) policy-making in general.

References

Brague, R. (2002). *Eccentric culture: A theory of western civilization.* South Bend, IN: St Augustine's Press.
Bratt, J. D. (2013). *Abraham Kuyper: Modern Calvinist, Christian democrat.* Grand Rapids, MI: Eerdmans.
Byrnes, T. A. (2006). Transnational religion and Europeanization. In Byrnes, T. A. and Katzenstein, P. J. (eds), *Religion in an expanding Europe* (pp. 283–305). Cambridge: Cambridge University Press.
Chaplin, J. (2011). *Herman Dooyeweerd: Christian philosopher of state and civil society.* Notre Dame, IN: University of Notre Dame Press.
Chaplin, J. (2009). God, globalization and grace: An exercise in public theology. In Goheen, M. W. and Glanville, E. G. (eds), *The gospel and globalization: Exploring the religious roots of a globalized world* (pp. 49–68). Vancouver, Canada: Regent College Publishing.
Chaplin, J. (2008). Beyond multiculturalism – but to where? Public justice and cultural diversity. *Philosophia Reformata*, 73: 190–209.
Chaplin, J. (2006). Rejecting neutrality, respecting diversity: From 'Liberal Pluralism' to 'Christian Pluralism'. *Christian Scholar's Review*, 35(2): 143–175.
Church of England. (2009). *Engaging with Europe: Turning hope into action.* London: Church of England.
Church of England. (2004). *The Church of England and Europe.* London: Church of England.
Church of England. (1990). *The Church of England and the challenge of Europe.* London: Church of England.
Church of England. (1972). *Britain in Europe: The social responsibility of the church.* London: Church of England.
Coupland, P. M. (2006). *Britannia, Europa and Christendom: British Christians and European integration.* Basingstoke: Palgrave Macmillan.
Dooyeweerd, H. (1953–58). *A new critique of theoretical thought* (4 vols.). Philadelphia, PA: Presbyterian and Reformed Publishing Co.
Fogarty, M. (1957). *Christian democracy in Western Europe 1820–1953.* London: Routledge and Kegan Paul.
Fountain, J. (2010). *Deeply rooted: The forgotten vision of Robert Schuman.* Heerde, Netherlands: The Schuman Centre for European Studies.
Gehler, M. (2004). The Geneva Circle of west European Christian democrats. In Gehler, M. and Kaiser, W. (eds), *Christian democracy in Europe since 1945* (pp. 207–220). London: Routledge.
George, S. A. (1998). *An awkward partner: Britain in the European Community* (3rd edn). Oxford: Oxford University Press.
Goudzwaard, B. (2001). *Globalization and the kingdom of God.* Grand Rapids, MI: Baker.
Goudzwaard, B. (2000). Globalization, regionalization, and sphere sovereignty. In Lugo, L. E. (ed.), *Religion, pluralism, and public life: Abraham Kuyper's legacy for the twenty-first century* (pp. 325–341). Grand Rapids, MI: Eerdmans.
Goudzwaard, B. (1979). *Capitalism and progress: A diagnosis of western society.* Grand Rapids, MI: Eerdmans.
Greschat, M. (1994). Der Protestantismus und die Entstehung der Europäischen Gemeinschaft. In Greschat, M. and Loth, W. (eds), *Die Christen und die Entstehung der Europäischen Gemeinschaft* (pp. 25–96). Stuttgart: Kohlhammer.

Gstöhl, S. (2002). *Reluctant Europeans: Norway, Sweden and Switzerland in the process of integration*. Boulder, CO: Rienner.

Hagevi, M. (2002). Religiosity and Swedish opinion on the European Union. *Journal for the Scientific Study of Religion*, 41(4): 759–769.

Herman, D. (2000). The New Roman Empire: European envisionings and American premillennialists. *Journal of American Studies*, 34(1): 23–40.

Hix, S., and Høyland, B. (2011). *The political system of the European Union* (3rd edn). Basingstoke: Palgrave Macmillan.

Kaiser, W. (2007). *Christian democracy and the origins of European Union*. Cambridge: Cambridge University Press.

Kaiser, W. (2004). Transnational Christian democracy: From the Nouvelles Equipes Internationales to the European People's Party. In Gehler, M. and Kaiser, W. (eds), *Christian democracy in Europe since 1945* (pp. 221–237). London: Routledge.

Keohane, R. O., and Hoffmann, S. H. (1991). Institutional change in Europe in the 1980s. In Keohane, R. O. and Hoffmann, S. H. (eds), *The new European Community: Decisionmaking and institutional change* (pp. 1–39). Boulder, CO: Westview.

Koyzis, D. T. (2003). *Political visions and illusions: A survey and Christian critique of contemporary ideologies*. Downers Grove, IL: InterVarsity.

Leustean, L. N. (2014). *The ecumenical movement and the making of the European Community*. Oxford: Oxford University Press.

Lijphart, A. (1999). *Patterns of democracy: Government forms and performance in thirty-six countries*. New Haven, CT: Yale University Press.

Luitwieler, S. (2015). The distinct nature of the European Union. *Philosophia Reformata*, 80: 123–139.

Luitwieler, S. (2014). *A community of peoples: Europe's values and public justice in the EU*. Amersfoort, Netherlands: Christian Political Foundation for Europe.

Madeley, J., and Sitter, N. (2003). Differential euroscepticism among the Nordic Christian parties: Protestantism or protest? Paper presented at the PSA Scandinavian Politics Specialists Group. Leicester, UK. April.

Mouw, R. J., and Griffioen, S. (1993). *Pluralisms and horizons: An essay in Christian public philosophy*. Grand Rapids, MI: Eerdmans.

Nelsen, B. F., and Guth, J. L. (2015). *Religion and the struggle for European Union: Confessional culture and the limits of integration*. Washington, DC: Georgetown University Press.

Nelsen, B. F., and Guth, J. L. (2003). Religion and youth support for the European Union. *Journal of Common Market Studies*, 41(1): 89–112.

Nelsen, B. F., Guth, J. L., and Fraser, C. R. (2001). Does religion matter? Christianity and public support for the European Union. *European Union Politics*, 2(2): 191–217.

Nelsen, B. F., Guth, J. L., and Highsmith, B. (2011). Does religion still matter? Religion and public attitudes toward integration in Europe. *Politics and Religion*, 4(1): 1–26.

Philpott, D., and Shah, T. S. (2006). Faith, freedom, and federation: The role of religious ideas and institutions in European political convergence. In Byrnes, T. A. and Katzenstein, P. J. (eds), *Religion in an expanding Europe* (pp. 34–64). Cambridge: Cambridge University Press.

Sandel, M. J. (2012). *What money can't buy: The moral limits of markets*. New York: Farrar, Straus and Giroux.

Taylor, C. (1989). *Sources of the self: The making of the modern identity*. Cambridge, MA: Harvard University Press.

ten Napel, H.-M. (1996). Van het continentale naar het Angelsaksische model van christen-democratie? Over de problematische europeanisering van de christen-democratische politiek. In Voerman, G. (ed.) *DNPP Jaarboek 1996* (pp. 229–244). Groningen, Netherlands: DNPP.

Vollaard, H. (2006). Protestantism and euroscepticism in the Netherlands. *Perspectives on European Politics and Society*, 7(3): 276–297.

Walzer, M. L. (1983). *Spheres of justice: A defense of pluralism and equality*. New York: Basic Books.

4 New worlds and new churches
The Orthodox Church(es) and the European Union

Peter Petkoff

Introduction

The Orthodox church(es) share a common commitment to the unity of dogma and spirituality. There is, however, no doctrinal formulation that comes close to a form of political theology at a pan-Orthodox level. This means that the Orthodox churches' attitude towards the European Union (EU) is driven by their ecclesial diversity and by complex inter-ecclesial relations. More fundamentally they share a fragmented and plural, theological objection to the very ideas of Europe and the West. This has been further complicated by the emergence of a substantial Orthodox diaspora from Eastern Europe, Russia, and the Middle East living across the breadth of the European continent. Consequently the ecclesial identity and self-perception of the autocephalous Orthodox churches is changing. These churches are becoming increasingly transnational and extra-territorial. With this, their perception of Europe and the West, as seen through the eyes of their diaspora communities, is altering from "threat" to "home" (Makrides and Uffelmann, 2003). The growing diaspora will not only impact the Christian demographics of Europe but will also transform the Eastern Churches' view of Europe and the EU (Leustean, 2009; 2011; 2013; 2014a; 2014b).

The Orthodox world and the idea of Europe and the European Union

The first challenge for the articulation of Orthodox theological terms of engagement with the EU, and with everything it represents, is to do with the very idea of Europe. The main point of reference for the Orthodox churches within and outside the EU is not Europe, but Christendom articulated visibly beyond Europe through the Pentarchy of the Ancient Patriarchates of Rome, Constantinople, Alexandria, Jerusalem, and Antioch, albeit fractured by the split with Rome. The Schism of 1054 and the hardening of relations with Rome after the sack of Constantinople by the Fourth Crusade in 1204 has made the idea of Europe and the Latin West a threat, something which remained politically, theologically, and culturally outside of the Byzantine Orthodox Commonwealth (Kazdhan, 2001). Although this opposition has often been exaggerated, and ironically re-articulated through the use of theological forms developed by the Reformation and the Counter-Reformation, it represents a powerful current which has shaped Orthodox engagement with the West in multiple contexts.[1]

These anti-Western and anti-European trends are mirrored in similar discourses about the East in Western Europe. A pre-European Community discourse that shaped the agenda of European integration was Pius XII's Christmas address of 1949 that blessed the Christian Democratic movements: 'Christian West and diabolical East'. In the aftermath of World War Two the Christian Democratic parties and their political discourse in predominantly Catholic countries dominated the early European integration discourse and thus the Orthodox churches did not have an opportunity to engage theologically with the idea of European integration at its inception. Greece joined in 1981, Cyprus in 1990, Bulgaria and Romania in 1995. Thus by 1995 there were four EU member states where Chalcedonian Eastern Orthodoxy was a majority religion. In all these countries at the time of accession the religious discourse equated Europe and the EU with something alien, hostile and different.

New worlds and new churches: Orthodox diasporas in the EU as a game changer

With a massive Russian diaspora after the fall of the Berlin Wall, with EU enlargement and an exodus from the Middle East, Europe is gradually becoming home to 85 per cent of the Eastern Christians (Thomas and O'Mahony, 2014). The 'West' has become home to a multinational Orthodox diaspora, which is presenting new challenges to the Orthodox hierarchies and transforming their approaches to the EU and its institutions. All major Orthodox churches now have representatives actively engaged in dialogue with the EU institutions in Brussels. *De iure* territorial Orthodox churches within and beyond the EU, which operate within their own canonical soil, demarcated through a consensus with other Orthodox churches, exercise what could be described as a *de facto* extra-territorial ecclesiastical jurisdiction amongst their diaspora communities in Europe. As a continuation of the League of Nations regime all territorial autocephalous Orthodox churches have a complex network of dioceses and parishes all over the world reaching out to the 'national' diaspora communities and coexist with other Orthodox parishes, sometimes even under the same roof.[2] This is not unproblematic – in theory the Orthodox Church has condemned phyletism, or the idea of a national or ethnic church, as a heresy. In practice almost all autocephalous churches are seen as a rock of the nation. This is particularly visible in the post-Ottoman nation-states, but also in Russia and Ukraine.

At the same time another trend is emerging in a number of EU countries – pan-Orthodox, transnational multi-jurisdictional episcopal conferences formed by representatives of all Orthodox jurisdictions operating within a particular country are seeking to overcome old ethnic and jurisdictional divisions.[3] In addition the Patriarchates of Constantinople and Moscow, although technically outside of the EU, actively engage in the Orthodox discourse within the EU and shape it directly or indirectly through their engagement with the Orthodox diasporas under their control. A number of Orthodox churches belong to the Conference of European Churches (CEC), where they cooperate with Protestant churches in Europe and develop fairly sophisticated ways of lobbying in the EU. It might seem that after the experience of Orthodox diasporas in Europe and through a profound mark on the European intellectual tradition shaped by the extensive interaction between Orthodox theologians and philosophers and their Catholic and Protestant counterparts, the sense of the West, as a foreign threat, might have disappeared.[4] It is, however, not that simple.

Confrontations and conversations: the Orthodox churches and the European Union

The Orthodox churches treat the EU as something outside of the church – something to pray for but not to engage with. Although all major Orthodox churches have representatives in Brussels, the conversations stimulated by Article 17 of the Lisbon Treaty are not always irenic. The economic meltdown in Greece and Cyprus evoked a number of statements of Orthodox hierarchs that were not particularly EU-friendly. The bishops of the Church of Greece described the bailout terms and agreement as a "foreign occupation" (Makris, 2010). In a similar vein the Archbishop of Cyprus declared that an EU exit would be an obvious choice since the EU is clearly not going to last (Rettman, 2013; Elder, 2013).

At the same time the economic crisis has contributed *de facto* to a more active engagement of the Orthodox churches within the EU. Historically these churches have been heavily dependent on state support and there have been very few legal provisions for those churches to develop their own charitable networks. The pressure on the churches to provide greater support to unprecedentedly impoverished populations, and the absence of the state infrastructure and financial support through which to conduct their charitable work in the past, has prompted the churches in Greece and Cyprus to develop their own grassroots networks, some of which will inevitably rely on funding streams from the EU. While these networks are in a nascent stage we can expect to see more cooperation between the local Orthodox charitable organisations and EU institutions (Roudometof and Makrides, 2010).

Another focus of the Orthodox critique of contemporary Europe is the rise of relativism and militant secularism.[5] Churches within the EU see European integration as both a threat and an opportunity. Those churches not within the EU but wishing to have visibility and an impact within the EU institutions speak through their traditional allies among the Orthodox churches of the different member states. In the case of the Russian Orthodox Church (ROC) this message is rather complex and multi-layered. Firstly, its engagement with the European, and indeed other international institutions, remains deeply sceptical and driven by the desire to protect the legacy of a Christian European *Kulturkampf* from militant secularism and the challenges of relativism. In this respect the position of the ROC comes very close to that of the Holy See. A second aspect of the Russian Orthodox Church's engagement with EU institutions is driven by a complex ecclesiastical foreign policy, which mimics and often parallels Russia's state foreign policy (Curanovic, 2012). In this respect the ROC spearheads, through its allies within the EU, Russia's policies towards Europe (Blagoev, 2014).

Furthermore, having developed its own social doctrine (unique within the world of the Orthodox churches) and its own 'Orthodox Bill of Rights' (Moscow Patriarchate, n.d.) the Moscow Patriarchate promotes some distinctly sceptical perspectives about existing human rights mechanisms and this includes the human rights culture of the EU. In this respect the Moscow Patriarchate's positioning towards the EU has to be seen as a wider project which links up with Russia's continuous attempts to reconceptualise international law as a sovereignty-driven rather than a rights protection-driven legal system. The 'Orthodox Bill of Rights' amplifies this argument and prepares the ground for the creation of an Orthodox *Kulturkampf* bound by different perceptions of international law and rights and driven by Orthodox culture.

What remains to be seen is how much traction these grand narratives would have amongst the other local Orthodox churches. After all, the Orthodox churches' engagement with political communities has always been pragmatic and since the fall of Constantinople and the 1917 Russian Revolution, normally not theologically driven. Moreover, the churches' engagement with political communities continues to be shaped by their inter-ecclesial dynamics and tensions. For example, the increasing tensions between Moscow and Constantinople over the primacy of honour of the See of Constantinople and over its extra-territorial jurisdiction, tensions between Moscow and other local Orthodox churches (Ukraine, Romania, Estonia) and very close relations with others (Bulgaria, Serbia, Georgia, Antioch), in many ways shape pragmatic alliances between particular local Orthodox churches and political communities. Because of this dynamic and multi-layered picture we can only speak about multiple Orthodox Christian perspectives towards the EU. Some Orthodox churches (Romania, Estonia) are quite openly pro-EU in their public statements. Others (Bulgaria, Greece, Cyprus) connect in a pragmatic fashion with the EU, at the same time remaining very critical towards certain EU positions and policies. A number of Orthodox churches within and outside the EU (Georgia, Bulgaria, Serbia) have maintained their close ties with Moscow. This has largely determined their approach to the EU and the international community. In addition, the Russian state has declared itself a *de facto* protectorate of Orthodox Christians in the Middle East (Valente, 2013) and the Moscow Patriarchate has invested a lot in building alliances with the Orthodox churches of Jerusalem, Antioch (based in Syria) and Alexandria as well as with the Oriental non-Chalcedonian churches.

Thus we can only speak of multiple Orthodox approaches to the EU driven by different configurations of local Orthodox churches, shaped by concerns about the integrity of their canonical soil, defensiveness against interventions from other Orthodox and sometimes non-Orthodox churches as well as by their own specific needs. Their relationships with governments and international organisations are driven by both principles and pragmatic responses to policies or to governments' engagements with international organisations and international affairs. This also means that different alliances or groupings emerge when different agendas or shared interests emerge. Some of the multi-layered inter-ecclesial relations may determine the formation of a particular grouping united around a specific agenda, or individual Orthodox churches could simply use open ecclesiastical channels to pursue particular agendas. When Russia banned EU food imports in response to EU sanctions over Ukraine the Churches of Greece and Cyprus used their open channels with the Moscow Patriarchate to lobby the Russian government to relax parts of the ban (Kalmouki, 2014).

These interactions suggest that foreign policy analysts cannot underestimate the potential impact and role an aspired Orthodox Commonwealth may have on the shaping of the interactions between the Orthodox churches and EU institutions. It presents analytical challenges to the existing foreign policy approaches, and perhaps also challenges and opportunities for the Orthodox churches themselves to rediscover or redefine the patterns of solidarity and exercise of soft power typical for the Byzantine Orthodox Commonwealth at this time in an EU context. Orthodox churches within the EU may discover that they would be able to operate more freely within an aspired domain of an Orthodox Commonwealth. They would certainly be attracted to the idea of asserting the levels of soft power within and beyond the Orthodox world that this commonwealth permitted and which closely guarded modern nation-states restricted. Understanding the grammar of the 'soft power' of the Byzantine Orthodox Commonwealth tells us a great deal about interdependence and complex relations between states (Nye, 2009) and of the complex interplay and interdependence between religion and the state.

It will be impossible to understand, and catastrophic to ignore, the positioning of the Orthodox churches in the public sphere today and in the past without a good grasp of the exercise of soft power in the Byzantine Orthodox Commonwealth, its fragmented manifestations in the modern period, and the claims for a full scale revival today in the foreign policy approaches of some of the Orthodox churches. The last figure to give expression to the idea of the Orthodox Commonwealth, Joachim III, Patriarch of Constantinople, died in the year of the outbreak of the Balkan wars. The end of the nineteenth century and the emergence of nation-states and *de facto* national churches was the end of the Byzantine Commonwealth (Obolensky, 2000), with Byzantium as a widely spread and varied complex with multiple centres, each with its own set of relationships and connections. It became a centre of concentric circles of influence and "soft power", with "horizontal" as well as hierarchical strands of connection through "its credible show of majesty and piety" (Shepard, 2006: 36–41) embodying the prestige of centuries of history. In a sophisticated 'symphony of powers', imperial office and the church together exercised soft power through their parallel and interconnected networks throughout the Byzantine Commonwealth. It is through this exercise of soft power that other rulers found their models for imitation and wanted to associate themselves with this glittering symbol of imperial and court life and of the Orthodox faith. The decline of the empire placed an increased emphasis on the role of the patriarch, both within Constantinople in relation to the imperial office and outside it through Mount Athos as a microcosm of the Orthodox commonwealth, and on the need to deal diplomatically and in other ways with a complex variety of external actors (Cameron, 2011: 21–24). After the fall of Constantinople it was the ecumenical patriarch and the monks on Mount Athos who still represented that shared consciousness (Cameron, 2011). The Ecumenical Patriarchate, Mount Athos, and Moscow's claim as 'The Third Rome', continue to serve that representative function today.

Orthodox networks and cooperation within the EU today are only a bleak resemblance of the Byzantine Commonwealth that survived the Ottomans (but not the Balkan Wars) and retained some fragments of cooperation in a contemporary context. It would nevertheless be naïve to underestimate the residual energy of the Orthodox Commonwealth, which is gradually being reconstituted in different contexts and has all the facilities to thrive within an EU context. Whatever one thinks of the legacy of the Orthodox Commonwealth from the point of view of foreign policy analysis it will be a grave error not to factor in existing ambitions and existing structures and political forms which are increasingly being deployed to establish continuity with the exercise of soft power of the Byzantine Orthodox Commonwealth.

Theological underpinning of the engagement with the EU: the absent political theology

The Orthodox churches, united in their shared understanding of the unity between dogma and spirituality, have always asserted that their political theology is summed up by praying for the temporal powers (indeed any temporal powers, Christian or Pagan) during the Great Entrance of the Holy Liturgy. Articulated primarily within a liturgical space demarcated by the beginning bidding prayer – 'Blessed is the Kingdom of the Father, the Son, and the Holy Spirit' – and by the sense that past, present, and the Second Coming of Christ are united within the boundaries of the liturgy. Orthodox political theology is in a sense perceived as something which transforms the world in the stillness of a moment which brings past, present, and future together, but much less so through social action. This does not mean that social action is not possible or desirable. But it could be argued that the church does not preach for political change outside of the context of the Eucharistic theology of the Orthodox liturgy. Striving for social change in the secular world would be perceived as a form of social engineering which would replace the imminent Second Coming and would be considered to be potentially idolatrous. Social and political action in this sense is driven by an internal spiritual transformation, not by following strategies of appropriate social or political engagement. The people of God therefore bear witness through patterns that are often difficult to assign to recognizable forms of social engagement. On that level, since the death of the last Christian emperor, the engagement with political authorities is counter-intuitive and merely pragmatic (Runciman, 1968; Sherrard, 1959, 1965).

And here lies the paradox. The Orthodox churches do not have a political role. Yet they have always depended on political organizations to legitimize their normative *corpus*. Most authors now agree that Caesaro-papism is an inappropriate formula to describe relationships between the Orthodox churches and the states they inhabit. But it will be very hard to deny that Orthodox churches have always been heavily dependent on the promulgation of church dogma through its incorporation within imperial law. Since the fall of Constantinople and the emergence of national Orthodox churches in eighteenth and nineteenth centuries, the community of Orthodox churches has never attempted to address the question of how they as a communion of churches genuinely relate to the idea of law as a normative structure parallel to their dogmatic normative corpus and body of ecclesiastical laws. Without engaging head-on with these questions, the Orthodox churches have developed pragmatic 'realist' relations with the political communities whose domains they inhabit. Those relations often border on compromise – Orthodox churches have always been accused of remaining silent about state persecutions (although such a view does not necessarily take into account the significant number of the members of those churches who did bear a silent witness and often paid, and continue to pay today, with their lives); churches often joined the process of national emancipation of a number of post-Ottoman states and effectively promote phyletism;[6] churches often adopt Protestant models of relationship between church and state, motivated by Lutheran or Catholic princes committed to modernizing their states and introducing political interference in the internal affairs of the national churches (Tsarist Russia and Greece).

One of the central challenges of engagement with the EU stems from the premise that the Orthodox churches approach the world through a theological lens inherently articulated via dogmatics. This focuses on 'ontology' as a way to fulfil human personality through particular perspectives and strategies about divine knowledge. This view is inherently suspicious of ethics-driven (rather than dogmatics-driven) approaches because of their overemphasis on 'mechanics' (i.e. properly applied principles of technical application) both in the context of theology but also in the context of social engineering (approaches which often merge with, and in some way debase, authentic theological enquiries that unify dogma and spirituality).[7] This is the reason

Orthodox theology has doubts about political, social, and economic projects which over-emphasise the mechanics of social cohesion. This is also the reason why large political, legal, or economic projects are viewed with suspicion not only by religious zealots but also by creative theologians. One of the key failures in religious organisations' engagement with any forms of regional or global political structures has been that they have often perceived institutional internationalization as a form of competitive theology (even though international institutional projects never were and were never intended to be theological paradigms) with which they have to engage theologically. This suspicion has extended to the EU. The Orthodox rapprochement as a result has been inherently utilitarian. Consequently there is nothing in terms of a substantive critique or a substantive apology that has distinctiveness which could be recognized as an original Orthodox contribution.

Between 'symphony of powers' and 'Babylonian captivity': prospects for Orthodox engagement with the EU

Having established that there has been little substantive engagement with the idea of the EU itself, we now examine the extent to which Christian Orthodox theological foundations might create an environment and opportunities for the future development of such engagement. Such an analysis would inevitably be external and such questions would be absent from those forms of Orthodox theological thinking that assume the EU is yet another political community the church prays for but does not engage with. A more interesting question is whether the EU would create an environment for thriving Orthodox communities and whether they are likely to appreciate that. Does the EU as a particular legal order fit into some of the central ideas/premises of Orthodox theology or does this particular legal order make Orthodox theology more difficult to articulate?

On several levels one could propose that the EU is a fertile ground for thriving Orthodox theology. It creates a melting pot that helps Orthodox communities come out of the Babylonian captivity of religious nationalism and compromising church-state relations driven by Enlightenment and Ottoman political forms. The EU also makes churches more engaged with one another and more ecumenical. It seems that the dilution of political boundaries has helped divided churches to join forces to pursue matters that concern them all. On another level the idea of EU integration does to some extent work with the distinctive understanding of social structures in Orthodox theology, articulated by the twin concepts of 'sociality' and *sobornost*. 'Sociality' refers to a complex amalgam of multiple and individualized 'I-Thou' (rather than 'I-It') interactions with the Other, which shape what is generally understood as social currents. *Sobornost* alludes to a dialogical and mystical 'I-Thou' encounter within the Body of Christ, making the above mentioned individualized interaction in the context of sociality more coherent and possible to exercise (Zizioulas, 2006; Frank, 1992). The EU may seem to offer prospects for this kind of social cohesion. Yet the growing Orthodox diaspora increases the awareness that a fragmentation of national belonging presents opportunities, challenges, and responsibilities that some local Orthodox churches simply cannot meet. Growing Orthodox diasporas in 'new lands' within the EU are likely to lead to the birth of new Orthodox churches shaped beyond ethnic divides.

For the EU this presents a new situation. The Orthodox churches do not engage at any level with the *raison d'être* of the EU. Or rather, they do not engage differently from the ways they engage with any other political community. Because the local Orthodox churches have accepted a status quo of existing within the context of non-Christian political regimes, it is no exaggeration to claim that their engagement with the cultural quality of laws and policies has somehow faded with the disappearance of the last 'Orthodox monarchies'.

At the same time this approach proposes that Christendom has not ended and Orthodox Eucharistic theology powerfully asserts this position by integrating the *entire* humanity into its liturgical drama. The limits of Orthodox political theology in some way present the opportunity to postpone the end of Christendom through its Eucharistic-political engagement with the world rather than through an 'evangelical' political engagement, which requires political communities to support the mission of the Church. This 'engaged dis-engagement' presents challenges for both ecclesial and political communities. At the same time it presents the possibilities of a 'living Christendom' where the salvation of souls pursued by the Church is not locked into a dependence on a political community that has to facilitate the mission of the Church. In the case of the Orthodox churches, a Thomist-style participation in public reason does not emphasise the conversion of political institutions, but rather the fulfillment of human persons. Attempts to convert political institutions are viewed with great suspicion because they may seem potentially idolatrous, utilitarian, and technology-driven, rather than 'ontological' projects, that is, projects which recognise and embrace the sacramental character of the world. Through an Orthodox theological lens "man's relation to God is not simply an intellectual and ethical relation, but a relation entirely and realistically based on the acceptance and use of created things; that is to say, on a eucharistic-liturgical utilization of the world" (Yannaras, 1973: 136). Such a primarily ontological stance is deeply sceptical towards any technological approaches to theology, philosophy, and any other intellectual strategies to social ordering.

> No matter how far technology develops, it never ceases to be a *utilization* of the world which is necessary, legitimate, and commendable. The absolute importance assigned to technology expresses an attitude of a particular kind of utilization of the world; a utilization which does not view the created order as the handiwork of a personal God, nor seeks to bring out the meaning of things (the *logos*) and the disclosure of the uncreated divine energies in the world; but a utilization which presupposes the

autonomy of man's needs and desires and man's arbitrary dominance over the physical world.

(Yannaras, 1973: 136)

Similarly, the reluctance to engage with questions of compliance of natural law with positive law may, perhaps, put Orthodox churches in a stronger position to be greater champions for international law and human rights as pragmatic legal tools than their Catholic and Protestant sister churches. This is partly because the latter have for many years entangled themselves in theological apologetics in relation to international law and human rights as if those represent a competitive theology which they have to reshape and with which they have to engage in theological disputation. The Orthodox churches in contrast have maintained that their authentic position in relation to civil law or any form of non-ecclesiastical law is always projected through the pastoral lens of canon law (civil law punishes, canon law heals). They engage with such parallel legal orders through parallel canonical approaches, but they are not expected to adopt, endorse, or reject any approaches of civil law, whether punitive or tolerant, in areas which would largely be considered in a Western Christian context to be broadly a clash between Divine, natural law and civil law.

This does not mean to say that Orthodox churches will not assert their theological positions in areas of concern in common with other churches. It is, however, less likely that these positions will be articulated as 'mechanical' Christian social engineering projects such as often emerge in the political theology of the Western Christian tradition (and to some extent in the methodological emphases of 'new natural law' theories of authors such as Finnis [2011] and George [1999]). In this respect the Orthodox churches remain and will probably remain uninterested in political or legal institutions. One of the reasons that this is unlikely to change is the inherently dialogical rather than hierarchical institutionalism of the Orthodox churches, a pattern that also extends to political and legal institutions. Another reason is the general decline of hierarchical institutionalism in the relationships between political and ecclesiastical authorities in Europe, particularly manifested by the trend towards disestablishment.

In this environment of declining hierarchical institutionalism, Orthodox churches have a real opportunity to reassert their authentic dialogical institutionalism. In the EU there is already a forum facilitated by Article 17 of the Lisbon Treaty. It might just be possible that this facility will create the environment needed for the Orthodox churches to get accustomed to engaging with political institutions beyond national boundaries and to overcome the stalemate of interdependency of national churches and national governments.

Such an engagement will also fit well with perceptions of authority which orient Orthodox theology more closely to 'personal authority', perceptions driven by a dialogical situation and which open up towards sociality and *sobornorst*. This approach, articulated by certain key Orthodox theologians, derives from the Christological formulations of the Council of Chalcedon (451 AD). It emphasizes the idea of the personal authority of each Christian, centred on the powers entrusted to each person though baptism ('priest', 'prophet', and 'king') and on the people of God together as 'shield-bearers of truth'. This dialogical dynamic between ecclesiastical hierarchy and people of God, one of promulgation and reception, can allow for many different forms of engagement in different situations and with diverse configurations of groups and individuals. The fulfillment of these roles within an ecclesiastical context means that relating to the world, individually or in a community, transforms the world through the transformation of the human beings in their ecclesial context. This amounts to a sacramental-ontological renewal of society and not necessarily a technological transformation of the political institutions.

Ware reminds us that what makes a church council universal is not simply an endorsement by the Pentarchy and the Emperor, but a reception by the People of God as 'shield-bearers of the Faith', a 'priesthood of all believers' co-responsible for shaping the church and the world (Ware, 1970). This is a role that the Orthodox laity may now extend to the forms through which its churches engage with the EU. This means that Orthodox theology has by default provided (at least in theory) greater space for the role of laity through the process of reception. It also suggests greater opportunities for dialogue rather than simply top-down clerical decision making. It implies that, outside as well as within the church, complex networks of clergy and laity will speak with a plurality of voices about the churches' engagement with the world. More importantly if the 'People of God' choose to exercise their role as 'shield bearers of truth' in a secular context, they and their associations may play a pivotal role in preventing ecclesiastical institutions from losing their theological voices by being too sceptical or over-confident about the benefits of their interactions with political communities. In order for this to happen the people of God have to awaken and acknowledge their responsibilities. This has already been happening, in differing degrees in different Orthodox churches. In some, reclaiming their ancestors' religion has been seen as a sign of a new freedom. But in many contexts this sense of freedom has led to complacency in treating their churches as cultural monuments or a plant they fondly grow in their back garden.

This is an untapped potential of the role of the 'People of God.' Following the Greek crisis, the growth of grassroots charities with strong EU connections and endorsement from the Church of Greece may be the first signs of greater lay engagement alongside that of ecclesiastical institutions. This trend, however, does not translate across all churches. In some Orthodox churches, local bishops refuse to endorse such grassroots developments and view them as threats to their own power. They may like the idea of interacting with the EU but see themselves as gatekeepers and middlemen who facilitate such contact.

It is very difficult to see how this could change unless EU institutional cooperation with lay Christian organisations is developed and strengthened. Moving in that direction would certainly make sense, particularly in countries where the Orthodox church is stagnated by declining ordinations and monastic vocations, ecclesiastical corruption, dilapidated parish structures, lack of education, and a hard-line hierarchical defence of a status quo beneficial for a particular brand of Orthodoxy. In such cases EU institutions should be reluctant to designate gatekeepers with whom they choose to work. Broadening the roster of interlocutors will strengthen the role and the forms of lay (re)engagement on the ground and will have an impact on the ways local Orthodox churches engage with current issues. At the same time, EU involvement in domestic ecclesiastical politics must proceed with a due care for religious autonomy. A complex case such as the right to access to Mount Athos on the negotiation table could easily kill *all* negotiations.

We see, then, that one of the main features of the engagement with the idea of the EU by Orthodox churches is a great diversity of voices not easy to reconcile. Some Orthodox bishops speak openly with anti-EU/anti-European positions (and these two are not always clearly distinguished). Others are openly pro-EU, others remain mysteriously silent, while a few hold views which could be described as fascist. All this presents a challenge of unpredictability in the ways Orthodox churches are likely to interact with the public institutions of the EU. On the one hand, they have less historical baggage compared to the Roman Catholic Church and a number of European Protestant Churches. These have seen their ecclesial identities shaped through an evolving expectation of being (albeit in a different way) co-participants in the articulation of public reason. To avoid such an expectation, Orthodox churches are perhaps theologically reluctant to spell out a particular contemporary commitment of engagement with the political.[8] On the other hand, because of the lack of an Orthodox political theology, Orthodox churches (and, for example, Orthodox MEPs) seem to adopt a plethora of political theologies. Some of those are fragments, others are hybrids, while most are borrowed either through historical circumstances, or through efforts at reconstruction, or simply by following what everybody else does. The result is that Orthodox voices within the EU institutions tend to articulate generic 'Christian' positions alongside those of other Christian churches rather than distinct Orthodox perspectives.

Urbi et Orbi: levels and forms of engagement in an EU context

EU institutions have provided an important context and a framework for an engagement with religious organizations. Orthodox churches actively pursue these opportunities, while their terms of engagement often display different attitudes towards the EU at home and abroad. Such diverse approaches are difficult to interpret. On the one hand they display a realist positioning of the churches engaging with different audiences, and, on the other, a possible shift away from church-state relations as a key *modus operandi* for the territorial Orthodox churches.

The Church of Greece, Cyprus, Romania, and the ROC have representations in Brussels. Those churches along with a number of other local

Orthodox churches are also represented by the CEC. The membership of CEC goes beyond the boundaries of the EU and indicates once again that the interplay between inter-Orthodox relations and Orthodox interactions with European institutions are complex. In addition, a Committee of the Representatives of the Orthodox Churches at the European Union (CROCEU) meets regularly and develops joint strategies. Their recent statement (coordinated with CEC policy) could be considered a blueprint about the future directions of engagement of the Orthodox churches with the European Union. The statement, agreed and issued prior to the upcoming elections for the European Parliament of May 2014, is indicative of the consolidation of an agreed pan-Orthodox agenda to be pursued before the European institutions. In it the enlarged responsibilities and competencies of the European Parliament according to the Lisbon Treaty are considered and the importance of the role of European citizens, particularly Christians, in the next elections, affirmed:

> The Orthodox Representatives would like to underscore that the European Union is not just another institution founded to safeguard individual and collective economic interests. It is rather the recipient encompassing the aspirations of hundreds of millions of people living in their own country who wish to be part of a larger family of nations that work together for the consolidation of social standards, dignity in life and security in society. All share a responsibility for building and developing institutions by all means socially, economically and environmentally sustainable. Christians are encouraged to take active part in the elections and, thus, to contribute to the improvement of the European project.
> (CROCEU, 2014)

The CROCEU statement commits Orthodox Representatives to work together with any competent authority in order to promote such goals. The document deals, *inter alia*, with sustainability-driven environmental policies, the protection of human dignity, the right to life, family life (marriage defined as a union between a man and a woman), gender equality, social investment policies tackling social exclusion, unemployment and poverty, guaranteeing a minimum wage, care for the most vulnerable members of the society and commitment to the common good of the people, and to a dialogue encouraging co-responsibility and cooperation with the European authorities in the spirit of Article 17 of the Lisbon Treaty. The document promotes a wider participation in the European elections and appeals to Orthodox Christians to exercise their democratic vote.

What is particularly significant in this document is that, among the commitments which spell out fairly predictable positions, the document also endorses a commitment on the part of the Committee of Orthodox Churches in Brussels to human rights, democracy, the rule of law and civic education. It calls for:

- Human Rights strategies for the protection of civil, political, social, economic and cultural rights. The aim is always to soften and not harden tensions in the society. Human rights must never become a battlefield. They rather have to be the firm ground to foster cohesion in the society and prosperity for its members. In particular, those who sustain freedom of religion, belief or conviction in fact work for promoting the values of peace and justice in the society. What is more, it is a duty for any state to secure access to efficient social services for all especially at a time of deepening crisis.
- Education strategies for democratic citizens who respect human rights and intercultural competences.
- Effective, humane, 'democracy and rule of law'-driven social inclusion policies towards migrants and refugees as well as policies tackling the problem of extremism and racism.

(CROCEU, 2014)

This is a very specific endorsement, spelling out more clearly than many other statements or position papers of individual Orthodox churches a pan-Orthodox position in relation to individual human rights. This endorsement of human rights is at odds with some fundamental positions of some of the local Orthodox churches, voiced as a religious critique of international law (albeit borrowed directly from a CEC statement).

Another reason this document is particularly significant for the Orthodox churches' engagement with EU institutions is that it shows both the ability and the commitment to engage with EU institutions on their terms and with language that is likely to have a greater traction in Brussels. A particularly fascinating feature is that the Orthodox churches have here expressed a political commitment to democratic elections, echoing the grammar of solidarity of the Christian Democratic movements of the early post-second world war period. Appropriation of such typically Roman Catholic political language is already significant enough. But what must be kept in mind is how differently the Orthodox churches relate to the EU institutions in Brussels as opposed to at home. While their representatives endorse the above values in Brussels, many of the national Orthodox churches have been historically silent during national parliamentary elections and have often endorsed fairly unsavory political elites. Papathanasiou (2013) even goes so far as to identify a national-socialist grammar in the statements of the Church of Greece and its alignment with the far right, especially after the economic downturn. This invites two possible explanations. One is that when engaging with EU institutions, policies and law at home and abroad, the Orthodox churches simply cater for different audiences. The other is that political and economic transformations, expanding Orthodox diasporas in Western Europe and a disillusionment with traditional alliances with governments at home, have brought the Orthodox churches genuinely closer to EU institutions – aided by the fact that such institutions, through the Lisbon Treaty, facilitate dialogue at a level which is no longer possible with national governments at home.

From a policy point of view this might be a significant development. It represents closer engagement by Orthodox churches with regional and international institutions and even a willingness to endorse human rights at a EU level, even while the same churches are quite reluctant to do so and often do exactly the opposite at a national level. Driven by their complex inter-ecclesial relations and inherent tensions, by complex and reconciled relationships with the states where their mother churches reside, and by pure pragmatism, the Orthodox churches articulate their positions in a highly contextualized fashion. The ROC would speak in one way as an autocephalous church responsible for the Russian Commonwealth and by pursuing foreign policy agendas aligned with the foreign policy agendas of the Russian state. At the same time it may speak very differently as a member of CEC or CROCUE before the European institutions. The same would apply to the churches of Romania, Bulgaria, Cyprus, Greece, Serbia, Albania, and the Ecumenical Patriarchate of Constantinople. While united in doctrine, these churches have been historically aligned in complex church-state relations and inter-ecclesial relations either close to ROC or to Constantinople, or acting fairly independently both in terms of relations with the major patriarchates and in terms of attitudes to Europe.

Thus it would be a gross oversimplification to try to consolidate this complex mosaic in order to adopt a common interpretation of all Orthodox churches (as it would be in the case of the Roman Catholic Church and the churches *sui iuris* in communion with Rome). A very important starting point would be to focus on what these churches share in common in terms of an understanding of unity between doctrine and spirituality and what are the examples of departure from their common tradition. On that level, issues such as homosexuality and biotechnology are negotiated to a greater extent at a 'constitutional level' by the ROC but contained at a level of penitential discipline by the other Orthodox churches. In other words, an engagement with the contemporary world would not be the common thread in Orthodox thought we might expect to see. Such an engagement takes different forms, picks different themes and rarely is endorsed by the whole local church or at a pan-Orthodox level.

Any engagement by EU institutions with Orthodoxy thus has to develop sophisticated tools to interpret these dynamics and to be aware of the inner diversity and independence of churches united by common doctrine. In doing so, EU institutions have to be aware of the inherent challenges of such a complex engagement. This would require balancing an awareness of the importance both of the hierarchical structures and of an independent, and at the same time properly endorsed and integrated, grassroots engagement with Orthodox laity. This might be pursued, for example, by championing programmes that would develop Orthodoxy's legitimate voice in the true spirit of the principle of subsidiarity. For one leading contemporary theologian, this includes paying attention also to the priority of the local parish itself:

Only the life of the parish can give a priestly dimension to politics, a prophetic spirit to science, a philanthropic concern to economics, a sacramental character to love. ... The liturgical unity of the faithful has to be the starting-point of all the things for which we hope: the transformation of the impersonal life of the masses into a communion of persons, the authentic and genuine (rather than the merely theoretical and legal) observance of social justice, the deliverance of work from the bondage of mere need and its transformation into an engagement of personal involvement and fellowship. Apart from the local parish all of these are but an abstraction, naive idealism, sentimental utopianism. But within the parish there is historical actualization, realistic hope, dynamic manifestation. The eschatological self-understanding of Orthodox theology cannot be actualized outside of the setting of the local parish. It is to this setting that the dialogue must return, leaving aside the challenge of the West. The role of Orthodox theology within the historical and cultural milieu of the West is to draw attention to the eschatological witness of the Church as embodied in the parish.

(Yannaras, 1973: 146)

It also means that EU interlocutors would need to acquire the necessary religious literacy enabling them to develop broader coalitions with Orthodox faith-based organisations (FBOs). This could involve the following: (1) identifying feasible conversations to pursue and distinguishing them from those that would be premature; (2) understanding the agenda of individual Orthodox FBOs as well as the group dynamics of all Orthodox FBOs in Brussels; (3) developing broader networks of interlocutors in each church rather than relying on representatives in the EU that often have a purely symbolic role quite different from the role of Papal Nuncios; (4) taking the measure of the unique challenges each Orthodox church is facing in its engagement with the EU and how these challenges could be addressed; and (5) grasping the geopolitical role that the Orthodox churches play and could play within the EU, the Council of Europe, and beyond, and using this knowledge in the EU's external action. But such forms of awareness cannot be reduced to mere statistics and demographics. EU actors would also have to incorporate an awareness of the pivotal role of the distinctive theological discourses and voices already touched on in this chapter.[9]

EU actors might also seek to recognise that some of the sceptical perspectives Orthodox (and other religious) voices raise about the work of international institutions are not completely misguided. International organisations and EU institutions will always face the challenge of teleological visions and the technological processes which are implemented to pursue such visions. Forms of multilateralism are often constrained by political contention and proceduralism. Well-informed and genuinely engaged religious voices may open new agendas for change in the ways regional and international organisations engage with the world, helping them take into account the complexities of polyphonic voices. A calibrated approach to political institutions through the ontological lens of Christian dogmatics can and should contribute, in the words of Jacques Delors, to reinvigorating the 'European soul' through a genuine social concern beyond a mere political and legal technological statecraft. A leap towards such a theological renewal rooted in the genuine ontological engagement with the world and a rediscovered relevance of religious voices could hardly be articulated better than in the words of Metropolitan Kallistos Ware of Diokleia (2015): "If Orthodoxy is to triumph ... it must be a humble, even humiliated Orthodoxy open to the needs of the world around us, sharing its sorrows, doubts and distress."

Notes

1 For example, the Slavophiles' anti-Westernism, Yugoslav anti-Westernism, Orthodox critique of the West as an extension of Communist propaganda during the Cold War, and critique of the West in the context of the Orthodox theological revival in Paris (particularly through the works of S. Boulgakov, N. Berdyaev, S. Frank, and V. Lossky), and Greece. See Yannaras (1973).
2 Since 1973 and until very recently the Orthodox Church in Oxford had two parishes with two bishops of two jurisdictions (Constantinople and Moscow) and two calendars.
3 Some of those include assemblies in the USA, France, UK, Spain, and Portugal.
4 In this respect, the Fellowship of St Alban and St Sergius, the Orthodox Theological Institutes in Paris and Munich, have been major hubs of dialogue and cross-fertilization of theological ideas.
5 This was apparent in the Inter-Orthodox Consultation on the Draft Constitutional Treaty of the European Union (Payne and Kent, 2011: 41).
6 On the current debates about Orthodox theology and nationalism, see *St Vladimir's Theological Quarterly* (2013).
7 Yannaras (1973: 131), for example, is prepared to link the theological presuppositions of modern theology with the medieval scholastic methodology and its intellectual effort to master the realm of accessible truth by defining and distinguishing the boundaries between man's capacities and the transcendent reality of God. A paradigmatic example of this 'technological' approach to theology is the definition of theology in Aquinas: "Nevertheless sacred teaching also makes use of human reasoning, not indeed to prove the faith (for that would do away with the merit of believing) but *to render manifest* some of the things which are delivered in this teaching." (*ST* I, Q 1, A 8, ad 2).
8 Strictly, the only appropriate form of government where the Church could actively engage remains a Christian theocracy. Other forms of government are seen as tolerating but not adequately facilitating a forum for the Church to participate in public reasoning.
9 For example, the 'I-Thou' theological strategies of encounter with the Other of John Zizioulas; the laity transformed by the authority vested upon them by Chalcedonian dogmatics in the theology of Kallistos Ware; the ontological corrective to social engineering in the theology of Christos Yannaras.

References

Aquinas, T. *Summa theologiae* [ST].
Blagoev, G. (2014). Rusia razmakha pr"st na ES chrez Bulgarskata Pravoslavna Ts"rkva Neofit m"lchi. Retrieved from www.faktor.bg/mnenia/lacheni-carvuli/22425-rusiya-razmaha-prast-na-es-i-chrez-balgarskata-pravoslavna-tzarkva-neofit-malchi.html%7D.

Cameron, A. (2011). Mount Athos and the Byzantine world. In Speake, G. and Ware, K. (eds), *Mount Athos: Microcosm of the Christian East* (pp. 11–27). New York: Peter Lang.
Committee of the Representatives of Orthodox Churches to the European Union (CROCEU). (2014). Strength comes out of unity. Statement in view of the European elections. 9 March. Retrieved from http://orthodoxru.eu/index.php?content=article&category=publications&id=2014-03-20-1&lang=en.
Curanovic, A. (2012). *The religious factor in Russia's foreign policy: Keeping God on our side.* London: Routledge.
Elder, M. (2013). Head of Cyprus's Orthodox Church urges exit before Eurozone collapses. *The Guardian*, 24 March 2013. Retrieved from www.theguardian.com/world/2013/mar/24/cyprus-orthodox-church-exit-eurozone.
Finnis, J. (2011). *Natural law and natural rights.* Oxford: Oxford University Press.
Frank, S. L. (1992). *Duhovnye osnovy obshtestva.* Moskow: Respublika.
George, R. (1999). *In defense of natural law.* Oxford: Clarendon Press.
Kalmouki, N. (2014). Greek Church appeals to Moscow patriarch over food ban. *Greek Reporter*, 25 August. Retrieved from http://greece.greekreporter.com/2014/08/25/greek-church-appeals-to-moscow-patriarch-over-food-ban/.
Kazhdan, A. (2001). Latins and Franks in Byzantium: Perception and reality from the eleventh to the twelfth century. In Laiou, A. E. and Mottahedeh, R. P. (eds), *The crusades from the perspective of Byzantium and the Muslim world* (pp. 83–100). Washington, DC: Dumbarton Oaks Research Library and Collection.
Leustean, L. N. (2014a). *Eastern Christianity and politics in the twenty-first century.* London: Routledge.
Leustean, L. N. (2014b). *The ecumenical movement and the making of the European community.* Oxford: Oxford University Press.
Leustean, L. N. (ed.) (2013). *Representing religion in the European Union: Does God matter?* London: Routledge.
Leustean, L. N. (2011). *Eastern Christianity and the cold war, 1945–91.* London: Routledge.
Leustean, L. N. (2009). *Orthodoxy and the cold war: Religion and political power in Romania, 1947–65.* Basingstoke: Palgrave Macmillan.
Makrides, V. N., and Uffelmann, D. (2003). Studying Eastern Orthodox anti-westernism: The need for a comparative research agenda. In Sutton, J. and van den Bercken, W. P. (eds), *Orthodox Christianity and contemporary Europe* (pp. 87–120). Leuven, Belgium: Peeters.
Makris, A. (2010). Greek Church denounces 'country governed by IMF'. *Greek Reporter*, 17 December. Retrieved from http://greece.greekreporter.com/2010/12/17/greek-church-denounces-country-governed-by-imf/.
Moscow Patriarchate. (n.d.). *The basis of the social concept.* Retrieved from https://mospat.ru/en/documents/social-concepts/.
Moscow Patriarchate. (n.d.). *The Russian Orthodox Church's basic teaching on human dignity, freedom and rights.* Retrieved from https://mospat.ru/en/documents/dignity-freedom-rights/.
Nye, J. S. (2009). *Soft power: The means to success in world politics.* New York: Public Affairs.
Obolensky, D. (2000). *The Byzantine commonwealth: Eastern Europe, 500–1453.* London: Phoenix.

Papathanasiou, A. N. (2013). Signs of national socialism in the Greek Church? *St Vladimir's Theological Quarterly*, 57(3/4): 461–478.
Payne, D. P., and Kent, J. M. (2011). An alliance of the sacred: Prospects for a Catholic-Orthodox partnership against secularism in Europe. *Journal of Ecumenical Studies*, 46(1): 41–66.
Rettman, A. (2013). Cypriot Archbishop calls for Euro-exit. *EU Observer*. 25 March. Retrieved from https://euobserver.com/economic/119555.
Roudometof, V., and Makrides, V. (2010). *Orthodox Christianity in 21st century Greece: The role of religion in culture, ethnicity, and politics*. Farnham: Ashgate.
Runciman, S. (1968). *The great church in captivity: A study of the patriarchate of Constantinople from the eve of the Turkish conquest to the Greek war of independence*. Cambridge: Cambridge University Press.
Shepard, J. (2006). The Byzantine commonwealth, 1000–1550. In Angold, M. (ed.), *The Cambridge history of Christianity, Volume 5: Eastern Christianity* (pp. 3–52). Cambridge: Cambridge University Press.
Sherrard, P. (1965). *Constantinople: Iconography of a sacred city*. London: Oxford University Press.
Sherrard, P. (1959). *The Greek east and the Latin west: A study in the Christian tradition*. London: Oxford University Press.
Special issue on Ecclesiology and Nationalism. (2013) *St Vladimir's Theological Quarterly*, 57(3/4).
Thomas, S., and O'Mahony, A. (2014). Postsecularity and the contending visions of the European political imagination in international relations. In Mavelli, L. and Petito, F. (eds), *Towards a postsecular international politics: New forms of community, identity, and power* (pp. 105–128). Basingstoke: Palgrave Macmillan.
Valente, G. (2013). Russia's 'protectorate' over Middle Eastern Christians. *Vatican Insider / La Stampa*, 24 October. Retrieved from http://vaticaninsider.lastampa.it/en/world-news/detail/articolo/russia-rusia-medio-oriente-28944/.
Ware, K. T. (2015). *Triumph of Orthodoxy: Sermon on the first Sunday of Lent*. 1 March. Oxford: Church of the Holy Trinity and Annunciation.
Ware, K. T. (1970). Primacy, collegiality, and the people of God. *Eastern Churches Review*, 3(1): 18–29.
Yannaras, C. (1973). Orthodoxy and the west. In Philippou, A. J. (ed.), *Orthodoxy: Life and freedom: Essays in honour of Archbishop Iakovos*. Oxford: Studion.
Zizioulas, J. (2006). *Communion and otherness: Further studies in personhood and the church*. London: T&T Clark.

5 The German social market economy
Its theological justification and role in European integration

Werner Lachmann

Introduction

Over the last few centuries European states developed markedly different economic philosophies. Britain was the first country to establish a free market economy based on a capitalist system, while France developed a bureaucratic model dating back to mercantilist times (Colbert). Germany initially followed an anti-liberal approach combined with a significant role for state interference (Bismarck). After World War Two, however, Germany became the economic liberal paragon of good behaviour – the model child of economic reforms – by introducing a Social Market Economy (SME), a compromise between socialist and liberal ideas. France, by contrast, introduced a model based on state planning ('planification française'). After the French-German reconciliation the two nations became the engine of European integration. On the way towards the creation of a Common Market for Europe, therefore, there was always going to be a need for a compromise between these contending economic approaches (Bilger, 1996). This chapter will explain the philosophical background, genesis, and policy implications of the SME; delineate the distinctively Protestant roots of this concept; offer a biblical-theological assessment of some leading ideas of the German SME; and outline the way in which the need for a German-French compromise continues to shape the development of the EU – using the creation of the euro as a leading example.

Theoretical background and economic policy implications of the SME[1]

Many of the core principles of the new concept of a SME go back to the ideas of classical liberalism, especially the assumption that a market system is best suited to regulate economic relationships. However, in contrast to *neo*classical economics, in the SME model government is also expected to play an important part – a point already recognised in the ideas of Adam Smith and John Stuart Mill who underlined the importance of a functioning government for the successful working of a market economy. The government was seen to be responsible for the economic framework if a country was to function well.

I begin with some historical remarks based on the German experience. The growing influence of liberalism in Europe during the nineteenth century led both to substantial industrial growth but also to what was termed the 'social question' (*Soziale Frage*). Not all people participated in the wealth created by industrialization, and, in the industrial centres, the poor lived a miserable life. In Germany, a group of economists, often disparaged as 'socialists of the chair' (*Kathedersozialisten*), demanded, therefore, social corrections of those negative side effects of liberalism. The *Verein für Socialpolitik* (Society for Social Policy) had been founded in 1872; their members (well-known economists, jurists, and businessmen) strove for an improvement of the social situation of the poor in the country. The best-known economists and administrators of those days in the German-speaking area understood themselves as liberals and supported the competitive market process. In contrast to the English classical economists, however, they considered the social question as a challenge for the national government. Already Gustav von Schmoller (the leader of the younger German historical economic school) in 1874 addressed this question in his famous paper '*Die soziale Frage und der preußische Staat* ("The social question and the Prussian state"). The Society for Social Policy later became the German Economic Association.[2]

The SME is not yet identical with the 'free market economy', a model which emphasizes only the traditional regulatory functions of the state, i.e. those necessary to provide external security, to guarantee the rule of law, and to provide an infrastructural framework – a model known as 'minimal state' or *Nachtwächterstaat* (nightwatchman state). Citizens may freely dispose of their resources restricted only by the rule of law. Such an economic order is more in line with the ideas of American liberal economists who pleaded for minimum state interventions and who are convinced that it is the best for the people to leave the economy largely to its own devices.

The founders of the SME could take into account some historical experiences such as the failure of economic policy after the First World War and the subsequent dictatorship. The erratic interventions of the German government during the Weimar republic (1919–33) only served to increase the already existing economic problems. The woeful experiences of fascism and war-time planning helped to drive home the importance of individual freedom and showed the danger posed by government interventions to the freedom of the people. Thus the 'ORDO-liberals' started considering anew the role of government in the market system. Market models were developed which put the spotlight on the relationship between business and government. It was the aim of those theorists to restrain political power as well as economic power – only a government that is self-restrained could be a strong one. A government that interferes too much into the economy will become dependent on the support of pressure groups, causing the loss of the political ability to follow economic policies that are best for the whole nation.

The originators of this new concept did not consider it to be pure theory but rather a framework of general rules governing the economy. They spoke of a '*Stilgedanke*' (an orienting concept), where the implementation of the framework always has to be adjusted to the economic problems of the time. One could compare this concept to a compass that helps government find the right direction, while actual policy has to take into account existing possibilities. Because they stressed in their analysis the reaction of the economic actors to the given economic framework, the very concept of a SME provides for its continual further development, leading to greater flexibility and adjustment capacity in facing new economic challenges.

The fundamental idea of this economic model consists of connecting the principle of freedom of the market with that of social responsibility and economic redistribution for the purpose of economic justice. The economic goal consists of the simultaneous realisation of economic efficiency and social justice. The market outcome is considered as fair – as long as the market rules are fair. Hence the government was seen to be responsible for competition in efficiency (*Leistungswettbewerb*). In contrast to other competition models, ORDO-liberals rely on rules that they consider as collective goods. Such rules must be set by government since (contra Hayek) they are not the result of the market process as such. Competition in efficiency should be to the advantage of the consumer – even though, as Adam Smith already indicated, the supplier dislikes this kind of competition and prefers a "gentlemen's agreement" on prices (1976: 145).

It will be helpful to spell out the distinctive economic policy implications of the SME in contrast to the neo-liberal economic model currently dominant in, especially, the USA. Whereas neo-liberal economists such as F. A. Hayek emphasized that the state cannot foresee the course of free market developments (in terms of structure, behaviour, and efficiency), the ORDO-liberals insisted that market freedom needs to be supplemented by carefully calibrated rules and institutions. Hayek tried to design institutional rules that reduced to a minimum the need for collective action. By contrast, ORDO-liberals and with them the advocates of a SME, declared it to be a task of government to lay down the framework for all parties involved in the economic game. The maxim was: 'policy to shape the economic system – yes; intervening into the market process itself – no'.

The ORDO-liberal Walter Eucken, leader of the Freiburg School, thus distinguished between the *economic order* (the legal and institutional framework of the economic system) and the *economic process* (the daily transactions of the economic agents).[3] Nothing that could be coordinated via markets and prices should be undertaken by the government. To this end, Eucken formulated a series of systematic principles, chiefly 'constitutive' and 'regulatory' ones (summarised and explained in the Appendix). Here we need only indicate some of Eucken's fundamental principles that proved crucial to SME thinking: first, the drive for competitive prices; second, the priority of price stability; third, the importance of open markets; fourth, the unity of '*Gestaltungsmacht*' (power for formative action) and liability (i.e. liability should not be limited, implying a clear relationship between ownership and control, such that whoever has the right and power to decide, the right to influence or create a legal relationship, should also bear the resulting economic consequences); fifth, the importance of limiting the power of interest groups by placing the priority on '*Ordnungspolitik*' over '*Prozesspolitik*'.[4] We will return to some of the principles later when we discuss the evolution of the euro crisis.

Yet in addition to correcting so-called market failures there is also a need to correct market outcomes. The need for social policy and for measures to stabilise the economy must also be considered. According to the German ORDO-liberal tradition, the government has to guarantee the working of the market process via an effective competition policy. There are yet further tasks for government underlined by the supporters of a SME. For example, some socially important goods might be under-consumed by people because they are not aware of the importance of the goods and will thus demand too little; there are information problems on the demand side, especially over time. Government must therefore supply 'merit goods' such as education and health services because people might not demand the optimal amount. In addition, because the capital market does not work perfectly it is very difficult to obtain credit for, for example, educational purposes when creditors do not know if they will get their money back. Government must overcome this deficiency by means of an effective education policy.

ORDO-liberals also underline the need for establishing a competitive order and the need of safeguarding competition. Chicago school liberals would not support this idea because they think that the market system only needs free access for potential competitors and do not believe in the long-run market power of incumbents. Often it is thought that competition will be the result of the free interplay of all individuals. However, advocates of SME hold that competition is not a 'weed' that grows by itself but rather a 'cultivated plant' that must be tended by government. Completely free competition might result in anarchy or in monopolies. For various reasons some companies seem to be more efficient than others. But business in general does not like competition for it means that its economic position is always vulnerable. Companies thus try to form cartels in order to protect themselves against competition.

Neoclassical economists nevertheless argue that a functioning system of market competition is beneficial for the consumer because it results in supplying the society with all the goods it needs at the lowest costs, as well as securing the optimal use of scarce factors of production. But defenders of SME point out that this neoclassical ideal of competition will never actually arise. In neoclassical theory (which is mostly static in design), competition policy would require many small competitors (perfect competition). But this is not in accord with reality. Competition arises if there are competitive partners, which can influence the market price. Yet even a large number of small producers (agriculture) are often not able to influence market prices. Thus SME critics of the neoclassical model speak of '*Schlafmützenkonkurrenz*' (day-dreamer competition).

Advocates of SME thus insist that it is the task of government to regulate the economy such that effective competition will actually prevail. This would mean that cartels and certain company mergers are not allowed and that the government has to screen the market to check if there are enough companies supplying a good and if there is rivalry. This results in preventing companies from growing too big in order to obtain market power. On the other hand, government should seek to help small- and medium-sized enterprises in order to grow to such a size that they can indeed compete with market rivals. For example, incentives are given to small-shop owners to unite together in a cooperative in order to obtain better prices from industry by combining their demand.

The Protestant roots of the SME and the *Freiburg Circle*

While this is not generally known (especially outside Germany), many of the foundational ideas of a SME are deeply rooted in Christian ethics. Most of the fathers of the German Social Market Economy were confessing Christians (indeed members of the Confessing Church[5]) and this made a genuine difference to their political and economic thinking. After World War Two, four opposition groups were seeking to impose their ideas on the economy that was to be reconstructed, but none was able to impose its ideas entirely on the others. The German SME can be understood as a compromise in the intellectual struggle going on between the exponents of socialist ideas (the labour movement), the ORDO-liberal group which partly reflected Catholic social teaching, and those that were influenced by ideas of 'brotherly assistance' (*Nächstenliebe*) advocated by social ethicists of the Lutheran church. The fourth group consisted of some liberals who spoke out for a more purely liberal reconstruction of Germany (neo-liberals favouring the anti-state stance of Hayek). None of these four groups could become dominant in West Germany after the war. The concept of a SME sought to accommodate the demands of all those groups but met none of them completely. The ORDO-liberals and neo-liberals got market freedom; the socialists secured recognition of the social responsibility of the state, while the whole model found support in the social teaching of the Catholic Church and in Protestant social ethics. Here I focus on the Protestant justification.[6]

Already towards the end of the war a group of (mainly Protestant) German economists, jurists, and theologians – the 'Freiburg Circle'[7] – began to explore the shape of a possible economic order after the war, which they presumed by then was lost. As confessing Christians they took biblical and theological insights on economic ethics into account. The 'Freiburg Imperative' of those ORDO-liberals was put into practise by Ludwig Erhard in June 1948, after the introduction of the deutschmark (DM). Due to a fortunate historical circumstance Erhard, the then-director of the economics division in the British-American Zone, could begin to implement the SME in June 1948 without waiting for the permission of the Allied High Commissioner.[8] A key influence at this moment was the economist and sociologist of religion Alfred Müller-Armack, who had been working to develop a Protestant economic ethic that would relate the world of economics to the realm of faith and to show how economic behaviour and the institutions of a society were shaped by religious convictions.[9] In 1946 Müller-Armack had already developed, in his book *Planned Economy and Market Economy* (*Wirtschaftslenkung und Planwirtschaft*), a policy programme for a concept he dubbed 'Social Market Economy'. In 1952 Erhard appointed Müller-Armack as Head of the Central Policy Unit at the Federal Ministry of Economic Affairs. The SME quickly proved to be highly successful. The British weekly *The Economist* spoke already in 1952 of a German 'economic miracle' – to the displeasure of Ludwig Erhard for whom it was no miracle at all but merely the obvious result of a sound economic policy.

The key objective of these Protestant founders of the SME was to design an economic system that would simultaneously realise the values of market efficiency (including monetary stability) and social justice. The memory of how the effects of the Great Depression of 1929–1930s – its hyperinflation and high unemployment – had caused a national catastrophe in Germany was still very much in their minds. Hyperinflation had impoverished the middle class, while high unemployment had destroyed the future prospects of German workers. Hence ORDO-liberals began to insist that economic justice included *both* price stability and full employment. Inflation was considered to be theft, while work was deemed necessary for human dignity – hence the political aim of full employment (not least because only in conditions of full employment would workers be free to choose their employer). The political goal of the SME was to promote the security and well-being of the people rather than secure a high growth rate. In pursuing these goals, Eucken in particular underlined the importance of a strong state that stood above the opposing social partners. The state should protect freedom via effective market competition while also protecting the poor; the solution of the social question was to be based on both freedom and morality. Yet the Catholic principle of 'subsidiarity'[10] was also appealed to in order to reinforce the emphasis on personal freedom and devolved responsibility: individuals were to be responsible for their own destiny, and only when they were not able to provide for themselves should a proximate social body support them, with the state intervening last (Brakelmann and Jähnichen, 1994; Lachmann, 2007b).

Although most of the founders of the SME belonged to the *Bekennende Kirche* (Confessional Church), many post-war Protestant theologians opposed the SME model because of its affinity with economic liberalism.[11] Many of them supported a socialist order and attacked the SME precisely because it was a variant of capitalism. The slogan was: 'A Christian should be a Socialist!' For example, Otto Dibelius, Bishop of Berlin and a leading post-war theologian demanded 'Christian Socialism' as the appropriate economic model for West Germany. Three specific points of criticism were levelled by many Protestant theologians. First, competition itself was criticised as unbiblical and instead it was argued that the basic principle governing economic relations should be brotherly love and charity. Helmut Gollwitzer claimed that altruism excludes the necessity of competition. Defenders of SME replied that where competition is absent, economic stagnation follows.[12] Second, the principle of private ownership was questioned as ethically illegitimate. Critics pointed out that the word 'private' comes from the Latin *privare*, which means to rob or to expropriate. Advocates of the SME responded that whenever there is no ownership of property, no one takes responsibility for it. Third, the market economy is blamed for the spirit of selfishness it assumes and promotes. Defenders of SME replied by arguing that selfishness is the consequence of the Fall, not of the economic order itself. Competition, they argued, neutralizes human selfishness and tempers its effects, for the good of all.

In contrast, the Lutheran theologian Helmut Thielicke, a member of the Freiburg Circle, supported the concept of a SME. Among others, he posed the question of what concept of human character is needed in devising a suitable economic order (Thielicke, 1964–86). From a theological point of view he argued that, since humanity today lives in the age between the Fall and the Final Judgment, political and economic institutions must reckon with the reality of the destructive consequences of a fallen world in which humans are prone to selfishness and 'sin'. Accordingly he developed a theory of 'compromises'. With the aid of human reason, humans can discover what is good or bad for human society. In so doing, humans would need to seek a balance between human freedom and, given the reality of human fallenness, the need to protect the vulnerable. Here Thielicke employed the metaphor of a 'shipping channel': God created humans as free, yet also commands social responsibility and justice; between these two buoys the ship can freely manoeuvre. His conclusion was that the SME was located appropriately between the buoys of freedom and social justice and was, against its theological critics, consistent with biblical principles. In the same vein, Swiss theologian Arthur Rich (1985–90) required that an economic order should be both *menschengemäß* and *sachgemäß*: the economic system should be 'fit for human beings', i.e. appropriate for the weakness of human nature, but should also take into account economic laws (i.e. be correct from the technical point of view). Those ethical requirements, he held, are met by the SME (see Doherty, 2014).

The Protestant State Church very much favoured socialism. Since the *goals* of socialism seemed to be in line with Christian thinking, many Christians, therefore, supported socialism. Protestant defenders of the SME held that recognising the limited altruism of human beings has clear economic and political consequences. If both citizens and bureaucrats are corrupt, socialism cannot work effectively. Arguing in the same vein as Adam Smith, they claimed that the competitive system entices 'sinners' to work for the good of his neighbour, albeit unintentionally. If someone seeks wealth, he can only achieve this private goal by offering the best services to his fellows, but only those services they demand. He must in this way serve them, but there is no need to love them as well. By means of an effective competitive system, the Christian demand of 'loving your neighbour' is unintentionally enforced, because each produces things the others want and need. The SME is hence justified as an 'economic order for sinners' (as it is for Novak, 1982). This does not, however, imply that utility maximisation is a divine intention; rather, the purpose of competition is actually the mitigation of the negative effects of utility maximisation.

A theological appreciation of some leading ideas of the SME

In seeking to overcome a narrow economic liberalism and in speaking up for social justice, the founders of the SME claimed to find support in Protestant ethics. In keeping with a typically Protestant emphasis on the Bible, they were particularly influenced by certain characteristic themes in biblical social ethics. In this section I will show how these themes can be seen to lend support to the founding principles of the SME.

Before expounding these themes, it may be helpful to explain that in the tradition of Protestant – notably Lutheran – ethics such as that influencing the founders of the SME, four interpretive assumptions are often at work. First, the Bible does not itself give any indication of the specific design of a proper economic system. There is no obligation to take the pattern and necessities of an ancient Palestinian economy as the benchmark for contemporary economic systems. There is, therefore, no direct biblical support for claims that a Christian must be conservative, socialist, or liberal in economic affairs. Second, historically Christians have survived in all kinds of political and economic systems.[13] Third, the starting point of a biblical economic ethics is an ethics of individual action and an ethics of motivation.[14] Virtuous ethical behaviour is required of both rulers and ruled, governors and governed, employers and employees. This seems to be the message of the New Testament. There are different kinds of positions (the Reformers spoke of them as 'callings'): rulers, priests, farmers, and so forth. Everyone must perform their roles responsibly ('faithfully') in order for a society and an economy to function well. Nevertheless, fourth, each economic or political system must also respect broader principles of social ethics. For example, governments must abide by the requirements of justice (otherwise, as Augustine wrote in *City of God*, Book IV, rulers become little more than 'robbers'); the principle of stewardship should govern the behaviour of consumers; private property should be protected; the poor should be provided for. The upshot of these considerations is that, although the Bible does not itself teach a specific economic system, overall, market societies are more in line with the pattern of biblical thinking than socialist ones. Thus, while defenders of the SME would not claim that it is the privileged 'biblical' model, they would propose that it corresponds better to biblical themes than other available contemporary models.

I will now briefly summarise six key biblical themes that have proved influential on the Protestant advocates of the SME.[15]

The first theme is human dignity, and the notion of personal responsibility implied by it. The creation of humans "in the image of God" (Genesis 1: 27) is understood as the fundamental basis of their dignity, a dignity that protects them against infringements of their rights. With this dignity comes a unique responsibility for stewardship of the earth. Thus, already in the Garden of Eden, humans are assigned the role of co-worker with God in the continuing creation. Human beings thus have a right, privilege, and obligation to work (to "till and keep" the Garden) (Genesis 2:15). This theme finds an echo in the SME in the attempt both to recognise individual freedom and responsibility in the use of economic resources and the pursuit of work and to honour the dignity of citizens by means of promoting employment opportunities, while also facing the consequences of their economic actions.

The second theme is economic 'blessing'. The divine will is that people enjoy sufficient means to live, receiving the rewards of their responsible "tilling and keeping" of the earth. The promise of blessing is repeated throughout the Old Testament (e.g. Deuteronomy 15:4–6). It is one of the frequent refrains of the prophets that if the people are 'faithful' – if they live responsibly – they will enjoy peace and prosperity. Thus the prophet Micah promises that "they shall sit every man under his vine and under his fig tree, and none shall make him afraid" (Micah 4:4). SME thinkers did not hold that a Christian ethic mandated asceticism. Indeed *Erhard*'s slogan had been '*Wohlstand für alle*' ('Prosperity for all').

Yet these two themes did not stand alone. Accordingly, the third and fourth themes are justice and love. Justice is both protective and social. God is depicted as intervening in a fallen world to prevent social chaos. Thus, he shows protective mercy, even in judgement: the murderer Cain is shielded from arbitrary revenge. The Old Testament also contained many regulations to protect the poor; these are implications of both justice and love. The original distribution of wealth (land) in Israel was supposed to be reinstated every 50 years (The Year of Jubilee), and debts had to be forgiven every seven years (The Sabbath of the Seventh Year).[16] The principle is reiterated in the New Testament, where love becomes the controlling norm. Christian love both redeems for achievements and obliges the sharing of wealth with the less successful. 'Achievers' and 'non-achievers' have the same value under God; hence the apostolic injunction to the early church to engage in economic redistribution (2 Corinthians 8: 14–15). The principles of justice and love find an echo in the welfare provisions implied in the SME, in which society and the state assume a responsibility for the poor. Thus, for example, following the principle of the sabbatical year, welfare benefits do not have to be paid back.

A fifth theme influencing the founders of the SME, already alluded to above, is the characteristic Protestant ethical commitment to human freedom. Humans are given freedom in creation, and they are then redeemed through Christ to rediscover the freedom they lost through the Fall (Galatians 5:1). Translated into contemporary society, SME thinkers held that this implies that citizens must be granted extensive political and economic freedom.

Citizens enjoy freedom, within the necessary framework of social order, to develop their full potentials. Yet they also recognised that freedom inevitably permits inequality: freedom and equality of material outcome cannot exist together, and the pursuit of economic equality by government leads to tyranny. Indeed creation itself already implies "inequality" in the sense of difference; everything is created "according to its kind" (Genesis 1: 25). In this respect the SME is understood to be in line with the will of the Creator.

A sixth influential theme is truthfulness. The imperative to act and speak truthfully and honestly is central to the biblical social ethics shaping SME thinkers. They placed a high value on the integrity and transparency not only of individuals but also of the economic system itself. Via the competitive process, the market player obtains (more or less) reliable information on goods. The price system signals if there is a scarcity or a glut. Conversely, the degree of corruption increases with the degree of bureaucracy and non-competitive sectors. SME advocates understood morality as a kind of capital; trust and truthfulness can be considered as factors of production. The more they are present, the better the market process functions. As Röpke argued, the preconditions for a successful SME lie 'beyond demand and supply'[17] – namely in the morality of citizens.

Conflicts and compromises on the way to the Treaty of Rome

So far this chapter has sought to explain the philosophical background, genesis, and policy implications of the SME; identify some roots of this concept in twentieth-century German Protestant ethics; and outline some core theological themes that SME thinkers drew upon in defending the SME. This final section will outline the way in which the need for a German-French compromise continues to shape the development of the EU – using the creation of the euro as a telling example.

In the Treaty of Rome, which established the Common Market in 1957, Germany was able to embed the principle of competition in the European integration process. As noted, from the outset there was a struggle over what economic philosophy would prevail in this process, with Germany supporting the federal and competitive principle and France arguing for a more bureaucratic system with extensive state interference. This struggle is still going on. In the beginning, German ideas prevailed, but, in my view, over recent decades the French position has grown stronger; even the euro was introduced more according to French than German principles. Newly created European institutions are becoming a source of new regulations, albeit in the name of integration, often leading to a reduction in competition. Yet I also acknowledge that for some heavily protected sectors in Germany – the banking and service sectors, for instance – the European Commission did succeed in opening them up for European-wide competition. Nevertheless, the procedure for merger control has turned out to have little bite and is *de facto* being increasingly undermined. There are various ways of bypassing it. In

Germany, for example, there are exceptions possible by waivers of the Federal Minister of Economic Affairs (*Ministererlaubnis*). Citing general macroeconomic concerns held to be in the public interest, the Minister can override any decision of the Federal Cartels Office. To advocates of the SME, this is no surprise: they would argue that history demonstrates that *law cannot protect law*, and that the source of harmony between law and regulations issued at the highest level is never to be found in the constitution itself but rather in the harmony of the leading social partners. Nor can any economic system survive if these partners reject it.

The concept of the SME is, however, often not understood by political decision makers. Politicians in Europe pay no more than 'lip service' to its aims and principles. But unfortunately nor have even German politicians abided by such principles. For example, in the 1960s and 1970s the social democratic Federal Minister of Economic Affairs Karl Schiller began to advocate what he termed an 'enlightened Social Market Economy' that would combine ORDO-liberal ideas with Keynesian ones. His goal was the integration of the 'Freiburg Imperative' with Keynesianism. Politicians began to imagine that they knew better than the market what kind of goods should be produced for the population, and in which way. Because of the influence of Keynesian macroeconomics and fiscal policy, increased government intervention in the market followed and the social democratic government began to increase government debt.

On the issue of European integration, in Germany two different political views even clashed in the ruling CDU. The more bureaucratically inclined Chancellor Adenauer supported regional integration (following France), while Erhard (Economics Minister, the father of the 'economic miracle') argued for an Atlantic free trade zone, relying on greater economic exchange with the USA. France wanted a deepening in economic integration whereas Germany (Erhard's position prevailed in the Rome negotiations) supported a widening of economic cooperation. The Treaty of Rome could be seen as a compromise between the French and the German (Erhard's) positions. Following German demands, the Treaty of Rome incorporated a strong competition policy; a competitive European economy was the goal. The French secured a state-controlled agricultural policy and an interventionist overseas development aid policy. Further conflicts arose between Erhard and de Gaulle. De Gaulle wanted to transmit French 'planification' into the European Common Market, but this was met with resolute resistance from Erhard.

At each step of the European integration process, there were frictions between the German approach stressing competition and monetary stability and the French approach aiming at industrial policy, government planning, and the priority of employment policy *vis à vis* monetary stability. The 'little European integration' (confined to the original six) and the political transition in Germany from a Christian democrat-liberal to a social-liberal coalition led to a policy change towards the 'enlightened market economy', eventually leading to a fading of the German economic miracle (Giersch, Paqué, and Schmieding, 1992).

It was a fact of political reality that progress in European integration always needed some kind of French-German compromise. In the creation of the euro, German and French positions clashed, and again the outcome was a compromise. A 'two-speed' Europe was effectively born. Germany insisted on fixed rules, and the French on a fixed timetable. I will now briefly outline the four stages creating the euro against the background of this ongoing French-German contest. Some 15 years ago the phrase '*Euro ad portas!*' ('the euro is at the gate!') terrified many citizens. The French economist Jacques Rueff once remarked: "L'Europe se fera par la monnaie ou ne se fera pas de tout" ("Europe will come into existence through a common currency or not at all"). The French pun 'Le Franc fort est fait à Frankfort' annoyed many French politicians. The goal of French policy has been to create a common currency in order to be rid of the dominance of the deutschmark. Moreover, a common currency – so it was hoped – would abolish exchange rate risks and increase efficiency and competitiveness. In addition, a common currency would help ensure peace in Europe.[18] The European Commission expected that following the French view would lead to an enlargement of its competences.

In the Treaty of Rome there were already hints of creating a common currency (see Lachmann, 2007a). Three approaches to creating a common currency failed, but the last one succeeded. The first approach has been the Programme of Action of the EC Commission of 1962. The following elements were aimed at:

- fixed exchange rates until 1965,
- common policy concerning the IMF and third-world countries,
- creation of credit assistance in relation to existing foreign exchange reserves,
- liberalization of the capital market,
- setting up a currency union after 1965, at the latest by 1969, and
- coordination of wage and fiscal policy to support monetary policy.

It was a futile attempt because of German reservations (especially those of the German Bundesbank and the economics and finance ministries). At the end of 1968 the Prime Minister of Luxembourg, Pierre Werner, took a second initiative that had been taken up in February 1969 by Raymond Barre. The European Monetary and Economic Union should be established in stages until 1978. The Werner Report (1969) aimed at free movement of goods and capital, full convertibility of all currencies, fixed exchange rates, and the delegation of authority for national economic policy to the Union level. This provoked a fierce discussion regarding the path towards a monetary and economic union. The position of the so called 'economists'[19] – supported by Germany and The Netherlands – spoke up for a harmonization of monetary and macro policies first. After having reached inflation conformity (at a low level), the exchange rates could be fixed. This led to a 'coronation theory' – the final act of harmonization would have been the common currency. The slogan was: Harmonization first – then a common currency.

The contrasting view was backed by France, Belgium, and Italy. They supported the 'locomotive theory'. Europe should start with fixed exchange rates. Economic restrictions would force national policies towards harmonization. Fixed exchange rates with then-possible balance of payment problems would become the engine of economic harmonization and integration. Harmony of economic policies would be the final product. Their slogan had been: Fixed exchange rates first and economic harmonization (similar inflation rates) later. But the oil price crises of 1973 thwarted this approach.

By March 1979, after secret negotiations between France and Germany, the European Monetary Systems (EMS) had been established. Arguments in favour of the EMS were as follows:

- Faster European integration was required for political reasons.
- EMS would provide greater security and consistent calculation bases for European enterprises via stable exchange rates.
- Before the EMS, France suffered high inflation rates and had to devalue the franc, which led to price increases of imported goods. Germany suffered from revaluation pressures on the DM, hindering German exports, but helping to keep inflation down. Both countries saw an economic advantage by creating the EMS.
- The expansive monetary policy of the USA led to a devaluation of the dollar and a further revaluation of the DM.

Because of the way the EMS was set up, the DM became the anchor currency. Therefore, after German Unification, many countries spoke up for the creation of a common currency. In February 1988 Germany took the initiative to create a common currency with an independent European central bank (like the German Bundesbank). At the European Council meeting in Hanover in June 1988, the French president of the European Commission was asked to prepare a report (Delors Report), which envisaged the creation of the European Economic and Monetary Union (EEMU) in three stages. The first stage (completion of the internal market) commenced on July 1st 1990, and lasted until December 1993. On January 1st 1994 the second stage began with a greater harmonization of economic policies. The European Monetary Institute (EMI) was founded in Frankfurt to prepare the introduction of the common currency. At the beginning of 1999, the EEMU came into effect for all those countries that fulfilled the Maastricht criteria.[20]

Conclusion: *quo vadis*, Europe?

The European crisis is not, as such, a euro crisis. The internal and the external value of the euro have remained stable overall. The inflation rates are low, even in countries that had high inflationary pressures before joining the euro zone. Until recently, the value of the euro did not fluctuate that much against the US dollar, the British pound, and the Japanese yen.[21] However, the linking of banking debt and government debts increased the risk of both. The increase of government default risk increases the risk ratio of banks because they have to keep government bonds and do not need equity capital for that. Thus the danger of insolvencies of banks increases the insolvency risks of governments – a vicious cycle. The crisis is the result of politicians who violated and are still violating European law. Only three euro countries are still meeting the deficit criteria of the Maastricht criteria. France and Germany also violated those rules. The high unemployment rate in Spain and Greece was the results of national not European policies; in particular, the property bubble in Spain and public debt in Greece were homemade.

In my view, the focal point of debate about the future of the euro, and indeed the future of the EU, will be on the proper balance between, on the one hand, a commitment to EU-wide solidarity and, on the other, a respecting of subsidiarity with the acceptance of national responsibilities that it implies. France stresses more European solidarity and Germany insists on subsidiarity. I would argue that economic problems must first be addressed on the national level. For example, as long as Europe does not have a common government and a common fiscal policy, the 'no bailing out' principle should continue to prevail. Banks ought also to cushion loans to government by equity capital. A naive solidarity which is taken to mean the bailing out of other nations will not strengthen self-reliance or responsible political action. In essence, this is the old quarrel between German and French models of political economy.

The last century can be characterized as a time of pathological learning: Europe had to learn by extremely costly mistakes. Two wars finally convinced most European nations to look for peacekeeping European institutions. The failures of socialism and state planning should have taught them the importance of freedom, market pricing, and competition. Moreover, the escalating expenditures for social policy should have taught them that debt has to be paid back. Nations and politicians could have learned that these economic laws will – if only in the long run – always prevail against bureaucracy and state interference. The ORDO-liberals posed the political dilemma: reliance on political power or economic laws? The EU should now devote itself to addressing this problem head-on. It can only survive in international competition if the priority of economic laws is accepted – and not only endured but intentionally designed (see also Schäfer, 2000).

Surviving in international competition requires the dominance of market efficiency against political restrictions and the priority of innovation and growth over social redistribution. Government support and social services nearly doubled in the last 50 years, yet we observe in Europe a redistribution from the not-so rich to the not-so poor. The new Political Economy has analysed the political process of how politicians in their desire to be re-elected increase government expenditures under the label of solidarity and social aid, while denouncing all who do not support the welfare state. Social policy, I would argue, is more and more based on a secularization of Christian solidarity under the protection of political correctness. Pushing back biblical and Protestant values, the affinity of many Christian politicians and political thinkers with socialistic goals led to an increasing critique of the market, competition, and resulting inequality. However, the increasing pace of globalization poses serious challenges to government intervention; for companies can today not only opt for voice but also for exit.[22] Lowering exit options may even increase their voice option.

I propose that the principle of subsidiarity must become the general policy norm. Individual nations should not only retain responsibility for social policy and fiscal policy but also take back responsibility for these policy areas (e.g. no bailing out) in order to effect responsible political decisions. Perhaps we need to embrace the idea of a multispeed Europe. According to 'club theory',[23] for example, member states with similar economic and political values should work together more deeply. Since too much harmonization of economic outcomes hinders development, perhaps those states that follow the dominance of economic laws should compete with those that prefer economic planning and bureaucratic governance. Nations that put priority on price stability should combine against those that do not; this would argue for a northern euro and a southern euro. Inflationary countries (as a club) then still have the option of a depreciation of their currency. This could lead to a peaceful Europe – not one doing everything under the same roof – and one marked by openness, differentiation, and economic freedom.

Appendix: Principles for a successful economic policy[24]

After World War Two, the ORDO-liberals hoped to introduce a third chamber of political decision making in the newly founded German Federal Republic. This chamber would examine the decisions of the government as to whether they were in line with the principles of the SME.[25] Politicians rejected this proposal. As an alternative solution, Walter Eucken hoped that churches and jurists would support the concept of a SME. Hence he formulated some main economic policy principles, i.e. in particular the competitive part of this new concept. Likewise all jurists would become familiar with these basic principles of the SME. However, those ideas also could not be realized. As a way out of possible economic dangers he was afraid of, Eucken formulated and published some principles of economic policy that the government should take into account in its decision making.[26]

There are four different groups of principles:

- constitutive principles
- regulative principles
- potential additional principles
- institutional principles

104 *Lachmann*

The *constitutive principles* [27] were:

- the principle of competitive prices
- the principle of priority of price stability and monetary stability
- the principle of open markets
- the institution of private property for the distribution and allocation of economic resources
- the principle of freedom of contract
- the principle of liability of the owner and the decision maker[28]
- the principle of a constant and transparent economic policy.

The following *regulative principles* [29] were:

- the principle of reducing and correcting market power (control of monopolies)
- incomes policy to correct for undue inequalities without hindering investments
- correction of externalities
- correction of abnormal supply reactions (backward bending supply function).

The *potential additional principles* for competition policy were:

- the principle of avoiding punctualism, i.e. the legislative authority, court decisions and the economic administration should be aligned towards the principles of the competitive order (conformability principle = *Denken in Ordnungen*)
- the principle of reluctance to use business cycle policy (or macroeconomic stabilization policy)
- the principle of aid for self-help, i.e. social policy should be conducted in a way that conforms with the market.

Lastly, the *institutional principles* concerning national policies (*staatspolitische Grundsätze*) were:

- the principle of reducing the power of interest groups
- the principle of compliance with the principle of subsidiarity concerning the tasks and possible interferences of the government
- the principle of the priority of '*Ordnungspolitik*' over '*Ablaufpolitik*' or '*Prozesspolitik*'.[30]

The constitutive principles are important to guarantee functioning competition. However, even if the constitutive principles are observed, the results are socially not always acceptable and therefore corrections are necessary. Consequently, regulative principles are needed to protect the working of the SME.

Alfred Müller-Armack especially emphasized that market conformity should be observed by formulating economic policies. However, it is not sufficient to formulate economic concepts; one has also to look at legal possibilities of implementation and compliance.

Notes

1 This part draws heavily on Lachmann (2013a). Space prevents a direct analysis of those writings. For background on the Social Market Economy, see Blumenberg-Lampe (1986), Farmer (2006), Jens (2013), Lachmann (1988), Lachmann (1995), Lachmann (2013b), Lachmann and Rösner (1995), Lampert (1993), Stützel et al. (1982), Vanberg (1988), Wagner (1994), and Watrin (1993).
2 The German Economic Association is still called *Verein für Socialpolitik*.
3 The ORDO-liberals were often called the *Freiburger Schule* (Freiburg School) since most of them taught at the University of Freiburg in South Germany.
4 *Ordnungspolitik* could be understood as institutional policy – setting the proper rules; whereas *Prozesspolitik* describes the interventions of the government into the economy in order to steer it.
5 The Confessing Christians (*Bekennende Kirche*) were persecuted by the Nazis. *Dietrich Bonhoeffer*, a leading Protestant theologian of the *Bekennende Kirche*, was executed shortly before the end of World War Two.
6 For example, the founders of the SME realized the 'irenic principle' (Müller-Armack) of a functioning market. They understood human beings as capable of being responsible for their own destinies.
7 The *Freiburg Circle* consisted of three groups that met mostly in Freiburg; but economists outside Freiburg were part of some circles. The German economists Walter Eucken, Constantin von Dietze, and Adolf Lampe were members of all three circles (Rieter and Schmolz, 1993).
8 On 20th June 1948 the three Military Governments enacted a currency reform – introducing the German Mark (DM). This *Erhard* took as an opportunity to start with liberal reforms (SME) since he was convinced that a currency reform without economic reforms would not work. For more details, see Giersch et al. (1992) and Lachmann (2004: 34–37).
9 He also argued that the lack of economic development in the East could be explained by the metaphysics of the Greek Orthodox Church (Watrin, 2003).
10 The principle of subsidiarity requires that a central authority should perform only those tasks that cannot be performed effectively by a local level. It determines a hierarchy of responsibility.
11 Helmut Gollwitzer was a leading proponent of this view; he was very influential on Christian students during the 1960s. According to him, God's concern for the poor speaks for a socialist economic system (Gollwitzer, 1976). A more radical voice is Ulrich Duchrow.
12 They noted that the apostle Paul drew positively on examples from the competitive sports of the Greek world (e.g. 1 Corinthians 9: 24–25).
13 They pointed out that, even under dictatorships, God's people could sometimes rise to important government positions, as with biblical figures such as Daniel or Nehemiah.
14 Thielicke argued that there was only individual ethics and denied the possibility of a social ethics. Political systems and orders should be determined by using reason. Against the slogan 'capitalism is a structural sin', he claims that structures are morally neutral and cannot 'repent'. For a contrasting Protestant theological approach also influential at the time, see Brunner (1978).

15 I offer here my own articulation of these themes but all can be found in the writings of the Protestant founders themselves. Space prevents a direct analysis of those writings. For treatments of these and other biblical economic themes, see Beed and Beed (2012), Clouse (1984), Lachmann (1992),
16 For the Sabbath of the Seventh Year and Year of Jubilee, see Leviticus 25. God remained the owner of the land he gave to Israel. The Israelites became the user only.
17 This is a book title of the ORDO-liberal Wilhelm Röpke (*Jenseits von Angebot und Nachfrage*).
18 Many German economists warned the government about introducing the euro – since the member states were not an 'optimum currency area'. They pointed out that early introduction would increase the tensions in Europe and that governments would not abide by the rules. Maastricht was seen as a '*Schönwetterregulierung*' (fair weather regulation), i.e. the rules will be abided by as long as there are no national interests against it.
19 The clashing positions were dubbed 'economists' (German view) versus 'monetarists' (French view).
20 For a summary of the criteria see http://ec.europa.eu/economy_finance/euro/adoption/who_can_join/index_en.htm.
21 In January 2007, the exchange rate was 6.6 GBP for 10 euro; by October 2013 it was 8.5 GBP – an appreciation of the euro of 28 per cent against the GBP. Against the US dollar the euro appreciated 5 per cent in the same period.
22 Companies can choose between trying to influence the public and economic policy – or leave the country.
23 The economic theory of clubs is based on two seminal papers by James Buchanan (1965) and Charles Tiebout (1956). Whenever in an integration of countries the value judgments differ, some countries can go ahead with integration – if they have similar value judgements. This will lead to integrations with different speeds.
24 This appendix is taken from Lachmann (2013a).
25 This suggestion resembles the third chamber that Hayek proposed. See also Grossekettler (1997).
26 See Lachmann (2004: 41–43) for an explanation of the importance of those principles. See also Eucken (2007: 254–291). Such principles are relevant for safeguarding a competitive environment.
27 See Lachmann (2004: 44–45) and Eucken (2007: 291–304).
28 Whoever has an advantage from an action should also bear a possible loss.
29 See Lachmann (2004: 45–48) and Eucken (2007: 304–324).
30 Under *Ordnungspolitik* the ORDO-liberals understood a rule-orientated policy. The government should institute a framework such that the free decision-making of the companies will lead to the desired result. In contrast, *Prozesspolitik* means interference into the market process in order to control the economic outcome. Ordo-liberals accept some government interventions; however, they should promote and impede the working of market forces.

References

Augustine. *The city of God.*
Beed, C., and Beed, C. (2012). The nature of biblical economic principles, and its critics. *Faith and Economics*, 59 (Spring): 31–58.
Bilger, F. (1996). Die Konkurrenz der Wirtschaftsstile und die Entwicklung der Europäischen Union. In Klump, R. (ed.), *Wirtschaftskultur, Wirtschaftsstil und Wirtschaftsordnung* (pp. 175–190). Marburg, Germany: Metropolis.

Blumenberg-Lampe, C. (1986). *Der Weg in die Soziale Marktwirtschaft: Referate, Protokolle, Gutachten der Arbeitsgemeinschaft Erwin von Beckerath 1943–1947.* Stuttgart, Germany: Klett-Cotta.

Brakelmann, G., and Jähnichen, T. (eds) (1994). *Die Protestantischen Wurzeln der Sozialen Marktwirtschaft: Ein Quellenband.* Gütersloh, Germany: Gütersloh Verlagshaus.

Brunner, E. (1978). *Das Gebot und die Ordnungen. Entwurf einer Protestantisch-theologischen Ethik* (4th edn). Zürich, Switzerland: Theologischer Verlag. [Available in English as The divine imperative: A study in Christian ethics. Wyon, O. (trans.)]

Buchanan, J. A. (1965). An economic theory of clubs, *Economica*, 32: 1–14.

Clouse, R. (ed.) (1984). *Wealth and poverty: Four Christian views of economics.* Downers Grove, IL: InterVarsity.

Doherty, S. (2014). *Theology and economic ethics: Martin Luther and Arthur Rich in dialogue.* Oxford: Oxford University Press.

Eucken, W. (2007 [1952]). *Grundsätze der Wirtschaftspolitik* (7th edn). Eucken, E. and Hensel, K. P. (eds), Tübingen. [Available in English as *The foundations of economics: History and theory in the analysis of economic reality*. Hutchison, T. W. (trans.)]

Farmer, K. (2006). Germany's social market economy and the new systems competition. *Journal of Markets and Morality*, 9(2): 317–336.

Giersch, H., Paqué, K.-H., and Schmieding, H. (1992). *The fading miracle: Four decades of market economy in Germany.* Cambridge: Cambridge University Press.

Gollwitzer, H. (1976). *Forderungen der Umkehr: Beiträge zur Theologie der Gesellschaft.* München, Germany: Kaiser.

Grossekettler, H. (1997). *Die Wirtschaftsordnung als Gestaltungsaufgabe: Entstehungsgeschichte und Entwicklungsperspektiven des Ordoliberalismus nach 50 Jahren Sozialer Marktwirtschaft.* Münster, Germany: LIT.

Jens, U. (2013). Quo vadis Soziale Marktwirtschaft? *Orientierungen zur Wirtschafts- und Gesellschaftspolitik*, 135 (March): 11–14.

Lachmann, W. (2013a). Just trade and the social market economy. *Zeitschrift für Marktwirtschaft und Ethik / Journal of Markets and Ethics*, 2(Winter): 95–115.

Lachmann, W. (2013b). Religion, Wirtschaft, Wirtschaftsethik: Ein Überblick. *Zeitschrift für Marktwirtschaft und Ethik / Journal of Markets and Ethics*, 1(Spring): 3–29.

Lachmann, W. (2007a). Stabiles Geld hat seinen Preis: Der weg zur Europäischen Wirtschafts- und Währungsunion. In Lachmann, W., et al. (eds), *Zur Zukunft Europas: Wirtschaftsethische Probleme der Europäischen Union* (pp. 178–205). Berlin: LIT.

Lachmann, W. (2007b). Religion, economics and economic ethics: A biblical view. Chair on Economic Policy and Development Economics Working Paper 7. FAU-University Nürnberg-Erlangen, Germany.

Lachmann, W. (2004). *Volkswirtschaftslehre 2 Anwendungen* (2nd edn). Berlin: Springer.

Lachmann, W. (2000). Protestantische wurzeln der sozialen marktwirtschaft und ihre biblische bewertung. In Resch, I. (ed.), *Mehr als Man Glaubt: Christliche Fundamente in Recht, Wirtschaft und Gesellschaft* (pp. 187–217). Gräfelfing, Germany: Resch.

Lachmann, W. (1995). The genesis and principles of social market economy. In Lachmann, W. and Rösner, H. J. (eds), *Social security in social market economy: Conceptual foundations and procedural principles* (pp. 18–33). Sankt Augustin, Germany: Konrad-Adenauer-Stiftung.

Lachmann, W. (1992). Ethics and the market: Basic theological and economic considerations. *European Journal of Theology*, 1(2): 151–161.

Lachmann, W. (1988). Ethik und Soziale Marktwirtschaft: Einige Wirtschaftswissenschaftliche und Biblisch-theologische Überlegungen. In Hesse, H. (ed.), *Wirtschaftswissenschaft und Ethik* (pp. 277–304). Berlin: Duncker & Humblot.

Lachmann, W., and Rösner, H. J. (eds) (1995). *Social security in social market economy: Conceptual foundations and procedural principles.* Sankt Augustin, Germany: Konrad-Adenauer-Stiftung.

Lampert, H. (1993). *The economic and social order of the federal republic of Germany.* Sankt Augustin, Germany: Konrad-Adenauer-Stiftung.

Novak, M. (1982). *The spirit of democratic capitalism.* New York: American Enterprise Institute / Simon and Schuster.

Oslington, P. (ed.) (2003). *Economics and religion* (2 vols.). Cheltenham, England: Edward Elgar.

Rich, A. (1985–90). *Wirtschaftsethik. Vol. 1: Grundlagen in Theologischer Perspektive* (2nd edn). and *Vol. 2: Marktwirtschaft, Planwirtschaft, Weltwirtschaft aus Sozialethischer Sicht.* Gütersloh, Germany: Gerd Mohn.

Rieter, H., and Schmolz, M. (1993). The ideas of German ordoliberalism 1938–1945: Pointing the way to a new economic order. *The European Journal of the History of Economic Thought*, 1(1): 87–114.

Schäfer, W. (2000). Zukunftsperspektiven des Europäischen Modells der Sozialen Marktwirtschaft. *List Forum für Wirtschafts- und Finanzpolitik*, 26(2): 121–132.

Smith, A. (1976 [1776]). *An inquiry into the nature and causes of the wealth of nations* (Vol. 1). Indianapolis, IN: Liberty Classics.

Stützel, W., et al. (eds) (1982). *Standard texts on the social market economy: Two centuries of discussion.* New York: G. Fischer [Ludwig-Erhard-Stiftung].

Thielicke, H. (1964–86). *Theologische Ethik. Vol. 1: Dogmatische, philosophische und kontroverstheologische Grundlegung* (5th edn); *Vol. II.1: Mensch und Welt, Entfaltung* (5th edn); *Vol. II.2: Ethisch des Politischen, Enfaltung* (4th edn); *Vol. 3: Ethik der Gesellschaft, des Rechts, der Sexualität und der Kunst.* Tübingen, Germany: J. C. B. Mohr. [Available in English as *Theological ethics* 2 vols. Lazareth W. H. (trans.) London: Adam & Charles Black.]

Tiebout, C. (1956). A pure theory of local expenditure. *Journal of Political Economy*, 64: 416–424.

Vanberg, V. (1988). "Ordnungstheorie" as constitutional economics: The German conception of a "social market economy". *ORDO Jahrbuch für die Ordnung von Wirtschaft und Gesellschaft*, 39: 17–31.

Wagner, R. E. (1994). ORDO liberalism and the social market economy. In Brennan, H. G. and Waterman, A. M. C. (eds), *Economics and religion: Are they distinct?* (pp. 121–138). Boston, MA: Kluwer.

Watrin, C. (2003). Alfred Müller-Armack: Economic policy maker and sociologist of religion. *Journal des Économistes et des Études Humaines*, 13(2/3): 289–311.

6 Market-state or commonwealth?

Europe's Christian heritage and the future of the European polity

Adrian Pabst[1]

Introduction

The crisis in the euro area is changing the foundations and finalities of the European Union (EU). Amidst the combined banking and sovereign debt crisis, eurozone members have begun to put in place a banking and a fiscal union that will ever-more fuse centralised state power with an increasingly interdependent single market. In their current configuration, the single market and single currency undermine the principles of solidarity (providing mutual assistance to the most needy among Europe's peoples and nations) and subsidiarity (self-government at the most appropriate level in accordance with the dignity of the person and human flourishing). Connected with this priority of the economic over the social is a tendency to subordinate interpersonal relationships to the central state and the global market that converge at the expense of intermediary institutions such as professional associations, trade unions, universities, free hospitals, friendly societies, artisanal producers, manufacturing and trading guilds, and religious communities. Thus the European integration and enlargement processes are part of a wider logic of disembedding the economy from society and re-embedding social relations in economic transactions, to use the conceptuality of Karl Polanyi (2001 [1944]).

This chapter argues that the European project blends bureaucratic collectivisation with commercial commodification, which Catholic Social Teaching and cognate traditions in Anglicanism and Eastern Orthodoxy reject as false alternatives. Thus the European 'market-state' undermines Europe's shared cultural identity and hollows out the universal values derived from the Christian synthesis of ancient with biblical virtues on which vibrant democracies and market economies ultimately depend. The chapter also argues the, to some, surprising thesis that Europe's Christian heritage is a source of both social solidarity and religious pluralism that offers key resources to shape the future of the European polity across the wider Europe and the whole world.

The first section traces the rise of Europe's secular 'market-states'. The second analyses the EU's contemporary crisis, which is not primarily about the 'democratic deficit' but rather a lack of legitimacy. The third section describes the emerging shape of Europe in terms of a multispeed EU and a multipolar polity, notably the centrifugal forces that deepen divisions between (1) the euro-area core and periphery; (2) eurozone members (and candidates) and the rest of the EU; (3) the Union and other European powers (e.g. Russia, Ukraine, and Turkey), as well as North African and Near Eastern countries that are part of the wider European orbit. The fourth section contrasts the EU's evolution towards a 'market-state' with a civic commonwealth: whereas the former transfers powers to the centre under the guise of a federal model that is supposed to provide a lock on centralisation, the latter is a voluntary association of nations and peoples with a shared 'social imaginary' that can command popular assent and address the legitimacy crisis. The final section suggests that the EU remains a vestigially Christian polity whose roots go back to Christianity's fusion of Greco-Roman thought with biblical revelation, in particular the blending of philosophy, law, and virtue ethics with the revealed *logos* and the theological virtues of faith, hope, and charity. This unique legacy has shaped a common culture that can help re-embed states and markets in the interpersonal relations of civil society and integrate other faith communities in a shared public realm.

Europe's secular 'market-states'

Across Europe there is an inchoate awareness that power and wealth are increasingly concentrated in the hands of small elites at the national and supranational levels. The convergence of state bureaucracy with market managerialism has produced a new hybrid of political and economic power that has been conceptualised as 'market-states' – the shift from nation-states and the post-1945 Keynesian settlement towards the neo-liberal system of globalisation (Bobbitt, 2003: 213–242; Robinson, 2006: 1–18; Gamble, 2006). Accordingly, the collusion of national states with transnational markets provides the conduit through which political sovereignty and economic transactions converge and supersede the social relations and civic bonds in which they were traditionally embedded. In turn, this reinforces the growing disconnection between people and elites that underpins the EU's current crisis of legitimacy.

Crucially, the market-state is characterised by three paradoxes that rest on a fundamental shift in the source of sovereign power: first, greater centralisation but weaker governments; second, more popular demands on the state but less civic mobilisation and participation; third, welfare retrenchment but more state protection against risk (Bobbitt, 2003: 234–235). Conceptually, one can go further than Bobbitt to suggest that 'market-states' radicalise Polanyi's double movement of disembedding and re-embedding insofar as they subordinate social ties to depersonalised values and abstract standards such as global economic exchange or top-down bureaucratic regulation. In this manner, 'market-states' replace the anthropological primacy of interpersonal trust and cooperation with the impersonal forces of right and contract that rest on the pessimistic ontology of the social contract tradition (see Michéa, 2009).

This applies not only to Hobbes's and Locke's assumption of a violent 'state of nature' that requires the artificial order of state coercion and market competition. It also holds for Rousseau's idea of freely born individuals whose egoism (born out of comparison and rivalry with others) needs to be mediated by a social contract – enforced by national republics or a cosmopolitan federation of nation-states (as for Kant). Either way, different social contract theorists share a gloomy outlook about the individual or the free association of people – or both at once. So if human beings (alone or in society) are selfish, greedy, distrustful of one another, and prone to violence, then the impersonal institutions of state and market are best positioned to minimise conflict and maximise security, freedom, and equality.

Polanyi long ago pointed out how absurd this anthropology is, and contemporary anthropologists comprehensively rebut the underlying pessimism (Godbout and Caillé, 1998; Mauss, 2000). For during most of human history human beings have been so radically and immediately dependent upon each other that the first thing they have looked for is mutual recognition as the precondition of both social status and economic stability. For this reason they have usually been content with economic arrangements of reciprocal balance (whether these be more egalitarian or more hierarchical). Reciprocity and distribution tended to guarantee the biological survival of the individual, which was thereby subordinated to the cultural and historical survival of the social group. Hence the lower was mediated by the supplement of something higher – individual virtue, public honour, social recognition, and the mutual bestowing of gifts. Of course gifts can involve forms of obligation that lead to exploitation or oppression, but the point is that gift-exchange (in the widest sense) *is* the most fundamental basis of social order. Since this tends to be a mutual affair, human beings are rarely either purely self-interested or purely disinterested. Rather, society is a spiral paradox of 'non-compulsory compulsion' in which the giving of gifts (and every act and speech-act is a gift) half expects but cannot compel a return gift. This is the very fabric of human society. It is at once a political, economic, and cultural fabric, so that when countries try to base their economy on de-sacralisation and individualism, society is gradually abolished and humanity starts to contradict itself (Caillé, 2007; Godbout, 2007).

Seen from this perspective, the recent history of European integration reflects much more the Enlightenment tradition of social contract based on egoism than it does the quest for mutual recognition, which partly shaped the thinking of Europe's founding fathers (see Kaiser, 2007). After centuries of nationalism and Europe's self-destructive civil war (1914–45), they sought to make good on the promise of peace and prosperity. But there are two reasons why the rise of European market-states has displaced this shared Christian and humanist vision in favour of a secular settlement. First, market-states promote an increasing centralisation of power and concentration of wealth at the expense of local government, small-, and medium-sized businesses (that are often family owned), and the autonomy of civil society as a whole. As such, state and market power transgresses the civic and ethical limits that have been defended by different religious traditions (e.g. prohibition of usury, the 'living wage', a ban on slave labour).

Second, market-states are grounded in an ideology that invests the secular sphere of power and wealth with quasi-sacred significance by sacralising either politics or economics (or again both at once). For example, the primacy of rights and contracts over interpersonal relationships subordinates virtue to the spirit of acquisitiveness and the commercial society – as R.H. Tawney already argued in relation to the nineteenth-century *laissez-faire* model that was the historical precursor of contemporary capitalism. In short, market-states subsume the sanctity of life and land under the secular sacrality of power and wealth. From the perspective of Christianity and other faith traditions, the logic that informs Europe's secular settlement profanes the sacred and sacralises the profane. Thus the current crisis was from the outset part of a much wider cultural and moral crisis.

The EU's current crisis

The euro is by no means the sole cause of the Union's present predicament. Rather, it has extended and reinforced the deterministic logic of neo-functionalism that underpins the entire European edifice set up by the 1957 Rome Treaty, notably the idea that economic cooperation 'spills over' into political integration (see Haas, 1958; Mitrany, 1965; Sweet, Sandholtz, and Fligstein, 2001). The project of creating a banking, fiscal and political union among the 19 eurozone members is an expression of the same economic determinism that led to the single market and the single currency in the first place. Instead of a reciprocal recognition of diverse and mutually augmenting practices, neo-functionalism imposes centrally determined standards on all member states and candidate countries through top-down legal and regulatory harmonisation driven forward by the European Commission in concert with the European Court of Justice. In consequence, neo-functionalist integration has produced a process of bureaucratic and managerialist homogenisation at odds with the purported aim of securing Europe's unity-in-diversity (*in varietate concordia*).

In turn, this has led to an increasingly interdependent European economy that is ever-more disembedded from each national polity and society. Moreover, the EU has in recent years operated as an engine of centralisation of power and concentration of wealth. Linked to this is the emphasis on individual, subjective rights without similarly robust responsibilities for mutual flourishing, and commercial contracts devoid of social purpose. Without instilling a sense of reciprocity, EU rules and regulations have supplanted the civic ties and social bonds that hold together nations and peoples. Here it could be objected that Europe's founding principles of solidarity and subsidiarity are enshrined in successive treaties, for example the commitment in the 2009 Lisbon Treaty to create a 'social market economy'.

However, neo-functionalism reduces these and other values to formal, procedural devices: solidarity is equated with little more than redistribution by central diktat while subsidiarity allows Brussels and national capitals to shift the burden of blame to devolved levels without transferring power to people.

For these reasons, the current turmoil in the eurozone intensifies and radicalises a very profound crisis of legitimacy, with popular support for the European project in sharp decline (Lamy, 2012). The EU's crisis of legitimacy goes far beyond the well-known (but poorly understood) 'democratic deficit'. Every system of representation is in 'deficit' compared with the rigorous standards of democracy and representative government. This is not the same as a crisis of legitimacy, which concerns the lack of public trust and popular assent. Legitimate rule transcends formal arrangements and procedures because it involves at least three core capacities: (1) to make a political system intelligible to its members; (2) to mobilise civic consent; and (3) to engage citizens. Currently, the EU falls well short on all three accounts.

There is an increasing institutional risk that national parliaments and the European Parliament (EP) will unwittingly succeed in discrediting each other, as Larry Siedentop (2001) has argued. For the increased powers of the EP are not counterbalanced by its enhanced authority. By contrast, national parliaments retain authority but have less and less power. The widening discrepancy between power and authority constitutes a very dangerous dialectic that is gradually eroding the remaining popular support for European integration. Under pressure from political parties and the media to defend the national interest, governments who make decisions in EU ministerial meetings seem increasingly unable to command consent. In turn, this creates a growing gap between Europe's ruling elites and its citizenry. This, coupled with the triumph of a vacuously centrist pragmatism, helps account for the recent upsurge in support for the extreme left and right that seek to fill the ideological vacuum. Thus Europe needs a political project that can shape political debate and reconnect political classes to popular sentiment and public opinion. The Union's crisis of legitimacy predates the eurozone turmoil and has been developing ever since the acceleration of the European integration and enlargement process following the fall of Communism and German reunification.

Crucially, the EU lacks what Charles Taylor calls a 'social imaginary'; that is, "ways people imagine their social existence, how they fit together with others, how things go on between them and their fellows, the expectations that are normally met, and the deeper normative notions and images that underline these expectations" (2004: 23). A social imaginary "is in fact that largely unstructured and inarticulate understanding of our whole situation, within which particular features of our world show up for us in the sense they have. It can never be adequately expressed in the form of explicit doctrines because of its unlimited and indefinite nature" (Taylor, 2004: 24–25). Accordingly, a social imaginary shapes the way people who share it view their coexistence, notably the normative dimensions of individual or collective hope and the mutual expectations that citizens have *vis-à-vis* each other. For this reason, social imaginaries involve common narratives, myths, practices, and patterns of behaviour – not hollowed-out values or procedural arrangements.

As Taylor suggests, the theory of social imaginaries must conform to reality, i.e. popular experience and assent to political rule – whether through constitutional settlements, in elected assemblies or other forms of human association such as faith communities. (In fact, the parish remains the most primary administrative and cultural unit around which most local communities and people in Europe associate.) Yet now that the reality of social imaginaries has changed, the theory neither describes nor explains the experience of Europe's citizens. The EU used to have an *imagined* social imaginary that rested on mutual market interest, state welfare, and European social models. But the post-war settlement no longer captures the reality that most European citizens face on a daily basis. Moreover, the Union faces the double danger of deconstructing both the nation-state and national identity while so far failing in the attempt to build the first transnational political community in modern history (see Cooper, 2007).

Herein lies the reason for political extremism and popular alienation from the European project. The breakdown of national social imaginaries is the source for radicalisation on both the left and the right, chief of all the excesses of multiculturalism and post-national citizenship whereby foreign minority claims seem to take precedence over indigenous majority interests. As a result, growing numbers of citizens across Europe question representative democracy and the institutions of both state and market that collude with special interests at the expense of ordinary people. But since there is no widely shared European social imaginary or European citizenship, people end up rallying around the nation-state and national myths (or populist versions that are filling the void). Without a proper democratic mandate, neither national governments nor the supranational decision-making bodies of the EU will be able to command popular assent and address the legitimacy crisis that threatens the post-war European project as a whole.

The emerging shape of Europe

The euro crisis is accelerating the emergence of a multi-speed EU and multipolar Europe that can be traced to the post-1989 era. Coupled with the failure to implement the 1990 Paris Charter and overcome the Cold War opposition between the West and Russia (Sawka, 2015), the three-pillar system that was enshrined in the Maastricht treaty introduced a division into the newly established Union. The EU did not build the right institutions to translate its political ambition into reality and transform the neo-functionalist logic at the heart of the integration process. Throughout the 1990s and 2000s, successive enlargement waves and treaty revisions failed to stop the rise of the European 'market-state' by building a proper polity that reflects the EU's diverse societies and can embed the increasingly interdependent national economies.

However, one fundamental difference between the post-1989 era and the post-2009 years is that the ongoing turmoil in the eurozone has shifted the dynamic from the centripetal forces that unified the Union between 1957 and the early 1990s to the centrifugal forces that now tend to divide it in three ways: first, between the euro-area core and periphery; second, between eurozone members (and candidates such as Poland) and the rest of the EU; third, between EU member states, candidate countries and the 'European non-West' (including Russia and the wider Europe that extends to the greater Caucasus, parts of the Middle East and North Africa).

In relation to the emerging eurozone arrangements, the proposed project of creating a banking, fiscal, and political union fails to resolve the economic problems of the current crisis and the constitutional deficiencies that successive treaty revisions have not addressed. The combined banking and sovereign debt disaster since 2008–09 is in large part the outcome of a balance of payments crisis associated with long-standing trade imbalances between surplus countries at the core (chief of all Germany) and deficit countries in the periphery (mostly Greece, Ireland, Portugal, and Spain and less so Italy). These imbalances are linked to significant differences in competitiveness and productivity. In turn, such differentials are exacerbated by private and public sector investment within and across eurozone countries and EU member states, including incentives to channel surplus capital (from the global 'savings glut' accumulated by emerging markets) into specific sectors such as finance, insurance, and real estate. Fuelled by low interest rates and fixed exchange rates, the single currency accelerated and amplified the divergence between the real, productive investment economy of the core and the speculative finance economy of the periphery. The banking union may help deal with banking debt and the fiscal union might limit unsustainable budget deficits, but both merely treat the symptoms of a wider structural crisis of booms, bubbles, busts, and bailouts that the single currency has exacerbated but did not create (Pabst, 2016).

The emerging arrangements within the eurozone also risk deepening the divisions with the non-euro members such as the UK, Denmark, or Hungary. First, the proposed banking union has the potential to weaken the financial system of the euro area *and* the City of London by widening the gap between them, e.g. by restricting non-EU financial firms based in the UK to do business across the eurozone. The provisions aimed at centralising supervision and extending supranational control to deposit insurance and resolution regimes lack the necessary regional and sectoral flexibility to counteract the formation of banking conglomerates that carry systemic risk.

Second, the fiscal union will concentrate decision making on national budgets in the hands of the Commission in ways that could either clash with the interests of non-euro members or undermine the common rules of the single market (or both at once). The fiscal union could lead to new institutions such as a joint assembly of national parliamentarians and MEPs that might weaken the unity of certain Community bodies such as the European Parliament. As Charles Grant (2012) has remarked:

A key question is whether the Eurozone . . . countries develop institutions that are distinct from those of the EU. If they think their interests are different to those of the [non-euro] tier, they may. If the Eurozone develops special secretariats or parliaments with lawmaking powers, it could adopt rules that clash with those of the EU, fracturing the single market.

The UK position of seeking to repatriate powers and securing opt-outs will undermine the unity of the single market guaranteed by the Commission, the European Parliament, and the European Court of Justice (ECJ) because any special deal for Britain is likely to be rejected by other member states, which would lead either to a UK veto of a new treaty (and thus another extra-Community treaty arrangement among the rest – just like the fiscal compact) or 'Brexit' following the British referendum on EU membership that will take place before the end of 2017. But the difference is that any new non-EU treaty would entail new institutions for coordinating the economic polices of its signatories, which would create legal and regulatory divergence across the single market.

Thus, the euro crisis marks the failure of the latest attempt to construct or sustain a monetary union without a coherent political union that defines the distribution of powers according to the twin Christian Catholic principles of solidarity and subsidiarity. Amid the centrifugal forces of division, debt, and demoralisation, the eurozone countries face a fundamental choice between two kinds of federalism: either a German- or US-style federal model with a substantial budget and a permanent transfer of actual, financial 'fire power' to the centre, including the welfare state (i.e. a 'transfer union'); or else "a fiscal federation by exception" (in the words of the former ECB President Jean-Claude Trichet) that gives the supranational level powers of control and intrusion whenever individual national budget deficits and debt levels threaten the euro area as a whole (Trichet, 2012). The latter constitutes an apparently more decentralised model than a permanent transfer of power to the centre. But in reality it obeys a far more centralising logic than the former, which allocates power clearly among the various levels and grants national (or sub-regional) components a far greater degree of autonomy to administer their affairs.

However, even such a classical form of federalism seems politically unpalatable to most eurozone countries, including Germany and France. One reason is that the rise of the market-state at national and European levels has undermined the social bonds and civic ties on which functioning democracies and economies depend. The principle of solidarity involves a measure of mutual sacrifice, which is the only way of overcoming Europe's economic, political, and ethical crisis. The trouble is that the various European countries cannot ask their citizens to make sacrifices as long as there is a lack of legitimacy. The EU has helped create a sense of Europe as an economic-political entity but no shared social imaginary that translates into mutual understanding and sympathy among European citizens.

All the present proposals to resolve the current crisis involve structures that lack legitimacy and fail to mobilise citizens into making the necessary sacrifices. For example, the two proposed solutions to the economic crisis are either austerity or a fiscal stimulus, but governments cannot demand from their citizens the necessary national sacrifices under a European diktat of austerity or a retrenchment of the welfare state. Strong growth in the eurozone and the rest of the EU requires stable public finances and a profound transformation of the various European social models that are all economically unsustainable. As long as the Union does not defend and promote the kind of interconnections, civic ties, and cultural links that bind citizens together, the nations that compose the Union will share little more than the economic rights of the single market and the political mechanisms of supranational institutions. But a polity based on mass consumption and elite cooperation without a shared social imaginary will not command the assent of its people.

Europe's civic commonwealth: an alternative vision for the future

To transform the EU into a proper polity, its members need to address three fundamental errors. First, the primacy of economic integration over political union, which has led to a market-state that is disembedded from society and a citizenry that is subordinated to the joint rule of the economic and the political. Second, the premature process of constitutionalisation that culminated in the rejection of the 2005 Constitutional Treaty and then led to the partially flawed 2009 Lisbon Treaty. Third, the current institutional arrangements that concentrate power in the hands of supranational institutions and national governments at the expense of the citizens. These three errors are underpinned by the two dominant methods of integration and enlargement, namely the supranational Community method (that rests on the logic of neo-functionalism) and the intergovernmental method (that is grounded in the logic of liberal institutionalism).

The former imposes an EU settlement from above, while the latter denies the import of constitutional norms and reduces cooperation to largely technical transactions. Both approaches favour formal, procedural values and process over substantive notions and policy. That is why the EU is associated with generic standards and top-down harmonisation that weaken relational values such as mutual human flourishing, the dignity of each person, and the common good. These and other principles can be a source of disagreement and discord, and their meaning is neither fully discerned nor fixed. In a plural context discernment is the work of decades and endlessly subject to further debate. However, without such values both market economies and democracies lack shared ends that can bind together individuals, groups, and nations. Therefore both crude federalism, which is based on the supranational Community method, and narrow 'sovereignism', which draws on the intergovernmental method, are unable to blend unity with diversity by upholding universal principles which are embodied in particular practices. On the contrary, the dominant models and methods continue to fuel the centrifugal forces that exacerbate both integration and enlargement fatigue and risk breaking the Union asunder.

Europe's diverse Christian heritage has the potential to renew and extend the shared social imaginary on which a functioning market economy and democracy rely. In a remarkable report on "The Spiritual and Cultural Dimension of Europe" published in 2004, a reflection group composed of European statesmen and intellectuals debunked the neo-functional myth that economic integration will lead to political union and that market forces can produce politically resilient solidarity: "The original expectation, that the political unity of the EU would be a consequence of the European common market has proven to be illusory. ... To function as a viable and vital polity, the European Union needs a firmer foundation" (Biedenkopf, Geremek and Michalski, 2004: 6). Rightly rejecting any arbitrary list of abstract values, the group argued that the role of Europe's common culture, which is a variety of traditions that are both intertwined and in tension with one another, grows in significance as the old, secular logic of integration unravels.

The shared cultural bonds that (can) unite Europeans draw on the Christian fusion of biblical revelation with Greco-Roman antiquity in order to promote notions such as peace, reconciliation, solidarity, subsidiarity, the dignity of the person, the virtue of free association, and the distinction of religious from political authority that avoids both aggressive secularism (masquerading as secular neutrality) and fanatical theocracy (masquerading as religious guidance). In the absence of such and similar principles, the professing of values associated with democracy and liberalism will sound increasingly hollow. Indeed, the professed pragmatism of many European elites masks a dangerous moral relativism, as Pope Benedict XVI (2007) argued:

> A community built without respect for the true dignity of the human being, disregarding the fact that every person is created in the image of God, ends up doing no good to anyone. . . . In this historical hour and faced with the many challenges that confront it, the European Union, in order to be a valid guarantor of the rule of law and an efficient promoter of universal values, cannot but recognize clearly the certain existence of a stable and permanent human nature, source of common rights for all individuals, including those who deny them. In this context, the right to conscientious objection should be protected, every time fundamental human rights are violated.

Universal values like freedom, equality, solidarity, and the will of the majority require transcendent finalities such as substantive notions of the good. For otherwise they lack specific content and are hollowed out by procedural process, or else they oscillate between the sovereign individual and the sovereign collective and are subject to state (and market) power. Either way, a pure liberal market democracy weakens and even destroys all the diverse interpersonal relationships and the variegated forms of human association that constitute society, as evinced by the erosion of trust in public institutions and the sharp decline in social capital (Bauman 2001, 2003; Putnam, 2000, 2002).

Faced with this danger, the Union needs to eschew abstract standards, formal values and the priority of process over policy in favour of a mutual recognition of particular practices, universal principles such as the common good and the primacy of both constitutionalism and 'mixed government' – distinguishing the three branches of government without fully separating them from one another and thereby leading either to permanent paralysis or a concentration of power in the hands of the executive (Agamben, 2005: 1–40). Here the legacy of Christianity is key: up to a point, Europe remains a vestigially Christian polity that is characterised by hybrid institutions, overlapping jurisdictions, polycentric authority, and multi-level governance, which are different from the characteristically ancient or modern concentration of power in the hands of a sovereign – whether an absolute monarch or a revolutionary republic. As Rémi Brague (1999) shows, the origins of this distinctly European model go back to a long tradition that views Europe not as the novel product of modernity but rather as the continuous unfolding of the Hellenistic fusion of Jerusalem with Athens and Rome (see also Gouguenheim, 2008).

Connected with this blending of diverse cultures within an overarching framework is the Judeo-Christian distinction of religious from political authority. Based on this distinction, a free 'complex space' emerged between political rule and society wherein politics is not monopolised by the state but pertains to the public realm in which individuals and groups participate (Milbank, 1997). The history of Christendom is replete with periods of religious coercion and persecution (including centuries of Christian anti-Semitism and imperial contempt for Islam). However, these horrors do not invalidate the role of the Church – together with local communities and professional bodies like guilds or universities – in defending the freedom of society against political coercion. A crucial part of Europe's Christian heritage is the blending of the principle of free association in Germanic common law with the Latin sense of equity and participation in the shared *civitas*. Thus Christianity defends a more relational account in terms of objective rights and reciprocal duties, not merely subjective individual entitlements upheld by the state (or maximised by the market). What underpins this is the idea of a free, shared social space for religious and non-religious practice – the 'realm' of civil society that is more primary than the market-state. As the 'corporation of corporations', the European polity rests on a common civic culture and on social bonds that are more fundamental than either formal constitutional legal rights or economic contractual ties.

The aforementioned report by the Reflection Group on the spiritual and cultural dimension of Europe puts this well:

Europe itself is far more than a political construct. It is a complex – a 'culture' – of institutions, ideas, expectations, habits and feelings, moods, memories and prospects that form a 'glue' binding Europeans together – and all these are a foundation on which a political construct must rest. This complex – we can speak of it as European civil society – is at the heart of political identity. It defines the conditions of successful European politics and the limits of state and political intervention.

(Biedenkopf, Geremek and Michalski, 2004: 9)

Contrary to common misconceptions, the EU is neither a federal super-state nor an intergovernmental structure. Instead, European nations pool their sovereignty and are more like regions within a pan-national polity that combines a political system *sui generis* with elements of a neo-medieval empire (Hix, 2005; Zielonka, 2006, 2008). The German constitutional court, in a landmark ruling on the Lisbon Treaty in June 2009, emphasised that the Union in its original outlook is not so much an international organisation or single state as a voluntary association of states. But now that the EU has been captured by the logic of the market-state, its members need to strengthen the associational model that combines vertical, more hierarchical elements with horizontal, more egalitarian aspects. Based on overlapping jurisdictions and a complex web of intermediary institutions wherein sovereignty is dispersed and diffused, such a model can help re-embed both politics and economics within the civic and social bonds of civil society. Amid the current crisis of legitimacy, this suggests that the EU should pursue a subsidiary *polis* that connects supranational institutions much more closely to regions, localities, communities, and neighbourhoods. Most of all, the Union requires a much greater sense of a common *demos* with a mutual *ethos* and *telos*.

Specifically, one of the clearest weaknesses of the EU's political system is the established modality of direct elections to the EP, which has broken the link between national political classes and the European project, giving national politicians and national parliaments a pretext to get involved less than they should do and might otherwise have done. Bound up with this is another structural weakness, namely the evolution of the Commission from being a pan-European civil service in support of cooperation among national governments towards a supranational institution that concentrates both legislative and executive powers in its hand. Both EP elections and the design of the Commission drive a wedge between EU and national politics and deepen the growing gap between the Union and its citizens.

For these reasons, the EU should create a parliamentary system of bicameralism – with a lower house representing the people and an upper house representing cities, regions, nations, professions, and faiths. For its part, the Commission should revert to being a high-level European civil service that supports the work of the EU's bicameral legislature and the EU's executive – the Council of Ministers and the European Council (and possibly nationally elected politicians on secondment to the EU to ensure the day-to-day running of the EU's executive). In this manner, a bicameral system and an executive rooted in national polities can once again bind national political classes to the European project. The objection that the EU already has a certain kind of second chamber in the form of the Council of Ministers ignores its role, which is to relate the European project to national governments but not to national parliaments and national polities in the manner that is needed.

Crucially, a bicameral parliament and the participation of nationally elected politicians in the EU executive would go some ways towards building a mixed government that is in line with the best traditions of European constitutionalism – notably the rule of law, limits on sovereign power, the interplay of the 'one', the 'few' and the 'many', as well as the distinction of powers without, however, an absolute separation, which ends either in paralysis or in the primacy of the executive over the other branches of government. What a proper European polity requires is a much stronger measure of popular assent, coupled with civic participation (through local, regional, and professional assemblies like town-halls or guildhalls) and the guidance of 'the wise' (based on the representation of professions and faiths). Only a commonwealth of nations and peoples with shared social imaginaries will be able to foster social ties and civic bonds that are key to re-embedding markets and states in the interpersonal relationships of trust and cooperation.

Externally, a commonwealth that reflects the mediating universalism of the Judeo-Christian and Greco-Roman traditions would contrast with the exceptionalism of old empires and new colonial powers such as the USA and China. However imperfectly, the EU remains so far the only serious attempt to inaugurate a transnational polity whose members come together to form a voluntary association of nations that pool their sovereign power for the common good of their people and others across the globe. Europe has a terrible colonial history, but it has also given rise to a set of institutions and practices that have transformed tribalism and nationalism at home and abroad. Moreover, Europe has shaped global history not through sheer size or military might but rather thanks to its inventiveness and the creation of 'force multipliers' (Coker, 2009). European inventiveness today is mirrored in the international order that reflects Europe's Christian heritage. For example, European Protestant theologians and Catholic figures played a decisive role in creating the League of Nations after 1919 and the United Nations in 1946. As the chapters by Gary Wilton and John Loughlin in this volume show, Christian Democrats from Italy, Germany, the Benelux countries, and even France led the way in setting up the project for European integration and enlargement in the late 1940s and 1950s.

In contemporary parlance, the Christian origin and outlook of the post-1919 world order is based on the idea of 'networking' and 'mainstreaming' Christian ideas and thus multiplying the power of European's vestigially Christian polity. The invention of international organisations and supranational bodies reflects the Christian commitment to create a *megalopolis* – a cosmic city that upholds universal, global principles embodied in particular, national, or regional practices. Arguably, Christianity – whose global spread outstrips that of Islam and other world religions (Jenkins, 2002) – is Europe's single most significant force multiplier.

A renewed Christian polity – bastion for people of all faiths and none

Critics will object that a revivified Christian polity would undo the achievements of Enlightenment progress and provide a license for discrimination of non-Christians and non-believers. However, it is far from clear whether secular liberalism can secure toleration, equality, the rule of law, and neutrality of the state vis-à-vis religious faiths. Where liberalism has shed its religious roots, it mutates from what Rowan Williams (2006) defines as "procedural secularism", which guarantees a proper distinction of political from religious authority, into a "programmatic secularism" that imposes secular norms and seeks to privatise faith. It does so by equating freedom with little more than Isaiah Berlin's (1969) 'negative liberty' and by defining the role of the state in terms of its ability to maximise individual choice. Thus the secular market-state reigns by proscribing debates about substantive values and shared ethical ends.

The hidden assumption is that in a context of cultural diversity people hold incompatible and even incommensurable values (especially believers in relation to non-believers). Therefore they can only 'agree to disagree' and must settle for formal rules and procedures (see Pabst 2015). Faced with a clash of values, which in reality is as much the result of real diversity as it is the outcome of enforcing programmatically secular norms, liberalism lays down rules for 'fair play' between isolated human beings who are thought to be naturally greedy, selfish, distrustful of one another, and prone to violence (Rawls 1971; 1993), as I suggested in the first section. In this way the liberal market-state more and more produces the 'war of all against all' that was its own presupposition. But this does not thereby prove that presupposition, because it is *really existing* liberalism that has produced in practice the circumstances that it originally and arbitrarily assumed in theory. The secular outlook of contemporary liberal models is atomistic because it privileges the negatively choosing and self-governing individual over voluntary associations and group identity (as both Burke and Tocqueville already argued in the nineteenth century), including faith communities. Contemporary Europe is no exception.

Amid the global resurgence of religion in political life, liberalism seems unable to integrate different faith traditions into the public sphere except on strictly secular terms (see Pabst 2012b). Such terms not only override legitimate religious objections on grounds of freedom of conscience and freedom of religion (e.g. closing Catholic adoption agencies in Britain for not selecting same-sex couples as potential foster parents) but also stop believers from expressing themselves in their own voice (e.g. head-scarves or wall-mounted crucifixes). Reasonable religious concerns about the programmatically secular outlook of European law and politics tie in with wider Western worries about the consequences of failing to integrate a growing, devout, and alienated Muslim minority within a relativistic and increasingly aggressive secular culture. However, the solution proposed by secular and religious liberals alike repeats the errors of 1960s multiculturalism.[2] In conjuring up the idea of communities sharing the same space but leading a separate life, the advocates of balkanising multicultural models endorse a scenario that entrenches segregation and fractures any conception of a common good binding together all citizens. It is precisely because of the remorselessly atomistic character of both liberalism and multiculturalism that European countries are struggling to find a way of accommodating their increasingly ghettoised and radicalised Muslim population.

Thus the integration of Islam into liberal democracies is a challenge that confronts Europe as a whole. Regrettably, there are problems with the existing models of integration. British and Dutch versions of multiculturalism hoped to defend the equal rights of all citizens, but both countries abandoned the idea of a mutual organic and national culture based around religion. In this process, they lost the very medium in which both majorities and minorities could share. Germany eschewed its own Christian legacy in favour of an ethnic account of its identity. Thus, Germany reserves national culture predominantly for its indigenous population. Even though it grants generous socio-economic rights, the German model continues to limit citizenship for Muslim 'guest workers' and immigrants and thereby curtails their participation in political and civic life. In France, the Republican ideal of liberty, equality, and fraternity appeals to immigrants, but its secular instantiation denies the primary religious form of their identity. Moreover, the Muslim population is heavily discriminated against on the labour market and tends to be confined to the no-go areas of the *banlieues*. The French refusal to recognise France's Christian origins and legacy prevents the country from broadening its account of what French identity is and integrating other faiths such as Islam.

The trouble with the different European models is that they enshrine the primacy of secular law over against religious principles. Far from ensuring neutrality and tolerance, the secular European state arrogates to itself the right to control and legislate in all spheres of life (including education, the family, and marriage). State constraints apply especially to religion and its civic influence: legally, programmatic secularism outlaws any rival source of sovereignty or legitimacy – even under the umbrella of universal law (see Pabst, 2014). Politically, programmatic secularism denies religion any substantive import in public debate and decision making. Culturally, programmatic secularism enforces its own norms and standards upon all other belief systems. In consequence, the liberal promise of equality translates more and more into a secular imposition of sameness. Thus contemporary liberalism is unable to recognise religions in their own right or grant them their proper autonomy.

Moreover, liberal appeals to legal equality for all are insufficient because this treats secular law as given and rules religious norms out of the court of public discussion. Yet how can citizens decide on what equality is if societies do not agree what constitutes a good and what ends human beings should pursue? Liberals will rightly object that there is no fixed or final knowledge of the good or ethical ends. But it is liberal 'negative freedom' that brackets such questions out of the picture by ignoring the inherited wisdom of cultural traditions, notably Europe's Christian heritage. Such traditions give societies some intimation of the nature of universal principles, something to begin to debate about – for example the meaning of human dignity in relation to beginning- and end-of-life issues.

In response to the crisis of secular liberalism, the philosopher Jürgen Habermas (2006a, 2006b) has advocated the notion of post-secularity as a way of allowing the moral intuitions of faith to be part of public discourse and contribute to the common good. His pluralist politics seeks to integrate religion on post-secular terms into the national-republican state or the global-cosmopolitan public square. However, the notion of post-secularity fails to overcome programmatic secularism (see Pabst, 2012b). Habermas convincingly contests the liberal public-private divide and the exclusion of faith from politics, but he defends the post-metaphysical outlook of the Enlightenment and a version of the hegemonic secularist settlement, which together rule out shared ethical ends. The transcendent is now permitted within the public sphere but merely as a source of morality and strictly limited to informal communication among citizens (Habermas, 1995, 2008).

In contrast, formal deliberations at the level of the state and its agencies must be protected from religion by an institutional filter, which suspends all metaphysical questions and reduces religious belief to a purely private decision. In this manner, Habermas (2010) draws an absolute line between both the public square and the state, on the one hand, and communities and groups, on the other hand – a divide that religious arguments are not allowed to transgress. Beyond discursive deliberation or the respectful listening to difference, Habermas has little to offer by way of mediating the clash of rival values (such as freedom and equality). He will not accept that shared substantive finalities, such as the common good or human flourishing, can be publicly adjudicated. This takes no account of the current revival of the claims of virtue-ethics (by MacIntyre, Taylor, Sandel, and others) and in fact dismisses them out of hand.[3] For Habermas views religious faith as irrational, and his Enlightenment philosophy is predicated on the separation of natural immanence from supernatural transcendence. As a result, only secular reason is ultimately permitted to define the procedural and majoritarian norms that govern the public realm.

Beyond programmatic secularism and post-secularity, my argument is that Europe's Christian heritage can integrate other religions and people of no faith into a shared European project by acknowledging what secular ideologies cannot: transcendent finalities that exceed human volition but are open to rational discernment and debate. Christianity outlines a non-secular model of the common good in which all can participate. Rather than trying to defend religion through the guise of secular multiculturalism, true liberals (i.e. those who defend the principles of liberality such as 'mixed government', constitutional corporatism, and ancient liberties) should promote political pluralism through the Christian legacy. What Muslims and other religious believers most object to is not a difference of belief but its absence from European consciousness and the political realm. Thus recovering Europe's Christian heritage is not a sectarian project but instead the best basis for peaceful coexistence of believers and non-believers alike. How so? Unlike programmatic secularism and post-secularity, Christianity can hold positive views of Islam or other faiths precisely as religious believers who realise that they have much in common with what Muslims and other followers believe – a sense of the sacred, the sanctity of life and land, the integral and holistic nature of human existence, or the distinction of religious from political authority without divorcing religion from politics (especially in the Shia and Sufi tradition of Islam).

Thus a vestigially Christian polity can go further in acknowledging the integral worth of a religious group as a group than a secular polity can. Christians can validly see analogies to churches in mosques and Hindu temples, similarities that lead them to accord a considerable measure of respect to these institutions. Conversely, Jews, Muslims, and other religious believers not only welcome the European tradition of civil law but also the political recognition of Christianity in Europe. Examples include the mention of God and the Christian heritage in national constitutions and EU treaties, and a constitutional status for Christian churches and indeed other faith communities. In this manner, both the law and the public realm can uphold a shared space for both religious and non-religious practice. Since no values are neutral, a truly principled pluralism requires the presence of an 'indigenous' religious tradition that provides a host culture and nurturing soil for critical engagement and mutual understanding among believers and non-believers alike. True liberals (whether more religious or more procedurally secular) realise that a genuinely 'religious culture' has to be religious in a *specific* way. Unlike US civil religion, in Europe there is no such thing in practice as a 'general religiosity' (see Pabst, 2012a). It is Europe's specifically Christian heritage that underpins the common cultural norms without which Europeans will struggle to build a polity with a shared *demos, ethos,* and *telos*.

Conclusion

This chapter has contrasted the secular 'market-state' with the Christian commonwealth. My argument is that Europe's Christian heritage is a source of both social solidarity and religious pluralism that offers key resources to shape the future of the European polity. Contemporary Europe remains a vestigially Christian polity that is to a large extent governed by the Catholic Christian principles of solidarity and subsidiarity. The EU is neither a federal super-state in the making nor a glorified free-trade area but rather a neo-medieval 'empire', which pools national sovereignty and views states more like 'super-regions' in a wider subsidiary association of nations and peoples. In such a polity with overlapping jurisdictions and multiple levels of membership, states are key because they balance the rightful claims of localities and regions with the rightful claims of Europe as a whole. Paradoxically, a Europe that applies the principles of mutuality, reciprocity, and solidarity will speak to its local needs and global responsibility – to "function as a 'leaven' for the entire world", as Pope Benedict XVI said on the fiftieth anniversary of the Rome Treaty (2007).

Notes

1 Support from James Madison Trust for this research is gratefully acknowledged.
2 A laudable exception is the work of Tariq Modood and G.B. Levey (2009).
3 For a longer exposition of this critique, see Pabst (2015).

References

Agamben, G. (2005). *State of exception*. Chicago, IL: University of Chicago Press.
Bauman, Z. (2003). *Liquid love: On the frailty of human bonds*. Cambridge: Polity.
Bauman, Z. (2001). *The individualized society*. Cambridge: Polity.
Benedict XVI. (2007). Address to the participants in the congress promoted by the Commission of Bishops' Conferences of the European Community (COMECE) on the 50th anniversary of the Treaty of Rome, 24 March. Retrieved from www.vatican.va/holy_father/benedict_xvi/speeches/2007/march/documents/hf_ben-xvi_spe_20070324_comece_en.html.
Berlin, I. (1969). Two concepts of liberty. In Berlin, I. (ed.), *Four essays on liberty* (pp. 118–172). Oxford: Oxford University Press.
Biedenkopf, K., Geremek, B. and Michalski, K. (2004). *The spiritual and cultural dimension of Europe: Concluding remarks*. Vienna, Austria: Institute for Human Sciences/Brussels: European Commission. Retrieved from http://ec.europa.eu/research/social-sciences/pdf/michalski_281004_final_report_en.pdf.
Bobbitt, P. (2003). *The shield of Achilles: War, peace and the course of history*. London: Penguin.
Brague, R. (1999). *L'Europe, la voie romaine* (Rev. edn). Paris: Gallimard. [Lester, S. (trans.) (2002). *Eccentric Culture: A Theory of Western Civilization*. South Bend, IN: St Augustine's Press.]
Caillé, A. (2007). *Anthropologie du Don: Le tiers paradigme*. Paris: La Découverte.
Coker, C. (2009). Rebooting the west: The US, Europe and the future of the western alliance. Royal United Services Institute for Defence and Security Studies (RUSI), 6 November, Whitehall Paper 72. London.
Cooper, R. (2007). *The breaking of nations: Order and chaos in the twenty-first century* (2nd edn). London: Atlantic.
Gamble, A. (2006). Two faces of neo-liberalism. In Robinson, R. (ed.), *The neo-liberal revolution: Forging the market state* (pp. 20–35). Basingstoke: Palgrave Macmillan.
Godbout, J. T., and Caillé, A. (1998). *The world of the gift*. Winkler, D. (trans.). Montréal, Canada: McGill-Queen's University Press.
Godbout, J. (2007). *Ce qui circule entre nous: Donner, recevoir, rendre*. Paris: Seuil.

Gouguenheim, S. (2008). *Aristotle au Mont Saint-Michel: Les racines Grecques de L'Europe Chrétienne*. Paris: Seuil.
Grant, C. (2012). A three-tier EU puts single market at risk. *Financial Times*, 26 October. Retrieved from www.ft.com/cms/s/0/eb4d532a-19dd-11e2-a179-00144fea bdc0.html.
Haas, E. B. (1958). *The uniting of Europe: Political, social and economic forces, 1950–1957*. Stanford, CA: Stanford University Press.
Habermas, J. (2010). An awareness of what is missing. In Habermas, J. et al. (eds), *An awareness of what is missing: Faith and reason in a post-secular age*. Cronin, C. (trans.). Cambridge: Polity, 15–23.
Habermas, J. (2008). Secularism's crisis of faith: Notes on a post-secular society. *New Perspectives Quarterly*, 25(4): 17–29.
Habermas, J. (2006a). On the relations between the secular liberal state and religion. In de Vries, H. and Sullivan, L. E. (eds), *Political theologies: Public religion in a post-secular world* (pp. 251–260). New York: Fordham University Press.
Habermas, J. (2006b). Religion in the public square. *European Journal of Philosophy* 14(1): 1–25.
Habermas, J. (1995). *Postmetaphysical thinking: Between metaphysics and the critique of reason*. Hohengarten, W. M. (trans.) Cambridge: Polity.
Hix, S. (2005). *The political system of the European Union* (2nd rev. edn). London: Palgrave Macmillan.
Jenkins, P. (2002). *The next Christendom: The coming of global Christianity*. Oxford: Oxford University Press.
Kaiser, W. (2007). *Christian democracy and the origins of European Union*. Cambridge: Cambridge University Press.
Lamy, P. (2012). Europe needs a legitimacy compact. *International Herald Tribune*, 9 July. Retrieved from www.nytimes.com/2012/07/09/opinion/europe-needs-a-legitima cy-compact.html?_r=0
Mauss, M. (2000 [1954]). *The gift: The form and reason for exchange in archaic societies*. Halls, W. D. (trans.). New York: W. W. Norton
Michéa, J.-C. (2009). *The realm of lesser evil: An essay on liberal civilisation*. Fernbach, D. (trans.). Cambridge: Polity.
Milbank, J. (1997). On complex space. In Milbank, J. (ed.), *The world made strange: Theology, language, culture* (pp. 268–292). Oxford: Blackwell.
Mitrany, D. (1965). The prospect of European integration: Federal or functional. *Journal of Common Market Studies*, 4(2): 119–149.
Modood, T., and Levey, G. B. (2009). *Secularism, religion and multicultural citizenship*. Cambridge: Cambridge University Press.
Pabst, A. (2016). Political economy of constitution: Eurozone pathways beyond ordo-liberal and neo-functional models. In Cardinale, I., Coffman, D., and Scazzieri, R. (eds), *The political economy of the Eurozone*. Cambridge: Cambridge University Press.
Pabst, A. (2015). 'A habitual disposition to the good': On reason, virtue and realism. *Global Discourse*, 5(2): 261–279.
Pabst, A. (2014). Commonwealth and covenant: The west in a neo-medieval era of international affairs. *Telos*, 168: 107–131.
Pabst, A. (2012a). The western paradox: Why the United States is more religious but less Christian than Europe. In Leustean, L. N. (ed.), *Representing religion in the European Union: Does God matter?* (pp. 168–184). London: Routledge.

Pabst, A. (2012b). The secularism of post-secularity: Religion, realism and the revival of grand theory. *Review of International Studies*, 38(5): 995–1017.
Polanyi, K. (2001 [1944]). *The great transformation: The political and economic origins of our time*. Boston, MA: Beacon.
Putnam, R. D. (ed.) (2002). *Democracies in flux: The evolution of social capital in contemporary society*. Oxford: Oxford University Press.
Putnam, R. D. (2000). *Bowling alone: The collapse and revival of American community*. New York: Schuster and Schuster.
Rawls, J. (1993). *Political liberalism*. New York: Columbia University Press.
Rawls, J. (1971). *A theory of justice*. Cambridge, MA: Harvard University Press.
Robinson, R. (ed.) (2006). *The neo-liberal revolution: Forging the market state*. Basingstoke, England: Palgrave Macmillan.
Sakwa, R. (2015). The death of Europe? Continental fates after Ukraine. *International Affairs*, 91(3): 553–579.
Siedentop, L. (2001). *Democracy in Europe*. London: Penguin.
Sweet, A. S., Sandholtz, W., and Fligstein, N. (eds) (2001). *The institutionalization of Europe*. Oxford: Oxford University Press.
Taylor, C. (2004). *Modern social imaginaries*. Durham, NC: Duke University Press.
Trichet, J.-C. (2012). Lessons from the crisis: Challenges for advanced economies and for the monetary union. Eleventh Annual Niarchos Lecture, 17 May. Washington, DC: Peterson Institute for International Economics. Retrieved from www.iie.com/publications/papers/transcript-20120518niarchos-trichet.pdf.
Williams, R. (2006). Secularism, faith and freedom. Lecture at the Pontifical Academy of Social Sciences, 23 November. Rome. Retrieved from www.archbishopofcanterbury.org/sermon_speeches/061123a.htm.
Zielonka, J. (2008). Europe as a global actor: Empire by example? *International Affairs*, 84(3): 471–484.
Zielonka, J. (2006). *Europe as empire: The nature of the enlarged European Union*. Oxford: Oxford University Press.

7 European Union, identity, and place

Joshua Hordern

Introduction

This chapter is an exercise in political theology exploring ways in which European Union citizens might think about political life. The chapter has four sections: first, a discussion of how people, especially Europeans, identify with their places and their politics – this section considers the chief threat to European peace, ethnocentrism; second, a discussion of two key civic tasks regarding the interrelation of European Union member states, 'adequate identity' and 'sufficient agreement'; third, a conversation between contrasting political analyses of human motivation and civic participation concerning these tasks; fourth and finally, an account of the distinctive contribution of ecclesial identity to European consciousness.

This chapter, while paying due attention to legal, historical, economic, and constitutional matters, will operate on the conceptual level supported by concrete illustrations. Concepts will be analysed theologically to raise questions for all citizens and engage in conversation with the 'secular' forms of expression proper to political discourse. For the word 'secular' signals a Christian belief, that political life is shared by those who, for various reasons, both value the many forms of relatively peaceful social coexistence and communicate with each other as fellow citizens just because they are fellow creatures of God.

Identification, people, and place: the threat of ethnocentrism

Many European Union (EU) citizens feel as though their politics operates six feet in the air, detached, and perhaps ignorant of citizens' own participation in the places and goods upon which their flourishing depends. Their politics do not seem like the politics of their place but like the politics of no place at all. The political noise and fury appear to go on above the ground level of daily experience, leaving behind bewildered citizens in confused places. While this has long been a reported experience, it has been peculiarly accentuated in recent years. A chief, though not sole, reason is that the European experience has appeared to portray politics as essentially reducible to financial affairs. Printing money and flickering computer screens seem to be the mode of communication by which nations are interrelated. Decisions about money and debts appear to some European citizens not as the wise counsel of neighbourly friends but as the diktats of far-away bureaucracies. Today's Greek inheritors of the traditions of Athenian democracy who chant slogans against German neighbours exemplify this widely held and deep-seated feeling, a discordant cry amidst the symphonic hopes of post-World War Two Europe. Such discord shapes political life as every politician, local, national, and European knows. For it challenges the possibility of a supranational unity of hearts, that 'concord' necessary for an 'ever-closer union' – a moral, not just a financial or legal union – to be substantially realised.

At the heart of the challenge is the issue of the identification of people and their leaders with places. Such identification is a practical, political, long-term endeavour and so requires *conceptualisation* lest political activities proceed without an awareness of how identification works.

In what does 'identification' consist? Consider a conceptual distinction between 'place' and 'space'. To identify with a 'place' is to participate in describing, deliberating about, and pursuing the welfare of that place's people. Such participation involves defending and developing the place *as* a place lest it become simply 'space'. A space is not a place if it cannot make people feel and act as if there is a common activity in which they share. Space is thus distinguished from place. In a place people share and value together the goods by which they realise an adequately common social identity. The identity must be *common* because, unless people feel they share the burden of life in purposeful activity, hostility emerges. But it need only be *adequately* common because what is required for politics is not maximum cooperation between all citizens but something more modest: cooperation sufficient to enable people peaceably to secure the social roles and vocations they desire.

'Places' are not necessarily very large. To be 'the people of a place' is not reducible to being the body of citizens who share a nation-state. Both nation-states and smaller communities must inspire people's common sharing and valuation of goods in a place. Without a place in which the welfare of people can be sought, achieved and sustained, all activity that might otherwise be called 'political' becomes a mere flailing of limbs, gesturing at a world other than the one in which we are given to live.

Politics' task is to enable peoples' identification with places and to maintain this strenuous vocation's attractiveness to citizens amidst alternative, hostile and incompatible allegiances. As such, making and sustaining places is an intensely practical, political endeavour. It does not have to be grandiose. For example in the United Kingdom (UK), making places will involve ensuring that the large amount of new housing required in the coming years is achieved by conserving and developing the goods which existing residents enjoy rather than degrading those goods. What is true of housing is also true of public institutions such as health services that are similarly under pressure.

In order to bring politics down to earth and seek harmony instead of the cacophony that alienates many from participative political experience, driving them into the old hatreds from which the EU was supposed to emancipate people, it seems necessary to learn again the importance of place. Place, one observer suggests, "is the social communication of space. ... Places are the precondition for social communication in material and intellectual goods ... a function of our social communications, extending as far as they extend" (O'Donovan, 2005: 255–256). This 'communication' in space involves *spoken* conversation about the value of common goods. But 'communication' goes beyond conversation to *activities* whereby things talked about as good are actively shared, enjoyed, adapted and preserved.

Places are made by the 'communications' of individuals and groups in their varied families, institutions, and associations. Through such interactions, traditions and social cultures are created and developed. Places may also be made, in principle, between *peoples*, represented by their leaders but in many other forms of economic and cultural interaction, via that basic feature of the EU, the nation-state. In this sense, the territory of the EU might conceivably be a 'place'.

But the realisation that a place is *our* place does not automatically follow from treaties or laws. Rather the first person plural 'our' by which many share a place must continually be reassessed so that places do not collapse under pressures into internal confusion and external enmities. The spreading battles in the UK, pressed by UKIP, about access to 'our' welfare and 'our' housing by citizens from accession states such as Bulgaria and Romania is a signal of just this effect.

The quest that space be liveable as 'our' place presents a special challenge for the EU in which the peoples of nation-states increasingly interpenetrate each other's social communications in innovative economic, military, cultural, legal, and political ways. From the seemingly trivial but deeply felt effects of the ban on imperial weights and measures in British fruit and vegetable markets to legal judgments about prisoners' voting rights and freedom of religion to the shared use of aircraft carriers by France and the UK to the complexities of a mobile labour force in institutions such as the UK National Health Service, the interrelation of these European nation-states poses deep challenges, not least because of the number of citizens from other nation-states beyond the EU (such as the Commonwealth nations) who also live and work within European borders.

Ethnocentrism and the threat to peace

To talk of a place for *a people* will trouble many. It recalls the European collective memory of the twentieth century, when the notion of a *pre-political* social entity, a *Volksnation*, was turned to the darkest purposes. Accordingly, a foreshortened retrospective on the European journey is needed, taken at the angle from which our enquiry departs. For dreams of a pure *volk*, a people undifferentiated by stock and culture, reigning in millennial splendour over

Europe, threatened to overwhelm civilisation in a nightmare of annihilation. Such history places an indelible question mark over the reconcilability of strong national identity with a liveable transnational peace. Ethnocentric nationalism is the extreme that constantly threatens to subvert the entire enterprise and discourse of the EU.[1]

For the EU, politics must be not ethnocentric but rather in the business of negotiating disagreements and bringing peaceful resolutions to disputes within and between nation-states. For this to happen, there must be some shared underlying commonality that makes dispute itself intelligible, a first person plural by which a dispute is owned as 'ours' inasmuch as it is a disagreement about goods and places in which two parties have a common stake. Ethnocentrism threatens the possibility of negotiation between nations about goods by displacing the goodness of the world in which all participate in favour of the superiority of one, ethnically uniform nation and a preference for the success of that nation's participation in the earth's goods over against all comers. Fuelled by such a bad idea, twentieth-century Europe witnessed the negation of the negotiation and compromise politics, which are basic to democracy and peace.

However, while recognising that religions, including Christianity, have corruptly sponsored some ethnocentric nightmares, this politics of compromise is arguably native to the best of European *Christian* wisdom. Over against those who see 'religion' as "essentially more prone to violence – more absolutist, divisive, and irrational – than [liberalism]" (Cavanaugh, 2009: 6)[2] and drawing on Europe's varied traditions concerning churches and civic authorities, Rowan Williams observes that the "distinctively European style of political argument and debate is made possible by the Church's persistent witness to the fact that states do not have ultimate religious claims on their citizens" (2012: 79). For Williams, the tension that energises negotiation and debate concerns whether ultimate identity is claimed by a political authority appealing to a pre-political *Volksnation or* by the Christian God whose concern is for *every* nation and tribe. On Williams' thesis it is only when the tension between God and government is vigorously maintained, when both secular national identity and politics itself are reckoned provisional and liable to eclipse by the Kingdom of God, that the ethos of compromise, debate, and discussion *combined with* a proper love of nation may take root and grow, creating the conditions for the development of robust nation-states in peaceful interrelation. On Williams' view, it follows that such an interrelation of politics and ultimate authority is well-suited to ready Europe to oppose the kind of horrors it has witnessed and hopes never, God forbid, to see again. The fact that 'God' *can* be co-opted by devilish ethnocentrism does not entail that religion must be banished from public recognition but rather the opposite.

To sustain a politics which aims at peace between nation-states by negotiation and compromise, much turns on three core questions: what counts as an *adequate* realisation of various political identities – local, national, and European; what should be reckoned as *sufficient* agreement about goods; and, extending Williams' observation, what role the *interplay of political identity and religious – especially Christian – faith* has to play. I will explore the contours of these questions in the rest of this section before turning to more extended political and theological responses to them in the third and fourth sections.

Adequate political identity

The notion of an adequate political identity raises the question: adequate for what or for whom? With respect to people and place, political identity is adequate if it enables citizens to conceive of the environment in which they live as their 'place'.

European citizens might reasonably conceive of their environment in a series of more-or-less concentric circles or ellipses, pivoting around themselves, encompassing local, national, and European 'places', perhaps incorporating other inflections and demarcations such as 'Mediterranean' (not just, for example, Italian, Spanish, or Cypriot), 'British' (not just, for example, Northern Irish or English) or, because place and work are interrelated, 'rural and agricultural' (as distinct from urban and financial). Politics has the gift of giving structure to elements of these self-conceptions, by no means exhausting their meaning but at least articulating their contours.

For example, politics articulates territorial-legal self-conceptions whereby people know what is required in order to leave the shores of Libya in a boat and arrive in Italy (or Spain) *legally*. It does this through immigration law, border control, and other evidences of its authority, supported, if necessary, by coercive force alongside missions of mercy. Politics also bears witness to and sustains constitutional commitments whereby a head of state such as the Queen of the United Kingdom is recognised as the Crown whose government directs the business of Parliament with respect to both England *and* Northern Ireland. Politics also provides ways for the competing interests of rural and urban populations to be brought into disciplined communication, conflict and compromise. Think, to return to a previous example, of government guidance concerning the construction of new homes; or, for a further illustration, the (much-contested policies) on renewable energy, especially on-shore and off-shore wind farms.

In each case, politics enables people to recognise their identities and so organise their actions with regard to their place. This process by which politics enables identity to emerge may be categorised using the headings *differentiation* and *construal*. Libya as non-European is differentiated from Italy and Spain as European but all three are construed together in the common matter of migration in their shared Mediterranean place. Northern Ireland is differentiated from England but construed together in the common affair of continuing cultural identity and shared laws. The rural and urban are differentiated but construed together in finding solutions, however hotly disputed, to changing housing and energy needs. The *sine qua non* of common construal, in each case, is differentiation of identities based upon the places that people see as 'their' places. When those construals become less plausible, contest emerges: for example, independence movements in Scotland and Catalonia seek what seems to them more plausible construals of their places; the Campaign to Protect Rural England desires to protect cherished landscapes from the effects of climate change and thoughtless housing developments.

It is from within the process of differentiation and construal that representation, debate, and persuasion emerge. The recognition of the self through the other quickens the self's identification with a place but, in so doing, readies the self for a discourse that has the capacity to decentre the self in favour of the common task. For example, when two distinct local council authorities recognise that, while retaining the same pattern of local elected representation, identity, and accountability, residents in both areas will be better served by one common structure and shared services across the one shared place, such decentring has taken place. As an elected local councillor in 2011, I observed this challenging process first-hand in the plans for local authority services being shared by St Edmundsbury Borough Council and Forest Heath District Council.

The appeal of differentiated identities is that they sustain the drive to self-determination. The first-person plural 'our' depends upon the 'you' and the 'I' of self-determining individuals and associations, communities, and institutions. In domestic politics, such associations might include churches, residents groups, Trade Unions, Local Enterprise Partnerships, or ethnically defined associations such as a Turkish, Filipino, or Pakistani community network. These associations are many, overlapping nationally and locally. Sovereign nation-states are the bodies *par excellence* that claim citizens' loyalty, supporting self-awareness, and self-determination by enabling such associations to flourish alongside national citizenship. In this lies the heart of their continued appeal in Europe and globally today.[3]

Ethnocentrism, by contrast, offers self-determination without the kind of differentiation and construal about the good that marks discursive relations between and within communities and nation-states. To do better, nation-states must support an identity for individuals adequate for an 'I', a national 'our', and also, in some tense, complementary fashion, a transnational 'our'. This identity is adequate not totalising, enabling identification with a territory, but not encouraging the impression that such identification exhausts the possibilities of human life.[4]

Thus it is national identity that grounds a meaningful cosmopolitanism, the privilege of those who have passports. No one is *in fact* a citizen of the world. Nation-states can claim allegiance because they can provide the self-determination people need. For, under the protection that nation-states provide, the space people occupy in differentiation from their neighbours, near and far, may be conceived of as a place liveable in social peace. Such peace precisely arises only when places are shared through orderly if at times boisterous discussion, compromise and negotiation (see Hordern, 2014). Such an ethos, giving rise to openness to disciplined negotiation with neighbouring peoples, is a chief fruit of an adequate political identity.

Sufficient agreement on goods

To conceive of oneself in a place and yet construe the concerns of one's national and international neighbours as shared requires sufficient agreement on the goodness of goods or, at least, sufficient agreement about how goods are evaluated. To the question 'sufficient for what?', therefore, comes the reply 'sufficient for the peaceful communication of neighbours with one another' when 'communication' bears the burden of meaning described above, incorporating both shared conversation and shared activity. Agreement depends on procedures for discussion whereby goods become commonly reckoned *as* good.

Goods come in at least four forms. A discussion of these forms will shed light on the interrelation of the EU with national identity.

First, there are goods whose value may be discerned in a market such as the EU's Single (Internal) Market. Other chapters develop this theme in more technical ways that draw out this market's strengths and weaknesses. I note here that peoples' communication in marketable goods is basic to a sense of place. Interdependent trade relations between cultivated places can establish social communications that make for peace. As the Danube flows through the nations of continental Europe, including member states of the European Union, trade communication may help in forming channels of peace, worn into the fabric of land and social relations. As the English Channel and the Thames form a historic trade route between Great Britain and other nation-states so communication is formed by the ebb and flow of trust and distrust, like an inland waterway tidal system circumscribed by steep banks of contract.[5]

Theologically speaking, it is through the goods of *creation*, worked on by humanity, that such communication, trust and peace are achieved and renewed. The notion of such 'goods' depends on the Christian doctrine that goods have their goodness on account of the creative work of God who *is* good. The question of what goods are good *for* invites the process of human practical reasoning as to how, in particular circumstances, such goods are to be enjoyed and what market value, if any, should be placed on them. What is required for the argument here is that sufficient agreement that *these* goods of creation are valuable and that there is some way of communicating about their value makes possible the process of negotiation, not least about the money value of goods. The Christian doctrine of creation offers a unifying account to interpret the way that the peoples of nation-states in the EU, having an adequate identity through identification with their places, may be bound together in sufficient agreement and negotiated compromise about the goods of the created order.[6]

Second, for these goods to be made available, one good must be in principle recognised, namely the good of labour in the single market which makes the created goods of the world accessible to people inside and outside the EU. Good work is at the heart of the identification with place that makes the Union plausible. Work's value is institutionalised variously but perhaps most starkly in the Schengen agreement. Accession to Schengen is a closely guarded crossing-point, whereby neighbours from diverse nation-states recognise one another as those who value the goodness of work and will not abuse open borders by becoming parasitic on fellow EU citizens' labour.

The opt-out exercised by Ireland and the UK signals that such recognition is hard-won among European citizens and governments, but hardly insulates such polities from the question (or problem) of free movement. Indeed, when member states fear that newcomers joining Schengen may abuse their welcome, as witnessed by the hesitant hand offered by Germany and the United Kingdom towards Bulgaria and Romania, such fear reveals underlying beliefs about national identity. The ethos of work itself stands as a humane vocation above and beyond the euro or pound sterling.[7] For it concerns the spirit and heart of each culture's citizen and associations. A nation that sees work as the pinnacle of its identity may look suspiciously at cultures where work has not produced similar levels of prosperity to its own or seems to occupy a lower place in the social ecology, prized but submitted to family, religion, or rest. Such social differences can all too easily become the occasion for sweeping judgments against international neighbours as feckless, lazy, or worse, judgments unsupported (or only ambiguously corroborated) by data about actual working hours or productivity, data which itself requires considerable interpretation.[8]

The EU's capacity to allow for significant cultural difference about how and why work is good is a test of its continued appeal. More subtly, there are the various ways in which different cultures adapt to the challenges of a modern economy *vis-à-vis* the manner of handling created goods. To conceive of the created goods of the world as demanding of us that *we* adapt our work to *them* shows a humility that commonly has the benefit of making nations prosperous, at least in the short term.

But flexibility is not only the ability to respond to emergent economic trends. Rather, it involves recognising that the costs for non-marketable goods of the adaptability required by economies heavily weighted towards financial services and banking rather than manufacture and technology may itself be a good reason for a culture's non-adaptation. For example, some traditional cultures might refuse adaptation to work that requires a high degree of abstraction from tangible goods. The speedy adaptability that the promise of prosperity in a modern globalised economy elicits *seems* to have been less in evidence in southern European nations, such as Cyprus, Portugal, and Greece, than in Germany, the Netherlands, or the UK, which have managed to combine financial services with more specialised and high-tech manufacturing. Differences in cultural attitudes towards work must shape the EU's aspiration to become a moral union of trust in which each carries its own load while having the wherewithal to support others who are struggling to carry theirs in a global market.

Third, there are other goods, beyond the good of work and cultural adaptability (or reasoned resistance to adaptation), which are not communicable according to normal market rules but about which sufficient agreement is important. Two examples, marriage and knowledge, will make the point.

Marriage has long been recognised as an important good by Europeans, though its practice has varied. Marriages may bind individuals from separate nations together but are not to be bought and sold. A European Union in which, through European citizenship, the love, friendship and fruitfulness proper to marriage are enabled to grow unhindered by national boundaries is humane. More controversially, where there is disagreement about the nature of 'marriage', the negotiation of transnational cultural change by individual nation-states – regarding, for example, same-sex marriage or adoption rights for same-sex couples – is significantly inflected by obligations real and perceived towards wider European mores. Though marriage itself may not be marketable, the social price of entry into the market may, for some at least, be rather high.[9]

Knowledge is a good that, through the growing trend of Open Access scholarly publishing agreements, is moving out from quasi-market rules into free-to-view patterns of participation. While the research agendas that drive the creation of new knowledge, in national and European research, are quite reasonably linked to member states' economic interests, knowledge gained through publicly funded research is losing its price tag by being made freely available. The European Research Area aims to model to the world a responsible attitude to intellectual goods, especially in science and technology. If it can do so while securing the necessary patents and in the face of nation-states' own economic interests, it will boost European hopes for tackling transnational challenges such as climate change and food security (see Eve, 2014).

In the goods of marriage and knowledge, there are commonalities which cross borders binding peoples together in sufficient agreements to address perceived grand challenges, whether social or scientific. But sufficient agreement is not total agreement. This is indicated, on the one hand, by the consistent and firm resistance of Poland to legal recognition of same-sex unions (*The Economist*, 2013) and, on the other, by Italy and Spain's sustained opposition to the official European preference for the translation of patents into German, French, and English (*Spain v. Council*, 2013). These disagreements indicate that commonalities in goods, which are not reducible to market value or which, like Open Access knowledge, break the mould of markets, provide special opportunities for the deliberative, democratic discourse that makes a European Union conceivable.

The fourth and final good is one that is neither commensurate with the market nor shareable across national boundaries nor easily adaptable to the development of supranational institutions or transcultural mores. It is the good of a place called 'home' from which people go out and to which they return. The goods of marital friendship and knowledge enable people to recognise home as home and to care for it with informed wisdom. A key challenge for the EU, especially those most mobile within its borders, concerns how motivation for action that supports adequate political identity and sufficient agreement on goods relates to the deep consciousness of this place called home. The *oikonomia* upon which the interrelation of member states depends and through which flows the trust which strengthens moral union seems dependent on what Roger Scruton (2013) has called *oikophilia*, the basic human motivation to care for and love one's home. Scruton sees in the great ecological challenges that face humanity a testing of people's capacity to identify with their homes sufficiently so as to act to preserve those homes as liveable places for future generations. This tension between near and far lies at the heart of the crisis of European identity and will occupy much of the rest of this chapter.

Adequate identity and sufficient agreement in theological perspective

As noted above, Williams has claimed that the theological *interplay* of ultimate and penultimate allegiances – towards the Kingdom of God and the state – has been the crucible of the distinctively European democratic vision. For Europeans the question of 'home' was traditionally rooted in being a pilgrim people seeking an eternal home in the age to come while resident in particular places in the here and now. The ancient Hebrew prophet Jeremiah's proclamation to the exiled Israelites in Babylon was to build houses and settle down while waiting for their restoration to the Promised Land (Jeremiah 29:1–23). Home was both near and far, here now but also yet to come.

For such a vision, the tasks of identity and agreement are actually *energised* by being adequate and sufficient, rather than comprehensive and complete. Over against the fear endemic in Europe's twenty-first century economic crisis, a theology which argues that the disclosure of true identity and total consensus is *deferred* until politics is no more, at the second Advent of Christ, frees citizens from fear to work and pray steadily for the peace of their member state and the states of their neighbours. Christian theology expects only *partial* agreement on the value of marketable goods between and within nation-states and only *partial* consensus, if any, about the *quality* of those goods that break the mould of markets, such as marriage and knowledge. The pronouncements of successive Bishops of Rome on this matter illustrate the kind of disagreements we should continue to expect.[10]

This theological position may be experienced as an unwelcome cold shower by those who expect steady 'progress' towards the ever-closer convergence of European minds. Such hope should properly be called an 'over-realised epistemology', inasmuch as it expects the perfectly integrated communion proper only to the Kingdom of God to be worked out in the here and now. But few European visionaries are quite so unrealistic. A chastened Europeanism, with reduced expectations about total agreement across member states and tolerance of those who reject 'progressive' policies, should enable a better quality of debate, especially as regards social institutions such as marriage.

Places to live

The preceding sections have explored the kinds of identity and agreement in political life that seem necessary for a peaceful interrelation between the citizens and governments of European member states. In these final two sections, two ways of understanding citizen motivation, participation, and identity in the EU will be examined and given explicitly theological analysis.[11] In this first section, I will discuss further a positive vision of European places for people to live well, beginning, however, with some pressures on those places.

Pressures on places

While large parts of European citizenry have become more mobile in their working practices and more global in their outlook, Europeans at large still hunger for an affective political experience through which natural human desires for place, rather than space, can be met. The interplay of mobility and love of place has contributed to the rise of a new notion of patriotism, developed to support an emerging European consciousness. Jürgen Habermas argues for a 'constitutional patriotism' that addresses the "tension between the universalism of an egalitarian legal community and the particularism of a community united by historical destiny [which] is built into the very concept of the national state" (1998b: 115). For Habermas, European cosmopolitanism undermines 'ethnocentric' self-interpretations and dangerous notions of a *Volksnation*. More controversially, he believes that global political conditions are bringing about the decline of the nation-state and the emergence of post-national forms of political identification (1998b: 105–107). As regards identity and agreement, his positive proposal is that

> constitutional rights and principles . . . form the fixed point of reference for any constitutional patriotism that situates the system of rights within the historical context of a legal community. These must be enduringly linked with the motivations and convictions of the citizens, for without such a motivational anchoring they could not become the driving force behind the dynamically conceived project of producing an association of individuals who are free and equal.
> (Habermas, 1994: 134)

For constitutional patriotism, what "unites a nation of citizens, as opposed to a *Volksnation*, is not some primordial substrate but rather an intersubjectively shared context of possible mutual understanding" (Habermas, 1998a: 159). This means that, as Muller puts it, "citizens are asked to reflect critically upon particular traditions and group identities in the name of shared universal principles." A national consciousness, with its "attachments and loyalties" should be constantly revised through a "critical, highly self-conscious back-and-forth between actually existing traditions and institutions, on the one hand, and the best universal norms and ideas that can be worked out, on the other", a process which involves "a critical distancing from inherited beliefs" (Muller 2007: 28–29). This is the route to an identity adequate to the twenty-first century and an agreement on goods suitable for global, cosmopolitan life.

This constitutional patriotism, in which universal principles both depend on and criticise traditions, puts pressure on the sense of place we have been considering in two ways. The first is that it requires "a continuous civic self-interrogation and open argument about the past" (Muller 2007: 34). For Muller, the process of "European integration has helped Western European countries to gain some distance from their own pasts, as these pasts ceased to serve the particular post-war function as moral foundations of individual nations; integration lessened the need for national self-assertion, for homogenous narratives of national continuity" (2007: 107). On this reckoning, mindfulness of tradition does not require *commitment* to the traditional forms of life that have depended on settled places. Instead, the course is steered towards a post-national, post-conventional political consciousness.

Second, if political life represents a compromise between a nation-state's forms of local life and European universal norms, then the nation-state – still less any local community – must not be seen as a sufficient arena for the development of a democratic consciousness. The question such constitutional patriotism presses is how traditions and places relate to the procedures whereby the peoples of nation-states debate and cooperate with each other across national boundaries. The concern that follows is whether attachment to place, whereby people begin to reflect and deliberate about sharing goods in common, can survive and thrive in a politics whose discourse operates on the level of essentially transnational procedures, themselves drawn from no tradition or place at all.

Oikophilia

Habermas's core concern is to explain "what will motivate people to engage in the self-critical, other-regarding practice of deliberation in a democratic community" (Laborde, 2002: 595–596). The question of motivation is also Roger Scruton's, although he answers it rather differently. He draws on the trans-generational, Burkean notion of *oikophilia* introduced above with respect to sufficient agreement about the good of home. For Scruton, motivation is bound up with the conservation of places in which individuals participate and social life flourishes. In contrast to the mythic social contractarian 'we', Scruton appeals to "ways of forming a first-person plural [that] are [not] so conscious" (2006: 6). He suggests that there are "other, more instinctive and more immediate, forms of membership ... which have the desired result of making it possible for people to live together in a state of mutual support." In particular, he describes how in England, the instincts of kinship and religion, under the influence of "home", that localised "focus of loyalty", have brought about remarkable cultural achievements (Scruton,

2006: 19). For example, the notion that the land has been held in trust as a place to be cared for and passed on to one's own descendants has gone deep down into English law shaping the sense of national identity. He cites as evidence in English law the law of trusteeship and the "law of the land", institutionalised in dispersed courts and the right, in serious cases, to jury trial (Scruton, 2006: 119).

Scruton believes that liberals, while outwardly despising this conservative, localised, trans-generational vision, secretly desire

> an experience of membership that will open the heart, and also close the mind. At a certain point the strain of living without an 'us' and a 'them' becomes intolerable. On the lonely heights of abstract choice nothing comforts and nothing consoles. The Kantian imperatives seem to blow more freezingly, and the unfed soul eventually flees from them, down into the fertile valleys of attachment.
>
> (1990: 326)

These valleys are the places in which adequate identity emerges and sufficient agreement can be sought. While Habermas avoids Scruton's critique to some extent because he argues for a constant movement between the valleys and the heights, the local and the universal, a life *between* facts and norms, Scruton and Habermas are, in the end, irreconcilable. For Scruton insists that every

> political order depends, and ought to depend, upon a non-political idea of membership. And to the extent that it emancipates itself from that idea ... to that extent does it lose its motivating force, just as individuals lose their moral identity and will, to the extent that their prejudices, pieties and moral instincts are cancelled by the abstract imperatives of the 'pure rational chooser'.
>
> (1990: 303)

The non-political is especially concerned with the localised rather than the dislocated. By contrast, Habermas' rejection of a pre-political *Volksnation* and recommendation of a post-national consciousness embodied in supranational, continental institutions together undermine the consciousness and motivation for participation which Scruton calls *oikophilia*, an awareness of being at home in one's place.

Ecology

This difference has significant practical ramifications. For Scruton, motivation to care for a place and participate in its politics comes from this domestic root. He argues that a humane notion of citizenship must be ecologically compelling. One rationale for closer union is that European nations should have sufficient common commitments to act together on global challenges such as climate change. And yet, Scruton argues, the only plausible source for the attitudinal change required is the *oikophilia* that much environmental policy ignores.

Furthermore, Scruton notes that while "we are reluctant these days to provide these [environmental] obligations with … theological backing … for religious believers, unchosen obligations are not only vital to building a durable social order, but also properly owed to God" (2013: 224). Unchosen obligations that incur special local loves are argued for by Nigel Biggar. Over against an indiscriminate, cosmopolitan love, Biggar has described how "an individual should feel special affection for, loyalty toward, and gratitude to those communities, customs, and institutions that have benefited her by inducting her into human goods" (2014: 7).[12] This is no ethnocentric jingoism but an affirmation of a shared created order, allowing for both the universal duties such an order imposes and the fact that enjoyment of that order involves being localised. Recall the earlier emphasis on the goods of creation as basic to adequate identity and sufficient agreement. The created order is always local first. Humans are spatial beings, engaging with creation always in its proximate forms, although they may also participate in more distant relations, especially now through electronic communication in goods. But an attention to locality is what makes transnational discussion about goods possible since goods must at the beginning and in the end be good *for us*; and we – you and I – are first and last local. The localisation of discussion of what is good is the necessary basis for citizens to engage in wider, even transnational debates.

As for ecological concerns, Scruton argues that aesthetically toned attachment is what motivates people to care for their place (2013: 383–385). He observes that the assault on aesthetics through initiatives in energy production, such as wind-farms, threaten people's love of place and therefore their ecological, transnational consciousness.[13] For love of place motivates people to take responsibility for their environment and internalise the costs attendant on such responsibility rather than externalising them to others, whether living, yet unborn or of another place.[14] Such a core motivation as *oikophilia* must not be taken for granted or ridden over roughshod. To do so is to invite precisely the alienated responses that the unrepresented feel. Politics must therefore be *humanely localised* as a protection against ethnocentric nationalism and as the only sure motivational route towards an ecologically just and peaceful life for all. The problem Scruton identifies is that such a politics conflicts with EU bureaucrats whose "edicts … are propagated without respect for national differences or existing sentiments of legitimacy, and with no real expectation that anyone will be motivated to obey them. The result is a gradual erosion of respect for law" exemplified in the failure of the Common Fisheries Policy which led to the overturning of traditional jurisdictions and the sharp decline in fish-stocks (2013: 312–313).

While this is certainly not an argument against all wind farms (for example), it is an argument for ecological planning which attends to the *oikophilia* that motivates people to care for the world in the first place. Even some offshore wind farms, when visible from the coast, can destroy a people's sense of place. Recent contentious examples have included the Navitus Bay wind farm off the Jurassic Coast of Dorset, an area that enjoys UNESCO World Heritage Status. The threat of an insensitive policy is the destruction of the common loves, associations, communities, and localities that offer the best hope of a participatory politics and indeed a sustainable ecologically harmonious life.

Christian churches and European consciousness

The preceding argument has juxtaposed two responses to the challenge of adequate identity and sufficient agreement through two different descriptions of citizen motivation – commitment to universal principles anchored in but supervening on national institutions; and *oikophilia*, threatened today by lukewarm affirmations of attachment and bureaucracies insensitive to locality. What is at stake is how humane motivation to seek the common good is understood, a crucial theme for the consciousness of citizens of the EU and for the peace and prosperity of its member states.

As Williams' analysis indicated earlier, politics has not been alone in seeking wisdom on such matters. Although various ethnocentrisms have in fact been sponsored by some churches (e.g. the 'German Christians' or the Serbian Orthodox church during the Balkan wars), Christian churches, shaped by the theology outlined thus far, have often construed local agency and transnational concerns together in their self-understanding and in their relation to the societies and governments in which they live. As peoples in places, churches are ideally equipped to disclose the humane creaturely life, which makes for a local, highly motivated participation that has a transnational horizon, a consciousness that might make the EU live and breathe afresh. Other religious communities may also bring their own gifts and, indeed, problematic pasts, to this discussion. But, as Williams suggests, the interplay of political identity and specifically *Christian* faith, properly informed by past excellences and properly chastened by past distortions, provides peculiarly important insight into the interrelation of multiple poles of allegiance. Ecclesial identity affirms the creaturely quality of a transnational aspiration while interrogating European consciousness, ensuring that it only ever aspires to a provisional place in human hearts. This affirmation and interrogation is motivated both by convictions about human destiny in the new heaven and the new earth, for which no political identity can substitute, and by convictions about what constitutes a humane vocation now. Some concluding reflections about the life of churches will illustrate what this might mean.

The life of the early church, as seen in the New Testament books of Luke and Acts, discloses rival ways of understanding the interrelation of government, law, and locality and the formation of social consciousness.[15] Luke's narrative describes how Roman authorities failed to enact justice in the trials of Jesus and Paul, due in part to the universal, imperial legal structure and political culture that dominated their consciousness. Jesus, an innocent man, was condemned to death by Pilate whereas Paul was wrongly imprisoned and deported without intelligible charges. Imperial authority, being drawn from far-off Rome, failed to do justice at the local level. In some ways, ironically, the Roman Empire attempted to allow for *more* local allegiance and legal variation for prudential purposes (e.g. the tetrarchy permitted in first century Palestine) than is allowed for by the margin of appreciation doctrine recognised by the European Court of Justice (ECJ), in judging cases according to the Charter of Fundamental Rights of the European Union under the Lisbon Treaty, and by the European Court of Human Rights (ECtHR), in judging cases according to the European Convention on Human Rights.[16]

The point at issue with Habermas is that, if a Union of nation-states is to flourish, the ability to ensure continued participation of peoples in the politics of their own places is paramount to the continuation of justice; and the failure of the Roman Empire to enact justice is shown up by the life of the church. Local churches at their best, as traditional communities *par excellence*, may be foci for thoughtful action towards renewing political life in each member-state and across the EU. As communities living that tension between penultimate and ultimate discussed above, they ought to be committed to gathering locally in order to worship God and to preserve and renew 'places', bringing their gifts to the development of *oikophilia*. Since the home for which Christians ultimately hope is already guaranteed in the new heaven and the new earth, they are free for self-donation now in service of their neighbours, both near and far. They are free to make a home while they wait for home. Such an ethos both combats and invites temptation. The dark side of hoping for home is to abandon care for where one is – this is a constant hazard for Christian faith in Europe or elsewhere. But the way to overcome this temptation is not to take one's eye off the ultimate horizon but to walk towards it *through* the contemporary landscape drawing wisdom and insight from what is to come and working it out in the current moment. The bodily life of the future age compels Christians to be concerned for the humanisation of the localities of the present in order that space become and remain a place to live in social peace, a place not only for churches but for all people. Place is not then, about some narrow 'religious freedom' but more broadly about human freedom to enjoy peaceful social relations. The freedom of Christian people, energised ultimately by the incarnate, death, and mighty resurrection of Jesus Christ, provides wisdom about what constitutes freedom for all people to love and renew their own places. In short, the life of local churches should issue in that typically European source of civic participation, adequate identity and sufficient agreement on goods.

I note that these Scriptural and contemporary political insights are in tension with Scruton's thought. Scruton's concern for pre-political membership resembles to some extent the freedom of the church and, by extension, the social freedom of people. It seems to track the distinction between political authority and the society that gives political authority its rationale (O'Donovan and O'Donovan, 1999: 109). However, unlike the pre-political dimension of member states of the EU, which is now inaccessible, being hidden beneath the necessities of coercion and law, churches signal the possibility and in some measure the reality of human emancipation from diverse political identities for life in the kingdom of God. In this sense, the pre-political is dependent on the disclosure of true human freedom beyond coercive politics that will only come about at the second advent of Christ. It is precisely this horizon of freedom that protects the democracy that Europeans rightly value. For it suggests the accountability of political authority both to the citizenry and to God. Scruton, though he gestures in this direction, does not provide sufficient distinction between church and nation to foster this freedom or this kind of accountability.

Conclusion

The task of all citizens is daily to work for the sustenance and renewal of their places. This is something many do quite unselfconsciously and without the need for recourse to a conceptualisation of place, still less with thought of the influence of Christianity on European political life. However, at the level of local government, national government, and local churches, the renewal of place towards the kind of social peace that this life affords is a worthy goal, for which churches are commanded to pray and act. The surprising, powerful logic of Christian faith is that seeing this life in light of the life of the new heaven and the new earth precisely offers *renewal* to a participative, local, national, and even European political consciousness.

Notes

1 For historical analysis of nationalism in Germany in the post-World War Two period, especially the 1980s, see Evans (1987). The article critically assesses questions such as the quasi-mythological deployment in German discourse of 'the' Jews and 'the' Germans and the problems of national guilt, in relation both to some 'conservative' historians' attempt to recast the Nazi past and to the critiques advanced by Jürgen Habermas (on whom see further below) and others.
2 Cavanaugh (2009: 5, italics added) observes how the "myth of religious violence ... provides secular social orders with a stock character, the religious fanatic, to serve as *enemy*."
3 For theological and philosophical reflection on this theme, see Buchanan and Margaret (2003).
4 "A people with no relations has no identity, and the government of those with no identity has no legitimacy" (O'Donovan, 2005: 214).
5 For recent discussion of 'capitalist peace', see Schneider and Gleditsch (2012).
6 For theological reasoning concerning such goods, see O'Donovan (1986, esp. Chapters 1–2) and Finnis (2011: 81–99).
7 For discussions of work, see Hughes (2007) and Hordern (2010).

8 OECD data on this matter require interpretation; long hours do not, of course, necessarily entail greater productivity.
9 For analysis see Brewer (2014) and Paternotte and Kollman (2013).
10 For example, Pope Pius XI, *Casti Connubii* (1930) and Pope Francis, *Lumen Fidei* (2013: § 52).
11 See Hordern (2013: Chap. 4–5). The discussion here resituates and extends that argument with respect to 'place' and ecological considerations.
12 Biggar (2014: 11–13) further appeals to the affirmation of the *multiplicity* of linguistic communities in the events of Pentecost, to the affirmation of national identity and natural goods in Paul and Jesus, notwithstanding the relativisation of such identity and goods (e.g. marriage) in the New Testament (2014: 2–5).
13 See Scruton (2013: 274–83) for the general discussion of aesthetics.
14 For the notion of externalisation, see Scruton (2013: 151–9); offloading the costs on to future generations is deeply contrary to the Burkean beliefs of a conservative like Scruton.
15 I note that imaginative construals of this sort are not altogether outlandish in contemporary politics. Twice-elected Conservative Mayor of London, Boris Johnson, colleague and rival to David Cameron, has construed current European political life through the lens of the low bureaucracy, high-productivity, sexually adventurous and – to some degree – religiously tolerant *pax Romana*. Johnson (2007) knows about the brutality of the pre-Christian Roman Empire but nonetheless finds its remarkable capacity to attract the allegiance of many millions of people, principally 'Europeans' but also 'Turks' to a single central figure, Caesar, strangely alluring. Johnson's classical and political interests take him into theological terrain. For Johnson, the Christian story is remarkable in tracking elements of the birth of Augustus Caesar. However, the *contrast* he draws misunderstands the eschatological point, as seen in his comment that the "worship of the emperor Augustus was in itself a political act, an act of loyalty to Rome. The act of Christian worship did not carry any such political implications" (2007: 193). The point, as Williams indicates, is that it is precisely the difference between Christ's and Augustus' kingdoms which maintains the tension that gives European political consciousness its characteristic flavour. The political implications of Christian worship are far more extensive than Johnson's lens of Anglican-lite Christianity allows readers to perceive.
16 The margin of appreciation doctrine allows for a degree of variation in the application of law according to particular EU member state's (in the ECJ) or Council of Europe signatory's (in the ECtHR) local cultural or philosophical commitments. With respect to our earlier analysis of toleration of a range of doctrines of marriage, but this time with respect to the ECtHR and Council of Europe, an interesting analysis of an inconsistency in the use of the doctrine emerges in Paul Johnson: "Since the early 1980s, the Court's jurisprudence has shown a progressive narrowing of the margin of appreciation afforded to states in respect of sexual orientation issues. Nevertheless, the application of the doctrine remains somewhat inconsistent in respect of complaints brought to the Court by homosexual applicants. A key source of this inconsistency is variability in the importance that the Court attaches to the existence of a European consensus of opinion when determining the relevant margin of appreciation available to a state" (2011: 589). Not only is there uncertainty about the *importance* of an existing consensus but also the nature of any consensus if it exists and consistency in applying any consensus across differing types of cases. Johnson's interpretation is that the consensus was unwarrantably judged to be different regarding same-sex adoption and same-sex marriage or at least that the same consensus has been differentially applied but without clear warrant.

References

Biggar, N. (2014). *Between kin and cosmopolis: An ethic of the nation.* The Didsbury Lectures Series. Eugene, OR: Cascade.
Brewer, P. (ed.) (2014). Public opinion about gay rights and gay marriage. *International Journal of Public Opinion Research*, 26(3): 279–396.
Buchanan, A., and Margaret, M. (eds) (2003). *States, nations, and borders: The ethics of making boundaries.* Cambridge: Cambridge University Press.
Cavanaugh, W. (2009). *The myth of religious violence: Secular ideology and the roots of modern conflict.* Cambridge: Cambridge University Press.
Evans, R. (1987). The new nationalism and the old history: Perspectives on the west German Historikerstreit. *The Journal of Modern History*, 59(4): 761–797.
Eve, M. P. (2014). *Open access and the humanities: Contexts, controversies and the future.* Cambridge: Cambridge University Press.
Finnis, J. (2011). *Natural law and natural rights.* (2nd edn). Oxford: Oxford University Press.
Francis. (2013). *Lumen fidei.* 29 June. Retrieved from http://w2.vatican.va/content/francesco/en/encyclicals/documents/papa-francesco_20130629_enciclica-lumen-fidei.html.
Habermas, J. (1998a). Does Europe need a constitution? Response to Dieter Grimm. In Cronin, C. P. and De Greiff, P. (eds), *The inclusion of the other: Studies in political theory* (pp. 155–161). Cronin, C. (trans.). Cambridge, MA: MIT Press.
Habermas, J. (1998b). The European nation-state: On the past and future of sovereignty and citizenship. In Cronin, C. P. and De Greiff, P. (eds), *The inclusion of the other: Studies in political theory* (pp. 105–127). Cronin, C. (trans.). Cambridge, MA: MIT Press.
Habermas, J. (1994). Struggles for recognition in the democratic constitutional state. In Gutmann, A. (ed.), *Multiculturalism: Examining the politics of recognition.* Princeton, NJ: Princeton University Press.
Hordern, J. (2014). Loyalty, conscience and tense communion: Jonathan Edwards meets Martha Nussbaum. *Studies in Christian Ethics*, 27(2): 167–184.
Hordern, J. (2013). *Political affections: Civic participation and moral theology.* Oxford: Oxford University Press.
Hordern, J. (2010). *One nation but two cities: Christianity and the conservative party.* Swindon, England: Bible Society/Cambridge: KLICE.
Hughes, J. (2007). *The end of work: Theological critiques of capitalism.* Oxford: Blackwell.
Johnson, B. (2007). *The dream of Rome.* London: Harper Perennial.
Johnson, P. (2011). Homosexuality, freedom of assembly and the margin of appreciation doctrine of the European Court of Human Rights: *Alekseyev v Russia. Human Rights Law Review*, 11(3): 578–593.
Laborde, C. (2002). From constitutional to civic patriotism. *British Journal of Political Science*, 32(4): 591–612.
Muller, J.-W. (2007). *Constitutional patriotism.* Princeton, NJ: Princeton University Press.
O'Donovan, O. (2005). *The ways of judgment.* Grand Rapids, MI: Eerdmans.
O'Donovan, O. (1986). *Resurrection and moral order: An outline for evangelical ethics.* Grand Rapids, MI: Eerdmans.
O'Donovan, O., and O'Donovan, J. L. (eds) (1999). *From Irenaeus to Grotius: A Sourcebook in Christian political thought.* Grand Rapids, MI: Eerdmans.
Paternotte, D., and Kollman, K. (2013). Regulating intimate relationships in the European polity: Same-sex unions and policy convergence. *Social Politics*, 20(4): 510–533.

Pius XI. (1930). *Casti connubii.* 31 December. Retrieved from http://w2.vatican.va/content/pius-xi/en/encyclicals/documents/hf_p-xi_enc_31121930_casti-connubii.html.
Schneider, G., and Gleditsch, N. P. (eds) (2012). *Assessing the capitalist peace.* London: Routledge.
Scruton, R. (2013). *Green philosophy: How to think seriously about the planet.* London: Atlantic.
Scruton, R. (2006). *England: An elegy.* London: Continuum.
Scruton, R. (1990). In defence of the nation. In Scruton, R. (ed.), *The philosopher on Dover Beach: Essays* (pp. 299–328). Manchester: Carcanet.
Spain v Council. (2013). C-274/11. European Court of Justice. Retrieved from http://curia.europa.eu/juris/documents.jsf?num=C-274/11.
The Economist. (2013). Uneasy bedfellows. 4 February. Retrieved from www.economist.com/blogs/easternapproaches/2013/02/polish-politics.
Williams, R. (2012). *Faith in the public square.* London: Bloomsbury.

Part 2
Religion and the policies of the EU

8 European religious freedom and the EU

Thomas Schirrmacher and Jonathan Chaplin

Introduction[1]

Religious freedom is one of the most distinctive hallmarks of the identity of contemporary Europe. That every person may have their own religion or belief, and may choose and change it, openly and not secretly, and that religious belief is neither prescribed by the state nor imposed by other societal forces, is a basic prerequisite of human freedom, and a momentous achievement of modern Europe (Ahdar and Leigh, 2013). Closely related to religious freedom is the principle of 'state neutrality towards religion', a central implication of which is that the state may not presume to adjudicate among rival religious truth-claims. As the European Court of Human Rights has put it, "the State's duty of neutrality and impartiality [among beliefs] is incompatible with any power on the State's part to assess the legitimacy of religious beliefs … and … requires the State to ensure mutual tolerance between opposing groups."[2]

The European Union (EU) has inherited this legacy. EU institutions themselves, however, came late to religious freedom, for understandable reasons.[3] As a treaty-based multi-national organization, the EU may only act where it has been given 'competence' by its member states. From the beginning it was assumed that the emergent institutions would defer to the jurisdiction of member states on matters such as religious freedom or church-state relationships. The EU is not, therefore, competent to challenge the divergent approaches of member states towards religion, many of which do not adhere to strict state neutrality but grant differential public status to particular denominations (Madeley, 2003). The EU's capacity to shape religious freedom directly is thus limited, and its posture towards religious freedom is determined both by the inherited traditions of its member states, and the wider legal framework of the European Convention on Human Rights (ECHR) as elaborated by the jurisprudence of the European Court of Human Rights (ECtHR).

The chapter will not consider, except by way of illustration, the diverse state-religion relationships or religious freedom practices of individual EU member states.[4] It will only outline in broad terms the impact of the ECHR and ECtHR on European religious freedom at large, on which a substantial literature exists.[5] Nor will it consider the multi-layered relationship between religion and the EU's wider public order.[6] The chapter has four sections. The first relates the neglected story of how the wider European regime of religious freedom derives substantially from the historical and theological struggle of minority religions – mostly dissenting Protestants – for toleration in the sixteenth and seventeenth centuries. The second identifies four theological arguments for religious freedom and state neutrality coming to the fore during that early modern struggle and still relevant today. The third sketches the framework of religious freedom in Europe, as principally shaped by the ECHR, which sets the parameters within which the EU operates. The fourth section traces how the EU itself has, since the 1970s, entered upon the terrain of religious freedom, notes some of its achievements in this field and identifies some of the challenges it faces today, especially those impacting upon religious minorities.

European religious freedom: a very short history

Today, religious freedom is extensively and intensively, if not uniformly or consistently, recognized in theory and practice across most member states of the EU and by the Union itself. Yet religious freedom, unknown for much of the world's history, evolved in the European context at great cost and required the defeat of what Zagorin (2003: Chap. 2) terms "the Christian theory of religious persecution."[7] How can this be explained? The dominant narrative is that religious freedom is the consequence of the secular Enlightenment's breaking out of the iron grip of archaic and intolerant European religious traditions, and this narrative can muster much evidence in its support (Zagorin, 2003).[8] In this part we recount the less familiar narrative of how the European achievement of religious freedom was substantially birthed in the historical struggle of minority religions – mostly dissenting Protestants – for religious toleration.

A first European step in the direction of religious freedom was the 1526 resolution of the Diet of Speyer, overturning the 1521 Edict of Worms in which Emperor Charles V had outlawed Lutheranism on pain of confiscatory penalties or death for anyone found in possession of Luther's writings. The resolution officially tolerated two religions, Catholic and Lutheran, for the first time in Europe for over a millennium. The 1555 Peace of Augsburg then established the principle *cuius regio, eius religio* (whose realm, his the religion) across the Holy Roman Empire. In the Edict of Nantes of 1598, the scope of toleration was extended in France to Calvinists. Yet neither Augsburg nor Nantes signaled a commitment to religious freedom for individuals but only a ratification of *de facto* religious diversity between states. It did not imply a principled recognition of religious freedom but only what Rawls terms a "modus vivendi", a pragmatic laying down of arms in response to exhaustion and stalemate (Rawls, 1996: 145ff). An entire century in the development of religious freedom was then squandered as enormously costly religiously fuelled wars ravaged Central Europe and then France, England, and Holland,[9] after which Europe only recovered the fragile pragmatic achievements of Augsburg via the Peace of Westphalia of 1648.[10]

Zagorin has argued that theories of toleration appearing in the late sixteenth and the seventeenth centuries "were the work of profoundly Christian if also unorthodox thinkers, not of minds inclined to religious indifference or unbelief" and were unintelligible apart from such work (2003: 9). Christian humanist Erasmus prepared the ground (Zagorin, 2003: 49–68), but arguments for religious toleration per se first emerged on the radical wing of Protestantism.[11] It was not the achievement of established Protestant churches but of free churches, sects, and spiritualists, ranging from the Puritans to the Quakers.[12]

Religious toleration was first openly advocated by the early sixteenth-century pacifist Anabaptists who, persecuted by both Catholics and Protestants, declared themselves firmly against all religious coercion (Estep, 1975: 194–8). The first explicit exponent of a *theory* of religious toleration, however, was Sebastian Castellio, a close associate of John Calvin who, aroused by Calvin's consent to the burning of Servetus in 1553, argued passionately for religious freedom and against the use of force to suppress heresy and indeed against the very concept of heresy itself (Zagorin, 2003: Ch. 4).[13] A major source of arguments for religious toleration appeared in England in the early seventeenth century. The first known tract that called for complete religious freedom, written by the English Baptist Leonard Busher, was published in 1614 at a time when most leaders of the dominant confessions of the time (Anglican, Catholic, Puritan) defended enforced religious uniformity (Busher, 1614). While the tract had little immediate impact, the arguments it advanced began to achieve greater sophistication and wider circulation during the period of the English Revolution. Subsequently the 1689 Act of Toleration established widespread religious freedom, at least for (Trinitarian) Protestants.

One of the most forceful theological arguments for religious freedom emerging in this period came from the Baptist-inclined and spiritualist minister Roger Williams. Williams migrated with the Puritans to Massachusetts in 1631 and founded the new colony of Rhode Island in 1636, serving as governor. His vigorous polemic against intolerance, *The Bloudy Tenent of Persecution*, was published in London in 1644 while he was visiting the city to seek a royal charter for the colony (Williams, 1644). The book argued, strikingly, for universal religious toleration and a full separation of church and state, and both on explicitly theological grounds. It was, Zagorin asserts, "not only the most sweeping indictment of religious persecution thus far written by any Englishman but one of the most comprehensive justifications of religious liberty to appear during the seventeenth century" (Zagorin, 2003: 196).

Following the devastation of a century of religious warfare, dissenting Protestant arguments like those of Busher, Williams, the Levellers, and others began to acquire greater momentum (if not invariably for theological reasons). They were to be substantially reinforced and extended, while also cast into a more 'rationalist' language, by Enlightenment thinkers and statesmen. In England the classic case for religious freedom was Locke's decisive *Letter Concerning Toleration* (1689), which utilized both theological and Enlightenment rationalist arguments.[14]

Gradually, the political and demographic incongruities of the Westphalian legacy began to show and modern European states took successive steps towards greater religious freedom, such as for Arminians in Prussia and Jews in Austria in the eighteenth century. Articles 10 and 11 of the French Revolutionary Declaration of the Rights of Man and Citizen (1789) proclaimed the principle of freedom of thought, expression, and religion as a universal right (although the Revolution was soon to descend into its own grotesque form of religious persecution). We will not rehearse the fitful history of the progressive expansion and consolidation of religious freedom in nineteenth- and twentieth-century Europe.[15] The purpose of this section has simply been to draw renewed attention to the decisive, if neglected, role of Protestant minority demands for religious toleration as a vital contributor to the achievement of European religious freedom. Religious freedom is very substantially the outcome of a theologically inspired struggle for freedom by Christian minority churches against Christian majority churches. It remains a struggle in which today's European religious minorities have a great deal at stake.

Theological arguments for religious freedom

Out of this turbulent post-Reformation history some recurring arguments for religious freedom came to the fore. While the political and legal conclusions of these arguments are largely familiar to modern readers (many will know them principally through the medium of Locke's *Letter*), such arguments should not be straightforwardly equated with those mounted later from the platform of the secular liberal rationalism of the Enlightenment. It is the latter that have dominated Western discourses of freedom and rights since the Universal Declaration of 1948. Here we briefly render in our own terms four of the decisive theological arguments for religious freedom that came to prominence in these dissenting minority Protestant traditions and which, we submit, remain pertinent today.[16] The key claim is that religious freedom is not to be accepted on 'modus vivendi' grounds as a temporary, pragmatic adjustment to lost ground but is a compelling mandate inherent to the Christian faith itself.

Four categories of argument can be distinguished: ethical, epistemological, ecclesiological, and constitutional.[17] The central *ethical* argument is that the Christian gospel – mirroring the life and explicit teaching of Jesus and the consistent practice of the early church – commits its followers to a stance of universal neighbourliness and peaceableness and prohibits religious hatred or coercion. Dissenting Protestants were painfully aware of how religious coercion, not only against themselves, invariably fed public strife.[18] They were among the first to press the case that religious freedom is essential to civic peace among rival believers. Peace would emerge, not by believers abandoning or moderating their truth claims, but by propagating them solely by means of respectful persuasion.

One of the key *epistemological* arguments appealed to the nature of genuine faith as a wholly free response to God (Luther, 1974: 51–71).[19] Here biblical texts were appealed to, which insisted that the only worship God finds acceptable is one borne of voluntary love rather than inducement or coercion.[20] The inner orientation of the conscience, the 'heart', of human beings may not and cannot, be compelled. Forced or induced conversion or conformity is thus a contradiction in terms. Some advocates of religious toleration combined this claim with the related one, that while there may be certainty on the 'essentials' of the faith, this was lacking in respect of 'secondary' matters of belief and practice, and that, in any case, the distinction between the two was often hard to determine. It was therefore impossible to appeal, as defenders of intolerance frequently did, to any notion of truths that must be known to all and that could thus only be denied perversely and culpably. Others also grounded the epistemological claim more broadly in a theology of the created nature of humanity. Since all human beings, not only Christians, are created in the image of God (Genesis 1:26–27), all possess not only an identical dignity and worth but also an identical capacity to seek and acquire knowledge of God, whatever they might do with that capacity (Waldron, 2010). To restrict the entitlement to religious freedom only to Christians (or only a certain type) would be an arbitrary frustration of a universal, divinely bestowed human possibility.[21]

The third claim is *ecclesiological*. Dissenting Protestants may have striven to sever ties with a dominant religious institution but, for most, this was only in order to reconstitute themselves as a distinctive ecclesial community liberated to practice an alternative, more 'faithful' form of communal obedience. The freedom to believe was both an individual and a collective entitlement; the former could only be authentically realized through intense participation in a believing fellowship, one that might impose high expectations of conformity to communal belief and behaviour. While most Protestant dissenters were committed to ecclesial voluntarism (they construed the church as a voluntary association), most also rejected spiritual individualism (a view implying that corporate religious practice was incidental to true faith).

The fourth, *constitutionalist* claim is that because genuine (God-pleasing) faith cannot be forced, government may not impose any type of civil penalty upon those who uphold or reject any particular faith. This claim had to be vindicated against the arguments of both the Catholic church and the magisterial Reformers and their followers who generally upheld the widespread contemporary view that enforced religious conformity "was necessary not only for religion's sake but for the preservation of political unity and peace" (Zagorin, 2003: 82). Most dissenting Protestants endorsed the long-standing Christian belief that rulers have been given a distinctive but limited mandate by God to establish an external ('worldly', 'temporal', or 'secular') civil order of peace and justice and were therefore deserving of obedience. Here St. Paul's affirmation of the pagan Roman state as "God's servant" was standardly invoked by all sides (Romans 13:1–7). Unlike the ancient Israelite polity that was divinely mandated to enforce religious obedience upon the 'people of the covenant', the polity as depicted by all New Testament writers lacked any such authority. Such an argument subverted the long-standing Christendom assumption that there could be officially 'Christian' (or 'chosen') territorial nations. While the modern notion of 'state neutrality' is not found explicitly in the writing of these Dissenters, their denial of any right on the part of the state to determine the truth of religion anticipates the ECtHR's repudiation of the competence of the state to "assess the legitimacy of religious belief."

Wolterstorff draws out a necessary implication by noting that, on such a view, membership of the church generates among its members a compelling new loyalty that undermines any fusion of political and religious identities: under the 'new covenant' the church "cannot express the shared religious identity of [a whole] people, since there is no such identity. ... Whenever the church enters a society, it destroys whatever religio-ethical unity that society may have possessed. Now there is only religious pluralism" (Wolterstorff, 2012: 123). The implication of this argument was that, where the state confined itself to the establishment of civil peace, dissenting and minority – even non-Christian – beliefs might also flourish; a plurality of faiths could peacefully coexist within the same territory. Some dissenters eventually concluded that there existed a *divinely conferred* universal right to religious freedom.

During the eighteenth century these theologically grounded arguments increasingly came to be framed in the secular Enlightenment's language of a natural individual right to free conscience or rational autonomy, seen as an inherent, rather than divinely conferred, ground of human dignity. Religious freedom was increasingly conceived as one implication of a wider freedom of the autonomous individual mind to follow the imperatives of reason wherever they led. Religious freedom "became largely separated from its religious roots and thus drained of ... religious inspiration. [It] also came to be more and more justified during the Enlightenment primarily as a natural right associated with other natural rights. These developments infused the idea of toleration with an increasingly secularized character" (Zagorin, 2003: 292–293).

Thus, while the notion that religious freedom was the condition of a free human response to a divine summons to seek the truth was upheld within Christian churches, it progressively lost ground in wider European human rights discourse. Yet the story of the earlier origins of European religious freedom serves as a confirming instance of Witte's wider claim that "the Enlightenment was not so much a wellspring of Western rights as a watershed in a long stream of rights thinking that began more than a millennium before" (2007: 23). While the massive contribution of secular Enlightenment arguments to the realization of modern European religious freedom cannot be gainsaid, the pioneering theological arguments advanced by dissenting

Protestant minorities anticipated much of their abiding political content. As we shall see, the EU today finds itself shaped by both powerful cultural streams, and its anxious religious minorities often find themselves caught in the middle.

Religious freedom and minorities under the ECHR

Religious freedom in the EU is determined both by the diverse state-religion traditions of individual states and by the ECHR and the ECtHR. While the former remain powerful, the latter two are increasingly influential in determining the shape of European religious freedom.[22] In response to the systematic violations of human rights under Nazism and Soviet Communism, the Council of Europe of 10 member states, founded in 1949, drew up the European Convention on Human Rights (ECHR) which came into force in 1953; all members of the Council of Europe must sign it. The ECHR was a major milestone in the evolution of the legal protection of religious freedom in Europe and the first attempt to make legally binding the aspirations of the 1948 United Nations Universal Declaration of Human Rights. The ECtHR is the key institution for ensuring compliance with the ECHR, including the protection of religious freedom.[23] Since all EU member states are members of the Council, their own very diverse commitments on religious freedom are being brought incrementally into convergence by their adherence to the ECHR.

The ECHR secures robust formal protections of religious freedom, of particular value to religious minorities. Article 9, entitled "Freedom of thought, conscience and religion", contains a powerful affirmation of religious freedom:

> 1. Everyone has the right to freedom of thought, conscience and religion; this right includes freedom to change his religion or belief, and freedom, either alone or in community with others and in public or private, to manifest his religion or belief, in worship, teaching, practice and observance.
> 2. Freedom to manifest one's religion or beliefs shall be subject only to such limitations as are prescribed by law and are necessary in a democratic society in the interests of public safety, for the protection of public order, health or morals, or for the protection of the rights and freedoms of others.
>
> (Council of Europe, 1950)[24]

Two important distinctions are implicit in these formulations. The first is that between the 'right to believe' – meaning the negative freedom (the absence of legal restraint on the ability) to choose, change, express (or not to reveal) and advocate one's religion and to practice it in private, in homes and religious institutions – and the 'right to manifest', meaning the positive ability to live out the implications of one's faith in public as well as private settings.

The second is that between individual and institutional religious freedom. The latter is important because, as McCrea puts it, "the flipside of holding religion at a certain distance from the state [as implied by state neutrality] is the internal autonomy of religious institutions" (2010: 130). The reference to public communal manifestation in Article 9.1 implies that religious freedom is construed not only as an individual but also as a corporate right. Similarly, Article 2 of Protocol 1 (added in 1952) in effect protects the religious freedom rights of families: "the State shall respect the right of parents to ensure such education and teaching in conformity with their own religious and philosophical convictions."[25]

A third important distinction has emerged over time, namely that between religious and non-religious belief. In *Kokkinakis v Greece* (1993) the ECtHR formally defined 'freedom of religion or belief' (FoRB) to include both religious and non-religious convictions: "freedom of thought, conscience and religion is one of the foundations of a democratic society" both for religious people and for "atheists, agnostics, and skeptics."[26] Freedom is now guaranteed for both types of conviction with no assumption that either is entitled to public privilege.

The Court's protection of *institutional* religious freedom against infringements by signatory states has often proved robust, even when having to be balanced against other considerations (Leigh, 2012: 125).[27] In this respect the Court, as Leigh points out, "endorses a vision of religious organizations free of state interference, allowed to take their place in civil society as one of the building blocks of pluralism" (Leigh, 2012: 114). In *X v Denmark* (1976) the Court asserted pointedly that "the church is not obliged to provide religious freedom to its servants and members, as is the State as such for everyone within its jurisdiction".[28] Importantly, it has also allowed signatory states to grant religious institutions exemptions from generally applicable, 'neutral' laws in order to allow them to uphold their own religious ethos (McCrea, 2010: 103, 130–132). In regard to the *individual* right to believe in private settings and the individual right not be directly discriminated against in public settings, the ECtHR has also been very protective, showing itself willing to rule against infringements of such individual freedoms by signatory states even when rooted in long-standing practices (Leigh, 2013: 45–46).

Yet two inclinations have sometimes inhibited the Court's protection of the 'right to manifest'. One is its tendency to view religion as a voluntary matter and religious freedom as an essentially private individual right. This has left it reluctant to insist that signatory states offer *individual* religious believers (as distinct to institutions) exemptions enabling them to manifest their religious beliefs in public settings, or to recognise *indirect* discrimination on religious grounds as a breach of Article 9 (McCrea, 2010: 122–127). The other is the Court's willingness to accord to signatory states a very wide 'margin of appreciation' in upholding their own traditions of state-religion relationships (although Leigh [2013] finds its recent decisions to be inconsistent on the point). This has permitted quite substantive limitations on the individual, and at times, the corporate right to manifest, especially in public settings (McCrea, 2010: 133–135).[29] The Court has, for instance, shown such deference towards a traditionally Christian state in *Lautsi v Italy* (2011), where the Italian policy of displaying crucifixes in the classrooms of state schools, impugned as breaching the Article 9 rights of a non-Christian student, came under (ultimately unsuccessful) challenge.[30] But it has shown equal deference in refraining from challenging the application of strict public secularism (*laïcité*) in France and Turkey. McCrea concludes that "it is clear that conflict between the right to religious freedom and that of the state to control and define the nature of public spaces and institutions will generally be resolved [by the ECtHR] in favour of the latter" (2010, 134). This amounts to a significant limitation of the Court's capacity to protect religious freedom, and it can leave Europe's vulnerable religious minorities without adequate protection.

Who are these minorities? They include the 'new', the 'old', and the 'strange'. The 'new' have arrived with the substantial wave of recent migration to Europe from parts of the Indian subcontinent, Central Asia, and Africa, and include, for example, Hindus, Sikhs, and Muslims. It is overwhelmingly the emergence of Muslims who are increasingly asserting their Convention 'right to manifest' in public that has thrust the issue of minority religious freedom most firmly upon the European agenda (even though Islam is itself an 'old' European religion).[31] 'New' does not, of course, mean 'non-Christian'. Among the 'new' minorities are also conservative Christians migrating to Europe from parts of Asia, sub-Saharan Africa, or Latin America. Equally, many indigenous Europeans who more or less share such conservative stances (especially Catholics, Evangelicals, and Pentecostals) now constitute minorities in states which hitherto had been predominantly Christian; this is the case in, for example, the UK, the Netherlands, Germany and, in the light of the 2015 same-sex marriage referendum, probably Ireland. Such believers are increasingly reporting feeling alienated from their apparently relentlessly secularizing states. The self-perception of conservative Christians in some Eastern European states which have recently acceded to the EU is also fast approaching that of their Western European co-religionists. Given that the proportion of conservative Catholics and Orthodox in such states is rapidly diminishing, hopes on the part of some that the 'new evangelization' initiated by Pope John Paul II might initiate a re-Christianization of the EU, inspired from Eastern Europe, have scarcely been realized (Casanova, 2006). While polls suggest that majorities in several European states still notionally identity as 'Christian', those among them who hold views that might bring their 'right to manifest' into conflict with prevailing secular norms are now in a shrinking minority across most of Europe. Conservative Christians thus now constitute one of Europe's religious minorities, and they include both the 'new' and the 'old'.

Prominent among the 'strange' religious minorities whose religious freedom is at risk is Scientology, a religion facing deep suspicion in several European states, including Belgium and Germany. Belgium, however, displays a strong antipathy to 'cults' in general, leading it to place restrictions on Sikh temples, African Pentecostal churches, communities that practice yoga, and the Anthroposophical Society. The Appeal Court in Brussels has repeatedly rejected the work of the Belgian Parliamentary Commission on Cults, as it has the description by state officials of the Anthroposophical Society as a 'harmful sect' (Frautre, 2011: 222). Another 'strange' minority is the Baha'i, which fully affirms religious freedom and comports itself peacefully across all of Europe but which, while experiencing complete freedom in most European states, faces serious constraints in others, such as registration refusal in Romania, and even, in Armenia, acts of violence towards temples.

Thus, in spite of robust formal ECHR protection of religious freedom, religious minorities still face notable obstacles both to their 'right to believe' and to their 'right to manifest' in several signatory states. It is the case, however, that such obstacles are most prominently found among nations deeply formed either by traditionalist strands of Orthodoxy or by secular modernist versions of *laïcité*. Religiously illiberal tendencies in certain Orthodox countries are well recognized and are increasingly coming under the spotlight of the ECtHR. For example, the Greek state not only offers substantial public privileges to the Greek Orthodox Church (McCrea, 2010: 39) but also inhibits aspects of the religious freedom of others, including Muslims (outside of Thrace). For example, the exercise of a religious office without state permission is disallowed. In *Kokkinakis v. Greece* (1993), the ECtHR declined to protect the Orthodox Church from competition from the proselytizing activities of newer religions – only one of several cases where the Court has ruled against Orthodox privileges (Leigh, 2013: 43–45). In Romania a 2006 law on religion has had the effect of granting rights to a few religious communities while denying recognition to several minority ones (Andreescu, 2008).[32]

By contrast, religiously illiberal tendencies in countries governed by strict public secularism are less under the spotlight of the ECtHR. Critics allege that, even aside from a proper deference to national traditions such as French *laïcité*, the Court itself displays a bias towards an individualistic and secularist conception of religious freedom (Trigg, 2012; Boyle, 2004; Plesner, 2012). This is not entirely surprising given that ECtHR judges can be drawn from any Council of Europe members, some of which are secularist-leaning. Zucca singles out one ECtHR judge, András Sajó, as espousing an "aggressive secularism" (Zucca, 2012: Ch. 2). The criticism is that, while the 'right to believe' is extensively protected across signatory states, the 'right to manifest' in public settings, and in both individual and institutional expressions, has been hedged around with unwarranted limitations in *laïque* states. While most critics recognize that individual and institutional religious rights, like all rights, must be balanced against other rights (both the religious rights of others, and other kinds of rights), the charge is that this balance is being struck in a way that is needlessly prejudicial to the former (Trigg, 2012; Coleman and Walinowicz, 2015).[33] Such critics do not necessarily question state neutrality as such, at least insofar as it means a denial to states of the right to adjudicate among religious truth-claims. Their concern is that neutrality is being read in a needlessly restrictive manner rather than in the capacious, inclusive sense of "positive neutrality" proposed by Monsma (1993). This restrictive stance often impacts more heavily on non-Christian religions because the ECtHR's understanding of 'religion' and 'manifestation' is so heavily indebted to the legacy of Christianity. This 'Western' bias leaves European legislators and judges struggling to comprehend forms of manifestation – such as the Hindu practice of open-air cremation, the use of Shari'a law in private arbitration, or the wearing of religious dress in public settings – that diverge from familiar expectations of religious devotion.

Consider two examples of unwarranted curtailments of religious freedom, one of a conservative Christian, the other of Muslim women. In 2013 the ECtHR upheld the dismissal of Lillian Ladele, a marriage registrar employed by a council in London for refusing to conduct civil partnership ceremonies for same-sex couples, a requirement introduced only after she first signed a contract of employment with the council (*Eweida and Ors v United Kingdom*, 2013).[34] In this case courts in effect took it upon themselves to decide what parts of Ladele's faith were essential to it,[35] and expanded the notion of harassment beyond objective harm to the subjectively defined hurt feelings of a few colleagues. Both stances amount to potentially significant constraints on the right to manifest in public.[36] Gibson has argued that this judgement missed an important opportunity to apply the principle of the 'reasonable accommodation' of religion and which would have the salutary effect of making "individuals of faith feel less alienated by law" (2013: 616).

The second example concerns Moslem women's right to manifest. In 2010 the Council of Europe's Parliamentary Assembly issued a unanimous resolution opposing any general laws banning the wearing of the full-face (or integral) veil, while allowing specific restrictions for security or professional reasons (Council of Europe, 2010a, 2010b). Yet the same year a bill banning the wearing of the *burqa* in any public place was, controversially, passed overwhelmingly in both chambers of the French parliament (Silvestri, 2012). In 2011, the Belgian parliament followed suit, a decision upheld by the Belgian Constitutional Court in 2012. In July 2014 the ECtHR upheld the French law on the grounds that it was pursuant to a 'legitimate aim' of the French government (Willsher, 2014).

This is only one of many European cases involving legal restraints on the wearing of various items of religious clothing in one or other public setting.[37] While some might suggest that the Court's 2014 French ruling merely maintained its long-standing deference to the 'margin of appreciation' doctrine, it can be argued that to show such deference in such a classic case of individual religious freedom disclosed the Court's own leanings towards a secularist version of *laïcité*. It is, perhaps, evidence of what Augenstein calls a "strategy of avoidance" in which the Court "undermines an effective transnational protection of religious pluralism against the backdrop of diverse national constitutional traditions" and uses the margin of appreciation doctrine "to water down the high burden of 'necessity' of interference to be discharged by the state" (2012: 272).

These trends evident in the jurisprudence of the ECtHR (and in some national courts, not least the UK's) would seem to confirm Alessandro Ferrari's broader conclusion that European secularism is "[ceasing] to be pluralism-oriented, instead becoming an instrument for repackaging public spaces by coercively reducing differences" (2012: 78). Equally, Silvio Ferrari warns that a rigid imposition of generic human rights norms upon the internal doctrine and organization of religious communities "can start a process of cultural homogenization that ... undermines the specificity of religious communities and the contribution they can give to building a plural society ..." (2012: 145). This is a troubling dimension of the complexly evolving framework of ECHR religious freedom jurisprudence within which the EU functions.

The EU and religious freedom

As noted at the outset, the EU has been bound to adopt a cautious approach to religious matters in view of the fact that competence on state-religion relationships (in keeping with the EU principle of subsidiarity) remains at national level. Thus, for example, the Treaty of Amsterdam's 'Declaration on the status of churches and non-confessional organisations' asserts that the EU "respects and does not prejudice the status under national law of churches and religious associations or communities in the Member States" and "equally respects the status of philosophical and non-confessional organisations" (European Union, 1997).[38] As recently as 2010, McCrea was able to assert that the EU "has no specific policy on religion, nor any explicit competence in relation to religious matters" (2010: 1), thereby restricting its capacity to develop its own approach to religious freedom (2010: 114). Since the EU is now also formally bound by the ECHR and the decisions of the ECtHR, its own stance towards religious freedom is also significantly constrained by Convention jurisprudence.

Yet notwithstanding these constraints, the EU as an independent transnational organization does have a degree of latitude to develop its own approach to religious freedom and has recently begun to flex its muscles in this area in ways that not only meet but also exceed the religious freedom practice of the ECtHR. It is beginning to emerge as an independent actor with the potential not only to consolidate but also to extend religious freedom, at home and abroad.[39] By 2015 it could no longer be said that the EU has "no policy on religion." Indeed, Doe notes that there is now an emerging EU "common law" on religion (Doe, 2013: 145–146), contained in diverse sources and disclosing eight operative principles, including religious freedom, religious neutrality, subsidiarity, institutional autonomy, and non-discrimination.[40] While these are understood in broadly similar terms to those guiding the ECtHR, some distinctive emphases are emerging.

Since the 1970s EU institutions have moved progressively towards a more formal and explicit affirmation of the principles of religious freedom enshrined in the ECHR (McCrea, 2010: 118–119). For example, in 1976 the European Court of Justice recognized that religious freedom was among the general principles of law it was committed to upholding. In 1977 a Joint Declaration on Fundamental Rights by the Council, the Commission and Parliament included an undertaking to respect the provisions of the ECHR, which include religious freedom. In 1992 this was reaffirmed in Article 6 of the Maastricht Treaty. In 2000 the Charter of Fundamental Rights of the European Union (CFREU) was adopted, incorporating the substance of the ECHR's commitments to religious freedom. This included the EU's first formulation of its own text on religious freedom, namely Article 10.1 (repeating almost verbatim clause 1 of Article 9 of the ECHR). In 2009 the Lisbon Treaty of the European Union permitted the EU (as distinct to its member states) formally to accede to the ECHR and negotiations to join are still in progress.

The EU has also entered upon the terrain of religious freedom indirectly, and perhaps inadvertently, in regulating the Single Market and, pursuant to that, in issuing a series of Directives on employment and anti-discrimination (McCrea, 2010: 145–152). Early on the Community prohibited discrimination on grounds of religion against its own employees and in a 1970s ruling the Court of Justice indicated that Community institutions were under an obligation to facilitate the religious identity of an employee – an early intimation of a duty of 'reasonable accommodation'. Such a duty was confirmed in 1993 and 2013 regulations exempting competent religious authorities from laws governing humane slaughter of animals. Among other examples are a 1989 Directive ruling out the use of important religious or other symbols as trademarks, and a Broadcasting Directive of 2007 prohibiting member states from permitting media under their jurisdiction to broadcast material that incited religious (or other forms of) hatred or from issuing advertising during religious services (McCrea, 2010: 157–8).

A significant step forward in the regulation of religious freedom was the Framework Directive of 2000. On the authority of Article 6a of the Treaty of Amsterdam of 1999, the Community issued Directive (EC) 2000/78 outlawing discrimination in employment on a range of grounds, including religion. The principle has been applied across a wide range of areas of EU activity, and has served as a stimulus to the development of non-discrimination legislation in some member states (Doe, 2013: 148–149). Again going further than the ECtHR, the Directive prohibits not only direct but also *indirect* discrimination on grounds of religion. It thereby "enshrines the formal neutrality of the Single Market" (McCrea, 2010: 151) across member states, while also providing for the accommodation of religious choices within the market sector in cases where facially neutral employment requirements put adherents to a specific religion or belief "at a particular disadvantage compared to other persons" (Article 2[2]).

McCrea rightly notes that this offers the prospect of adherents of minority religions claiming protection against restrictive workplace practices that reflect a member state's dominant (mostly Christian) religion (2010: 152). Presumably, however, it should in principle also offer protection of any religious minorities (including Christians) against the adverse impact of a dominant secularism, something that the ECtHR, and some national courts, have been less willing to countenance. These emerging accommodation entitlements are, of course, expected to be balanced against the need to protect the religious rights of others on the one hand, and the legitimate imperatives of the market sector or state regulation on the other. Pursuant to the latter, the Union has properly laid down that such accommodation should not override the legitimate requirement of employers that an employee be capable of performing the essential functions of a post or impose on employers intolerable burdens (McCrea, 2010: 154–5). Accommodation is rightly understood as a reciprocal and mutually limiting obligation between employers and employees (Gibson, 2013).

The Union has also shown itself willing to extend the principle of accommodation beyond individuals to religious institutions. Its primary motivation (like that of the ECtHR) has been to defer to the right of member states to permit such institutions to govern themselves in ways consistent with their religious (or other) ethos, including some offering public services such as education or health (McCrea, 2010: 160–168). This is implied in the 1997 Declaration's disavowal of any right to override the public status of religious associations granted them under national laws; respect for the autonomy of religious institutions has long been assumed in various regulatory instruments (Doe, 2013: 146–149). Accommodation of institutional autonomy rights is affirmed in the Framework Directive's specification that such associations (as well as non-confessional ones) may enjoy exemptions from anti-discrimination laws, made by their national governments, permitting employers to insist on a "genuine, legitimate and justified occupational requirement," such as adherence to a particular religion or belief, as a condition of employment, and to require employees to "act in good faith and with loyalty to the organisation's ethos."[41] As McCrea puts it, these provisions "ensure that religious bodies exercising public functions can protect the religiously specific nature of the public services they provide by granting scope within EU law to exempt them from otherwise applicable non-discrimination norms" and thereby protecting a "broad, collective, institutional identity in public contexts" (2010: 163, 164).

However, troubled by the apparently capacious scope of the provisions of the exemption, McCrea ventures the unfounded and speculative assertion that they appear to "place religion outside of the norms governing the public behavior of institutions in modern liberal societies and to characterize religion as a kind of non-rational, non-modern phenomenon whose actions cannot be regulated or assessed according to generally applicable modern norms without impinging on its essence" (2010: 164). None of this is implied in the wording of the provisions, which extend the exemption to 'non-confessional' organizations, and also cite 'religion or belief'. Puzzlingly, McCrea suggests that it applies exclusively to religious bodies (2010: 162–166). He notes that "one does not find … publicly funded socialist, environmentalist, or fascist hospitals and schools at Member State level" (2010: 165). But that is an entirely contingent matter and the wording of the exemption does not in any way rule such bodies out. While he notes in passing the reference to 'belief' as well as 'religion', he suggests it is merely "rhetorical." On the contrary, it seems to convey (as he himself puts it) "an implicit denial that religion is by its nature entitled to privileged status to which other belief systems are not" (2010: 165).

A strategically important initiative in the extension of EU religious freedom policy was the European Foreign Affairs Council's explicit adoption of a global religious freedom mandate in 2013.[42] Following on from the 2007 Lisbon Treaty and the creation of the European External Action Service (EEAS), the EU has sought to strengthen its role as a global player, and this has included its 'soft power' promotion of human rights, including FoRB. This move led to the adoption by the European Council of the EU *Guidelines on the promotion and protection of freedom of religion or belief* (European Council, 2013). The Guidelines are intended as binding on the European diplomatic service.[43] But they are more broadly relevant as an indication of what the EU may come to expect of its member states in their own internal religious affairs. The Guidelines reaffirm much of what is already contained in the ECHR's Article 9 and in the EU's Charter.[44] The Conclusion of the Council when adopting the Guidelines reveals that threats to religious minorities were at the heart of its concerns:

> "The Council reaffirms the strong commitment of the European Union to the promotion and protection of freedom of religion or belief.
>
> The Council recalls that freedom of thought, conscience, religion or belief applies equally to all persons. It is a fundamental freedom which includes all religions or beliefs, *including those that have not been traditionally practiced in a particular country, the beliefs of persons belonging to religious minorities*, as well as non-theistic and atheistic beliefs. The freedom also covers the right to adopt, change or abandon one's religion or belief, of one's own free will.
>
> The Council underlines that States have a duty to protect everyone, *including persons belonging to minorities*, from discrimination, violence and other violations. States must ensure that their legislative systems provide adequate and effective guarantees of freedom of thought, conscience, religion or belief to all without distinction".
>
> (European Council, 2009, emphasis added)[45]

The Guidelines also include a robust affirmation of institutional religious freedom. Clause 19 asserts that religious freedom "includes rights for communities to perform acts integral to the conduct by religious groups of their basic affairs. These rights include, but are not limited to, legal personality and non-interference in internal affairs, including the right to establish and maintain freely accessible places of worship or assembly, the freedom to select and train leaders or the right to carry out social, cultural, educational and charitable activities." This is highly important for religious minorities, especially those whose claims to 'manifest' may appear 'new' or 'strange' to western lawmakers and courts.[46]

The European Parliament (EP) is becoming increasingly active in the area of religious freedom. The EP has shown particular concern with violations of religious freedom abroad (Oliver-Dee, 2014). In 2011 it adopted a resolution urging EU institutions to use the TFEU Article 17 framework for dialogue with religious groups to highlight the issue of religious persecution and called on the High Representative for Foreign Affairs to develop a permanent EEAS capacity to monitor global restrictions on religious freedom and to report annually to Parliament. In a similar vein it adopted a resolution on 'Religious Freedom and Cultural Diversity' (European Parliament, 2014). In 2012 the European Parliament Working Group on Freedom of Religion or Belief (EPWG on FoRB) was established, issuing its first Annual Report in 2014. Now upgraded to the European Parliament Intergroup on Freedom of Religion or Belief and Religious Tolerance, it issued its first Annual Report in 2015 (European Parliament IFROBRT, 2015). Both reports urge the EEAS and other EU actors to accord much greater attention to global religious freedom than they had done so far, indirectly confirming Mandaville and Silvestri's judgement that in the EU's external handling of religion is "timid" and that its "voice and capability as a foreign policy actor remains weak and fragmented" (2015: 2).

Conclusion

Collectively, therefore, EU institutions now offer a robust political affirmation of, and formal framework of legal protection, for religious freedom. In adopting such commitments, it has set itself a high bar by which its own performance, as a major regional and global political entity with significant scope for independent action in this area, may be critically assessed. EU organs should thus be urged to follow through, within the limits of their own competencies, on such commitments and to encourage member states to do the same. Cumulatively, these contain robust affirmations both of the right to believe and of the right to manifest, clear opposition to both direct and indirect religious discrimination, support of both individual and institutional religious freedom, and an endorsement of the principle of reasonable accommodation of religious persons and institutions.[47] These commitments have repeatedly conveyed a special concern for minority religious freedoms.[48]

These two challenges have been, and will continue to be, made more pressing by the arrival of 'new' religious citizens following expansion and as a result of migration and by the new activism of 'old' religious minorities.

Responding to the presence and public claims of Islam within the EU will likely prove the toughest performance test of the EU's commitments to religious freedom and state neutrality. On the one hand, the EU is already formally committed to granting religious freedom as generously to Islam as it does to other religions, even to the point (*contra* the ECtHR's highly tendentious remarks in *Refah Partisi v. Turkey*) of protecting freedom of speech for those Islamist groups which do not themselves defend the full suite of liberal democratic norms, but which advance their views lawfully. On the other, there are mounting concerns across many EU states – concerns that must be critically interrogated, not fearfully deferred to – that even adherents to 'mainstream' or 'moderate' Islam might seek for themselves a position of illicit public privilege, or secure 'exemptions' from generally applicable laws which could be invoked to cover religiously-based oppression – of women in 'Sharia tribunals', for example (Ahdar and Aroney, 2010) – thus breaching the Union's own fundamental Community values.[49] These are among the anxieties surrounding the accession of Turkey to the EU.[50] But these challenges only illustrate the wider task confronting the EU – which could arise from the public demands of any of its minority communities of religion or belief – of seeking a judicious balance between the legitimate FoRB aspirations of all its citizens across very diverse member states and the baseline norms required to sustain constitutional democracy.

These challenges present the Union with two daunting tasks. The first is to shore up its legitimacy as an actor in the area of religion-state relationships and religious freedom policy. The legitimacy of member states as primary actors in this area derives from the established authority of their own long-standing cultural and religious traditions. But, as McCrea cautions, the political legitimacy of the Union is limited in this area just by virtue of its lack of such an established cultural tradition (2010: 3, 9–10, 50; cf. Katzenstein, 2006: 24–30). Securing greater legitimacy for religious freedom policies will inevitably be a slow, incremental process, requiring concerted action on several fronts. Part of that task will be making good the persisting democratic deficit facing all EU institutions, and the remedies to this deficit must surely include granting wider powers to the central representative body in the Union, the European Parliament. Since it is already presenting itself as a committed champion of religious freedom, an empowered Parliament (reformed, perhaps, along the lines suggested by Pabst in Chapter 6) could prove decisive in elevating the legitimacy of the Union as a whole on matters of religious freedom. As a modest first step, the Parliament might extend the exclusively non-EU remit of its own Intergroup on religious freedom to internal EU matters.

The second task is to work towards greater clarity and consistency of religious freedom policy, across all religions, especially minority ones, across all relevant areas of policy (non-discrimination and human rights, the Single Market, religious dress, religious hatred, immigration, etc.) and across all relevant organs (Court of Justice, Council, Commission). This will require the

Union to acquire a much more sophisticated understanding of how it sees the place of religion and belief in its own public spaces. This in turn will require the Union to clarify its relationship to the wider ECHR legal framework. While the Court of Justice is formally bound to, and shows great deference to, ECtHR jurisprudence (McCrea, 2010: 232–235), both it and other EU institutions have shown themselves willing to go beyond minimal ECtHR requirements on, for example, the question of reasonable accommodation (McCrea, 2010: 141–142). While the ECtHR itself defers to signatories' existing models of state-religion relationship, Doe discerns in recent EU religion policy a growing affinity with 'cooperationist' rather than 'separationist' models of this relationship (2013: 151). That, we suggest, is promising for its future practice of religious freedom. But for that promise to be fulfilled, the Court of Justice will need to develop its own mind on religious matters.[51] As Augenstein suggests, it should not content itself merely with meeting a "floor" of minimum ECtHR standards but rather fulfil its own stated declaration that it is indeed a truly independent source of law able to interpret the Union's fundamental rights in an autonomous way (2012: 274–278).

The EU should embark upon a more self-conscious and religiously literate engagement with religious freedom issues, with the aim, as Alessandro Ferrari puts it, of "giving the right to religious freedom more substance and efficacy [and] making it a real paradigm of a pluralistic society" (A. Ferrari, 2012: 87). It should enact in its own deeds, and model to member states, an attitude of constructive, engaged even-handedness (as opposed to cool detachment) towards all faiths, especially minority ones, who are willing to accept the constraints arising from state neutrality in a context of pluralism (S. Ferrari, 2012: 145–146). In forging such a space, it might profitably revisit the political insights bequeathed to modern Europe by the dissenting Protestant minorities who, in openly theological voice, and at considerable cost, first projected the demands for religious toleration upon the European stage.

Notes

1 We are indebted to Gary Wilton, Julian Rivers, and Sean Oliver-Dee for valuable comments on earlier drafts of this chapter. The usual disclaimers apply.
2 *Refah Partisi v Turkey* (2003), paragraph 91. On the concepts of religious freedom and state neutrality see Leigh (2013), Bielefeldt (2012) and Trigg (2012).
3 For example, the EU was not until recently able to be a signatory to the ECHR since it was not a state.
4 See Ahdar and Leigh (2013: Ch. 4); Monsma and Soper (2009); Robbers (2005).
5 See Leigh (2013); Ferrari and Pastorelli (2012); Doe (2010); McCrea (2010: Ch. 4); Ovey and White (2006); Taylor (2005); Evans, C. (2001); Evans, M.D. (1997).
6 McCrea (2010); Leustean and Madeley (2013); Leustean (2013).
7 This is the theory that "it is right and justified to maintain religious unity by force and to kill heretics and dissenters if necessary" (Zagorin, 2003: 3).
8 There are other narratives, such as Witte (2007).
9 Cavanaugh (2009) questions that these can straightforwardly be termed 'religious' wars.

10 Strictly, it returned territories to the religious confessions that had prevailed in 1624.
11 Witte (2007) argues that liberal readings such as Zagorin's, which accentuate the intolerant character of the magisterial Reformation, overlook the crucial longer-term influence on religious freedom of the wider constitutionalist theory of rights emerging from early Calvinism.
12 As Protestant theologian Troeltsch put it over a century ago: "It is at this point that the stepchildren of the Reformation finally had their hour in world history (1911: 62).
13 Castellio's argument was denounced by both Calvin and Theodor Beza, his successor as leader of the Genevan church (Zagorin, 2003: 114–132).
14 See also Zagorin (2003: Ch. 7).
15 In Germany, for example, general religious freedom was only secured since 1919 under the Weimar Constitution.
16 Such arguments were not unprecedented. See Nederman and Laursen (1996); Witte (2007: Chs. 1–3).
17 Trawling a longer stretch of history, Ahdar and Leigh (2013: 34–50) identify eight theological arguments and, in the liberal tradition, four types (2013: 69–84). See the four "modern European" justifications discussed by McCrea (2010: 106–115).
18 For contemporary empirical confirmation, see Grim and Finke (2010).
19 Luther's *The Freedom of a Christian* (1520) was only concerned with internal freedom and did not prevent him from appealing to the elector of Saxony to suppress Catholicism. Calvin was more forthright that it was the duty of rulers to suppress false religion (Zagorin, 2003: 75–6; 79–82). In his earlier period, however, Calvin placed much stronger emphasis on religious liberty, a point Zagorin overlooks (see Witte, 2007: Ch. 1).
20 Zagorin observes that while the New Testament knew something like the concept of 'heresy', it "never enjoins any coercion or silencing of those who introduce heresies and cause divisions" (2003: 19).
21 This resembles what Forst calls the "respect" conception of toleration as distinct to the "permission" conception held by early modern 'tolerating' states (2012: 59–64).
22 This and the next part owe much to the comprehensive account in McCrea (2010), although the interpretations put upon it are ours.
23 The Organization for Security and Co-operation in Europe (OSCE), established in 1975, and its Office for Democratic Institutions and Human Rights (ODIR), function in parallel to the ECtHR, assisting members on the implementation of human rights, including religious freedom.
24 For the history of Article 9 see Evans (1997: 262–362).
25 On the history of this article see Ovey and White (2006: 1–3).
26 The focus of this chapter is on religious convictions but at several points we also imply 'freedom of religion or belief'.
27 Autonomy of religious institutions is one of three guiding principles Ringelheim (2012) discerns emerging from the Court's religion jurisprudence (up to 2011). The other two are the religious neutrality of the state and the secularity of the foundations of law.
28 Quoted in Leigh (2012: 115).
29 Not all deviations from state neutrality infringe minority religious freedom. In *Darby v Sweden* (1991) the Court recognized that the state establishment of a particular faith did not in itself violate Article 9.
30 The Court did not accept that a state may officially recognise the truth claims of a particular faith but tolerated crucifixes as part of a cultural tradition, concluding that they did not breach the child's Article 9 rights.

31 See Silvestri (2009; 2013); C. Schirrmacher (2013); Ferrari and Pastorelli (2012); Durham et al. (2012), Zucca and Ungureanu (2012); Tibi (2009); Maussen (2007); Saeed and Saeed (2004); T. Schirrmacher (2003).
32 The legal situation of some Eastern European Orthodox countries has actually regressed since joining the EU, to the detriment, especially, of Muslim religious freedom. On Greece, however, see Delikostantis (2007).
33 For a measured empirical study of the UK situation, see Weller et al. (2013).
34 The judgement did, however, contain other provisions that strengthened religious freedom. See Cranmer (2013).
35 It had already done so in *Ahmad v UK* (1982). See McCrea (2010: 126).
36 Referring to *Ahmad*, McCrea accepts this critique of the Court on the first point (2010: 127), but fails to interrogate its approach to harassment in *Ladele* (2010: 153).
37 See Ferrari and Pastorelli (2012); Durham et al. (2012: Part II).
38 Quoted in McCrea (2010: 61 n 37). Its substance of is reaffirmed in Article 17 of the Lisbon Treaty.
39 Our focus is on matters of religious freedom internal to the EU. On its external activities in this area, see Oliver-Dee (2014).
40 He identifies three phases of EU engagement with religion: an early phase marked by an absence of norms; 1976–1992, when the "side-effects" of economic law on religion emerged; 1992–2007, in which a "growing body of substantive norms" appeared (2013: 153 n1).
41 Article 4(2). Quoted in McCrea (2010: 163).
42 This followed the adoption of European Council (2012). See Oliver-Dee (2014).
43 Oliver-Dee notes that initiatives on global religious freedom had (at least prior to 2013) been "Parliament-led, rather than Commission-led, and of an ad hoc nature" (2014: 30).
44 They also strongly affirm the right to change one's religion, a crucial issue in EU relations with officially Muslim states and certain Muslim-majority states.
45 The Copenhagen Criteria defining the prerequisites for EU membership also include a general commitment to the protection of minorities (McCrea, 2010: 94 n173).
46 Yet even claims from 'old' minorities can baffle judges, as they did in the Jewish Free School case of 2009 where the UK Supreme Court ruled that the admissions policy of the school, rooted in ancient Jewish tradition, violated the Race Relations Act 1976. The Court held that the school's policy was after all not based on religion but on ethnicity. Ferrari suggests that this judgement "implies that the membership rules of a religion are subject to the scrutiny of State courts ... thus limiting its collective religious freedom right" (S. Ferrari 2012, 142).
47 See also Resolution 1928 of the Parliamentary Assembly of the Council of Europe (2013). Against the charge that reasonable accommodation 'privileges' religion, Zucca asserts that it is a "grave simplification" to suppose that "one law for all" means "one rule for all" (2012: 109), and that, by contrast, "One legal framework can easily encompass a plurality of rules that apply differentially" (2012: 133)
48 The Lisbon Treaty provision for dialogue with religions also embraces Scientology (Foret, 2010: 33), but EU bodies have so far failed to condemn the discriminatory treatment of Scientology by some member states. On the precarious global context of minority faiths, see Ghanea (2012).
49 By contrast, 'honour killings' and 'forced marriages' are, essentially, practices embedded in shame-based cultures rather than being religious injunctions. In the UK prominent Muslim leaders have forcefully condemned both as 'un-Islamic.'
50 See Doe (2010: 146); McCrea (2010: 205–208); Haynes (2011).
51 This could signal what Doe anticipates would be a distinct fourth phase in the evolution of its thinking in the field, marked by "a more rigorous and critical understanding and articulation" (2010: 153) of its general principles.

References

Ahdar, R., and Aroney, N. (eds) (2010). *Shari'a in the West.* Oxford: Oxford University Press.
Ahdar, R., and Leigh, I. (2013). *Religious freedom in the liberal state* (2nd edn). Oxford: Oxford University Press.
Andreescu, L. (2008). Romania's new law on religious freedom and religious denominations. *Religion, State and Society,* 36(2): 139–161.
Augenstein, D. (2012). Religious pluralism and national constitutional traditions in Europe. In Zucca, L. and Ungureanu, C. (eds), *Law, state and religion in the new Europe: Debates and dilemmas.* Cambridge: Cambridge University Press, 261–280.
Bielefeldt, H. (2012). Freedom of religion or belief: A human right under pressure. *Oxford Journal of Law and Religion,* 1(1): 15–35.
Boyle, K. (2004). Human rights, religion and democracy: The Refah party case. *Essex Human Rights Review,* 1(1): 1–16.
Busher, L. (1614). Religious peace: Or a plea for liberty of conscience. In Underhill, E. B. (ed.), *Tracts on liberty of conscience and persecution 1614–1661.* London: 1846.
Casanova, J. (2006). Religion, European secular identities, and European integration. In Byrnes, T. and Katzenstein, P. J. (eds), *Religion in an expanding Europe* (pp. 65–92). Cambridge: Cambridge University Press.
Cavanaugh, W. (2009). *The myth of religious violence: Secular ideology and the roots of modern conflict.* Oxford: Oxford University Press.
Coleman, P., and Walinowicz, K. (2015) *Europe: The problem of intolerant equality laws. Report 2014: Cases of intolerance or discrimination against Christians.* Vienna, Austria: Observatory on Intolerance and Discrimination against Christians in Europe. Retrieved from www.intoleranceagainstchristians.eu/.
Council of Europe. (2010a). *Parliamentary Assembly, Islam, Islamism and Islamophobia in Europe, Resolution 1743.* Strasbourg, France: Council of Europe.
Council of Europe. (2010b). *Parliamentary Assembly, Islam, Islamism and Islamophobia in Europe, Recommendation 1927.* Strasbourg, France: Council of Europe.
Council of Europe. (1950). *European Convention on Human Rights.* Strasbourg, France: Council of Europe. Retrieved from www.echr.coe.int/Documents/Convention_ENG.pdf.
Cranmer, F. (2013). Chaplin, Eweida, Ladele and McFarlane: The judgement. *Law & Religion UK,* 17 January. Retrieved from www.lawandreligionuk.com/2013/01/17/chaplin-eweida-ladele-and-mcfarlane-the-judgment/.
Delikostantis, K. (2007). Die Menschenrechte im Kontext der Orthodoxen Theologie. *Ökumenische Rundschau,* 56: 19–35.
Doe, N. (2010). Towards a 'common law' on religion in the European Union. In Leustean, L. N. and Madeley, J. T. S. (eds), *Religion, politics and law in the European Union* (pp. 141–160). London: Routledge.
Durham, Jr., W. C., Torfs, T., Kirkham, D. M., and Scott, C. (eds) (2012). *Islam, Europe and Emerging Legal Issues.* Farnham: Ashgate.
Estep, W. R. (1975). *The Anabaptist story* (Rev. edn). Grand Rapids, MI: Eerdmans.
Evans, C. (2001). *Freedom of religion under the European convention on human rights.* Oxford: Oxford University Press.
Evans, M. D. (1997). *Religious liberty and international law in Europe.* Cambridge: Cambridge University Press.

European Council. (2013). *EU guidelines on the promotion and protection of freedom of religion or belief.* Retrieved from http://consilium.europa.eu/uedocs/cms_data/docs/pressdata/EN/foraff/137585.pdf.
European Council. (2012). *EU strategic framework and action plan on human rights and democracy.* Retrieved from www.consolium.europa.eu/uedocs/cms_data/docs/pressdata/EN/foraff/131181.pdf.
European Council. (2009). Council conclusions on freedom of religion or belief. 2973rd General Affairs Council meeting Brussels, 16 November 2009. Retrieved from europa.eu/rapid/press-release_PRES-09-328_en.doc.
European Parliament (with Intergroup on Freedom of Religion or Belief and Religious Tolerance [IFROBRT]). (2015). *The state of freedom of religion or belief in the world.* Retrieved from www.religiousfreedom.eu/file/2015/06/2014-Intergroup-Report-FINAL.pdf.
European Parliament. (2014). Resolution B7–0365/2014. Retrieved from www.europarl.europa.eu/sides/getDoc.do?pubRef=-//EP//TEXT+MOTION+B7-2014-0365+0+DOC+XML+V0//EN.
European Union. (1997). Declaration No 11 to the last act of the Treaty of Amsterdam [1997] *OJ C340/133*.
Ferrari, A. (2012). Religious freedom and the public-private divide: A broken promise? In Ferrari, S. and Pastorelli, S. (eds), *Religion in public spaces: A European perspective* (pp. 71–91). Farnham: Ashgate.
Ferrari, S., and Pastorelli, S. (eds) (2012). *Religion in public spaces: A European perspective.* Farnham: Ashgate.
Foret, F. (2010). Religion: A solution or a problem for the legitimation of the European Union? In Leustean, L. N. and Madeley, J. T. S. (eds), *Religion, politics and law in the European Union* (pp. 31–44). London: Routledge.
Forst, R. (2012). Two stories about toleration. In Zucca, L. and Ungureanu, C. (eds), *Law, state and religion in the new Europe: Debates and dilemmas* (pp. 49–64). Cambridge: Cambridge University Press.
Frautre, W. (2011). Belgien/Belgium. *Journal for the Study of Beliefs and Worldviews*, 12(1), 209–225.
Ghanea, N. (2012). Are religious minorities really minorities? *Oxford Journal of Law and Religion*, 1(1): 57–79.
Gibson, M. (2013). The God 'dilution'? Religion, discrimination and the case for reasonable accommodation. *The Cambridge Law Journal*, 72(3): 578–616.
Grim, B. J., and Finke, R. (2010). *The price of freedom denied: Religious persecution and conflict in the twenty-first century.* Cambridge: Cambridge University Press.
Haynes, J. (2011). Politics and Islam in Turkey: From Ataturk to the AKP. In Haynes, J. and Hennig, A. (eds), *Religious actors in the public sphere: Means, objectives and effects* (pp. 192–212). London: Routledge.
Katzenstein, P. J. (2006). Multiple modernities as limits to secular Europeanization? In Byrnes, T. A. and Katzenstein, P. J. (eds), *Religion in an expanding Europe* (pp. 1–33). Cambridge: Cambridge University Press.
Leigh, I. (2013). The European Court of Human Rights and religious neutrality. In D'Costa, G. et al. (eds), *Religion in a liberal state* (pp. 38–66). Cambridge: Cambridge University Press.
Leigh, I. (2012). Balancing religious autonomy and human rights under the European convention. *Oxford Journal of Law and Religion*, 1(1): 109–125.

Leustean, L. N. (ed.) (2013). *Representing religion in the European Union: Does God matter?* London: Routledge.
Leustean, L. N., and Madeley, J. T. S. (eds) (2013). *Religion, politics and law in the European Union.* London: Routledge.
Locke, J. (1983 [1689]). *A letter concerning toleration.* Indianapolis, IN: Hackett.
Luther, M. (1974 [1523]). Temporal authority: To what extent it should be obeyed. In Porter, J. M. (ed.), *Luther: Selected political writings* (pp. 51–71). Philadelphia, PA: Fortress Press.
McCrea, R. (2010). *Religion and the public order of the European Union.* Oxford: Oxford University Press.
Madeley, J. T. S. (2003). European liberal democracy and the principle of state religious neutrality. In Madeley, J. T. S. and Enyedi, Z. (eds), *Church and state in contemporary Europe: The chimera of neutrality* (pp. 1–22). London: Frank Cass.
Mandaville, P., and Silvestri, S. (2015). Integrating religious engagement into diplomacy: Challenges and opportunities. *Issues in Governance Studies,* 67 (January). Washington, DC: Brookings Institution.
Maussen, M. (2007). The governance of Islam in Europe: A state of the art report. IMISCOE Working Paper 16. Amsterdam: UVA Institute for Migration and Ethnic Studies.
Monsma, S. V. (1993). *Positive neutrality: Letting religious freedom ring.* Westport, CT: Greenwood Press.
Monsma, S. V., and Soper, J. C. (2009). *The challenge of pluralism: Church and state in five democracies* (2nd edn). Lanham, MD: Rowman and Littlefield.
Nederman, C. J., and Laursen, J. C. (eds) (1996). *Difference and dissent: Theories of tolerance in medieval and early modern Europe.* Lanham, MD: Rowman and Littlefield.
Oliver-Dee, S. (2014). The European Union's awkward embrace of religious freedom. *Review of Faith and International Affairs,* 12(3): 25–32.
Ovey, C., and White, R. C. A. (2006). *The European convention on human rights.* Oxford: Oxford University Press.
Parliamentary Assembly of the Council of Europe. (2013). Safeguarding human rights in relation to religion and belief, and protecting religious communities from violence. Resolution 1928(2013), clause 9.9. Retrieved from http://assembly.coe.int/nw/xml/XRef/Xref-XML2HTML-en.asp?fileid=19695&lang=en.
Plesner, I. T. (2012). The European Court of Human Rights: Between fundamentalist and liberal secularism. In Durham, Jr., W. C. et al. (eds), *Islam, Europe and emerging legal issues* (pp. 63–74). Farnham: Ashgate.
Rawls, J. (1996 [1993]). *Political liberalism* (Rev. edn). New York: Columbia University Press.
Ringelheim, J. (2012). Rights, religion and the public sphere: The European Court of Human Rights in search of a theory? In Zucca, L. and Ungureanu, C. (eds), *Law, state and religion in the new Europe: Debates and dilemmas* (pp. 283–306). Cambridge: Cambridge University Press.
Robbers, G. (ed.) (2005). *State and church in the European Union* (2nd edn). Baden-Baden, Germany: Nomos Verlagsgesellschaft.
Saeed, A., and Saeed, H. (2004). *Freedom of religion, apostasy and Islam.* Farnham, England: Ashgate.
Schirrmacher, C. (2013). *Islam und Demokratie.* Holzgerlingen, Germany: SCM Hänssler.

Schirrmacher, T. (2003). *Feindbild Islam*. Nürnberg, Germany: VTR.
Silvestri, S. (2013). *Europe's Muslim women: Beyond the burqa controversy*. London: Hurst.
Silvestri, S. (2012). Comparing burqa debates in Europe: Sartorial styles, religious prescriptions and political ideologies. In Ferrari, S. and Pastorelli, S. (eds), *Religion in public spaces: A European perspective* (pp. 275–292). Farnham: Ashgate.
Silvestri, S. (2009). Islam and religion in the EU political system. *West European Politics*, 32(6): 1212–1239.
Taylor, P. M. (2005). *Freedom of religion: UN and European human rights law and practice*. Cambridge: Cambridge University Press.
Tibi, B. (2009). *Euro-Islam*. Darmstadt, Germany: Primus.
Trigg, R. (2012). *Equality, freedom and religion*. Oxford: Oxford University Press.
Troeltsch, E. (1911). Die Bedeutung des Protestantismus für die Entstehung der Modernen welt. Vortrag, Gehalten auf der IX. Versammlung Deutscher Historiker zu Stuttgart am 21. April 1906, in *Historische Zeitschrift* , 97.1(1906), 1–66.
Waldron, J. (2010). The image of God: Rights, reason, and order. In Witte, J. and Alexander, F. S. (eds), *Christianity and human rights: An introduction* (pp. 216–236). Cambridge: Cambridge University Press.
Weller, P., Purdam, K., Ghanea, N., and Cheruvallil-Contractor, S. (2013). *Religion or belief, discrimination and equality: Britain in global contexts*. London: Bloomsbury.
Williams, R. (1644). *The Bloudy tenent of persecution, for cause of conscience discussed in a conference betweene truth and peace*. London.
Willsher, K. (2014). France's burqa ban upheld by human rights court. *The Guardian*, 1 July. Retrieved from www.theguardian.com/world/2014/jul/01/france-burqa-ban-up held-human-rights-court.
Witte, J. (2007). *The reformation of rights: Law, religion and human rights in early modern Calvinism*. Cambridge: Cambridge University Press.
Witte, J., and Alexander, F. S. (eds) (2011). *Christianity and human rights: An introduction*. Cambridge: Cambridge University Press.
Wolterstorff, N. (2012). *The mighty and the almighty: An essay in political theology*. Cambridge: Cambridge University Press.
Zagorin, P. (2003). *How the idea of religious toleration came to the west*. Princeton, NJ: Princeton University Press.
Zucca, L. (2012). *A secular Europe: Law and religion in the European constitutional landscape*. Oxford: Oxford University Press.
Zucca, L., and Ungureanu, C. (eds) (2012). *Law, state and religion in the new Europe: Debates and dilemmas*. Cambridge: Cambridge University Press.

Cases

Ahmad v UK (1982) 4 EHRR 126
Darby v Sweden (1991) 13 EHRR 774
Eweida and Ors v United Kingdom (2013) ECHR 37
Kokkinakis v Greece (1993) 17 EHRR 397 [31]
Lautsi v Italy, Appl. No. 30814/06, Grand Chamber, 18 March 2011
Refah Partisi (The Welfare Party) and Others v Turkey (2003) 37 EHRR 1
X v Denmark (1976) 5 DR 157

9 The representation of religion in the European Union

Lucian N. Leustean

Introduction

In a secularised continent, the construction of the European Union (EU) has been predominately bureaucratic with religious actors more visible at the local level. The signing of the Treaties of Rome in 1957 and the merging of the executive bodies of the three European Communities (EC) in the late 1960s occurred at a time when academic scholars announced the inevitable death of religion and the emergence of various secularisation models.[1] One of the most widely circulated comments came from sociologist Peter Berger who pointed out that, if the trend persisted, in the twenty-first century "religious believers are likely to be found only in small sects, huddled together to resist a worldwide secular culture" (Berger, 1968: 3; see also 1999).

Despite the widespread perception that religious actors were passive to the construction of the European project, relations between churchmen and politicians at the local and supranational levels have been a constant mark from the Schuman Declaration until today. What mattered were not only the religious communities' views of political dynamism in Brussels and Strasbourg but also their involvement in policy-making as societal actors in the EU. This chapter focuses on the mobilisation of religious networks in the process of European integration. It examines the typology of transnational religious structures, compares the main policy areas for religious/convictional actors, and provides a list of religious/convictional actors in dialogue with European institutions.

Religious dialogue with European institutions

As a general trend, Christian churches remained quiet on the process of European integration. In a report presented at a meeting organised by the Christian Study Group on European Unity in 1968, Hans Hermann Walz attempted to provide an explanation of the lack of churches' official response from the Treaties of Rome until then. He pointed out that during this period

> not one church synod, no single official speaker of any one of our churches have ever issued a statement of encouragement, criticism or even

warning in the matter of the Common Market and its problems. This is to be compared with the fact that in these months hardly any official or semi-official church gathering goes away without a more or less enlightened pronouncement on the Vietnam war and that in recent years at least seven official statements have been made about one or two cinema-pictures of Swedish origin which seemed to offend moral sentiments about sex.

(Walz, 1968: 13)

In Walz's opinion, the limited public involvement of churches towards the European Communities was due to two major factors. Firstly, churches seemed "to be incompetent in European matters" (1968: 16) The European Community was regarded a purely economic and political project and technical details and disputes on agricultural subsidies and economic quotas did not have a theological substance which could raise interest among local congregations. Instead, churches were eager to take a stand on issues on which they could easily identify between the terms "good" and "bad." Secondly, "individualism, Puritanism and secularism" had a strong impact on Western European churches (1968: 16). Churches could not easily distance themselves from the past and the process of Western integration was perceived by many churchmen as an opposite movement to the communist regimes of the East. In conclusion, Walz suggested that although churches remained largely quiet, the most successful engagement with the EC was done by transnational reflection groups. In his opinion,

[w]hat the churches as corporate bodies will not do at present, can and must be done by Christian groups of people willing to sacrifice honoured values for the future and being able to accept their European heritage. These groups connected with one another from country to country must try to change the atmosphere in which our churches largely live. For this purpose they should not restrain themselves to political argumentation – which of course is very necessary. They must go into theological, historical and sociological arguments. Moreover, they should not only speak in general to a general church public, but they should try to convince church leaders and theological thinkers person by person and step by step.

(Walz, 1968: 16)

The establishment of the 'Ecumenical Commission on European Cooperation' was the most appropriate example in this sense. A few months after the Schuman Declaration, in September 1950, a transnational group of Protestant and Anglican politicians and churchmen set up a highly selective group titled the 'Ecumenical Commission on European Cooperation' (ECEC), which provided expertise to churches on the process of European integration.[2] At the pressure of churchmen from the World Council of Churches (WCC), the group would change its name twice: in 1953 to the 'Committee on the

Christian Responsibility for European Cooperation' (CCREC) and in 1966 to the 'Christian Study Group on European Unity' (CSGEU), lasting until the Roehampton Conference in 1974.

The ECEC was informally affiliated with the WCC and had an international membership with churchmen and politicians from the European Coal and Steel Community (ECSC) and other Western European countries which later joined the EC (Britain, Denmark, Sweden). Its selective membership represented a wide political and religious spectrum in Western Europe bringing together experts affiliated with both the EC and the Council of Europe. In addition, the expertise of the group would become more influential with some of its members acquiring prime positions of leaderships in Western Europe, such as Jean Rey, European Commissioner in charge of External Relations (1958–67) and President of the European Commission (1967–70); Gustav Heinemann, President of Federal Republic of Germany (1969–74); and Max Kohnstamm, General Secretary of the High Authority of the European Coal and Steel Community (1952–56) and Vice-President of the Action Committee for the United States of Europe (1956–75).[3]

Furthermore, in the 1960s, the CCREC members were instrumental in supporting the establishment of ecumenical bodies in Brussels. This was particularly visible in 1964 when leading churchmen from the six EC countries, Britain, and Switzerland established a transnational network in Brussels, titled the 'Consultative Committee of Churches for the European Communities'.[4] In 1966 the Consultative Committee was paralleled by the establishment of a lay office at the initiative of officials working in European institutions, 'the Ecumenical Centre in Brussels'.[5] Both ecumenical bodies shared the same office and monitored the policy-making of the European Communities. Their main functions were both to inform churches of decisions taken at European level but also to involve national churches on reflecting on the process of European integration.[6]

While concrete steps were taking place in Brussels, the non-public response of churches towards European integration was mainly due to the impact of the Cold War. From their beginning the European Communities were a political project with a defined regional scope and, consequently, this regionalism was perceived by churchmen as an obstacle to the dialogue between East and West. However, despite official reticence, the political drive of the EC would gradually lead to an increasing Europeanisation of religious transnational networks.

Although ECSC countries as a whole were predominantly Catholic, relations between European institutions and the Roman Catholic Church developed on the initiative of local dioceses, at least in France and Belgium, rather than as the policy of the Holy See towards European federalism. Between 1950 and 1952 the diocese in Strasbourg had a small office monitoring the Council of Europe; however, the office was closed due to financial reasons and lack of interest from the Holy See.[7] A new office was opened by Jesuit clergy in Strasbourg in 1956 that aimed to provide a link between the Council of Europe and the Roman Catholic Church. This office, named the 'Catholic European Study Information Centre' (*Office Catholique d'Information sur les Problèmes Européens* – OCIPE), opened a branch in Brussels in 1963. OCIPE ran in parallel with the 'European Catholic Centre' (*Foyer Catholique Européenne*), which was established in the same year looking after the pastoral needs of EU officials and their families in Brussels.[8] After the Second Vatican Council a large number of religious bodies entered into contact with European institutions, some of which opened offices in Brussels to provide expertise and a global network on education, development, humanitarian aid, and diplomatic relations, such as the Council of the Bishops' Conferences of Europe in 1963;[9] the CIDSE – International Co-operation for Development and Solidarity in 1967; the Catholic International Education Office in 1974; and, the European Committee for Catholic Education in 1974. The increasing number of Catholic offices in Brussels was supported by the appointment of a Papal Nuncio in charge of diplomatic relations between the Holy See and the European Community in 1970.

The first elections to the European Parliament in 1979 encouraged further developments in the Brussels strategy of churches. The Quaker Council for European Affairs opened an office in 1979 while the Holy See established an official representation named 'the Commission of Bishops' Conferences of the European Community' (COMECE) in 1980 which provided a direct link between Catholic bishops in the European Community and European institutions.

Both the Catholic and Protestant offices in Brussels and Strasbourg operated with a small number of personnel, mainly appointed by national religious hierarchies, and with limited financial support from their churches and from the European Commission. These offices brought together not only churchmen from EC member states but also officials working in European institutions who provided expertise in areas traditionally considered outside the interest of churches, such as agriculture and migration.

This exchange of information and knowledge between churches and European institutions reflected the private–public nature of religion. The concept of 'religion' was associated with the personal interests of some EU officials while religious representations were regarded as part of the increasing number of civil society organisations lobbying in Brussels. The EU officials' involvement in religious organizations had a double impact. Firstly, it led to increasing contact between Catholic and Protestant offices that culminated with the 1974 Roehampton Conference. The conference represented the climax of inter-religious relations in Western Europe and was dedicated to the process of European integration. Secondly, the Conference led to the establishment of a Joint Protestant-Catholic Working Group in Brussels to provide a theoretical investigation of the 'purpose' (*finalité*) of European integration and a practical analysis of the role of churches, particularly in the field of development policy. This Group became an established representation named the 'European Ecumenical Commission on Development' (EECOD) and ran from 1975 to 1996.

A new turn in relations between European institutions and religious communities took place in the early 1980s. On the recommendation of Secretary General Émile Noël, President Gaston Thorn of the European Commission appointed Umberto Stefani, Director at the Secretariat General, as Special Counsellor on 13 September 1983 in charge of compiling a census of religious organisations and as an informal liaison officer with the Holy See. Stefani also retained this position later during the first years of Jacques Delors's presidency and was instrumental in organising the visits of Pope John Paul II to European institutions in 1985 and 1988.

Delors's interest in religious and ethical issues and the increasing mobilisation of religions on European issues in the context of the Single European Act led to an increasing number of meetings with religious and ethical organisations. New religious bodies set up offices in Brussels and engaged in an informal type of dialogue. These included the European Union of Jewish Students, which opened an office in 1982, while the European Commission received delegations from the European Jewish Congress in 1987 and the Ecumenical Patriarchate in 1989. After the death of Jean-Louis Lacroix, who worked on ethical issues and was one of Delors's closest advisors, Delors appointed the so-called 'Lacroix Group' of advisors in 1987. Although the group did not have an official mandate to liaise with churches, on 8 March 1989 Delors established a new advisory group named the 'Forward Studies Unit' (FSU) (*Cellule de prospective*) under the leadership of Jean-Claude Morel, a former Director-General, and Jérôme Vignon, Coordinator of Studies. The FSU continued the Lacroix Group's previous expertise and was asked to establish regular contact with churches and religious communities.[10]

The FSU's official mandate on religion led to the appointment of Marc Luyckx as Secretary in charge of religious dialogue in September 1990. Luyckx was a former Catholic priest with a doctorate in Russian and Greek theology from the *Pontificio Istituto Orientale*. He served as Secretary of the EECOD from 1985 until 1989, being involved in the work of Catholic-Protestant representations in Brussels. In 1990, he wrote a report on a comparative analysis of the Abrahamic religions and atheist communities and concluded that, despite the process of secularisation, there was an increasing interest in spirituality coupled with science and technology (Luyckx, 1992).

Luyckx's drive in favour of closer relations between the Commission and a wide range of religious and convictional communities that needed to be better organised at pan-European level was paralleled by a large number of new religious representations. They included churches (the Brussels Office of the Evangelical Church in Germany in 1990; the Jesuit Refugee Service Europe in 1991; the Liaison Office of the Orthodox Church to the European Union in 1994, under the jurisdiction of the Ecumenical Patriarchate), religions (CEJI – A Jewish Contribution to an Inclusive Europe in 1990; the Forum of European Muslim Youth and Student Organization in 1996; the European Bahá'í Business Forum in 1993) and communities of conviction (European Humanist Federation in 1991).

In October 1996, Luyckx was replaced by Thomas Jansen, Secretary-General of the European People's Party, who retained his position during Santer's presidency. In the same year, the Forward Studies Unit was renamed as the Group of Political Advisors to the European Commission (GOPA). During Romano Prodi's presidency, Michael Weninger, a former Austrian diplomat with studies in theology and philosophy was appointed in charge of contact with churches and religious communities within GOPA.

Both Jansen's and Weninger's leaderships coincided with the establishment of a European programme titled 'A Soul for Europe: Ethics and Spirituality', which was intended to promote religious dialogue between Christians, Jews, Muslims, and Humanists and was administered by the European Ecumenical Commission for Church and Society. The programme had its origins in Delors's meeting with religious leaders in 1990 in which he suggested that Europe needed 'a soul'. However, it failed to lead to a unified European stance on religious and convictional issues.[11]

The establishment of the Convention on the Future of Europe in 2001 and discussions on the *Treaty Establishing a Constitution for Europe* brought new religious actors in contact with European institutions. The decision to exclude references to 'God' and 'Christianity' in the Preamble of the Constitution, and debates in the intergovernmental conference between 2003 and 2004 revealed that despite an increase in religious lobbying in Brussels, national governments continued to have a powerful voice in issues related to religion.[12]

The institutionalisation of religious relations was the product of intergovernmental negotiations during the Convention. In 2005, GOPA was renamed the Bureau of European Policy Advisors (BEPA).[13] In 2007, Jorge César das Neves, a Portuguese official with a background in philosophy, was appointed in charge of relations with religions and 'convictional communities'; he retained the position until January 2012 when he was replaced by Katharina von Schnurbein, a German national who was previously the Commission Spokesperson for Employment, Social Affairs and Equal Opportunities and the Chair of the European Affairs Committee at the German Bundestag in Berlin. Katharina von Schnurbein remains the only EU official in European institutions with a direct mandate to coordinate religious dialogue, although recent proposals have been put forward to create a similar position in the European Parliament. On 1 November 2014, President Jean-Claude Juncker delegated the implementation of religious dialogue to Vice-President Frans Timmermans. At the same time, the Bureau of European Policy Advisors has been replaced by a European Political Strategy Centre, which advises the President of the European Commission. For the first time after the 1992 Maastricht Treaty, the issues of 'religion' and 'faith' have been excluded from the attributions of this Centre and have instead been placed within the Directorate-General Justice and the newly established European External Action Service.[14]

The functional breakdown of representations

A comparative analysis of the material collected from the archives and public documents issued by the European Commission, Catholic, Protestant, and Humanist bodies reveals that 120 actors have been in dialogue with the European Commission from 1957 until today, 82 of which have opened representations in Brussels. Although not definitive with many other religious and convictional organisations having approached European institutions informally, these numbers demonstrate the increasing interest in issues of 'religion' and 'faith' among a wide range of policy makers.

Before the 1950s Brussels already had offices of a number of Catholic bodies, such as the European Young Christian Workers and the Conference of International Catholic Organizations. The most significant increase in the number of Catholic organisations is visible after the establishment of the European Coal and Steel Community in 1951 and after the Merger Treaty of the European Community in 1966. However, the latter increase is also directly linked to the Second Vatican Council, which led to a new stage in church policy towards European institutions. After the Maastricht Treaty in 1992, new Catholic bodies, which are in contact with European institutions, tend to have representations in Brussels rather than outside Belgium.

The Protestant, Anglican, and Orthodox communities mobilised extremely slowly in the early years of the process of European integration. In particular, Delors's call for finding 'a soul for Europe' led to the parallel establishment of new bodies and offices in the EU and in Brussels. While the Catholic presence represented a coordinated engagement of the Holy See in dialogue with the European Community, the other Christian confessions became more directly involved only after the European institutions opened their doors to a wide range of interest groups. An overview of all religious representations in Brussels reveals that the increase in their numbers has been directly linked to the political evolution of the EU. While the Roman Catholic Church remains the dominant confession in terms of the number of religious representations, after the Single European Act the non-Catholic, other religions, and convictional actors witnessed a steep increase.

Religious representations in the EU are divided into diplomatic representations, official representation of churches, inter-church organisations or networks, confessional or convictional organisations, religious orders, and single-issue organisations.

Diplomatic representations

The Roman Catholic Church is the only religious confession with a diplomatic representation in Brussels, with a Papal Nuncio for the European Community appointed in 1970. According to diplomatic law, the Papal Nuncio not only represents the Holy See but also has a symbolic mission as the Doyen of the Diplomatic Corps accredited to European institutions.

Concurrent with the increasing number of representations after the Maastricht Treaty, the Order of Malta entered into contact with the European Commission in the early 1990s and opened a diplomatic representation in 2003. However, the Order of Malta is not recognised by all EU member states; its diplomatic relations are recognised only by the European Commission and not by the other European institutions. In 2006, the European Commission opened an EU diplomatic delegation to the Holy See and, in the following year, the delegation was given diplomatic attributions regarding the Order of Malta.

Official representations of churches

A distinct entity is the 'official representation of churches'. Churches have been firstly represented by either pastoral bodies or by inter-church organisations. Although the Catholic Church was in contact with European institutions through OCIPE, the European Catholic Centre and other Catholic agencies, it opened an 'official' representation only in 1980, namely the Commission of Bishops' Conferences of the European Community (COMECE). The COMECE is in direct contact with a large number of Catholic bodies and represents the official voice of the Roman Catholic Church to European institutions.

The first Protestant church to have an independent office was the Evangelical Church of Germany (*Evangelischen Kirche in Deutschland* – EKD) in 1990.[15] The office provides legal expertise to the Church and Society Commission of the Conference of European Churches (CSC/CEC) and represents the EKD to European institutions.

After the Maastricht Treaty, a large number of churches followed a similar pattern to the EKD. Although they were and remained part of inter-church structures, they have gradually opened their own offices. In some cases, churches have chosen to be more visibly part of the structure of an inter-church organisation by sending an officer representing them (for example, representatives from Sweden and Finland working in the CSC/CEC). Other churches have decided to maintain contact with their previous inter-church partners while having set up offices of their own, such as the Ecumenical Patriarchate (1994), the Orthodox Church of Greece (1998), the Romanian and the Cypriot Orthodox Churches (2007), and the Church of England (2008).

Inter-church or convictional organisations/networks

Inter-church or convictional organisations/networks have a large membership and represent most confessions within a specific branch of a faith. From the beginning of the process of European integration, churches were grouped in inter-church organisations or networks that represented their interests. The World Council of Churches (1948) and the Conference of European Churches (1959) had informal contact with offices in Brussels.[16] In addition, some inter-church networks separated from these organisations and established their own representations, such as the European Evangelical Alliance (1994) and the Pentecostal European Fellowship (2005).

A number of non-Christian and convictional communities have established their own offices in Brussels. The main distinction between this type of structure and those above is in the membership. The confessional/convictional organisations/networks represent either only a community within a larger confession (for example, B'nai B'rith Europe) or a group of confessional/ convictional organisations (for example, the European Union of Jewish Students or the European Humanist Federation). A large number of these organisations/networks were established before the European Coal and Steel Community but only became engaged in dialogue with European institutions after the Single European Act.

Religious orders

Although religious orders are associated only with the Roman Catholic Church, they do not fit into one of the above categories due to their nature and operation. Their prime activity is pastoral, some of them carrying out advocacy work which is independent of the official policy of the Holy See. The Jesuit order has been the most active in monitoring the activities of European institutions, opening a religious office in Strasbourg in 1956 and in Brussels in 1963. A European office of the Jesuit Refugee Service was opened in 1990 while the Dominican order established a centre (ESPACES – Spirituality, Culture and Society in Europe) in 2001.

Single-issue organisations

The majority of religious and convictional organisations represent single-issue groups, such as education, humanitarian aid and advocacy. They operate either on an exclusive 'single' issue or are engaged in a few issues at the same time. The single-issue organisations span across all churches, religions, and communities of convictions and are actively engaged in EU policy areas. Most of them are in dialogue with European institutions either through diplomatic representation, official representation of churches, or inter-church or convictional organisations/networks. For example, the majority of Christian single-issue organisations maintain close relations and are represented by the COMECE and the CSC/CEC in their dialogue with European institutions.

Policy considerations on 'religion' and 'faith' in the European Union

Which are the main policy areas of interest to religious and convictional communities as part of their dialogue with European institutions? How have these policy areas changed during the construction of the European Union?

An insight into the policy interests of religious communities is provided by the annual statements published in *European Issues* produced from 1950 until 1974 by the Ecumenical Commission on European Cooperation (ECEC), the first transnational religious network in dialogue with European institutions. The analysis in these statements, of topics circulated among churchmen and EU officials, demonstrates that in the 1950s the main policy area of consideration was the rather broad topic of 'the meaning of Europe'. Finding a commonly agreed view in relation to this on how to engage with the process of European integration continued throughout the 1960s until the ECEC's dissolution in 1974.

The ECEC was particularly interested in raising awareness among churches at the national level, and most statements were directed towards identifying the benefits and weaknesses of EC membership for existing and prospective EC member states. This type of policy engagement, which placed a considerable emphasis on national awareness rather than a systematic supranational dialogue, was influenced by both the limited engagement of national churches with the European Communities and the evolution of the Cold War. As highlighted in Walz's statement at the beginning of this chapter, the process of identifying concrete policy areas in which churches could have made a specific contribution were underdeveloped in the 1950s and the 1960s. Topics such as 'youth' and 'aid' appeared sporadically during this period. Although the ECEC ended its annual meetings in 1974, the Roehampton Conference, which took place in the same year bringing together Catholic and Protestant participants, led to the establishment of a transnational religious network on 'development issues'. A more visible engagement of churches with EC policy areas became evident in the 1970s and the 1980s when, in addition to 'development', churches raised concerns on the impact of inter-European 'migration' as a common area for both churches and European institutions.

President Delors's encouragement of dialogue between the EU and a wide range of religious and convictional organisations, particularly after 1990, led to the emergence of a professionalized type of religious and convictional organisation in Brussels. This professionalized type involved not only churches but also Muslim and Humanist organisations which were invited in the early 1990s to mobilise themselves at the European level and sent representatives to Brussels to participate in religious dialogue with the European Commission.[17] New policy areas were consequently put forward as areas of interest for European institutions and religious/convictional bodies, including 'education', 'institutional and legal affairs', 'bioethics', 'advocacy', 'inter-cultural and inter-religious dialogue', 'climate change', 'humanitarian aid', 'technology', and 'investment'.

In terms of numbers, an overview of 120 religious and convictional actors which were in dialogue with European institutions from 1982 until 2012 reveals that the Roman Catholic Church has the largest number of bodies in Brussels. However, this number is very close to that of other Christian communities. The main difference between these bodies is that the number of

Catholic single-issue organisations is significantly higher than those of other Christian churches. On the other hand, the number of official representations of churches is almost half that of single-issue organisations revealing that churches tend to become more specialised, working on policy issues directly with European institutions.

While a large number of 'religions' and 'communities of conviction' have entered into dialogue with European institutions, they mostly belong to the category of organisations/networks with a limited number in single-issue organisation indicating that they lack the policy expertise and direct implementation at the national and international levels of EU programmes.

Although a clear framework has not been established to indicate the ways in which dialogue between European institutions and religious representations should take place, the Lisbon institutionalisation implies that working on specific EU policy issues is the common denominator.

With the exception of official meetings between 1982 and 1990 that have been recorded by the Commission, it is difficult to obtain a detailed record of all encounters between EU officials and religious bodies. However, the data reveals that the European Commission tends to have a similar number of meetings with the Roman Catholic Church and Protestant/Anglican communities taken together as a bloc. Protestant/Anglican and Orthodox communities have been mainly represented by the CSC/CEC and the Roman Catholic Church by COMECE. If the figures only accounted for one particular Protestant/Anglican church, such as the Evangelical Church of Germany, the Church of England, or the Church of Scotland, they would indicate the predominance of Catholic meetings. However, this perception has to note that the CSC/CEC dialogue with European institutions accounts for a large number of churches while, similarly, COMECE accounts for a significant number of Catholic faithful.

After 2005 the number of meetings to include all churches, religions and communities of conviction witnessed an increase, reflecting the decision of President Barroso to organise annual high-level meetings with their religious and convictional leaders. The increase also reflects the fact that Orthodox churches established their own offices in Brussels rather than being represented by the CSC/CEC,[18] while dialogue with Muslim representatives has witnessed a comparable increase especially after the July 2005 London bombings. Dialogue with Jewish communities was constant from the 1980s onwards with a similar increase after 2005. In 2007, the European Commission decided to have separate meetings between, on the one hand, churches and religions, and, on the other hand, communities of conviction. Since this date, the number of communities of conviction in dialogue with the European Commission has witnessed an increase, in particular the number of Masonic lodges.

The Lisbon institutionalisation of religious dialogue builds on a long history of relations between institutions and religious/convictional actors. Although the number of representations in Brussels increased considerably after the Maastricht Treaty not all of them are officially engaged in dialogue with the European Commission. Small religious communities acting independently or those that are perceived as controversial in the eyes of EU officials are not invited to be part of the official dialogue. However, by maintaining an office in Brussels, they participate in policy programmes developed by the EU. This trend is most visible after 2007 and demonstrates that the Commission has become more selective in choosing its partners of dialogue.

Currently, meetings are organised as working groups (bringing religious and convictional experts based either in Brussels or at the national level together with EU officials working on specific issues), dialogue meetings (seminars) and meetings between the highest level of political and religious leadership in Europe. The topics for discussions within working groups indicate that representations are required to provide expertise on a wide range of European policy issues, such as climate change, migration, development, and financial reform. Most representations operate with a small office in Brussels supported by only a few members of staff. The number of meetings with the European Commission suggests that only those religious and convictional representations that are able to adapt their agenda according to new topics within working groups are invited to be part of official discussions. In addition, the Commission is interested in acquiring expertise from representations on policy issues while ensuring that there is a direct communication between national and supranational institutions.

Conclusion

Religious communities have had a timid relationship with the European institutions. Although officially churches were attached to national politics and influenced by the evolution of the Cold War, religious transnational networks were present from the first days of the ECSC and the EC. They engaged in dialogue with EC officials and politicians involved in the process of European integration and aimed to bring their national congregations in direct contact with European institutions.

The degree of European public support for religious engagement with European institutions remains an open area for further analysis. Although Article 17 of the Lisbon Treaty institutionalises a mechanism of religious dialogue, it is unclear if this dialogue could be perceived as 'business as usual' or only an attempt to increase the public image and visibility of the EU.[19] The European Commission remains the only institution which has set up a direct mandate of dialogue with 'churches, religions, and communities of conviction'; however, finding a common balance on how to engage with religious and convictional representatives in Europe and beyond remains a contested issue.

Acknowledgments

Data in this chapter has been corroborated from interviews with former and current religious practitioners and civil servants and material from the following bodies and archives: the Bureau of European Policy Advisers (BEPA) of the European Commission, Brussels; the Church and Society Commission of the Conference of European Churches (CSC/CEC), Brussels; the Commission of the Bishops' Conferences of the European Community (COMECE), Brussels; the Jesuit European Office – OCIPE, Brussels; the European Catholic Centre (*Foyer Catholique Européen*), Brussels; the Quaker Council for European Affairs, Brussels; *Centre d'Action Laïque*, Brussels; the Historical Archives Service of the European Commission, Brussels; Lambeth Palace Archives, London; and, the Archive of the World Council of Churches, Geneva. I am grateful to the staff in these organisations for permission to read their documents. This chapter does not reflect the official position of any of the above organisations. The chapter draws on Leustean (2013a).

Notes

1 For secularisation in post-war Europe, see Martin (1978) and Davie (2000; 2002).
2 For the history of relations between ecumenical organisations and European institutions see Greschat and Loth (1994), Leustean (2014) and Burton (2015).
3 Among the founders of the ECEC in 1950 were André Philip, the French Economic Minister (1946–47) and head of the French delegation to the European Economic Commission of the United Nations in 1947; Connie L. Patijn, the Dutch delegate to the United Nations Economic and Social Council; Max Kohnstamm, Counsellor in the Dutch Ministry of Foreign Affairs; Gustav Heinemann, German Minister of Interior, member of Bundestag representing the CDU and President of the Synod of the Evangelical Church of Germany; Kenneth Grubb, Chairman of the Churches Commission of International Affairs office in London; Denis de Rougemont, a writer and leader of the cultural section of the European Movement; and Pierre Mahillon, a Belgian Magistrate.
4 The Consultative Committee of Churches in the European Communities was established by Protestant churches in the ECSC and the UK in 1964. It was renamed the Commission of Churches in the European Communities in 1972; the Ecumenical Commission for Church and Society in the European Communities in 1979; the European Ecumenical Commission for Church and Society in 1985; and was integrated into the Conference of European Churches in 1999. An office was opened in Strasbourg in 1986.
5 The Ecumenical Centre in Brussels was registered as an *Association internationale sans but lucratif* in *Moniteur belge* no 2734 on 20 May 1965. In 1966 the Centre employed the Reverend Marc Lenders as Secretary, a position he retained until 1999.
6 See also Coupland (2006) and Zeilstra (1995).
7 For OCIPE in the early 1950s see, Chenaux (2007). For Catholic mobilisation in the European Communities in the early 1960s, see Leustean (2013b).
8 For Christian democracy, see Kaiser (2007) and van Hecke and Gerard (2004).
9 The Council of the Bishops' Conferences of Europe had its headquarters in St Gallen, Switzerland, and some of its members entered into contact with European institutions, without opening an official representation in Brussels.
10 The FSU was placed directly under the President's authority and was composed of eleven Brussels officials, two experts, five interns, and one national official (Pour mieux se connaître, 1991).
11 The programme was set up in 1993 and ended in 2004. For the minutes of the 1990 meeting see Leustean (2013a).

12 For the position of various churches on the Preamble and Article 17 see Leustean (2007 and 2014); Foret and Schlesinger (2006); Foret (2015); and Nelsen and Guth (2015); and Milton's chapter in this volume.
13 For an overview of religious dialogue with European institutions see, Jansen (2000), de Charentenay (2003), Weninger (2007) and Massignon (2007).
14 For more on religion and politics in the European Union, see Vincent and Willaime (1993), Leustean and Madeley (2010), Nelsen, Guth and Fraser (2001), Robbers (1996), Berger, Davie and Fokas (2008), Byrnes and Katzenstein (2006), McCrea (2010), Madeley (2009), Messner (1999) and Werkner and Liedhegener (2013).
15 The EKD has been one of the founding members and the largest financial contributor to the establishment of the Consultative Commission of Churches in the European Communities in 1964. After the Merger Treaty, the EKD aimed to establish an independent office in 1969, but this was discouraged by the President of the European Commission who suggested that churches are better represented by an inter-church organisation.
16 The official positions of both the World Council of Churches and the Conference of European Churches towards the process of European integration were affected by Cold War divisions.
17 For the dialogue between Muslim organisations and European institutions see Silvestri (2009). On Islam in Europe, see Roy (2004), Ramadan (2005) and Tibi (2012).
18 In December 2014, the CSC/CEC fully merged with the Conference of European Churches.
19 Article 17 of the Lisbon Treaty states: "The Union respects and does not prejudice the status under national law of churches and religious associations or communities in the Member States. The Union equally respects the status under national law of philosophical and non-confessional organisations. Recognising their identity and their specific contribution, the Union shall maintain an open, transparent and regular dialogue with these churches and organisations."

References

Berger, P. (ed.) (1999). *The desecularization of the world: Resurgent religion and world politics*. Grand Rapids, MI: Eerdmans.

Berger, P. (1968). A bleak outlook is seen for religion. *New York Times*. 25 January.

Berger, P., Davie, G., and Fokas, E. (2008). *Religious America, secular Europe? A theme and variations*. London: Ashgate.

Burton, W. (2015). *The European vision and the churches. The legacy of Marc Lenders*. Geneva, Switzerland: Globethics.net with CEC.

Byrnes, T. A., and Katzenstein, P. J. (eds) (2006). *Religion in an expanding Europe*. Cambridge: Cambridge University Press.

Chenaux, P. (2007). *De la Chrétienté a l'Europe: Les Catholiques et l'idee Européenne au XXe Siècle*. Tours, France: CID Editions.

Coupland, P. (2006). *Britannia, Europa and Christendom: British Christians and European integration*. Basingstoke: Palgrave Macmillan.

Davie, G. (2002). *Europe, the exceptional case: Parameters of faith in the modern world*. London: Darton, Longman and Todd.

Davie, G. (2000). *Religion in modern Europe: A memory mutates*. Oxford: Oxford University Press.

de Charentenay, P. (2003). Les relations entre l'Union européenne et les religions. *Revue du Marché Commun et de l'Union Européenne*, 465: 90–100.

Foret, F., and Schlesinger, P. (2006). Political roof and sacred canopy? Religion and the EU Constitution. *European Journal of Social Theory*, 9(1): 59–81.
Foret, F. (2015). *Religion and politics in the European Union: The secular canopy.* Cambridge: Cambridge University Press.
Greschat, M., and Loth, W. (1994). *Die Christen und die Enstehung der Europäischen Gemeinschaft.* Stuttgart, Germany: Kohlhammer.
Kaiser, W. (2007). *Christian democracy and the origins of European Union.* Cambridge: Cambridge University Press.
Jansen, T. (2000). Europe and religions: The dialogue between the European commission and churches or religious communities. *Social Compass*, 47(1): 103–112.
Leustean, L. N. (2014). *The ecumenical movement and the making of the European Community.* Oxford: Oxford University Press.
Leustean, L. N. (2013a). Does God matter in the European Union? In Leustean, L. N. (ed.), *Representing religion in the European Union: Does God matter?* (pp. 1–32). London: Routledge.
Leustean, L. N. (2013b). Roman Catholicism, diplomacy and the European communities, 1957–1964. *Journal of Cold War Studies*, 15(1): 53–77.
Leustean, L. N. (2007). The place of God: Religious terms in the debate on the European constitution. In Cohen, A. and Vauchez, A. (eds), *La constitution Européenne: Elites, mobilisations, votes* (pp. 113–127). Brussels, Belgium: Presses de l'Université de Bruxelles.
Leustean, L. N., and Madeley, J. T. S. (eds) (2010). *Religion, politics and law in the European Union.* London: Routledge.
Luyckx, M. (1992). Religions confronted with science and technology: Churches and ethics after Prometheus. Gordon, D. and Cooper, T. (trans), *European Commission.* Brussels, Belgium: Forecasting and Assessment in Science and Technology [FAST]. Retrieved from http://vision2020.canalblog.com/archives/religions_science_and_technology/index.html.
McCrea, R. (2010). *Religion and the public order of the European Union.* Oxford: Oxford University Press.
Madeley, J. T. S. (2009). *E unum pluribus*: The role of religion in the project of European integration. In Haynes, J. (ed.), *Religion and politics in Europe, the Middle East and North Africa: Challenges to citizenship, secularisation and democracy* (pp. 114–135). London: Routledge/ECPR Studies in European Political Science.
Martin, D. (1978). *A general theory of secularisation.* Oxford: Blackwell.
Massignon, B. (2007). *Des dieux et des fonctionnaires: Religions et laïcités face au défi de la construction Européenne.* Rennes, France: Presses Universitaires de Rennes.
Messner, F. (1999). La législation culturelle des pays de l'Union Européenne face aux groupes sectaires. In Champion, F. and Cohen, M. (eds), *Sectes et démocratie* (pp. 331–358). Paris: Éditions du Seuil.
Nelsen, B. F., Guth, J. L., and Fraser, C. R. (2001). Does religion matter? Christianity and public support for the European Union. *European Union Politics*, 2(2): 191–217.
Nelsen, B. F., and Guth, J. L. (2015). *Religion and the struggle for European Union: Confessional culture and the limits of integration.* Washington, DC: Georgetown University Press.
Pour mieux se connaître: La cellule de prospective. (December, 1991). *Courrier du Personnel*, 533.
Ramadan, T. (2005). *Western Muslims and the future of Islam.* Oxford: Oxford University Press.

Robbers, G. (ed.) (1996). *State and church in the European Union.* Baden-Baden, Germany: Nomos.
Roy, O. (2004). *Globalized Islam: The search for a new Ummah.* Cambridge: Cambridge University Press.
Silvestri, S. (2009). Islam and religion in the political system of the EU. *West European Politics* 32(6): 1210–1239.
Tibi, B. (2012). *Islamism and Islam.* London: Yale University Press.
van Hecke, S., and Gerard, E. (eds) (2004). *Christian democratic parties in Europe since the end of the cold war.* Leuven, Belgium: Leuven University Press.
Vincent, G., and Willaime, J.-P. (1993). *Religions et transformations de l'Europe.* Strasbourg, France: Presses Universitaires de Strasbourg.
Walz, H. H. (1968). Why is the importance of the integration process so little understood in the churches? *European Issues*, (23): 13–16. [The Archives of the World Council of Churches: Churches Commission on the International Affairs, CSGE, 1965–68].
Weninger, M. H. (2007). *Europa ohne Gott? Die Europäische Union und der Dialog mit den Religionen, Kirchen und Weltanschauungsgemeinschaften.* Baden-Baden, Germany: Nomos.
Werkner, I.-J., and Liedhegener, A. (eds) (2013). *Europäische Religionspolitik: Religiöse Identitätsbezüge rechtliche Regelungen und politische Ausgestaltung.* Heidelberg, Germany: Springer.
Zeilstra, J. (1995). *European unity in ecumenical thinking 1937–1948.* Zoetermeer, Netherlands: Boekencentrum.

10 God and the Constitution

Guy Milton

Introduction: the issue

The United States Declaration of Independence (1776) – probably the most familiar of all foundational documents – opens with words that are among the best known in the English language. It states that all men are "created equal" and "endowed by their Creator with certain inalienable Rights", qualifying this statement as "self-evident".

It is less obvious in a twenty-first century European context that any basic common values, however widely they might be shared, would be universally accepted as self-evident by reference to a creator God. It is therefore perhaps not surprising that, when the European Union (EU) attempted in 2002–03 to draw up a draft Constitution, the suggestion to refer in the preamble to God or Christianity proved to be a significant stumbling block to reaching agreement on the text. The Convention that drew up the draft Constitution spent much of its time debating potentially far-reaching changes to the way in which power is exercised at the European level. But towards the end of its mandate, it also spent time on the issue of the wording of the Constitution's preamble, and in particular on the controversy over the appropriateness of appealing to a transcendent God in a modern legal text (*invocatio dei*),[1] or even of recognising the role of Christianity and the Christian tradition in the development of Europe and its political culture. This discussion served to highlight issues about the identity of Europe, the foundational values of the European Union, and the origins of those values.

This chapter examines this debate and assesses the outcome. It begins by looking at the context of the Constitutional debate, and in particular asks why the issue of *invocatio dei* arose for the first time more than four decades after the signing of the Treaty of Rome[2] – the original founding document of the European Economic Community (as it then was). It then examines the process by which the Constitution was drafted. This was a radical departure from the traditional method of treaty drafting, allowing for the first time the opportunity for input from those outside the EU's institutional framework. The chapter therefore looks at the various participants in this process and the contributions they made to the debate. It examines the dynamics of the negotiating process, both as played out within the formal structures but also as a function of a larger debate. Finally it seeks to evaluate the outcome and how it can help increase our understanding of the wider issue of the relationship between Christianity and the EU, which is the subject of this book.

The context

The 1950 Schuman Declaration, which led directly to the creation of the European Coal and Steel Community and then in 1957 to the Treaty of Rome establishing the European Economic Community (EEC) (Schuman, 1950), proposed the creation of a community in which closer economic cooperation would lead to shared common interest which would help consolidate post-war European reconciliation. The Treaty of Rome was, as a result, a somewhat technocratic and functional text. It had a preamble, but even this was rather prosaic, with the exception of the opening clause that read, "Determined to lay the foundation of an ever closer union among the peoples of Europe" (Preamble).

For the first 45 years of the existence of the European Community (then Union), and despite significant and substantive changes to the original Treaty of Rome, the preamble attracted little attention; in particular few questioned what was meant by an "ever closer union". The preference for continuity (or at least for evolution over revolution) can be explained in part by the fact that the starting point for discussions on further integration was always the existing treaty text. This meant that the onus was on those member states that wanted changes to treaty articles not only to provide justification but also persuade the others to agree. This led to an instinctive reluctance to re-open the existing text unless there were very good arguments for doing so. For more than forty years no one saw any good reason to make any fundamental changes to the preamble.

Yet, despite the inherent conservatism of the process, successive treaty changes have gradually but inexorably led to a significant transfer of power from national to EU level and have resulted in a Europe which is more economically and politically integrated than was probably ever imagined by its founders. Increased integration prompted questions about the extent to which individual European citizens identified with the EU and how to ensure sufficient democratic legitimacy at the European level. The introduction of direct elections to the European Parliament in 1979 was an attempt to address these issues, but in itself was not enough for those who remained uneasy about what they saw as the Union's "democratic deficit" (as it was later coined) despite the fact that over the years the powers of the directly elected European Parliament had steadily and significantly been increased whenever the treaties were amended.

One way of addressing the issue of identity is through an identification of shared values. So in 1999, prompted by concerns that the EU continued to lack a sufficiently clear proclamation of the shared values on which it was founded, the European Council meeting in Cologne agreed to draw up a Charter setting out an exhaustive list of fundamental rights applicable at Union level. The Charter of Fundamental Rights (2010), which was agreed and solemnly proclaimed the following year, begins with a reference to the basic values on which the EU is founded. However, as Casanova points out, the proclamation of these values is "a basic social fact ... the common normative framework shared by most Europeans" (2006: 81). It does not address their origins, transcendent or otherwise, and does not offer any explanation as to why, if at all, these values are particularly European.

A further development was the EU's increasingly rapid enlargement from the original six founding members to fifteen by the turn of the millennium, and a firm commitment to accept 10 more countries – mostly from former communist states in central and eastern Europe – who joined in 2004. Furthermore the European Council meeting in Helsinki in 1999 agreed to accept Turkey as a candidate country, which it described as "destined to join the Union ..." (§12). The first tentative steps had been taken to admit a large and predominantly Muslim country into the European Union.

The combination of these various developments placed an increasing focus on the question of the nature of the political identity of the EU. What does it mean to be European? What is the origin of Europe's values and moral heritage? Where are the limits to Europe's identity and what is it that defines these limits? It should not be surprising that the nature of these questions would increasingly draw the churches into the debate. The decision in 2001 to organise a Convention to address these issues and the subsequent initiative to draw up a Constitution for Europe gave the churches for the first time a more direct voice at the EU level and an opportunity to influence directly the discussions.

It would however be a mistake to assume that religion had been entirely absent for the first few decades of European integration. As earlier chapters of this book have set out in more detail, many of the individuals who were instrumental in the establishment of the original European Community, not least Robert Schuman, were men of faith, products of the Christian Democratic political movement, which has strong roots in the Roman Catholic tradition. Furthermore, the founding principle which lay behind the European project and which is the dominant theme of Schuman's Declaration (1950) is 'solidarity'. Solidarity has both moral and political implications. It implies burden-sharing in the quest for the common good, and in very practical terms underpins an approach to European integration which recognises the equal value of every state to have a voice, to be heard and to play a role in the decision-making process. It is also closely linked to the social teaching of the Roman Catholic Church, which has had a strong influence in the development of the EU.

Perhaps more surprising is the EU's appropriation of the Catholic Church's principle of subsidiarity, included in the treaties for the first time in 1992.[3] Intended to ensure that decisions are taken as closely to the citizen as possible (and so avoid unnecessary 'interference' at the European level), the EU adapted for its own purposes a principle first set out explicitly by Pope Pius XI (1931),[4] who sought to find a balance between non-interference in the natural rights attributed to families and individuals and a recognition of the state in addressing issues of social justice.

But if religion had not been absent, it had certainly been discreet. Only in 1997 was the role of churches explicitly recognised in an EU foundational text. Declaration no. 11 annexed to the Amsterdam Treaty states that "The EU respects and does not prejudice the status under national law of churches and religious associations or communities in the Member States" (it makes the same statement with regard to philosophical and non-confessional organisations) (Treaty of Amsterdam, 1997).

Even though this declaration went largely unnoticed, it was a point of departure for churches and religious organisations. The fact that their existence and role was acknowledged in the treaties for the first time gave them increased confidence to look for opportunities to influence the future development of the EU. The Convention process was just such an opportunity. It was a radical departure from the traditional approach to changing the treaties, and its impact on the outcome was almost certainly much greater than the governments of the member states had ever expected. Furthermore the very public debate – in particular on the preamble to the Constitution – served to bring the churches, whether they sought it or not, very much into the limelight.

The process

Treaty change takes place within the framework of an Inter-Governmental Conference (IGC) bringing together the representatives of the governments of all the member states, and requires their unanimous agreement. In 2000 an IGC was convened to address in particular some key outstanding institutional issues that needed to be settled in advance of the accession of the 10 new member states in 2004. The negotiations were even more difficult than usual, and the outcome (in the form of the 'Nice Treaty') was widely considered as falling short of expectations (Treaty of Nice, 2001).

The experience led member states to agree not only to revisit some key issues in the treaties, but to do so in a very different way. The next IGC was to be preceded by a Convention, which would bring together not just government representatives but also members of national parliaments and representatives of the EU institutions.

Furthermore it was to consult widely, sounding out public opinion and civil society on what exactly they wanted from the EU and how they wanted it to deliver. The mandate given to the Convention left open both the form and content of the outcome. It certainly did not specify that it should result in a Constitution. Nevertheless former French President Valerie Giscard d'Estaing (2002), who in December 2001 had been appointed President of the

Convention, made clear from the outset that he was ambitious and that a complete Constitution for the EU should be the outcome.

The Convention began its work in February 2002 and ended some 15 months later. However the outline of a possible Constitution was only presented by Giscard d'Estaing after the summer break of 2002, and the drafting of the text only started at the beginning of 2003. Because the Convention (at Giscard's insistence) had no rules of procedure, it was unclear from the outset when and how the Convention would consider its work to be complete. Voting was excluded, which meant that the work had to proceed on the basis of consensus. However what exactly was meant by consensus was never defined collectively, but left to Giscard himself to decide. Once the Convention had completed its work, the Constitution was handed over to the member states where it had formally to be approved in an IGC. Those member states who had expected a second chance to negotiate were to be disappointed. The collective political pressure not to re-open the text was huge. The Constitution survived almost intact, was approved by the IGC, and was then submitted, as is always the case, for ratification according to the internal procedures of each Member State.

At first sight the openness of the Convention process looked impressive. All the plenary sessions were open and accessible to the public via web-streaming, an entire session was devoted to hearings of representatives from civil society, all documentation was available on a dedicated website, and a separate Forum website published over 1,200 submissions which were received from a wide range of interested parties.[5] Yet despite these considerable efforts, surveys indicated that the general level of knowledge in the member states about the Convention and its work was disappointingly low. Those who participated in the public hearing or who prepared written submissions were for the most part Brussels-based. The majority represented interest groups whose bread and butter is to follow the EU institutions and attempt to influence the decision-making process. Even the Youth Convention turned out to be far less inspiring than Giscard had hoped.

Despite these criticisms, the openness of the Convention process made it relatively easy for the churches and religious organisations, particularly those with a permanent presence in Brussels, not only to follow closely the work of the Convention but also, where appropriate, to bring their voice to bear on the negotiations. Most obviously that voice was directed at ensuring that – at the least – some recognition was given to Europe's Christian heritage, and therefore focussed on the text of the preamble.

The issue would probably have not arisen at all had Giscard not taken the ambitious decision to draft a Constitution from scratch. His was an innovative approach. It rejected the traditional method of amending the existing treaties, which would instead be repealed in their entirety and replaced with a new consolidated text. The Convention was in effect being invited to go back to basics and re-design the EU. In the event the outcome was not quite as radical as the process implies; indeed a significant part of the existing treaties was transferred wholesale to the draft Constitution. It did however mean that when the text was submitted for ratification in the member states, it looked to be more ambitious than it actually was, and as a result Giscard's approach proved in the longer term to be the undoing of the Constitution.

For Giscard (and for the majority of Convention members) the drafting of a European Constitution also provided an opportunity to place modern European political and economic union in its historical context. This meant going back to first principles, and seeking to identify a shared culture and common values. This in turn raised the issue of whether it was appropriate or desirable to use the preamble of the Constitution to refer to Europe's Christian heritage or even to a transcendent God as the source of those values. The question was not academic: several member states had similar references in their national constitutions. Others did not and rejected the idea from the outset. The stage was set for a lively, confused, and at times very public, debate.

The actors

Even if the Convention process meant that the governments of the member states were not in complete control, they were still the most influential actors in the negotiations, not least because the final say, once the Convention was over, would lie with them alone. And nowhere more than in relation to the issue of the preamble and the discussions over an *invocatio dei*, were the national interests, backgrounds, and traditions of the member states such an important factor in setting the terms of the debate.

All EU member states are signatories of the European Convention on Human Rights (Council of Europe, 1950). In doing so, they have committed themselves to the freedom of thought, conscience and religion. Article 9 of the Convention, which clearly sets out this principle, also recognises that freedom to manifest one's religion may be subject to limitations, but only where there are specific interests in doing so: "in the interests of public safety, for the protection of public order, health or morals, or for the protection of the rights and freedoms of others" (§2).

The commitment to these provisions has ensured a largely consistent approach to the practice of religion across the EU, although there have been some differences over the interpretation on where exactly to set the limitations, not least (as Chapter 8 shows) where these are invoked on the grounds of "the protection of the rights and freedoms of others". The controversy over legislation in France and Belgium over the banning of *burqas* that cover a woman's face entirely is one example. The broad consistency of approach to the principle of the freedom to practise religion however belies a wide variety of attitudes to the role of religion and in particular its relationship with the state. At one end of the spectrum France preaches and practises an approach that calls for a complete separation not just between church and state, but between personal faith and the public sphere. Its constitutional tradition has, ever since the revolution, been resolutely secular (or *laïque*). At the other end lie the United Kingdom and Denmark, both of which have established state religions (although in the case of Denmark this is combined with some of the most liberal legislation almost anywhere in the EU in areas such as free speech and limits on censorship).

Member states' attitudes to the preamble to the Constitution and in particular to whether to include an *invocatio dei* were significantly, but not exclusively, influenced by their own national constitutional traditions. Five of the current 28 member states contain an *invocatio dei*, and more include a reference to Christianity. The German Basic Law adopted in 1949 opens with the words: "Conscious of their responsibility before God and man, ... the German people, in the exercise of their power, have adopted this Basic Law" (Germany, 1949). The Irish Constitution, which is perhaps the most fulsome in its acknowledgment of its Christian tradition, begins by invoking not God but the Holy Trinity: "In the Name of the Most Holy Trinity, from Whom is all authority and to Whom, as our final end, all actions both of men and States must be referred, We, the people of Eire, humbly acknowledging all our obligations to our Divine Lord, Jesus Christ, who sustained our fathers through centuries of trial, ... do hereby adopt, enact, and give ourselves this Constitution" (Ireland, 1937).

The text contains a significant number of further references to God, recognising in particular that all powers of government derive, under God, from the people. Furthermore the practice of religion is not simply protected, but religion itself is "respected and honoured" (Art. 44). Similarly, the Greek Constitution opens with the words "In the name of the Holy and Consubstantial and Indivisible Trinity" (Greece, 1975)

The more recent Polish Constitution (adopted in 1997), although referring to God, takes a more inclusive approach to religious faith, despite its strong Catholic tradition. It states that: "We, the Polish Nation – all citizens of the Republic, both those who believe in God as the source of truth, justice, good and beauty, as well as those not sharing such faith but respecting those universal values arising from other sources ..." (Preamble). Despite accepting the diversity of opinion in the area of faith, it states unequivocally the nation's debt to its Christian heritage: "beholden to our ancestors ... for our culture rooted in the Christian heritage of the Nation and in universal human values, ... recognising our responsibility before God or our own consciences, hereby establish this Constitution of the republic of Poland" (Preamble) (Poland, 1997).

It is perhaps not surprising that, against this background, the representatives of the governments of Ireland and Poland were amongst the staunchest defenders of the inclusion of an *invocatio dei* in the European Constitution. Yet support came also from Italy and Spain, neither of which have any such references in their national constitutions. Both of course are countries with strong Catholic traditions, but more specifically, both were governed at the time by centre-right parties that draw their inspiration from the Christian democratic tradition.

Party affiliation also played a important role in determining the outcome of the Convention's work. If the member states' representatives were largely, but not exclusively, driven by national interest, national and European parliamentarians were motivated to a great extent by party political interest. So the MEPs from the European People's Party (EPP) group in the Convention drew support from their position as the largest political group in the European Parliament, and on a wide range of issues sought alliances with national members from the same political family. It is not therefore surprising that centre right national parliamentarians from Spain, Poland, and Italy were some of the more vocal in calling for a reference to God or to Europe's Christian heritage in the preamble. The strongest opposition to such a reference came from the Socialist political family, with French and Belgian parliamentarians taking the lead in defending a defiantly secular approach.[6]

By bringing together representatives of member-state governments and of both national parliaments and the European Parliament, the Convention became a debating chamber where both national and party political interests found a voice. But the Convention was not insulated from a wide range of other interests that found their voice through public hearings and consultations. Amongst these other interests were those of the churches, which had the Brussels-based structures needed to function effectively as a lobbying mechanism able to resonate with sufficient members of the Convention to influence the outcome of its work, even if, in the case of the preamble, the final result fell short of expectations.

From early in the Convention's work, cooperation between different denominations and church-based organisations was good, beginning with a joint letter to the Convention's President from a range of Christian churches and church-related agencies in the summer of 2002 setting out an agreed list of aspirations. However, during the course of the negotiations the main church actors in the process were, not surprisingly, the Catholic Church, represented by COMECE (the Commission of the Bishop's Conferences of the European Community) and an affiliation of various protestant churches operating under the umbrella of CEC (the Conference of European Churches). Both organisations have strong representational offices in Brussels. COMECE was founded in 1980 in the wake of the first direct elections to the European Parliament, and replaced the existing Catholic Pastoral Information Service. It consists of Bishops delegated by the 26 Catholic Bishops' Conferences (of whom 24 are based within the EU) and seeks both to monitor developments in the EU and maintain a dialogue with the EU institutions. It has a large secretariat based close to them.

The Conference of European Churches is a broad ecumenical organisation representing a range of Protestant denominations. It was founded in 1959 and adopted its first constitution in 1964. Its original purpose was to provide mutual support between the churches across Europe in order to promote reconciliation after the Second World War. The Church and Society Commission, which is part of CEC, has particular responsibility for addressing church and society issues, and monitors developments in various international organisations, including the EU. It has offices in both Brussels and Strasbourg.

All of these actors, both those who were formally part of the Convention process, as well as those, including the churches, who were outside but nevertheless seeking to influence the outcome, played a role in the story of how the EU embarked on a process of drafting a constitution and in so doing began to ask searching questions about Europe's identity, values, and purpose. The next section charts the story of that process by looking at the negotiations on the constitution, and in particular the discussions which centred on whether faith and religious heritage can provide some guidance in the search for answers.

The negotiations

The first six months of the Convention were dedicated to what Giscard (2002) called the "listening phase". Conscious of the very varying degree of awareness of EU issues amongst Convention members (many national parliamentarians were for example unfamiliar with the workings of the EU), he sought to use this time to bring everyone up to a similar level of knowledge. At the same time this phase was useful for him in gauging where the centre ground lay, and so to assist when it came to drafting a text. However the fact that Giscard had already called for a Constitution for Europe in his opening speech to the Convention meant that the parameters of the debate had been fixed from the outset, unless a consensus emerged from within the Convention to embark on a very different path. The disparate composition of the Convention made this unlikely; and Giscard knew this.

The listening phase included a session in June 2002 organised with a view to hearing the views of civil society, although – as already pointed out – this turned out to be less inclusive than had been intended. It was however an opportunity to stimulate interest in the Convention's work and an invitation to any interest groups to offer their contribution. The churches' first substantive reaction was by means of a letter sent in June 2002 and signed by representatives of COMECE and CEC, but also a number of church-based agencies such as Caritas and the European Federation for Diaconia. The letter referred to seven issues: (1) the importance of the EU seeing itself as a community of values, (2) the acknowledgment of Europe's religious heritage, (3) the incorporation of fundamental rights into a future constitution, (4) the need to reflect the churches' social teaching, (5) the importance of contributing to a fair and just system of global governance, (6) the establishment of a structured dialogue with churches and religious communities, and (7) the incorporation of Declaration 11 (on the respect for the status of churches and religious communities) into the text of a constitution.

Two of these issues relate specifically to the role of the churches, and were, in addition to the debate over the preamble, their main priorities. In both cases the requests were accepted and incorporated into the constitution. Article I-52 specifically referred to the status of churches and non-confessional organisations (the latter added at the insistence of those who sought to avoid giving the churches any sort of 'privileged' status) and included both a reference to need for their status to be respected (thereby taking over the language from the existing Declaration 11), as well as adding a commitment to the EU to "maintain an open, transparent and regular dialogue with these churches and organisations" (Treaty Establishing a Constitution for Europe, 2004).

The question of whether or not to acknowledge Europe's Christian heritage (which became subsumed into the wider debate over the preamble), was of a different order given that, unlike the two issues referred to above, it had no practical implications. Yet the provision in Article I-52, giving churches the possibility of influencing directly the EU's decision-making process, attracted virtually no attention, unlike the very public debate over the preamble. Some have even seen this as a conspiracy by the church: the Secretary-General of the European Humanist Federation at the time saw the discussion over the preamble as a deliberate tactic by the churches to divert attention from their real priority of securing a commitment to dialogue with the institutions (Schlesinger and Foret, 2006: 59).

The sense of frustration from members of the Convention in the run-up to the summer holiday period in 2002 at the lack of any substantive work on texts was to some extent mitigated by Giscard's promise to present an outline treaty after the summer break. This he duly did in October, but by then the Convention had embarked on a more detailed examination of specific policy areas through dedicated working groups. It was only in early 2003 that the text of the Constitution began to take shape.

The process of drafting the constitution began with the drafts of individual articles or groups of articles being drawn up by the Convention Secretariat. These were then sent to the Praesidium, which was chaired by Giscard, and composed of his two Vice-Presidents, three government representatives, two representatives of national parliaments, two MEPs, and two members of the Commission. Once examined (and where necessary, modified) by the Praesidium, the texts were circulated to all Convention members. They were then debated, and members were able to submit proposed amendments in writing. The debates and amendments enabled the Praesidium to adjust the texts, which were gradually refined to the point where it was considered they reflected as closely as possible a consensual view.

The preamble was handled slightly differently, and left to nearly the end of the process. Giscard had invited members of the Praesidium to try their hand at a text. Six rose to the challenge, but their contributions were set aside when Giscard himself presented his own text to the Praesidium at the beginning of May 2003. The text drafted by Giscard was not uncontroversial.[7] It began with a reference (in Greek) from Thucydides (Pericles' funeral oration), recalled Europe's cultural, religious and humanist inheritance, set out its calling to continue along a path of civilisation, progress and prosperity, and referred to the proposed motto for Europe of "united in its diversity".

The second paragraph, which subsequently became the focus of the debate over the reference to God or Christianity bears quoting in full:

Drawing inspiration from the cultural, religious and humanist inheritance of Europe, which, nourished by the civilisations of Greece and Rome, characterised by spiritual impulse always present in its heritage and later by the philosophical currents of the Enlightenment, has embedded within the life of society its perception of the central role of the human person and his inviolable and inalienable rights, and of respect for law.

The text as a whole was received with very mixed feelings by the Praesidium. For some it came across as overbearing and pompous, and bore all too obviously the hallmarks of a deeply secular and French approach. The suggestion that the Convention might end the preamble by thanking itself looked particularly smug. However the debate in the Praesidium focussed on the second paragraph and the absence of any reference to God or Christianity (the latter being perhaps surprising given Giscard's well-known opposition to Turkish accession of the EU). Several members argued, on the grounds that it would be a simple statement of fact, for a reference to the role played by the Christian church in the history of Europe. The most vocal proponents were John Bruton, former Irish Prime Minister, who argued strongly both within the Praesidium and publicly for such a reference, and Inigo Mendez de Vigo, the MEP representing EPP interests. The response of Giscard was that the reference to religious heritage in the second paragraph of his text must necessarily refer to Christianity (even if it did not say so) given that it was situated chronologically between the classical civilisations and the Enlightenment. Others considered that referring solely to the Christian tradition could justifiably be criticised on the grounds that it ignored the important contribution throughout European history of other religions and cultures (not least Judaism and Islam). The response would be either to say nothing or end up with a text that, in an attempt to satisfy everyone, risked becoming an unwieldy catalogue. In spite of, or perhaps because of, the clear split in views within the Praesidium, Giscard's text was circulated to Convention members on 28 May 2003 almost unchanged.

Following the circulation of the Praesidium text, a total of 18 written proposals for amendment were received (Reactions to the Draft Articles, 2003). The majority called for the inclusion in one form or another of a reference to Europe's Christian heritage; very few specifically requested an *invocatio dei*. Most notable was an amendment drafted by the Polish members of the Convention (of different political backgrounds) which suggested referring to Europe's Judeo-Christian heritage and which was supported by a total of 37 Convention members. Very similar amendments were received by Gianfranco Fini, the right-wing Italian government representative, and Elmar Brok MEP on behalf of the EPP Group in the Convention.

The Praesidium nevertheless felt it inappropriate to amend the text in response to these calls. The issue was by now a matter of public debate, and sensitivities on both sides were running high. Giscard doubtless calculated that the 18 amendments received still represented a minority of Convention members, that his original text had therefore been close to the mark, and that accepting a change in the text at this late stage would have prompted an even stronger reaction from the opposing camp. When a revised text of the preamble was circulated on 12 June, the changes were relatively modest, and did not respond directly to the written amendments. The new text no longer contained references to the civilisations of Greece and Rome, or to the Enlightenment. It read simply (and – it has to be said – more clearly):

> Drawing inspiration from the cultural, religious and humanist inheritance of Europe, whose values are always present in its heritage, and which has embedded within the life of society its perception of the central role of the human person and his inviolable and inalienable rights, and of respect for law.
> (Revised Texts, 2003: 2)

Many saw the new text as more balanced, but for the proponents of an explicit reference to Europe's Christian heritage, this offered little succour. Furthermore, when the Convention met the following day (13 June), there was no opportunity for further discussions on the preamble. The draft constitution was adopted by acclamation (albeit with an opposing report from a number of dissenting sceptics). Giscard presented the text to EU Heads the following week, and although it was not quite the end of the Convention's work (there were several more meetings devoted to tidying the more detailed policy provisions which formed Part III of the proposed Constitution), members had no further opportunity to discuss the preamble. It seemed that twenty-first century Europe was not going to be able to acknowledge its Christian roots.

The outcome

However, the Convention was not the end of the process (indeed the end was a lot further away than anyone imagined at the time). The representatives of the member-state governments who gathered for the Inter-Governmental Conference found they had little scope to amend the text, and although it took a further year to finalise the negotiations, the work was mainly about details; the Constitution remained largely intact.

Because the Convention was not the end of the process, churches and religious organisations continued to argue that the preamble should be amended. The highest profile intervention came at the end of June 2003 as the Convention was completing its work when Pope John Paul II delivered his Apostolic Exhortation entitled *Ecclesia in Europa*. In it he described the Christian church as being a "central and defining element" in Europe's history which had "shaped the culture of the continent", and therefore appealed for the inclusion in the constitution of a reference to the religious "and in particular the Christian heritage of Europe" (2003: §114). Some member states also continued to harbour hopes that a way could be found for the IGC to address this lacuna in the preamble. At a ministerial meeting in Naples in December

2003, several continued to press the point, but without success. A number of delegations had in any case never really liked the preamble (on the grounds that it was pretentious and unnecessary), and the Finns even called for it to be scrapped altogether. Partly in response to these concerns, it was decided to delete the quotation from Thucydides, despite reluctance from the Greek delegation.

Further pressure came from a French centre-right MEP, Elizabeth Montfort, who launched an appeal in advance of the final meeting of the IGC on 17–18 June 2004. She had initiated a petition in Malta back at the end of 2002 and claimed to have received over a million signatures from across the EU by May 2004. Despite this, neither the campaign nor the petition attracted much attention. Poland, one of the member states most committed to this issue, was in fact preoccupied with the more arcane but politically sensitive issue of vote weighting in the Council, which dominated the final months of the IGC. A last attempt in the form of a letter from seven member states (Portugal, Italy, Slovakia, Poland, Malta, Lithuania, and the Czech Republic) in June 2004 had no effect (Pilette and de Poncins, 2007: 295). The final text of the Constitution – with the preamble unchanged (apart from the loss of Thucydides) was signed in Rome in October 2004.

The Constitution was in effect an international treaty, and once signed had to be ratified by all member states. The choice of procedure for ratification is a matter for each Member State. The majority were either obliged or chose to go for parliamentary ratification. A small number opted for a referendum. The Spanish people approved the Constitution with a strong majority in February 2005, but the bombshell hit at the very end of May when the French voted to reject the text. Only three days later the Dutch followed suit. The Constitution was, at least in its current form, dead.

It is not the place here to analyse why French and Dutch voters rejected the Constitution. The reasons were many and varied, and would almost certainly have led to similar rejections in other member states. But the decision to replace the existing EU treaties with a Constitution, which in itself created the political pressure to hold referendums, certainly played an important role. The title of 'Constitution' was misleading, and explains why the debates in the referendum campaigns were shot through with distortion and intellectual dishonesty. It looked to many as if the EU was appropriating for itself the trappings of a sovereign state, and for some this was a step too far.

But the huge investment in the Convention process, and the vested interests of several member states, not least the Germans, meant that there was weight behind the constitution text, even if it clearly could not survive in its current form. After 18 months of soul-searching within the EU, Germany, which took over the Presidency of the Council of ministers in the first half of 2007, launched a process to retrieve the constitution. The aim was two-fold: to retain as much of the substance of the constitutional text as possible, but to do so in a way which meant that it no longer gave the impression of bringing about a sea-change in the development of the EU. So work began on transforming the text. Gone was the title 'Constitution'. Gone was an approach that meant replacing the existing treaty framework. Instead lawyers and civil servants toiled over the task of transforming the provisions of the Constitution into an amending treaty. The result would look more like a minor evolution than a major revolution. And in so doing, it would not – for most member states – require a referendum; which was precisely the point.

If the work was technical, some of the political issues – including the content of the preamble – never completely disappeared. When Chancellor Merkel, the daughter of a Protestant pastor, visited Pope Benedict XVI at his summer residence in Castel Gandolfo in August 2006, she underlined her attachment to a reference in the preamble to Europe's Christian heritage. Some nine months later, having witnessed the reality of negotiations, she had to express her regret to a meeting of religious leaders in Brussels that the new text would not be able to include such a reference (Rettman 2007).[8]

One of the consequences of rejecting the trappings of a constitutional approach was to return to the original format of the existing treaties. That included jettisoning the new preamble and instead sticking with the existing text that had its origins in the original preamble to the 1957 Treaty of Rome. But it was quickly obvious that, in the light of the Convention's work, and with residual pressure to maintain a reference to Europe's Christian heritage, the absence of even a generic reference to religion would be seen by some as a step backwards. The solution was simple: the existing preamble would be preserved, but the second paragraph from the preamble of the Constitution would be discretely inserted. In this way the new text, or Lisbon Treaty as it became known following its signature in Lisbon in December 2007, preserved a small legacy from the Convention process: religion generally, if not Christianity specifically, was recognised as part of the heritage of Europe. No one objected, but no one cried victory. Such is the nature of compromise.

An assessment

In 2005 COMECE published an evaluation of the original Constitution text. The preamble is seen as something of a mixed result. COMECE states that "an explicit mentioning of God or Christianity would have been a strong signal supporting the identity of Europe", and regrets the absence of any such reference. Yet it takes some comfort from the fact that the Constitution "implicitly accepts the predominant contribution made by Christianity to today's Europe" (2005: 14).

Both the negotiations on the preamble and the very public debate at the time reveal much about the attitudes towards the function of religion in modern Europe, and the churches' role, both current and historical, in giving substance to European identity. The debate was essentially about whether to include a reference to the Christian church in the preamble. Only a small minority were committed to pressing for a reference to God (an *invocatio dei* in the proper sense). Yet the media persisted in framing the debate as one about God, and did so frequently in a way which poked fun – albeit usually rather gently – at the churches. The headlines were the most revealing: one striking example was *The Economist*, which, on 4 December 2003 carried an article entitled 'God meets the lawyers'. In practice the focus of the lobbying of the churches and Christian-based organisations was on securing a reference to the Christian heritage of Europe rather than to God, largely because the former looked more likely to be accepted (even if ultimately this proved not to be the case). For other religious groups, such as the Jews and Muslims, a reference to God would have been more acceptable than singling out the Christian church: Aiman Mazyek, the Secretary General of the Central Council of Muslims in Germany, speaking in 2007, said that German Muslims were disappointed that Christians had not been able, despite their strong lobby, to push through a reference to God (Bolivar, 2007). The dominance of the Christian church as opposed to other religious groups should not be surprising. The church had powerful backers in a number of member-state governments, who are ultimately the masters of treaty texts. Opposition came more from those member states with strong secular traditions than any other religious groups.

The initiative to draft a Constitution for the EU took place in the absence of any serious discussion about European identity. Yet the Constitution – unlike the treaties which had preceded it – sought to go beyond the functional and articulate a sense of community based on a shared history, identity and polity. But when Giscard produced his preamble, it turned out that his own interpretation of what it meant to be European (which left out the Christian church) was not shared by other Europeans. The debate, in trying to establish a common identity, succeeded only in highlighting its limits. And attitudes towards the role of the Christian church in the history of Europe were shown to be determined largely by reference to national culture and tradition.

The debate pitted the religious against the secular, but was asymmetrical. The Christian church, and those member-state governments backing its calls, had no problem with including, alongside its own contribution to European development, explicit references to those of others (e.g. classical civilisation and the Enlightenment). Yet for countries with a strong secular tradition such as France, as well as for secularist and humanist organisations, any inclusion of a reference to the Christian church was a problem. For them, an explicit acknowledgment of the historical role of the Christianity would not only have recognised the churches' contribution to European integration and indirectly to the values on which the EU it was founded (both historical facts), but would also have given some legitimacy to their continuing place in modern (and 'enlightened') society, and called into question their insistence on a complete separation between church and state.

The excessive attention to the essentially symbolic language of the preamble was in stark contrast to the almost cursory attention devoted to other aspects of the Constitution text. So the churches successfully (and with almost no discussion) secured a commitment in the Constitution to an open and regular dialogue with the EU institutions. This gives the churches direct access to EU leaders, and an opportunity to bring the voice of the Christian churches to bear on European policy-making. It would have been nice to have been recognised in the preamble, but this pales into insignificance by comparison with a mechanism which enables the churches to speak Christian values into the future development of the European Union and how it impacts the lives of every one of the half a billion individuals living within it.

Notes

1 *Invocatio dei:* A reference to God in a legal text where the text itself is proclaimed in the name of the deity.
2 The Treaty of Rome (Treaty Establishing the European Economic Community) is available in facsimile format on the EU database of legal texts (http://eur-lex.europa.eu). All subsequent treaties have been published in the Official Journal (OJ) of the European Communities (subsequently European Union) and are also available through the same website. Throughout this chapter, references to treaties include the relevant OJ number and date.
3 See Article 2 of the Treaty on European Union.
4 The principle, however, is implicit in Pope Leo XIII's encyclical *Rerum Novarum* (1891).
5 The Forum website is no longer extant. It invited submissions from third parties and divided these into four categories: Political/public authorities, organisations with socio-economic interests, academia and think tanks, and other representatives of civil society, e.g. NGOs.
6 See the European Convention (2003) document 814/03 for the Secretariat's report of discussions of the plenary session, although this gives only a hint of the differences of views expressed.
7 The first draft from President Giscard d'Estaing is no longer accessible. However, as the above text makes clear, the Praesidium accepted the draft with virtually no changes. The text as approved by the Praesidium can be found in document CONV 722/03 (Preamble, 2003).
8 This happened on the same day that the meeting took place.

References

Bolivar, L. (2007). Most European nations keep God out of constitution. *Deutsche Welle*, 9 September. Retrieved from http://dw.de/p/BbyX.
Casanova, J. (2006). Religion, European secular identities and European integration. In Byrnes, T. A. and Katzenstein, P. J. (eds), *Religion in an expanding Europe* (pp. 65–92). Cambridge: Cambridge University Press.
Charter of Fundamental Rights of the European Union. (2010). 30 March. *OJ C83*.
Church and Society Commission of the Conference of European Churches, Commission of the Bishops' Conferences of the European Community (Secretariat), Caritas Europa et al. (2002). Joint letter to the President of European Convention. Brussels, 28 June. Retrieved from www.eurodiaconia.org/files/PDF/GOV_03_02_Joint_letter_to_President_of_European_Convention_2002.pdf.
Commission of the Bishops' Conferences of the European Community [COMECE]. (2005). The treaty establishing a constitution for Europe: Elements for an evaluation,

11 March. Retrieved from www.comece.org/content/site/en/publications/pubsec/index2.html.
Council of Europe. (1950). *European Convention on Human Rights*. Strasbourg: Council of Europe. Retrieved from www.echr.coe.int/Documents/Convention_ENG.pdf.
European Convention / The Secretariat. (2003). Summary report of the plenary session, 11 and 13 June. Brussels. *CONV 814/03*.
Germany. (1949). *Basic Law for the Federal Republic of Germany*. 23 May.
Giscard d'Estaing, V. (2002). *Introductory speech by President V. Giscard d'Estaing to the convention on the future of Europe*. 26 Feb. Retrieved from http://european-convention.europa.eu/docs/speeches/1.pdf [also part of Document CONV 4/02].
Greece. (1975). *The Constitution of Greece*, 11 June.
Helsinki European Council. (1999). *Presidency conclusions, 10–11 Dec*. Retrieved from www.europarl.europa.eu/summits/hel1_en.htm.
Ireland. (1937). *Constitution of Ireland*, 29 Dec.
John Paul II. (2003). *Ecclesia in Europa. Post-Synodal Apostolic Exhortation*. 23 June. Retrieved from http://w2.vatican.va/content/john-paul-ii/en/apost_exhortations/documents/hf_jp-ii_exh_20030628_ecclesia-in-europa.html.
Leo XIII. (1891). *Rerum Novarum*, 15 May. Retrieved from https://w2.vatican.va/content/leo-xiii/en/encyclicals/documents/hf_l-xiii_enc_15051891_rerum-novarum.html
Pilette, A., and de Poncins, E. (2007). Valeurs, objectifs et nature de l'Union. In Amato, G., Bribosia, H., and De Witte, B. (eds), *Genèse et destinée de la constitution Européenne* (pp. 287–310). Brussels, Belgium: Bruylant.
Pius XI. (1931). *Quadragesimo Anno*, 15 May. Retrieved from http://w2.vatican.va/content/pius-xi/en/encyclicals/documents/hf_p-xi_enc_19310515_quadragesimo-anno.html.
Poland. (1997). *Constitution of the Republic of Poland*, 2 April.
Preamble. (2003). Presidium to Convention, 28 May. *CONV 722/03*.
Reactions to the Draft Articles of the Revised Text of Part One (Volume I): Analysis. (2003) Secretariat to Convention, 4 June.*CONV 779/03*.
Revised Texts. (2003). Presidium to Convention, 12 June. *CONV 811/03*.
Rettman, A. (2007). Merkel gives up on God in the EU Treaty. *EU Observer*, 15 May. Retrieved from https://euobserver.com/enlargement/24066.
Schlesinger, P., and Foret, F. (2006). Political roof and sacred canopy? Religion and the EU Constitution, *European Journal of Social Theory*, 9(1): 59–81.
Schuman, R. (1950). Declaration of 9 May. Robert Schuman Foundation. Retrieved from http://europa.eu/about-eu/basic-information/symbols/europe-day/schuman-declaration/index_en.htm.
Treaty Establishing a Constitution for Europe (2004) *OJ C310/1*.
Treaty Establishing the European Economic Community [Treaty of Rome]. (1957). 25 March. *298 UNTS 11*.
Treaty of Amsterdam amending the Treaty on European Union, the Treaties Establishing the European Communities and Certain Related Acts. (1997). 10 Nov. *OJ C340/1*.
Treaty of Nice amending the Treaty on the European Union, the Treaties Establishing the European Communities and Certain Related Acts. (2001). 10 March. *OJ C80/1*.
Treaty on European Union [Maastricht Text]. (1992). 29 July. *OJ C191/1*.
United States Declaration of Independence. (1776). US National Archives and Records Administration. College Park, MD. Retrieved from www.archives.gov/exhibits/charters/declaration_transcript.html.

11 Christian economic ethics and the euro
Which way to go?

Johan Graafland

Introduction

Since the collapse of Lehman Brothers in 2008, it was 'all hands on deck' for economic policy makers. What began as a crisis in the housing market in the United States, first expanded into an international financial crisis, then into an economic crisis with a significant drop in GDP and a deterioration in government finances, and later into a European debt crisis. A common element in many countries is that the combination of a deterioration in the financial sector and a deterioration in government finances created an explosive situation, which led to various flywheel effects (Blundell-Wignall and Slovik, 2011). Governments in countries like Ireland, Belgium, France, and Spain had to support their banks to prevent an implosion of the financial sector. The resulting impairment of government debts brought the banks that had invested in government bonds into deeper problems. Studies show that since 2007, the financial markets have increasingly imposed punishments on high government deficits and debts through higher interest rates (risk premiums) (Attinasi et al., 2009).

One of the many effects of the crisis was a growing divergence in confidence in the economic situation of various European countries. These differences put European policy makers under great pressure to come up with additional policy measures to reverse the situation. Because there was a continuous threat in some countries that government finances would get completely out of hand and/or banks would go bankrupt, European policy makers decided to put important steps in place towards European integration. The chosen path is controversial, however. There is an important undercurrent of economists who strongly object to this form of integration forced by the economic situation. The fact is that the economies that are united in the European Monetary Union (EMU) differ greatly from each other. Real convergence in economic performances is needed to make a common currency zone successful. But there is serious doubt whether it will be possible to reverse the divergence and the ever-growing debts and credits through economic reforms.

In this chapter, I will evaluate five policy options for the euro as a way out of the euro crisis from a set of four Christian values: human dignity, common good, justice, and solidarity. Besides the current policy of a further integration of the European economies through a coherent set of institutional measures for the euro countries, I analyse four other policy options where one or more countries leave the EMU, the euro is split into a northern and a southern euro or where all EMU countries return to a national currency. The structure of the chapter is as follows. Section two briefly introduces five Christian values. Section three describes the roots of the euro crisis. Section four introduces the policy options that are examined in the chapter. Section five presents a qualitative analysis of their economic effects. Section six evaluates these options from the standpoint of the five Christian values.

Christian values

The economy is an area of life where many values are present and expressed; it is not a value-free zone. Economics is about describing and studying choices that people make in situations of scarcity, on the basis of all possible trade-offs. All those choices are of great importance for human well-being. Great damage to such well-being is caused when it is assumed that economic activity is only about money making and that only materialistic values and standards matter. In the Hebrew and Christian scriptures and in diverse Christian theological traditions there is a wealth of sustained reflection on the moral dimension of economics. In this chapter I identify just five of the core values in these traditions and apply them to the crisis in the eurozone: human dignity, common good, justice, solidarity, and subsidiarity (Graafland, 2014; Dutch Council of Churches, 2013). My account of these values draws especially on the tradition of Catholic Social Teaching.

Human dignity originates from the creation of humans 'in the image and likeness of God' (Genesis 1:26). This central biblical text provides a religious foundation for human dignity and respect for human rights. Human dignity is not a matter of social convention or a self-grounded possession, but essentially conferred by God. Every person is unique and has an intrinsic, inalienable value. In Hebrew wisdom literature, the figure of Job witnesses that he has not despised the rights of his servants, because "The same God who created me created my servants also" (Job 31:13–15). Every human has a right to a life that can express the image of God. Being a 'person' implies that one is able to formulate one's own thoughts and actions and be capable of self-awareness and community with others. Personhood implies freedom. The freedom of the will is the ability to decide in self-determination in the face of different possibilities, without being driven in psychic determinism. Freedom is foundational for many other values in human interaction, such as love and responsibility. If people do not have freedom of choice, they cannot be held morally responsible for their deeds (Galatians 6:4–5). Without personal freedom of will, moral responsibility is impossible, so that guilt and atonement, reward and punishment lose their meanings.

The *common good* relates to those social conditions under which people can realise their destinies. Everyone has the right to enjoy the fruits of the common good. God intended the earth and all that it contains for the use of every human being and people, without excluding or favouring anyone. This means that each person must have access to the level of well-being necessary for his or her full development and that there should be an acceptable degree of equality. The common good is indivisible and only in community can human society attain it; it does not simply consist of the sum of the particular goods of each subject of a social entity. An individual cannot achieve the good life alone, but only in conjunction with others at various levels of social life, such as the family, company, city, region, country, European, or global community. Realizing the common good is therefore a responsibility for all people, each according to their possibilities. That implies that all should stand at the service of others; it requires a constant ability and effort to seek the good for others.

The principle of *justice* requires that everyone receive what is their due. Justice entails reciprocity, i.e. the Golden Rule: "Do unto others as you would have them do unto you" (Luke 6:31). But biblical justice is not confined to this so-called commutative justice, which focusses on reciprocal obligations. It is also connected to 'charity'. This is expressed by, for example, the term 'preferentional option for the poor'. It demands that we place the care of the needy at the centre of community life, on the understanding that if a person's development is impeded by poverty or unemployment, the quality of community life is also affected. God is in a special way the God of the destitute, the poor, the exploited, the wronged, and the abused (Psalm 146:7–9). Jesus did not only identify himself with the poor (Matthew 25:40), but proclaimed that he will do justice to the oppressed, give bread to the hungry, free the prisoner, and restore the sight to the blind (Luke 4:18). A generalization from this is the principle of *solidarity*, which rests on the assumption that we form a community of people where we are interdependent and responsible for one another.

Finally, the principle of *subsidiarity* has been formulated in the social encyclical *Quadragesimo Anno*.[1] This principle protects people from abuses by higher-level social authorities and calls on the same authorities to help individuals and intermediate groups to fulfil their duties. Society not only consists of individuals but also of a plurality of lower and higher communities. The state has, as the highest community, the right to intervene in the lower communities if the common good is threatened and lower communities are not able to realise their responsibilities. But at the same, it should take care that the freedom and responsibility of lower communities is respected. Thus the principle applies in two ways (Graafland and Blok, 2004). On the one hand, in a negative sense it states that larger entities should not assume the roles and functions of smaller entities if these are able to perform them by themselves. The freedom and responsibility of the lower communities that function in between the state at the top and family life at the bottom should be respected and promoted so that each remains at the service of the common good. The unwarranted assumption of roles and functions by larger authorities often lessens social participation. The subsidiarity principle thus aims to oppose unnecessary centralization, bureaucratization and the excessive power of the state. On the other hand, the subsidiarity principle has a positive dimension, namely that larger authorities should help lower order authorities if these are not able to perform their roles and functions on their own (Höffner, 1983). Although the lower communities have their own duty to serve the common good, in some cases the help from higher organisations is necessary. The principle thus honours two other principles, namely respect of human dignity and the principle of solidarity or mutual service. It is, one might say, the organisational implication of these two other principles.

Roots of the euro crisis

The euro project started with the Treaty of Maastricht in 1992 and the creation of the European Monetary Institute (EMI) in 1994. Table 11.1 shows that since the introduction of the euro in 1999, convergence between the euro member states has occurred for several economic parameters, but not for all. The current account in particular shows divergence for different countries. Greece, Portugal, and Spain exhibit a current account deficit that is larger than in the period before 1999. To a lesser extent, this also applies to Ireland, France, and Italy. In contrast, Germany, Finland, Luxembourg, and the Netherlands and, to a lesser extent, Austria and Belgium show a current account surplus and have not deteriorated since 1999 (except Belgium). Berger and Nitsch (2010) therefore conclude that the magnitude and the persistency of the current account imbalances have increased since the introduction of the euro. This indicates that large differences in competitiveness between the various EMU countries continued between 1999 and 2011. This is partly due to the fact that northern European countries developed more innovative industrial products and services than southern European countries (which depend more on agriculture and tourism). A recent study by Wierts et al. (2012) shows that the exports of the northern European countries (Belgium, Luxembourg, Germany, France, the Netherlands and Austria) to emerging markets in Eastern Europe, Asia and South America are much higher than the exports of southern European countries to emerging markets. As emerging countries have a higher growth in income, the northern European euro countries benefit from this. Wierts et al. (2012) explain this difference in export performance by the share of technological advanced products, which is much lower for southern European than for northern European countries.

Another reason is the higher productivity growth in Northern Europe as a result of the automation and digitization of industrial production and commercial services. The labour costs per unit of product are consequently much lower (Rodenburg and Zuidhof, 2012). Between 1998 and 2011, the labour costs per unit of product increased in France (28 per cent), Ireland (36 per cent), Spain (38 per cent) and Italy (40 per cent) much more than in Germany

Table 11.1 Economic developments within the eurozone[a]

	Annual GDP growth	Inflation[b]	Unemployment rate[c]	Government budget surplus (% of GDP)[d]	Gross government debt (% GDP, 2010)[e]	Balance of payments (% GDP)[e]
1999–2011						
Belgium	1.8	2.1	7.8	−0.4	96	2.7
Germany	1.2	1.5	8.8	−2.2	83	4.7
Finland	2.4	1.8	8.5	4.1	48	5.4
France	1.5	1.8	9.0	−2.7	82	0.0
Greece	2.4	3.3	10.1	−5.4	144	−9.1
Ireland	3.7	2.5	6.1	1.5	95	−1.9
Italy	0.7	2.2	8.2	−2.9	118	−1.5
Luxembourg	3.7	2.6	3.8	2.3		9.4
The Netherlands	1.9	2.2	3.8	−0.6	63	5.3
Austria	1.9	1.8	4.3	−1.6	72	1.8
Portugal	1.2	2.5	7.6	−3.7	93	−9.6
Spain	2.6	2.8	11.9	0.3	61	−5.7
1991–99						
Belgium	4.4		8.5	−2.9	124	5.3
Germany	1.4	1.8	8.1	−2.2	59	−0.7
Finland	3.9	1.9	13.2	−2.4	54	4.6
France	1.9	1.5	10.3	−3.9	58	1.9
Greece					97	−2.9

	Annual GDP growth	Inflation[b]	Unemployment rate[c]	Government budget surplus (% of GDP)[d]	Gross government debt (% GDP, 2010)[e]	Balance of payments (% GDP)[e]
Ireland			12.7	0.4	67	2.1
Italy	1.4	3.9	10.3	−5.0	118	2.5
Luxembourg			2.6	2.7	7	10.7
The Netherlands	3.2	2.4	5.6	−3.3	71	5.3
Austria	2.5	1.8		−3.5	66	−2.5
Portugal			5.9	−4.5	56	−4.9
Spain	2.8	3.9	18.1	−4.9	65	−0.5

[a]Source: Eurostat.
[b]For 1991–1999: based on national currencies, consuption price index.
[c]For 1991–1999: average in 1991–1998.
[d]For 1999–2011: average in 2000–2007; source: Teulings et al. (2011), p. 15. For 1991–1999: average in 1995–1998.
[e]For 1991–99: average in 1995–98

(6 per cent). Since all countries had the same exchange rate, northern and southern European countries actually had an undervalued and overvalued currency respectively, causing increasing divergence in their trade balances.

However, one cannot only blame southern European countries for these growing trade imbalances. One can also argue that the northern countries based their economic growth one-sidedly on exports and that growth of domestic expenditures lagged too much behind (Rajan, 2010). Further, government deficits were kept rather low in Germany. The high national savings were invested in southern European countries, which put downward pressure on the real interest rates in these countries. This provided an incentive to easy borrowing in southern European countries, not driven by excess demand but rather by excess supply of financial means worldwide. Research has shown that the interest levels determined by the ECB were not in accordance with the fundamental economic developments in various countries, such as Germany (Hayo and Hofmann, 2006), Greece (Arghyrou, 2009) and Spain (Arghyrou and Gadea, 2012).[2] Especially for Spain, this is striking, because Table 11.1 shows that Spain had a relatively high economic growth and no big public deficit or public debt. But inflation was relatively high, causing a real appreciation (i.e. a rise in the value of the currency in relation to other countries, adjusted for inflation differentials). As a result, the real interest rate was even negative. This not only caused a trade deficit, but also led to a large bubble in the real estate market, making the economic growth of Spain, in retrospect, very one-sided and therefore vulnerable. If Spain had not been part of the EMU, the Central Bank of Spain would probably have set a higher interest rate to reduce the inflationary pressures (Arghyrou and Gadea, 2012). This would have slowed down the bubble in the real estate market. It is precisely because of the unified monetary policy within EMU that Spain has become so vulnerable to the economic crisis from 2008. Given the institutional setting of the EMU, the ECB could also do little else than pursue price stability for the EMU as a whole. There was no room to combat macro imbalances of specific countries.

Under-spending in the northern euro countries and excess spending in the southern euro countries also explain the differences in inflation rates that determine the competitiveness of a country. These differences in inflation rates already date back from the period before the EMU. Already in the 1980s, the Netherlands had an inflation rate similar to that in Germany, but countries like Italy, Spain, and Greece had a consistently higher inflation rate. As a result, they regularly devalued their currencies relative to the German mark in order to maintain their competitiveness. In fact, the introduction of the euro has not radically changed this trend, because since 2002 the southern European countries have consistently had higher inflation rates than the average of the euro zone (Rodenburg and Zuidhof, 2012). Consequently, between 1970 and 2012, the index of labour costs per unit of product drifted apart substantially, from 255 for Germany (1970 = 100) to 4560 for Portugal and 7905 for Greece (DNB, 2012). Although the degree of divergence is less than in the period before 1998, the relative unit of labour costs also increased substantially in southern European countries after 1998. The reason for these persistent differences in inflation is often sought in the various institutions of the labour and goods markets, such as those concerning lay-off protection and entrance barriers on goods markets. According to Rodenburg and Zuidhof (2012), it is difficult to fight the structural differences between countries like Greece and Germany because they reflect the culture of a country. This is because Greece not only has an inflexible labour market but also other problems, such as corruption, poor tax morality, bureaucracy and patronage, which restrict the growth capacity of the country. Nevertheless, the members of the Monetary Union hoped that its creation would boost economic reforms. But looking back, we must conclude that the convergence in per capita income in the past 10 years has been more the result of rising spendings, made possible by cheap credits, than of reform policies that improved competition on the labour market or the goods market (ING, 2012).

Another structural difference concerns the public deficits and debts, which are particularly high in Greece and Italy. For some countries, national debts have risen to over 90 per cent of GDP. A debt of 90 per cent of GDP is often considered as critical, because such a high debt hampers economic growth and, hence, the capacity to pay off the debt. In part, the increase in debts has been the result of the economic downturn since 2008. Until 2007, countries like Spain and Ireland even had a budget surplus. But also before the crisis, the structural budget deficits in some countries increased. Countries that had large deficits before the crisis have faced a larger increase in their structural budget deficits after the crisis (Gilbert and Hessel, 2012). As mentioned before, one of the reasons that structural debts were allowed to rise so high before the crisis is the convergence in interest rates on government debts in all EMU countries since 1995. This took away the incentive to limit borrowing for countries with a large deficit. The euro and the uniform monetary policy, resulting in confidence of the financial markets within the whole euro zone, in this way enforced the divergence between countries. The Maastricht Treaty did not provide for mechanisms ensuring budgetary convergence. While some rules (the 3 per cent norm for the government deficit and the 60 per cent standard for the debt ratio) should have provided for this, they were soon violated by Germany and France, which made discipline and credibility disappear. This also gave other countries room for moral hazard. In this way, Germany and France contributed to a situation in which budget deficits and public debts could rise in the southern European countries. This shows that the euro as a common currency has certainly played a role in the rise and development of the euro crisis.

Five policy options

Even though the economic crisis has made clear that the EMU has failed, this does not necessarily mean that the best way forwards is to return to the old situation of national exchange rates. In this analysis, I have chosen to explore five policy options.

Further integration of the current euro zone

The policy option of further integration comes down to a continuation of the current euro zone in combination with a permanent emergency fund, banking union, budgetary union and a macroeconomic imbalance procedure. The exact interpretation of this policy option obviously depends on the realization of the above elements. Cliffe (2012) even distinguishes 6 different scenarios, which focus to a greater or lesser extent on the possibilities of further integration.

Grexit

Besides the option of further integration of the current euro zone, the first variant that we distinguish is the exit of Greece from the euro zone. The reason to investigate this policy option is that it is probably the most likely alternative.

Several countries leave the euro zone

The third option is that several countries leave the euro zone. As with the previous variant, we assume that this exit will be permanent.

Splitting the euro into a neuro and zeuro

In the fourth place, we will examine the policy option in which the euro is split into a common currency for the northern European countries (neuro) and a common currency for the southern European countries (zeuro).

Complete return to national currencies

The final policy option is the most radical variant, in which all EMU countries return to national currencies.

Two important assumptions will be made in what follows. The first is that an exit from the euro zone does not mean that countries should leave the EU as well. EU treaties do not make statements about the possibility to exit the euro zone without having to give up their EU membership. According to the CPB, it is conceivable that European rules on this point will be rewritten or simply put aside (Teulings et al., 2011). The second is that the position of EU countries that do not belong to the euro zone will not change. It is conceivable that a reconfiguration of the euro zone will trigger non-euro countries to step in, especially in the northern euro zone. The current problems with the euro and the great dynamics in various countries make this unlikely in the short term, however. Finally, this study will not answer the question how a possible break-up of the euro should be managed. There are interesting studies available that take this question as a starting point (Capital Economics, 2012).

Qualitative economic analysis

The economic-political analysis of the five policy options is very complex and subject to a substantial degree of uncertainty. In Graafland (2013) I present an extensive analysis of the consequences of various options in the short and in the long term. In this section, I will only summarize the main findings of this report.

General analysis of breaking-up of euro

Based on the criteria from the theory of the Optimal Currency Area (OCA) (see Table 11.2), the current euro zone has performed moderately to badly.[3] Firstly, labour mobility between countries is very low, because of large cultural differences (including language barriers), while the flexibility of the labour markets of many countries is limited. Secondly, the production structure of euro countries varies substantially (Baldwin and Wyplosz, 2012). As a result, economic shocks affect the economies of euro countries in very different ways, as we have seen during the recent economic crisis. Thirdly, the degree of openness and the intensity of trade relations between euro countries differ. The exports of Finland, France, Greece, Italy and Spain to other euro countries amount to less than 10 per cent of their GDP. Also, since the introduction of the euro, the share of exports from southern European countries to northern European countries has unexpectedly not increased (Wierts et al., 2012). Fourth, financial transfers between euro countries are low. The total budget of the European Union amounts to around 1 per cent of EU GNP, of which (in 2011) 42 per cent was spent on direct aid to farmers and

Table 11.2 OCA criteria for a common currency union

Economic	
1. labour mobility	People move easily between the countries of the union
2. product diversification	Countries have a widely diversified production structure that is comparable to other countries within the union
3. openness	Countries have intensive trade relations
Political	
4. budgetary transfers	Countries agree to compensate each other for adverse shocks
5. homogeneous preferences	Countries share a wide consensus on how to deal with shocks
6. solidarity	Countries accept costs with regard to a common destiny

Source: Baldwin and Wyplosz (2012).

market related expenses and 45 per cent on cohesion, growth and employment. Political preferences of financial-economic policies are heterogeneous and the policy response to economic shocks quite different (Bohn and de Jong, 2011). Cultural diversity also limits European solidarity. The current Eurobarometer shows that only 16 per cent of the people answer the question 'Do you ever think of yourself as not only nationalistic, but also European' with "often", whereas 43 per cent of the people answers with "never" and 38 per cent with "sometimes".

Given the fact that the euro zone meets the criteria of the OCA theory only moderately to badly, one would expect that the contribution of the euro to the economies of euro countries has been rather small. This is confirmed by various empirical investigations. The CPB estimates that for the Netherlands, the euro has generated a structurally higher GDP of 2 per cent, which is about a quarter of the contribution of the internal market (Teuling et al., 2011). Other studies also indicate that the trade effects of the EMU have been rather weak. Wierts et al. (2012) discuss various economic studies. Some studies showed that the euro initially increased the trade intensity within the euro zone, but later studies reported much smaller effects. Berger and Nitsch (2008) even conclude that, after correcting for a trend-like growth in trade integration, the effect of the euro on trade in the euro zone seemed to be entirely absent. The small contribution of the euro is also indicated by the fact that, since the introduction of the euro, euro countries do not show higher economic growth than non-euro countries (Graafland, 2013). Taking into account the current high costs of stabilizing the euro zone, it is likely that the net contribution of the euro to the economy of the euro zone has been negligible or even negative.

However, a reconfiguration of the euro zone comes with potentially high transition costs. Apart from the costs of reintroducing national coins (which amounts to about 1 per cent of the GDP of the exiting country), there is a risk that this break-up will lead to speculative capital flows that will endanger the financial sector.[4] Some studies present a bleak scenario in which the exit of Greece alone will be reason enough to put the already vulnerable banking sector in Europe under even more pressure, resulting in a deeper recession in Europe with substantial effects on the rest of the world (Buiter, 2011; ING, 2012). Other studies estimate that these negative effects can be largely prevented, provided that the reconfiguration of the euro zone is managed well.

Apart from these predictions, one could question in how far transition costs should be taken into account in policy considerations. This depends on the time horizon of policy makers. Because politics is often driven by a short-term horizon and because economic growth is already fragile as a result of the overall vulnerable economic situation in the world, there is a strong inclination to give priority to short-term interests, making transition costs very dominant in policy considerations. Thus, there is a danger that the long-term costs of some policy options will not be sufficiently taken into account. However, if one aims at a sustainable and optimal currency union in the long term, the costs in the long term (>20 year) should be the key factor during the policy-making process.

Provided that the exit is well managed, the big advantage for a country that leaves the euro zone is that the prospects of economic recovery will greatly improve due to the reduction of the exchange rate and strongly improved competitiveness. Recent research shows that the exports of southern European countries depend more on price competition than the exports of northern European countries (Wierts et al., 2012). A decline in the exchange rate is therefore of great potential importance for the competitiveness of southern countries. The effects depend, among other things, on the inflationary response to the devaluation.[5] Experiences in other countries show that it is unlikely that a devaluation will be completely neutralized by high inflation. In some cases, devaluations led to a substantial recovery, as in Britain in 1992 and in several Asian countries, like Korea, Singapore, Taiwan, and Thailand (Kim and Ying, 2007). Because of high excess supply and unemployment in southern European countries, there will be sufficient production capacity and labour available to meet the extra demand for production, caused by the increase of exports and the decrease of imports. Therefore, inflationary pressures will be limited. Devaluation then provides a means to fight the main underlying cause of the current euro crisis, i.e. the difference in competitiveness between various countries. A comparison with Iceland, Ireland, and Latvia shows that (in addition to the amortization of debts) external devaluation is more effective than a tedious process of internal devaluation through wage moderation and that the social costs with respect to unemployment are lower (Darvas, 2011). One of the reasons is that strengthening competitiveness through structural reforms only creates better prospects in the very long run, whereas it remains uncertain whether the measures will be permanent.

Although the devaluation of the currencies of one or some southern euro countries will initially affect the competitiveness of the northern euro countries, in the long term, the northern euro countries will benefit from the recovery of economic growth in the southern euro countries, because the demand from these countries will recover. It will also challenge the northern countries to strengthen their own competitiveness.

A disadvantage of the exit of countries from the euro zone is that it puts the repayment of loans by the exiting countries at high risk. Depending on which country exits, large to very large sums of money will be involved. If the exit is badly managed, write-offs on loans can bring the European economy into a deeper recession, because of the precarious economic situation in other euro countries and the vulnerability of the financial sector. In that case, high legal costs are to be expected, caused by complex settlements of debts that are denominated in euros. In how far these risks should affect policy considerations depends on the counter-factual. This is because even if no country leaves the euro zone, substantial write-offs on loans to vulnerable euro countries have been and will be inevitable. This will be necessary and desirable in order to give weak euro countries sufficient prospects for recovery. Moreover, there is a real risk that the commitment to keep a country within the euro zone will generate very high costs in the long term, because the support needed for that purpose leads to a permanent dependency relationship (*The Economist*, 2012b). In contrast, an exit from the euro zone offers the prospect that in the long term, a country will be able to partly meet its commitments and repay its debts because of recovered competitiveness. Therefore, it is difficult to predict whether the loss on loans will be larger or smaller if a country stays within the euro zone (and therefore is unable to regain its competitiveness within a reasonable time span), than if it leaves the EMU (and devalues its national currency relative to the euro).

Analysis of five policy options

In this section I apply the foregoing qualitative analysis to each of the five policy options.

First, further integration of the euro zone will have a higher chance of success if euro countries better meet the criteria of the OCA theory. This means that if the euro zone is able to create a clear institutional framework that makes it better meet the criteria of the OCA theory, this policy option is preferable. However, it is highly uncertain whether the euro zone will succeed. Increasing labour productivity through reforms is a very difficult process: it would be quite an accomplishment if a government, by good policy, could make annual labour productivity growth increase by 0.5 per cent, but even then it would take decades to catch up with its competitors if they lag behind by 30–40 per cent (Capital Economics, 2012). There is a high risk that structural reforms will only be partly implemented. Another substantial risk is that the intended European institutions will not perform optimally in view of the economic and political functions for which they have been designed.

Second, a Grexit has advantages and disadvantages, depending on how it is implemented. If the exit is carefully managed and euro countries offer Greece sufficient financial support and write-offs on loans in order to give Greece a good starting position, this option has the advantage that Greece can recover its competitiveness. The introduction of a parallel currency, as proposed by Andre ten Dam (2012), can contribute to a smooth transition. After the exit, Greece should remain a full member of the EU and should still be entitled to make use of structural funds. This possibility would increase the chance that Greece will choose for a voluntary exit and would offer prospects of higher economic growth in Greece as well as in the euro zone. Another important advantage is that the exit of Greece will increase the chance of successful further integration and convergence within the euro zone. If not carefully managed, however, the advantages of the exit of Greece as described above will be overwhelmed by the disadvantages that are related to large transition costs. It is uncertain whether the Grexit option will demand more write-offs on loans to Greece than the option of further integration of Greece within the euro zone. This depends on how well the exit is managed and how the attitude of Greek politicians and citizens will be towards both options. A great danger of further integration is the creation of a permanent dependency relationship, which will involve very high costs in the longer term. The biggest disadvantage of a Grexit is the danger of contamination of other southern European countries. This will increase uncertainty, and financial markets will demand an additional risk premium on bonds of other weak euro countries. The expectation that other southern European countries could also exit will increase the capital flow from those countries. According to Buiter (2011), it is very likely that, due to the financial chaos resulting from this, Europe will fall into an even deeper recession.

Third, the expected effects of the exit of Greece, Spain, Portugal, and Cyprus (GSPC) are qualitatively similar to the effects of a Grexit: improved competitiveness through devaluation of the new currencies and a bigger chance of successful integration of the remaining euro zone. *The Economist* (2012a) prefers this major adjustment of the euro zone over an exit of Greece alone, because it would enhance the viability of the euro zone. Because the proportion of technically high-quality products in the exports of peripheral countries is relatively low, devaluation can make an important contribution to exports by improving price competitiveness. As the remaining European countries better meet the criteria of the OCA theory, the stability of the euro zone will increase. In addition, keeping GSPC countries in the euro zone and further integrating the euro zone will make the support to the GSPC countries endless and will also entail considerable risks in the long term. *The Economist* (2012a) estimates the potential costs will amount to €250 billion annually. Negative effects are that the chance of structural reforms in the exiting countries will decrease and that the devaluation of their currencies will endanger the competitiveness of Italy and France. This may destabilize the smaller euro zone. Because this policy option will lead to a very significant reconfiguration of the euro zone, the risks are much higher than for a Grexit.

Fourth, based on the OCA theory, the following countries would qualify for a new neuro zone: Germany, Austria, the Netherlands, Finland, and Belgium (Capital Economics, 2012). Estonia, Ireland, Slovenia, and Slovakia might also be included. The remaining countries – Greece, Cyprus, Italy, Spain, and Portugal – would qualify for a zeuro zone. Based on the criteria of the OCA theory, France could also best participate in the zeuro zone and play an integrating role.[6] The additional advantage would be that the neuro zone and the zeuro zone are more equivalent in size. However, for political reasons, this seems unrealistic and it is more likely that France will be classified as a member of the neuro zone. The expected economic effects of splitting the euro in a neuro and zeuro thus defined, are similar to the effects of the exit of Greece, Spain, Cyprus, and Portugal. Nonetheless, it is expected that the prospects of economic growth would be less favourable, because the countries that belong to the zeuro zone meet the criteria of the OCA theory only moderately to badly. The benefits of a common currency union in the zeuro zone will therefore not outweigh the disadvantage of loss of flexibility with regard to monetary policies and exchange rates.

222 *Graafland*

Finally, some argue that if any country's exit from the euro zone is contemplated, it is best instantly to decide on a complete return to national currencies, because as soon as a country leaves the euro zone this will be a signal for markets that the euro is reversible (Capital Economics, 2012). This will provide ammunition to put pressure on other structural weaknesses in the euro, which will be a recipe for continuing crisis. But, based on the OCA theory, a complete break-up of the euro into national currencies will be unnecessarily harmful to the economies of the neuro zone. For the countries in the neuro zone, a complete break-up will lead to higher transition costs and more permanent economic disadvantages, like less competition and productivity growth.

Insights from recent unemployment trends

The analysis in the previous sections is based on my report from 2013 (Graafland, 2013). Since then (apart from Greece), the euro zone seems to have been stabilized. Are there indications that we must update the conclusions?

To answer this question, I examine recent developments in unemployment. The unemployment rate is an important indicator, not only from an economic point of view but also from social and political perspectives and from the standpoint of the Christian values discussed in my second section. How did the euro zone perform since 2010?

Table 11.3 shows that, after unemployment started to rise in 2008 when the crisis unfolded, it stabilized and declined after 2010 in all European countries that do not belong to the euro zone. But not so in the euro zone. In 11 out of 15 euro countries the unemployment rate further increased between 2010 and

Table 11.3 Development unemployment rate: January 2010 – January 2014 (in per cent)

Eurozone:				Non-eurozone: 18.5	
Belgium	8.2->8.5	Italy	8.5->12.7	Denmark	7.4->6.9
Cyprus	6.6->16.6	Luxembourg	4.7->6.1	Latvia	20.2->11.6
Germany	7.5->5.2	Netherlands	4.5->7.2	Poland	9.7->9.7
Estonia	18.3-> 8.2	Austria	4.5->4.9	Czech republic	7.8->6.9
Finland	8.7-> 8.4	Portugal	11.5->15.2	UK	7.9->6.7
France	9.4->10.3	Slovenia	6.6->9.8	Iceland	7.4 -> 5.4
Greece	11.3->26.6	Slovakia	14.7->14.0	Sweden	9.0->8.2
Ireland	13.1->11.9	Spain	19.0->25.3		

Source: Eurostat.

2014, with Greece, Portugal, and Spain as the most dramatic examples. Furthermore, in half of the euro countries the unemployment rate still exceeds 10 per cent of working population in 2014, whereas in the non-euro countries this is only the case in Latvia.

Based on these recent developments, the clear impression emerges that the euro zone faces greater difficulties in recovering from the economic crisis than do EU countries outside the euro zone. A possible explanation is the lack of flexibility to improve competitiveness through exchange rate mutations. As a result, the labour market is completely dependent on internal deflation, which is a much slower channel to reduce unemployment.

Evaluation

So far, my analysis has focused on the economic effects of the five policy options. It is obvious, of course, that economic factors have a major impact on realizing the Christian values introduced above. I now illustrate this in relation to each of these five values.

First, the economic crisis shows that a strong decline in prosperity and persistent high unemployment harms the common good and hence crowds out an important condition for respecting human dignity. This must be factored directly into evaluations of policy options and not considered as an external, optional consideration. Particularly mass unemployment may have devastating consequences for the common good. Because of the extraordinary reduction in economic activity, many people were dismissed and thereby disconnected from the working community in the enterprise where they used to work. Because of mass unemployment, many of them had very few opportunities for finding new work. Severed from their working community with no opportunity for (finding new) creative work, unemployed workers are more likely to experience psychological problems such as depression, low subjective well-being, and poor self-esteem (Paul and Moser, 2009). Unemployment also affects families. The stress and depressive symptoms associated with job loss can negatively affect children, and depression in children and adolescents is known to be linked to multiple negative social outcomes. Widespread unemployment also influences the health of wider supporting neighbourhoods by reducing resources, leading to low-quality housing, underfunded schools, restricted access to services, and public transportation, and limited opportunities for employment (Brisson, Roll, and East, 2009). High unemployment and resulting growing income inequalities are therefore key factors in a declining social climate and fuel social unrest and a growing sense of unfairness. The severe economic circumstances and the reduction in social assistance also greatly impacted the lives of old people, particularly in southern European countries.[7] The suicide rate in the EU has increased on account of the economic crisis. In Spain suicide was the largest non-natural cause of death in the post-crisis years.[8] This shows how the current hard economic conditions take away people's sense of control over their own lives. From this point of view, it is of utmost importance that economic policies are selected that prevent high unemployment for a long period and, if maintaining the current euro zone hampers such restoration of the labour market, alternative currency exchange systems should be given serious consideration.

From the perspective of communitative justice, the euro zone only functions well if the participating countries all positively contribute to its benefits. Of course, countries may temporarily be offered help from other countries, but reciprocity requires that this help is not structurally one-sided. It should be a matter of give and take. This reciprocity is not experienced by many. This is because when it comes to mutual support, it is predominantly one-way traffic from the north to the south and there is little expectation that this will change in the near future. Since the help offered to troubled countries is often conditioned on the acceptance of severe cutbacks in public expenditures, privatization of government services and other economic reforms, the people of these countries experience the humiliation of the loss of their national autonomy. The advantage of a free currency exchange system is that the market rewards the productivity of a country on a largely anonymous basis through multiple micro transactions instead of through political decisions. If a country becomes less competitive and the trade balance deteriorates, the value of its currency will decline and purchasing power will adjust automatically by making imports more expensive. But people might experience this circumstance as showing more respect for their freedom rights than when the economic destiny of their country is largely forced upon it by foreign entities (like the troika).

When we consider the value of solidarity, it should be noted that the vision of the European Community has always involved more than an economic project. The central idea behind European integration was to prevent a new war on the European continent. Founders like Schuman (as Gary Wilton's chapter shows) have always stressed that the European peace project is rooted in shared values and comprehends more than shared interests. Despite all the diversities, there also exists a common European culture and history that is reflected in everything that Europe has produced. The question is whether this 'big' story behind the European project has sufficiently taken root in the 'hearts and minds' of European citizens. A major obstacle to solidarity is the high degree of cultural diversity within Europe. In recent decades, the emphasis on the economic dimension of European integration has increased due to the advantages of the internal market, the free movement of persons, services, goods and capital. But since economic benefits are now decreasing and pressure on countries increasing, support for the euro, and thus the EU, is declining. Although the political elite within Europe is aware of the need for a common future, its citizens – especially less educated people – are far less willing to give up national sovereignty. Especially in times of crisis, national sentiments are getting much stronger. Because of this, substantial redistributive social policy at a European level is not feasible. Moreover, solidarity does not necessarily imply that countries should remain within the euro zone.

As discussed above, giving up the membership of the euro zone does not mean that the membership of the EU should also be given up. As noted, on the contrary, if Greece, for example, would exit the euro zone, it could, and in my opinion should, remain a full member of the European Union and still be entitled to make use of structural funds. If the transition to non-membership is carefully managed and facilitated by the ECB, and if this allows Greece a new start and substantially faster improvement of its economy, solidarity with Greece would actually require a Grexit.

Finally, seen from the angle of the principle of subsidiarity, it is relevant to note that the euro zone will only become more robust and better able to meet the criteria of the OCA theory if a process of further integration takes place. But given the cultural heterogeneity within the euro zone, such integration will constantly be experienced as a limitation of the individual freedom of countries. One can doubt if there is sufficient reason to pay the high price of limiting the freedom and responsibility of individual states and their citizens in order to protect the Euro, particularly since the economic and political benefits of the euro have not proven to be very favourable. Also for the next decades, it is likely that cultural differences and different economic preferences – such as the commitment of countries to preventing inflation, government deficits or debts or to combatting unemployment, the institutional design of the economy, fiscal policy, the role of the state, the role of unions, the role of the ECB, styles of leadership, and political culture – between euro countries will persist.

Given the cultural and political heterogeneity between euro countries, the subsidiarity principle implies that it is extremely important that European policies have sufficient democratic legitimacy. During the economic crisis the democratic legitimacy of the EU has been, however, considerably under pressure because of the dominant role of the ECB. Due to the independence of the ECB, democratic politics cannot control the ECB. The ECB's independence can therefore only function properly if it abstains from interventions that require political considerations and democratic legitimacy. Despite its limited monetary mandate, the ECB more and more took on a financial stability role by generously providing loans to European banks and by demanding qualitatively low requirements to the collateral for these loans. Whereas the ECB was explicitly modelled after the German Central Bank, the crisis brought about an increase in its political role through the buying of bonds from southern European countries. Also by setting requirements in the form of necessary reforms, the ECB went beyond its authority and took over the role of national governments without having the democratic legitimacy for this. According to de Jong (2012), the goal behind the measures taken by the ECB was to make the euro irreversible. This is confirmed by the following statement of Asmussen (director of the European Central Bank and successor of Jürgen Stark): "Our starting point is that the euro is irreversible. And that we have to repair the flaws in the currency union. That is indeed politics, yes. … We have to complete the monetary union … work on a banking union and an economic, financial and political union" (quoted in De Gruyter, 2012). But it is up to politicians and parliaments to make such decisions. This is not a goal of the ECB and nor should it be. Countries that leave the euro zone would regain more control of their own monetary and economic policies. As the citizens of such countries would have more influence on their own politics, their autonomy over the design of economic institutions and economic policies would be more respected. Further, countries that remain in the euro zone after others have left will be able to strengthen the democratic legitimacy of monetary and economic policies, because if there is more stability in the euro zone, there will be less urge to minimize the role of the EU parliament and national parliaments.

It is, of course, difficult to derive definitive conclusions from these five Christian values with regard to the way the EU should go. Much depends on the economic consequences of the five economic policies, which are highly uncertain. But the fact that unemployment in the euro zone is still very high relative to non-euro European countries makes clear that the present policy of continuing the euro project to safeguard the many financial and political interests that depend on it, has imposed a very high price. My own conclusion is that, under certain conditions, the option of Greece leaving the euro zone should be seriously considered, since it might be more attractive for Greece as well as the rest of the euro zone than further integration of the current euro zone, including Greece. These conditions are: (1) the exit is well managed; (2) Greek debts are substantially diminished through the amortization of debts; (3) Greece is financially supported during the transition period; (4) Greece should acknowledge the advantages of an exit and prefer it itself; (5) after the exit, Greece should remain a full member of the EU and should still be entitled to receive support from Europe's structural funds; and (6) the exit should take place at a moment where the financial markets have been stabilized and the economic prospects for other European countries are positive, so that the probability of contamination will be low. Under these conditions, it can be expected that economic growth will increase both in Greece and the euro zone and that the amortization of debts will be lower in the long run. The stability of the euro zone will increase in the long run, because it will better meet the criteria of the theory of optimal currency area. This will increase the probability that it will be more able to face new, major economic shocks in the world economy. The Grexit will provide Greece more opportunities for economic recovery. During the transition towards the Greek drachma, one can possibly make use of a parallel currency system. The exit of Greece should be accompanied by a design of exit conditions for euro countries. This will discipline other countries and will increase the chance of a successful integration of the remaining euro zone.

Notes

1 Pius XI, *Quadragesimo Anno*, 1931, in J. Verstraeten and G. Ginneberge (2000).

2 Nechio (2011) shows that before 2008, the target rate of the ECB was too low for the peripheral European countries (Greece, Ireland, Portugal, and Spain), but after the economic crisis in 2008, it was too high.
3 For earlier applications of the OCA theory to the euro zone, see Eichengreen (1990), de Grauwe and Vanhaverbeke (1993), Bayoumi and Eichengreen (1997) and Artis (2002).
4 Rose (2007) shows that in the 69 countries that have left a currency union since the Second World War, no major macroeconomic consequences occurred before, during or after the break-up. New coins were introduced without major disruptions. Capital Economics (2012), however, notes that these examples are not comparable with a break-up of the euro zone, because the analysis of Rose concerns many small, post-colonial economies, which subsequently linked their currency to stronger currencies and had no large foreign or public debts.
5 This corresponds with simulation results of Garcia-Solanes and Torrejon-Flores (2010) with a general equilibrium model, which show that the impact of devaluations on domestic consumption and production prices for countries with large debts is limited. They conclude that devaluation for this type of countries is a good means to adjust the real exchange rate.
6 *The Economist* (2012b) even considers the weak economy of France as the biggest potential danger for the euro at the moment.
7 An extreme example is the suicide of a 77-year-old man in Greece. He saw no other way out and wanted a 'worthy end before I have to look for food between the garbage', he wrote in a farewell letter. Source: www.nu.nl/griekenland/2779740/man-pleegt-zelfmoord-grieks-parlement.html.
8 Source: www.spanjevandaag.com/nationaal/zelfmoord-grootste-niet-natuurlijke-doodsoorzaak-in-spanje/. See also: www.ine.es/ss/Satellite?L=1&c=INEPublicacion_C&cid=1259924963420&p=1254735110606&pagename=ProductosYServicios%2FPYSLayout&tittema=Society.

References

Arghyrou, M. G. (2009). Monetary policy before and after the euro: Evidence from Greece. *Empirical Economics*, 36(3): 621–643.
Arghyrou, M. G., and Gadea, D. M. (2012). The single monetary policy and domestic macro-fundamentals: Evidence from Spain. *Journal of Policy Modelling*, 34(1): 16–34.
Artis, M. J. (2002). Reflections on the optimal currency area (OCA) criteria in the light of EMU. Working Paper 193, Central Bank of Chile.
Attinasi, M. G., Checherita, C., and Nickel, C. (2009). What explains the surge in euro area sovereign spreads during the financial crisis of 2007–2009? Working Paper 1131, European Central Bank.
Baldwin, R., and Wyplosz, C. (2012). *The economics of European integration* (4th edn). London: McGraw-Hill Higher Education.
Bayoumi, T., and Eichengreen, B. (1997). Ever closer to heaven? An optimum-currency-area index for European countries. *European Economic Review*, 41(3–5): 761–770.
Berger, H., and Nitsch, V. (2010). The euro's effect on trade imbalances. Working Paper 226. IMF.
Berger, H., and Nitsch, V. (2008). Zooming out: The trade effect of the euro in historical perspective. *Journal of International Money and Finance*, 27(8): 1244–1260.
Blundell-Wignall, A., and Slovik, P. (2011). A market perspective on the European sovereign debt and banking crisis. *OECD Journal: Financial Market Trends*, 2: 1–28.

Bohn, F., and de Jong, E. (2011). The 2010 euro crisis stand-off between France and Germany: Leadership styles and political culture. *International Economics and Economic Policy*, 8(1): 7–14.

Brisson, D., Roll, S., and East, J. (2009). Race and ethnicity as moderators of bonding social capital for employment in low-income neighborhoods. *Families in Society*, 90 (4): 368–374.

Buiter, W. (2011). A Greek exit from the euro area: A disaster for Greece, a crisis for the world. *Global Economics View*, 13 September.

Capital Economics. (2012). *Leaving the Euro: A practical guide*. Retrieved from www.policyexchange.org.uk/images/WolfsonPrize/wep%20shortlist%20essay%20-%20roger%20bootle.pdf.

Cliffe, M. (2012). *Roads to survival: How EMU break-up could be avoided*. ING Financial Markets Research, June. Retrieved from www.ing.com/About-us/Our-stories/Features/Feature/ING-publishes-report-on-how-EMU-breakup-could-be-avoided.htm.

Darvas, Z. (2011). A tale of three countries: Recovery after banking crises. *Bruegel Policy Contribution* 2011/19. December. Retrieved from www.bruegel.org/publications/publication-detail/publication/663-a-tale-of-three-countries-recovery-after-banking-crises/.

de Grauwe, P., and Vanhaverbeke, W. (1993). Is Europe an optimum currency area? Evidence from regional data. In Masson, P. and Taylor, M. (eds), *Policy Issues in the Operation of Currency Unions* (pp. 111–129). Cambridge: Cambridge University Press.

de Gruyter, C. (2012). Men praat te makkelijk over een Griekse exit. *NRC*, 22 September. Retrieved from www.nrc.nl/handelsblad/van/2012/september/22/men-praat-te-makkelijk-over-een-griekse-exit-1155133.

de Jong, E. (2012). Euro behouden is onderdeel politieke agenda ECB. *MeJudice: Economen in Debat*, 14 September. Retrieved from www.mejudice.nl/artikelen/detail/euro-behouden-is-onderdeel-politieke-agenda-ecb.

DNB. (2012). Inhaalslag vereist voor achterblijvende eurolanden. *DNBulletin*, 19 January. De Nederlandsche Bank. Retrieved from www.dnb.nl/nieuws/nieuwsoverzicht-en-archief/dnbulletin-2012/dnb266973.jsp.

Dutch Council of Churches. (2013). *Faith and economics: Perspectives on the economic crisis*. Amersfoort, Netherlands: Author.

Eichengreen, B. (1990). Is Europe an optimum currency area? Working Paper 90–151, University of California. Retrieved from http://escholarship.org/uc/item/40m5g6pp.

Garcia-Solanes, J., and Torrejon-Flores, F. (2010). Devaluation and pass-through in indebted and risky economies. *International Review of Economics and Finance*, 19(1): 36–45.

Gilbert, N., and Hessel, J. (2012). De Europese overheidsfinanciën tijdens de crisis. *Economisch Statistische Berichten*, 97: 166–169.

Graafland, J. J. (2014). Christian faith, economy and the economic crisis. *Philosophia Reformata*, 78: 108–114.

Graafland, J. J. (2013). *The future of the Euro: A comparative analysis of five policy options*. Amersfoort, Netherlands: European Christian Political Federation.

Graafland, J. J., and Blok, M. (2004). Subsidiariteit, soevereiniteit in eigen kring en de bouwfraude. *Philosophia Reformata*, 69: 2–13.

Hayo, B., and Hofmann, B. (2006). Comparing monetary policy reaction functions: ECB versus Bundesbank. *Empirical Economics*, 31(3): 654–662.

Höffner, J. (1983). *Christian social teaching*. Bratislava, Slovakia: LÚC.
ING. (2012). Roads to survival: How EMU break-up could be avoided. June.
Kim, Y., and Ying, Y. -H. (2007). An empirical assessment of currency devaluation in East Asian countries. *Journal of International Money and Finance*, 26(2): 265–283.
Nechio, F. (2011). Monetary policy when one size does not fit all. Economic letter 2011–2018, Federal Reserve Bank San Francisco. Retrieved from www.frbsf.org/publications/economics/letter/2011/el2011-18.html.
NU.nl. (2012). Man pleegt zelfmoord voor Grieks parlement. 4 April. Retrieved from www.nu.nl/griekenland/2779740/man-pleegt-zelfmoord-grieks-parlement.html.
Paul, K. I., and Moser, K. (2009). Unemployment impairs mental health: Meta-analyses. *Journal of Vocational Behavior*, 74(3): 264–282.
Rajan, R. (2010). *Fault lines: How hidden fractures still threaten the world economy*. Princeton, NJ: Princeton University Press.
Rodenburg, P., and Zuidhof, P. W. (2012). De euro en structurele verschillen in de Eurozone. *Economisch Statistische Berichten*, 97: 170–174.
Rose, A. K. (2007). Checking out: Exits from currency unions. Discussion Paper DP6254. CEPR. Retrieved from www.cepr.org/active/publications/discussion_papers/dp.php?dpno=6254.
Spanje Vandaag. (2011). Zelfmoord grootste niet natuurlijke doodsoorzak in Spanje. 16 November. Retrieved from www.spanjevandaag.com/nationaal/zelfmoord-grootste-niet-natuurlijke-doodsoorzaak-in-spanje/.
ten Dam, A. (2012). The Euro-crisis and 'The Matheo Solution (TMS)'. Retrieved from www.thematheosolution.eu/BVMW.pdf
Teuling, C., Bijlsma, M., Gelauff, G., Lejour, A., and Abbing, M.R. (2011). *Europa in crisis: Het centraal planbureau over schulden en de toekomst van de Eurozone*. Amsterdam: Balans.
The Economist. (2012a). Breaking up the euro zone. The Merkel memorandum, 11 August. Retrieved from www.economist.com/node/21560252.
The Economist. (2012b). France and the euro. The time-bomb at the heart of Europe. Why France could become the biggest danger to Europe's single currency/ So much to do, so little time, 17 November. Retrieved from www.economist.com/news/leaders/21566640-why-france-could-become-biggest-danger-europes-single-currency-time-bomb-heart.
Verstraeten, J., and Ginneberge, G. (2000). *De sociale ethiek van de Katholieke Kerk in de encyclieken van Leo XIII tot en met Johannes Paulus II*. Brussels, Belgium: LICAP.
Wierts, P., van Kerkhoff, H., and de Haan, J. (2012). Trade dynamics in the euro area: The role of export destination and composition. Working Paper 354. DNB. Retrieved from www.dnb.nl/en/binaries/Working%20Paper%20354_tcm47-280101.pdf.

12 The greening of the EU?

A Christian assessment of the EU's environmental policies for biodiversity and nature

Janice Weatherley-Singh, Tiago Branco and Marcial Felgueiras

Introduction

The aim of this chapter is to assess the effectiveness of the European Union's environmental policy and legislation for biodiversity and nature and to analyse the values underlying them from a Christian theological perspective. This will be achieved in two stages: firstly, by analysing the evolution of European Union (EU) nature conservation legislation and biodiversity policy, the extent to which they are becoming 'greener', and the values underlying such policy; secondly, by exploring the role of values in the application of EU environmental law to a case study in Portugal. Policy-making is ultimately rooted in underlying principles and values, and EU environmental policy is no exception. Debates about environmental protection turn significantly on how much value the natural environment is given compared to other policy priorities and why. The case study examined here reveals a growing parting of the ways between the utilitarian economic agenda increasingly driving official EU environmental policy and an assumption that certain environmental goods have an 'intrinsic value' – an assumption that remains widely endorsed among EU citizens and that finds robust support in a Christian environmental ethic.

Given the wide scope of EU environmental policy, in this chapter we focus on the specific policy area of nature and biodiversity, one of the largest and most important policy areas dealt with by the European Commission's Environment Directorate-General. Climate change policy, another very important area of environmental policy-making, is not included within this analysis, as this has not been dealt with by the EC Environment Directorate-General since 2010 when the new EC Climate Action Directorate-General was created. Additionally, in recent years climate change has received much greater attention from Christian authors than the issue of biodiversity loss.[1]

According to the UN, "biodiversity is the variability amongst living organisations and the ecological complexes of which they are part, including diversity within species, between species and of ecosystems" (United Nations, 1992). The fact that biodiversity is seriously under threat today is recognised by many scientists and policy makers.[2] The statistics show an alarming picture, with 20 per cent of the world's coral reefs now lost and 50 per cent at risk, and 13 million hectares of tropical forest being lost each year. European citizens currently consume twice as much as Europe's land and seas can produce with an increase in the European Ecological Footprint of 33 per cent in the last 40 years (European Environment Agency, 2010). The European Commission recognises the serious stress that species and habitats are now under and states that:

> biodiversity loss has accelerated to an unprecedented level, both in Europe and worldwide. It has been estimated that the current global extinction rate is 1,000 to 10,000 times higher than the natural background extinction rate. In Europe some 42 per cent of mammals are endangered, together with 15 per cent of birds and 45 per cent of butterflies and reptiles.
> (European Commission DG Environment, 2015a)

According to the then EU Environment Commissioner Stavros Dimas (2008), biodiversity loss is a global threat that is just as serious as climate change and needs to be faced with the same urgency.

Although an analysis of the EU's efforts to protect biodiversity does not reflect all of its environmental protection work or all the values driving the full range of EU environmental policy, it provides a useful case study for one of its most important environmental policy areas. In this chapter we assess the effectiveness of EU environmental policy and legislation and the values underlying it from a Christian theological and ethical perspective. This perspective will not be elaborated or defended here – an extensive scholarly literature on the theme already exists[3] – but some of its main contours can be briefly outlined. Such a perspective proceeds from the assumption that not only human beings but also the natural world have an intrinsic value[4] deriving from their having been created, sustained, and redeemed by a transcendent God who enters into a covenant relationship with his creatures (Bookless 2008, 2014; Bauckham, 2010). Scholars such as Stuart et al. (2005) argue that a Christian environmental ethic, rather than ceding to humans unrestricted dominance over the rest of creation to master it entirely for their own purposes, strongly affirms the responsible human stewardship[5] of the natural environment. The confession that humans have been 'made in the image of God' mandates their trusteeship of everything that God has made. As Van Dyke puts it: "the purpose of stewardship is to reconcile the human and non-human creation on earth to a productive, beneficent and loving relationship" (2006: 59).

A Christian environmental ethic thus supplies a robust ground for attributing to non-human species an 'intrinsic value' and not merely an instrumental value as means to human ends. It does not, of course, deny that non-human nature also serves vital human ends. Indeed, much human interaction with nature is motivated by the theologically legitimate desire to meet human needs. Nor does it deny that there are often difficult judgements to make when the environmental consequences of meeting particular human needs seem to collide with human duties to protect intrinsically valuable environmental goods. The issue becomes problematic when economic arguments and the relentless pursuit of human material satisfaction – notably the maximisation of economic growth – are given precedence over environmental policy-making, making it difficult or even impossible to honour any environmental goods as having an intrinsic value at all.

A perspective informed by notions of 'intrinsic value' and 'stewardship' is now widely endorsed by most theological traditions as the core of a Christian environmental ethic.[6] As the case study will show, such a perspective also provides a specific ground among Christian environmental practitioners for hope that positive change in the area of biodiversity protection is worth striving for even against many odds. This Christian perspective will form the background for analysing whether the EU's biodiversity and nature policy is contributing to the 'greening of the EU'; or, in the theological language cited above, whether it is promoting the 'reconciliation of the human and non-human creation to a productive, beneficial, and loving relationship'.

Our assessment will show that whilst the EU does hold the view that environmental protection is necessary and important, its policy responses are increasingly driven by economic objectives at the expense of a recognition of the intrinsic value of nature. Our case will be that the EU's increasing use of economic arguments to justify biodiversity protection is undermining its effectiveness and limiting the extent to which it is contributing to the 'greening of the EU'.

The development of EU environmental and biodiversity policy

As recognised by governments around the world, effective legislation and policies are needed to prevent biodiversity loss. Policies are needed that create protected areas to give biodiversity space to retreat and regenerate, and biodiversity protection also needs to be integrated within other policy areas to reduce the pressures upon it (Spangenberg, 2007a). This is also the case at EU level, at which many policies are implemented that have a considerable impact on biodiversity, such as agriculture, fisheries, and regional development.

The European Commission Environment Directorate-General began in 1973 with a team of five people at a time when environmental consciousness was growing in Europe. EU environmental policy subsequently grew and was given greater legitimacy in 1987 when it was included in the Single European Act Treaty (Scheuer, 2005). By 2010, the Environment Directorate-General comprised a team of more than 500 people who together oversee over 200 pieces of environmental legislation currently in force at the European level (European Commission DG Environment, 2010).

The EU began legislating for nature protection by creating protected areas in 1979, through the adoption of the Wild Birds Directive (more commonly known as the Birds Directive). This was based on the growing recognition that many wild birds are migratory and do not recognise national borders and therefore require international action to protect them effectively in the face of population declines (European Commission DG Environment, 2015b). The Directive is still in force today and provides a legal system of protection for all wild bird species within the EU (European Union, 2009). As well as outlining measures to protect species, for example through hunting restrictions, the Birds Directive also outlines the need to protect habitat areas that are particularly important for the conservation of wild birds, by providing a legal framework for the designation, management, protection, and restoration of important habitat areas, known as Special Protection Areas (SPAs). A study by Donald et al. (2007) showed that the Birds Directive has been effective and has provided measurable conservation benefits.

A further important and complementary piece of EU legislation to protect nature came in 1992 with the adoption of the Directive 'on the conservation of natural habitats and of wild fauna and flora' (more commonly known as the Habitats Directive). This Directive aims to protect over 1,000 animal and plant species and more than 200 habitats of European importance (European Commission DG Environment, 2015c). Like the Birds Directive, it includes specific species protection measures and has extended the network of protected areas by designating sites to protect the EU's most important habitats and species, called Special Areas of Conservation (SACs). Together, the protected areas designated under both the Birds and Habitats Directives are known as Natura 2000. Scheuer (2005) noted that implementation of these two Directives has been very slow, with member states often missing deadlines for site designation. Additionally their implementation has been undermined by contradictory EU infrastructure and agricultural funding policies. Nevertheless, since these two pieces of legislation were adopted, 26,000 Natura 2000 sites have been designated as protected areas, covering an area of 750,000 km^2 (18 per cent of the EU's land area), making it the largest network of protected areas in the world, an undoubted achievement (European Commission DG Environment, 2015d).

The then EU Environment Commissioner Potočnik expressed the Commission's view on this achievement in a speech at an event organised by environmental organisations in 2012:

> [T]he Habitats Directive can be credited, to a large extent, for preserving our most precious natural assets and beginning to address the crisis in biodiversity. I can say with confidence that its biggest success lies in the creation of the Natura 2000 network. These areas of high biodiversity value embrace over 26,000 nature sites and cover almost a fifth of our land territory as well as substantial marine areas. This makes it the largest coordinated network of protected areas in the world. This is an achievement we can all be proud of.
>
> (Potočnik, 2012)

Despite widespread acknowledgement of the success of the EU Birds and Habitats Directives in achieving their objectives, they have recently been included within the European Commission's Regulatory Fitness and Performance Programme (REFIT), an ongoing evaluation that aims to determine whether various pieces of EU legislation are "fit for purpose" (European Commission, 2013). The main rationale behind this evaluation is to determine whether EU legislation is stifling business and economic growth. Depending on the outcome of this review, there is now a risk that the Directives will be modified in future so as to become less effective in achieving conservation objectives. Environmental issues were high on the global political agenda in 1992 when the Habitats Directive was adopted, with the UN Conference on Environment and Development, also known as the Rio Summit or Earth Summit, taking place the same year in Rio de Janeiro, Brazil. The Rio Summit was unprecedentedly large for a UN conference, attended by 172 governments and 108 Heads of State or government (United Nations, 1997) and was notable for promoting the concept of 'sustainable development'. The Rio Summit certainly influenced EU environmental policy-making: sustainable development was included as an EU objective in the 1997 Treaty of Amsterdam and an EU Sustainable Development Strategy was adopted in 2001. The Treaty of Amsterdam characterised sustainable development as intended to ensure a harmonious balance between economic activities and the environment, implying a high level of environmental protection and a requirement for environmental mainstreaming into other EU policy areas (Morgera, 2010).

The Rio Summit also led to the adoption of three UN Conventions to protect the environment, covering desertification, climate change, and biological diversity. The EU ratified the UN Convention on Biological Diversity in 1993, and as part of its commitment to the convention, adopted a EU Biodiversity Strategy in 1998 to address biodiversity loss (European Commission, 1998). The Biodiversity Strategy recognised that establishing protected areas and introducing targeted species protection measures was not enough to prevent biodiversity declines. They therefore also included measures to mainstream biodiversity conservation objectives into other EU policy areas that were negatively impacting it, such as agriculture, fisheries, and development assistance.

Further, very significant global political commitments were made in 2002 during the UN World Summit on Sustainable Development and the Conference of the Parties to the Convention on Biological Diversity, to reduce the rate of biodiversity loss by 2010 (Mace and Baillie, 2007). The European Heads of State went even further and adopted a tougher target to halt the loss of biodiversity by 2010. A new EU Biodiversity Communication was published in 2006 to further progress the agenda of mainstreaming biodiversity into other EU policy areas. Yet, despite all these efforts, biodiversity loss continued rapidly and the EU 2010 biodiversity target was not met (European Commission, 2011). A further EU Biodiversity Strategy was therefore adopted in 2011 to continue efforts to mainstream biodiversity objectives into other EU policy areas by 2020 (European Commission, 2011).

Whilst the Birds and Habitats Directives have resulted in considerable conservation successes (Donald et al., 2007; Potočnik, 2012) the Biodiversity Strategies have so far mostly failed in their efforts to successfully mainstream biodiversity objectives into other EU policy areas. Unlike the Directives, the Biodiversity Strategies have not been legal instruments, making them difficult to enforce. Hey (2005) argues that EU environmental policy-making initially set out with an ambitious and optimistic set of environmental goals, which, whilst recognising that the economy and environment are interdependent, also justified environmental policies on their own terms, without subordinating them to economic objectives. However, this hope of achieving far-reaching policy change was frustrated during the following decades of policy-making as member states rallied against the Commission's attempts to strengthen environmental policies and fought to maintain their focus on economic growth. Morgera (2010) also notes that the EU has suffered from an 'implementation gap' due to a continuous lack of compliance with and enforcement of EU environmental law by the member states.

Spangenberg underlines the claim that biodiversity must be mainstreamed into other areas of EU policy if it is ever to be effectively protected: "changing the modus operandi of our societies is a huge challenge, but a necessary one: for the safeguarding of biodiversity, end-of-the-pipe solutions and compensation such as establishing protected areas are simply not enough, as long as the pressures on biodiversity continue unabated" (2007b: 345). Yet when it comes to integrating biodiversity into other EU policy sectors, there appears to be a continuing lack of political will to achieve this effectively. Spangenberg et al. (2012) are not confident that the new EU 2020 Biodiversity Strategy will help in integrating biodiversity objectives into other policy areas. They note that while the European Council claims that biodiversity should be fully reflected in EU policies and strategies, it is not included, for example, in the EU's overarching Europe 2020 strategy for economic growth, which does not include any biodiversity targets. Other policy areas, such as transport, not only ignore biodiversity but threaten to increase the pressures upon it.

Values influencing the development of EU environmental and biodiversity policy

According to the European Environment Agency (2012), the values behind the protection of natural areas in Europe have shifted over time. Historically, areas were first protected for game or timber but already by the sixteenth and seventeenth centuries they also came to be valued for their natural beauty. In the late nineteenth and early twentieth centuries the rationale changed again to respecting the intrinsic value of nature. It was only following the Second World War that the emphasis was increasingly laid upon the need to maintain biodiversity. Finally, in more recent years, a mixed model has emerged in which a range of values underlies the rationale for protected areas, including aesthetics, biodiversity protection, and economics.

The justification provided in the preambles to EU biodiversity legislative and strategy documents offers an indication of the values driving EU nature protection. The preambles to the Birds and Habitats Directives (from 1979 and 1992 respectively) emphasise the need to protect declining species in order to safeguard a shared European heritage, and assert that environmental preservation is an essential Community objective and important for achieving sustainable development. In the case of these Directives, an underlying value for protecting the environment is that of increasing integration and pursuing common goals that benefit the whole European community. In the preamble to the Birds Directive, the focus is on the Community's responsibility to conserve the natural environment. Likewise, the Habitats Directive states that "the preservation, protection and improvement of the quality of the environment, including the conservation of natural habitats and of wild fauna and flora, are an essential objective of general interest pursued by the Community" (European Union, 1992).

The rationale described in the 1998 EU Biodiversity Strategy highlights that biodiversity should be protected both for its 'intrinsic value' as well as its importance to humans. It refers to the inherent worth of biodiversity as well as its value to people because of its contribution to social, economic, scientific, educational, cultural, recreational, and aesthetic goals. The 'intrinsic value' rationale is not explained in detail but is said to be included in response to the "expectations and aspirations of its citizens, which in addition to the proven economic and environmental values of biodiversity, include the ethical principle of preventing avoidable extinctions" (European Commission, 1998: 2). The later 2006 Biodiversity Communication took a similar line, claiming that biodiversity loss "is of concern not just because of the important intrinsic value of nature, but also because it results in a decline in 'ecosystem services' which natural systems provide" (European Commission, 2006: 3). Much of the rationale provided in this document was taken from the Millennium Ecosystem Assessment report (2005), a ground-breaking and influential scientific report launched by the UN Secretary-General that demonstrated the drastic decline in the many ecosystem services provided by the natural environment. In answer to the question, "Does it matter if we drive more and more species to extinction?," the Communication presents an ethical argument that many people care about biodiversity loss because they believe that humans do not have the right to decide the fate of nature. Yet it also provides utilitarian arguments: biodiversity matters because many people value it for the pleasure and inspiration it provides and for its contribution to the economy and the provision of ecosystem services.

While the most recent Biodiversity Strategy adopted by the Commission in 2011 again outlines both an 'intrinsic value' and a utilitarian rationale for conservation in its vision for biodiversity, it gives much greater prominence to the utilitarian justification for conservation, particularly its potential contribution to economic development. Throughout the document, nature is referred to in predominantly economic terms, such as 'natural capital' or 'green infrastructure'. The strategy draws on the findings of the 'The Economics of Ecosystems and Biodiversity' report (TEEB Report, 2009) that resulted from a project part-funded by the European Commission that aimed to calculate the economic values of biodiversity. This approach of calculating the economic benefits of biodiversity and its contribution to the economy is relatively new but is gaining momentum within the conservation movement. For example, Jones-Walters and Mulder (2009) argue that society's failure to place a value on nature has led to a decline in biodiversity and that providing better information to policy makers on the valuation of ecosystem services should improve the outlook for biodiversity. Pullin et al. (2009) also argue that the TEEB study may be a first step in generating awareness that biodiversity has an economic value that surpasses the short-term income to be generated from unsustainable development and exploitation. This move towards an economic approach to environmental protection is also reflected in global policy-making. For example, the 2012 UN Conference on Sustainable Development (commonly referred to as Rio+20 as it took place 20 years after the original 1992 Earth Summit), made the 'green economy' one of its two major themes.

One reason for this new trend in framing the arguments for biodiversity protection in economic terms is to counter arguments from critics of environmental policies who argue that they are bad for the economy, bureaucratic, disproportionately costly, and reduce business competitiveness (Scheuer, 2005). The inclusion of the EU Birds and Habitats Directives within the Commission's current REFIT process reflects this perception and demonstrates a shift by the Commission to further prioritise economic growth and business interests over nature protection. However, according to Scheuer, there is in fact no empirical evidence of EU biodiversity policies negatively impacting the economy; and, rather than being bureaucratic, in comparison to other EU policies such as agriculture, environmental legislation is relatively simple. This assertion is backed up by Verschuuren, who states that:

> neither ... the Birds or Habitats Directive necessarily halt economic development. These legal provisions do, however, bring an end to rash decision-making in favour of activities or projects that may harm biodiversity or landscape diversity. Only after thorough assessment, as to the effects of activities or projects on habitats, and of the economic benefits of these activities, can decision-making proceed. If there are alternative solutions that do not harm biodiversity, or do so but to a lesser extent, these solutions must be chosen. However [...] it is possible for a project to proceed if there is no reasonable alternative.
>
> (2004: 64)

A review of the implementation of the Birds and Habitats Directives by the UK government in 2012 also showed that, far from being a burdensome barrier to development, wildlife protection measures under the EU Directives had very rarely blocked business developments. Just one example was cited in the review, the development of a wind-farm that was prevented from going ahead because of the impacts it would have had on an important population of 50,000 wild ducks (DEFRA, 2012: 13–14).

It therefore appears that the EU is increasing framing its arguments in favour of biodiversity policy and legislation in economic terms in order to make them more politically acceptable and to counter unsubstantiated arguments from others that 'biodiversity is bad for business'. But there are limits to such an approach. An overdependence on economic arguments to justify nature conservation generates its own problems, because it is often difficult to demonstrate the value of the benefits (often long term) derived from protecting environmental goods and services over the value of profits (usually short term) that can be derived from industry and economic development, even if this has a damaging impact on the environment. If nature is not recognised as having intrinsic value, the decision to use or even destroy it to maximise a speedy return on investment is almost impossible to avoid. Baillie points out that it is indeed possible to conserve the 100 most endangered global species if we want to, but that, realistically, if they are allowed to go extinct this will have little discernible impact on the global economy, jobs or security. Baillie poses the simple question: "the future of these species depends on our values, are they priceless or worthless?" (2012: 16). The difficulty of justifying conservation predominantly on economic grounds is especially problematic given the challenging financial crisis the EU is currently facing, for in such a political climate the option providing the greatest short-term profit is most likely to prevail.

A Christian perspective on biodiversity protection

It may surprise some to hear that Christians were involved in some of the earliest conservation initiatives. For example, already in the 1600s and 1700s, the British naturalists John Ray and Gilbert White perceived a clear link between their faith and a responsible stewardship of the natural world on account of its intrinsic value. Well-known Christian leaders such as John Wesley, William Wilberforce, and Charles Spurgeon were also involved in preaching on action to protect animals and recognise their value as God's creatures. It is possible that this early Christian involvement influenced the commitment of later conservation movements to these values. However, Christians played a less prominent role in the modern-day conservation movement that gained traction in Europe during the 1970s and 1980s, and in some cases they regarded it with suspicion and negativity.

At that time, many environmentalists believed that religion was a major contributor to the current ecological crisis and considered that the Judeo-Christian ethic in particular – notably the ideas that there is a fundamental distinction between humanity and all other species and living things, and that humans have 'dominion' over the earth – had exercised a very negative impact on human behaviour in the West. A widely cited essay by White put this critique forcefully, asserting that "Christianity is the most anthropocentric religion the world has seen" (1967: 4). From the 1990s, however, increasing numbers of Christians have recovered a theology of environmental stewardship along the lines outlined earlier and committed themselves to engaging in what is now widely referred to as 'creation care.'[7] The Roman Catholic Church has been prominent in this revival of interest in environmental concern. The Vatican held a major conference on climate change in 2007 and has declared its intention to become the first carbon-neutral state (Vidal and Kington, 2007). Already in 1990, Pope John Paul II spoke on the importance of creation care on World Peace Day in a message entitled 'Peace with God the Creator, Peace with all of Creation'. This message was reaffirmed in 2010 in a speech by Pope Benedict XVI on World Peace Day, entitled 'If You Want to Cultivate Peace, Protect Creation'. Pope Francis has maintained this commitment and released a major encyclical on the theme in summer 2015 (Pope Francis, 2015).

'Care for creation' has become a central part of the work of the ecumenical World Council of Churches, which has also been present at UN climate change conferences since they began in the 1990s (World Council of Churches, n.d.). More recently, a growing number of evangelical Protestants have taken the issue up, for example in the 2012 consultation on 'Creation Care and the Gospel' organised by the Lausanne Conference and World Evangelical Alliance (see Lausanne Movement, 2012). At the same time, environmentalists are increasingly acknowledging the positive role that religious communities can play in responding to the environmental crisis (Bell, Chaplin, and White, 2013). For example, the Society for Conservation Biology (n.d.) has claimed that "it is increasingly recognized that religions can help make essential and substantial contributions to rethinking and responding to the world environmental crisis" (Paragraph 1).

As noted, the interest in environmental issues by the EU and other global decision-makers around the time of the 1992 Rio Earth Summit already emphasised the need to achieve a harmonious balance between economic activities and the environment. This was reflected in the adoption of the EU Habitats Directive, which ensures that areas of land are designated for the conservation of threatened species and habitats, and in which socio-economic activities are permitted as long as they do not cause environmental damage. This approach seems to fit well with a Christian ethic of "reconciling the human and non-human creation to a productive, beneficent and loving relationship". In subsequent years, the increasing emphasis on the utilitarian value of nature and biodiversity and its potential contribution to economic development by the EU and other international bodies as a way of justifying its conservation, with a lower emphasis on its intrinsic value, represents a move away from the Judeo-Christian ethic.

Writing from a Christian perspective, Van Dyke criticises the increasing dependence on utilitarian arguments as a justification for conservation because of the underlying assumption that the only value in preserving biodiversity integrity is its usefulness or attractiveness to humans and equating the intrinsic value of the entity to be conserved with the personal benefit this gives to those doing the conserving, namely humans. He argues that "the purpose of their (species) conservation is not the satisfaction of human preference, and the value of a species' existence is not based on the benefit that humans might derive from it" (2006: 56). He claims, moreover, that this view is not peculiar to Christians but is close to the moral orientation of most people.

Within a utilitarian ethical framework there can, strictly speaking, be no 'intrinsic' values (whether transcendently grounded or not) that could trump the outcomes of an economic cost-benefit analysis of an environmental decision. Instead, the value of a particular species or place depends on the balance between calculated advantages and disadvantages. For example, people may agree with the moral judgement that 'it is morally wrong to kill'. A traditional Christian justification for this statement would be grounded in a transcendently grounded truth-claim, as distinct to a utilitarian justification that killing is, contingently and all things considered, destructive for society. Equally, people may agree that 'we have a moral imperative to protect the environment'. Yet there is a deep difference between a moral argument based on a belief in the claim that creation has an intrinsic value, and a morality based on the view that it will be an economic loss to me, my children, and my grandchildren if our environment is destroyed. The difference between the former approach and the latter is disclosed by the ranking given to some principles in comparison to others. Whilst a Christian ethic affirms the (transcendently grounded) worth of the entire created world, a utilitarian approach is only able to consider the balance between the potential socio-economic costs and benefits of environmental protection. Without some concept of intrinsic value, the task of justifying biodiversity protection always has to compete against, and is often overruled by, other socio-economic interests and other principles, especially the political aim of maximising economic growth.

In contrast to the increasingly economic approach being taken by environmental policy makers, it appears that many EU citizens are concerned about biodiversity loss and believe that ethical arguments (whether transcendently grounded or not) provide sufficient rationale for its protection. In a poll for the European Commission by Gallup (The Gallup Organization, 2010), 84 per cent – 93 per cent of EU citizens felt that biodiversity loss was a *very* or *fairly* serious problem at national, European, and global levels. They also saw the conservation of biodiversity, first and foremost, as a moral obligation: 70 per cent of EU citizens agreed *very much* with this idea. Furthermore, the EU's dominant focus on economic growth seems at odds with the desires of European citizens. When asked which measure the EU should prioritise in order to protect biodiversity, the largest proportion (30 per cent) selected introducing stricter regulation of economic sectors that had an adverse impact on nature.

It is possible to identify a broad spectrum of reasons why citizens commit to caring for the environment. Some of these reasons have an explicit moral basis but they do not, of course, necessarily come from a shared Christian ethical framework or a recognition of Europe's Christian heritage. They might reflect a 'romantic' or even pagan appreciation of nature, or indeed more instrumental or utilitarian considerations, especially in local contexts that greatly benefit from environmental resources. One of the most powerful utilitarian motives is catastrophism – the fear that the human race may not be able to survive, or that it may only survive in an apocalyptic condition. Often, the slogans from environmental movements (both moderate and radical) are based on this line of reasoning, according to which dramatic climate change and biodiversity loss, along with its unpredictable consequences, are the most pressing and essential arguments for looking after the environment.

As noted, Christian theology provides very strong reasons to protect the environment, the basis of which is distinct from the reasons that motivate governments and much of civil society. This basis affects the approach that Christians take to biodiversity conservation, as demonstrated by the following case study concerning the work of Christians involved in implementing the EU Habitats Directive in Portugal.

A case study of Christian involvement in the implementation of EU nature legislation

One of the Christian organisations practically involved in tackling environmental problems over the past few decades, and in supporting the implementation of environmental policy, is the international conservation organisation A Rocha. Since its establishment in 1983, A Rocha has grown into a global network of 19 national Christian conservation organisations with a shared 'creation care' mission to be realised through a combination of scientific research, community conservation, and environmental education. Its work has resulted in demonstrable benefits for biodiversity conservation and poverty alleviation in several countries (Sluka et al., 2011).

This case study, focused on A Rocha's work in Portugal, reveals a commitment to the two elements of a Christian theology of the environment already noted above: the intrinsic value of nature as 'creation', and a distinctive motivation arising from the theology of hope, in which individuals are primarily committed to care for creation as an act of faithfulness to God and a desire to participate in the redemptive work of Christ in all creation. This belief led A Rocha to fight a battle to save the environment that many others considered to be unimportant compared to the effort involved.

A Rocha began its work in the 1980s at the Ria de Alvor in the Algarve, Portugal, an environmentally important estuarine site with considerable opportunities for environmental studies and conservation. At that time there was relatively little environmentally damaging economic development, although the tourism industry was just beginning to enter its first boom. The Ria de

Alvor is formed by the confluence of two rivers. It is surrounded by farmland and is partially separated from the sea by two spits of land composed of sand dunes and salt marsh. A Rocha established a field study centre at the site and conducted scientific surveys of the flora and fauna, alongside environmental education. These scientific studies subsequently contributed to its designation as a Natura 2000–protected area under EU law following the adoption of the EU Habitats Directive in 1992 (Santos, 2012).

Despite being less than 1,500 hectares in size, the site contains 19 different habitat types, three of which were recognised to be of priority conservation importance under the Habitats Directive.[8] It also harbours many plant and animal species recognised to be important under the Directive. One plant, the Camphor Thyme (*Thymus camphoratus*), is of priority conservation importance, while six species are listed in Directive Annex II B, and seven in Annex IV B (ICNB, 2006). In 1996, the Ria de Alvor received further recognition as an internationally important wetland, and it was designated under the intergovernmental Ramsar Convention[9] which recognised it to be an important stop-over site for migrating birds with nationally important numbers of several species as well as valuable aquatic life.

Despite the international importance of the Ria de Alvor and its designation as a protected wildlife area under EU law, a property in the heart of the site was bought by a real estate company, which in 2006 destroyed 36 hectares of marshland habitat, allegedly for 'ground clearing and farm rehabilitation activities'. This included a small area of habitat recognised to be of European priority conservation importance. Additionally, one-third of the area covered by Camphor Thyme, the plant of priority conservation importance, was completely removed. A Rocha tried to open a discussion with the company regarding these activities, but they refused to engage. Instead they continued to conduct environmentally damaging and illegal actions over a period of almost two years, during which time A Rocha presented complaints to the relevant authorities. Although the authorities repeatedly visited the site, no convictions of any kind were made and the destruction continued.

It appeared that whilst the site was supposedly protected under EU law, and therefore also under Portuguese law, in practice the site designation was ineffective and failed to provide any real protection; A Rocha Portugal knew that this had been the case at other Natura 2000 sites in Portugal. For them, protecting the Ria de Alvor also represented a wider issue of justice based on a conviction that local people deserved to have environmental laws that served their real welfare. A Rocha therefore decided to begin a campaign in partnership with other environmental organisations, and to take legal action to fight for the protection of the Ria de Alvor, beginning with a legal injunction to prevent any further destruction, followed by a legal action in the Algarve Administrative Court.[10] However, despite the legal injunction that A Rocha secured for the site, the owners continue to cause further damage to the habitat on repeated occasions.

Biodiversity conservation is in essence very local and comes down to particular places and species, in very different contexts. The challenges associated with implementing EU environmental policies are therefore mainly encountered at the local level. Upon entering this legal process it became clear that a large gap existed between environmental policy-making decisions at the European level and implementation at the member-state and local levels. This was also demonstrated by the very slow transposition of the Habitats Directive into Portuguese law following its adoption at Community level in 1992. This also led to Portugal being referred to the European Court of Justice by the European Commission in 2001 for the incorrect transposition of one of the Directive's Articles (Verschuuren, 2004). Issues such as a lack of communication between administrative entities, a lack of understanding of the legal requirements and a lack of political will at national level to implement EU law, have added to the implementation challenges.

This legal case was interpreted by A Rocha in terms of the theological principle that what to many seems to be insignificant, weak, and small may actually be very important.[11] A Rocha Portugal itself was established by a very small group of people who shared the straightforward aim to practise Christian faith in an environmental context. Their early studies were quite unsophisticated, including bird counts, bird ringing, and plant surveys and usually undertaken by amateurs, volunteers, and students. However one of these small studies, a published survey on the distribution of the toadflax plant in the Algarve (Simonson, 1994), turned out to play an unexpectedly important role by providing crucial court evidence.

In the midst of these challenges, A Rocha Portugal aimed to respond in a way consistent with its Christian identity and values. In addition to the two theological commitments already mentioned, A Rocha Portugal sought to put the local community at the centre of its actions (Felgueiras, 2005), due to their conviction that a concern for the local environment and wildlife cannot be separated from a concern for the welfare of the local community and for the quality of the physical 'place' in which its identity is rooted (a theme developed in Joshua Hordern's chapter).[12]

In the same way that conservation cannot be reduced to a concern for a particular species or habitat without taking local people's needs into account, neither does it mean that addressing economic issues, creating jobs, or pursuing prosperity should be prioritised at any environmental cost. A Rocha Portugal was convinced that local people were being subjected to a drive for economic development that did not serve their real welfare. Many companies were buying land with a view to construction for tourism with a total disregard for environmental laws, but with a promise of local economic development and job creation. However, in many cases, such construction was leading to the creation of low-paid, seasonal jobs with few long-term prospects and little security, or else was resulting in jobs and profits for foreign companies and workers and relatively few economic prospects for local people. Maintaining a close relationship with the people living near to and using the Ria de Alvor provided an opportunity to engage in a dialogue, albeit sometimes a heated one, concerning the best solutions for environmental protection and local development that also assured the well-being of local people.

Throughout the campaign, A Rocha Portugal found itself drawing on the theology of hope alluded to above as a source of motivation in the face of numerous obstacles such as stress and financial challenges. They were also inspired by the biblical motif, found in the Hebrew scriptures, of the 'healing of the land'[13] rather than a desire for the payment of financial compensation – not least because the payment of fines has in any case proved to be an ineffective deterrent for companies making huge profits from environmentally destructive activities. Unusually, the legal outcome that they pursued was therefore not for punishment in the form of a fine but rather a full restoration of the habitat. However, whilst A Rocha began a court case focused on the restoration of the habitats, the Attorney General opened a second case focused on the conviction of the administrator of the company, which if successful would result in a fine.

Eventually, after a protracted legal battle, the company administrator was finally convicted in February 2012 of an environmental crime, given a two-year suspended prison sentence and ordered to pay a fine of 150,000 euros, in response to the case opened by the Attorney General. In making this decision, the court also recognised the unethical tactics employed by him and others in the building industry: "tactics like these over recent decades have constituted an assault on the Algarve coastline by the building industry" (A Rocha International, 2012) Furthermore, in June 2012, under the court case begun by A Rocha, the company was ordered to restore completely the destroyed habitat areas. This means that the land-owning company is forbidden to undertake any work on the protected habitat areas, thereby allowing the wetland to recover (Marsh, 2012). The company administrator and the company both tried to appeal these outcomes and were able to replace the suspended prison sentence with a fine but the sentence to restore the habitats prevailed. So A Rocha Portugal thereby achieved the result it had hoped for, namely 'the healing of the land'. This successful outcome is a direct result of the designation of the site under the EU Habitats Directive; without this legal protection, damage to the internationally important wildlife habitats would have certainly continued.

Conclusion

This case study demonstrates the practical operation in a very specific context of the particular Christian environmental insights and motivations noted above. It suggests that, even with very limited resources and influence, organised Christian environmental efforts may be one of a number of faith-based initiatives positioned to make a significant contribution to the future implementation of EU nature legislation. The outcomes of the two court cases show the importance of the principle of protecting species and habitats for their intrinsic rather than their economic value, a principle consistent with a Christian environmental ethic. This principle influenced EU decision making during the design and adoption of the EU Habitat Directive in 1992 and meant that sites were designated as part of the Natura 2000 network regardless of their economic usefulness to people. In the case of the Ria de Alvor, the EU priority conservation species found there, the Camphor Thyme, is a small plant with medicinal uses, but worth very little economically in comparison to the potential real estate value of the site.

As the EU moves towards a deeper dependence on economic justifications for biodiversity conservation in policy documents such as the EU 2020 Biodiversity Strategy, there is a danger that this will lead to less effective conservation outcomes. This is especially evident when it comes to mainstreaming biodiversity conservation into other EU policy areas, for this inevitably involves difficult decisions and trade-offs between environmental and economic objectives. Furthermore, the Commission's recent decision to review the Birds and Habitats Directives because of their perceived restrictions on business development demonstrates an increased prioritisation of economic growth above biodiversity protection and thereby represents a step backwards from a 'greening of the EU'. As mentioned earlier, this move also seems to go against the wishes of many EU citizens who primarily view biodiversity conservation as a moral obligation.

There is, therefore, a significant gap between the EU's stated objective to protect the environment and biodiversity, and the actual action it is taking to do so. Whilst there are a number of values underlying EU environmental policy-making (European solidarity; the ethical/moral preferences of EU citizens; the socio-economic/utilitarian benefits of species), it seems that in many cases, apart from the exception of the largely successful Birds and Habitats Directives, EU policies are increasingly giving the greatest value to promoting short-term economic profits at the expense of environmental protection. Whilst the EU Birds and Habitats Directives largely grew from a rationale based on the intrinsic value of species, this value-basis for conservation is losing ground to predominantly economic arguments.

The EU still acknowledges there is a moral imperative for nature conservation, but when this comes into conflict with or creates challenges with other policy sectors and economic objectives, these moral arguments are usually overruled in favour of short-term economic gains. However, despite these political limitations, many European citizens remain, encouragingly, strongly in favour of the EU taking action to protect the intrinsic value of the environment and biodiversity, and many are now voicing their support for the EU's nature legislation.[14] The need to encourage the EU to protect biodiversity for its intrinsic value is more important than ever, given the intensifying pressures it is now under. As illustrated by this case study from Portugal, when committed individuals and organisations with strong faith-based motivations get involved, it is possible for them, even with limited resources, to support the implementation of EU environmental legislation and thus contribute to the 'greening of the EU' – to 'the healing of the land'.

Notes

1. See, for example, Spencer and White (2007), Northcott (2007), Northcott (2013).
2. For example in the UN Convention on Biological Diversity (1992), the Millennium Ecosystem Assessment (2005), the TEEB Report (2009), and the European Commission biodiversity strategies (1998, 2006, 2011).
3. Among Protestant theologians alone, see, e.g. Boumer-Prediger, 2001; Bookless, 2008; Bauckham, 2010; Northcott 2013. Biblical passages frequently cited in this literature include, e.g. Genesis 2.15, Psalm 24.1, Colossians 1.15–19, Matthew 6.28–29.
4. Strictly speaking, the value of both human and non-human creatures is theologically contingent (upon God) rather than intrinsic (to themselves). However the term intrinsic is commonly used to refer to value that is independent of human valuation, and it is used in that sense here.
5. The term 'stewardship' is not used in the Bible to refer to the human relationship with non-human creation, and there is academic debate about its use (Palmer, 2006). However, as understood by Van Dyke et al. (2006), it retains widespread use within the global Christian community.
6. It is worth noting that this is also increasingly true of the largest and fastest-growing wing of global Christianity, namely evangelicalism. Contrary to the perceptions of many, Stuart et al. assert that "evangelical Christians are committed by their biblical beliefs not only to the conviction that God himself cares for his universe in a daily and ongoing way but also that he helps and guides people in their conservation efforts" (Stuart, Archibald, Ball et al., 2005: 1690).
7. Oelschlaeger (1996). The term 'creation care' refers to a divinely delegated responsibility to human beings to care for the earth, not to a theology of origins (Sluka, Kaonga, Weatherley et al., 2011).
8. EU Habitats Directive habitat codes: 1150, 1510, and 2130
9. The Convention on Wetlands (Ramsar, Iran, 1971), known as the Ramsar Convention, is an intergovernmental treaty that commits member countries to maintain the ecological character of their Wetlands of International Importance and to plan for the 'wise use', or sustainable use, of all of the wetlands in their territories.
10. Campaign website: www.riadealvor.org/ria-en/index.html.
11. The biblical story of the widow's mite in Luke 21.1–4 was an important reference point for A Rocha.
12. Biblical passages to which A Rocha often referred in this regard included Jeremiah 29.4–7, 11, and Acts 17.26–27.
13. See, for example, 2 Chronicles 7.13–14.
14. According to the RSPB (reported via twitter), as of the 19th May 2015 over 100,000 people had signed their "defend nature" petition calling for the EU Birds and Habitats Directives to be kept intact.

References

A Rocha International. (2012). Legal judgement gives hope for Algarve. 2 March. Retrieved from www.arocha.org/int-en/news/top-stories/12213-DSY.html.
Baillie, J. E. M. (2012). Priceless or worthless: You decide. In Baillie, J. E. M., and Butcher, E. R. (eds.), *Priceless or worthless? The world's most threatened species* (pp. 16–17). London: Zoological Society of London.

Bauckham, R. (2010). *The Bible and ecology: Rediscovering the community of creation.* London: Darton, Longman and Todd.
Bell, C., Chaplin, J., and White, R. (eds) (2013). *Living lightly, living faithfully. Religions and the future of sustainability.* Cambridge: Faraday Institute and KLICE.
Benedict XVI. (2010). If you want to cultivate peace, protect creation. For the celebration of the World Day of Peace [speech]. 1 January. Retrieved from http://w2.vatican.va/content/benedict-xvi/en/messages/peace/documents/hf_ben-xvi_mes_20091208_xliii-world-day-peace.html.
Bookless, D. (2014). The Bible and biodiversity. *Cambridge Papers*, 23(3): 1–6. Cambridge: Jubilee Centre. Retrieved from www.jubilee-centre.org/bible-and-biodiversity.
Bookless, D. (2008). *Planetwise: Dare to care for God's world.* Nottingham: InterVarsity Press.
Boumer-Prediger, S. (2001). *For the beauty of the earth: A Christian vision for creation care.* Grand Rapids, MI: Baker Academic.
Department for the Environment, Food and Rural Affairs (DEFRA). (2012). Report of the habitats and wild birds directives implementation review. Retrieved from www.defra.gov.uk/habitats-review.
Dimas, S. (2008). EU nature policy: Challenges in a changing world. Launch of BirdLife International (Speech), 14 February. Retrieved from http://europa.eu/rapid/press-release_SPEECH-08-82_en.htm?locale=en.
Donald, P. F., Sanderson, F. J., Burfield, I. J. et al. (2007). International conservation policy delivers benefits for birds in Europe. *Science*, 317: 810–813.
European Commission. (2015). *Europe 2020: Europe's growth strategy.* 2 March. Retrieved from http://ec.europa.eu/europe2020/index_en.htm.
European Commission. (2013). REFIT – Fit for Growth. [Press release]. 2 October. Retrieved from http://europa.eu/rapid/press-release_IP-13-891_en.htm.
European Commission. (2011). Communication from the Commission to the European Parliament, the Council, the Economic and Social Committee and the Committee of the Regions; Our life insurance, our natural capital: An EU biodiversity strategy to 2020, *COM/2011/244 final.*
European Commission. (2006). Communication from the Commission: Halting the Loss of Biodiversity by 2010 – and Beyond – Sustaining Ecosystem Services for Human Well-being, *COM/2006/0216 final.*
European Commission. (1998). Communication from the Commission to the Council and the European Parliament: on a European community biodiversity strategy. 4 February. *COM/1998/42 final.*
European Commission DG Environment. (2015a). What is diversity? Last update 1 April. Retrieved from http://ec.europa.eu/environment/nature/biodiversity/intro/index_en.htm.
European Commission DG Environment. (2015b). About the Birds Directive. Last update 22 April. Retrieved from http://ec.europa.eu/environment/nature/legislation/birdsdirective/index_en.htm.
European Commission DG Environment. (2015c). About the Habitats Directive. Last update 22 April. Retrieved from http://ec.europa.eu/environment/nature/legislation/habitatsdirective/index_en.htm.
European Commission DG Environment. (2015d). Nature and Biodiversity. Last update 26 May. Retrieved from http://ec.europa.eu/environment/nature/index_en.htm.
European Commission DG Environment. (2010). Retrieved from http://ec.europa.eu/environment/pubs/pdf/factsheets/dg_environment.pdf.

European Environment Agency. (2012). Protected areas in Europe: An overview. *EEA Report* 5/2012. 22 October. Retrieved from www.eea.europa.eu/publications/protec ted-areas-in-europe-2012.
European Environment Agency. (2010). EU 2010 Biodiversity baseline: Post 2010 EU biodiversity policy. *EEA Technical Report* 12/2010. 19 October. Retrieved from www.eea.europa.eu/publications/eu-2010-biodiversity-baseline.
European Union. (2009). Directive 2009/147/EC of the European Parliament and of the Council on the conservation of wild birds (codified version). 30 November. *OJ L 20/7*.
European Union. (1992). Council directive 92/43/EEC on the conservation of natural habitats and of wild fauna and flora. 21 May. *OJ L 206/7*. Retrieved from http://eur-lex.europa.eu/legal-content/EN/TXT/?uri=CELEX:31992L0043.
Felgueiras, M. (2005). Entertaining angels in community living. In Tillett, S. (ed.), *Caring for creation: Biblical and theological perspectives* (pp. 114–115). Oxford: Bible Reading Fellowship.
Hey, C. (2005). EU environmental policies: A short history of the policy strategies. In Scheuer, S. (ed.), *EU environmental policy handbook: A critical analysis of EU environmental legislation* (pp. 18–19). Bruxelles, Belgium: European Environmental Bureau.
ICNB. (2006). *Sítios de importância comunitária, from instituto de conservação da natureza e das florestas*. Retrieved from https://docs.google.com/viewer?url=http%3A%2F%2Fwww.icnf.pt%2FNR%2Frdonlyres%2F70B26E05-B362-4E7E-986C-481393833DE4%2F0%2FSIC_Ria_Alvor.pdf.
John Paul II. (1990). Peace with God the creator, peace with all of creation. For the celebration of the World Day of Peace [speech]. 1 January. Retrieved from http://w2.vatican.va/content/john-paul-ii/en/messages/peace/documents/hf_jp-ii_mes_19891208_xxiii-world-day-for-peace.html.
Jones-Walters, L., and Mulder, I. (2009). Valuing nature: The economics of biodiversity. *Journal for Nature Conservation*, 17(4): 245–247.
Lausanne Movement. (2012). Lausanne global consultation on creation care and the gospel: Call to action. St. Ann, 9 November. Retrieved from www.lausanne.org/content/statement/creation-care-call-to-action.
Mace, G. M., and Baillie, J. E. M. (2007). The 2010 biodiversity indicators: Challenges for science and policy. *Conservation Biology*, 21(6): 1406–1413.
Marsh, S. (2012). Developer made to restore trashed wetland. Royal Society for the Protection of Birds [website], 15 June. Retrieved from www.rspb.org.uk/community/getinvolved/b/specialplaces/archive/2012/06/15/developer-made-to-restore-trashed-wetland.aspx.
Millennium Ecosystem Assessment. (2005). *Ecosystems and human well-being: Synthesis*. Washington, DC: Island Press.
Morgera, E. (2010). Introduction to European environmental law from an international environmental law perspective. *University of Edinburgh School of Law Working Paper Series 2010/37*, Edinburgh, Scotland.
Northcott, M. S. (2007). *A moral climate: The ethics of global warming*. Maryknoll, NY: Orbis.
Northcott, M. S. (2013). *A political theology of climate change*. Grand Rapids, MI: Eerdmans.
Oelschlaeger, M. (1996). *Caring for creation: An ecumenical approach to the environmental crisis*. New Haven, CT: Yale University Press.

Palmer, C. (2006). Stewardship: A case study in environmental ethics. In Berry, R. J. (ed.), *Environmental stewardship: Critical perspectives, past and present* (pp. 63–75). London: T & T Clark.
Pope Francis. (2015). *Laudato Si'*. 24 May. Retrieved from http://w2.vatican.va/content/ francesco/en/encyclicals/documents/papa-francesco_20150524_enciclica-laudato-si.html
Potočnik, J. (2012). 20 years on: The importance of EU nature protection. Three for the Tree [Speech]. Brussels, 25 September. Retrieved from http://europa.eu/rapid/p ressReleasesAction.do?reference=SPEECH/12/647&format=HTML&aged=0&lang uage=EN&guiLanguage=en.
Pullin, A. S., Báldi, A., Emre Can, O., et al. (2009). Conservation focus on Europe: Major conservation policy issues that need to be informed by conservation science. *Conservation Biology*, 23(4): 818–824.
Santos, H. P. (2012). Um justo agradecimento à associação A Rocha. *Ambio: Blogue de Reflexão sobre Ambiente e Sociedade*. Retrieved from http://ambio.blogspot.pt/ 2012/02/um-justo-agradecimento-associacao-rocha.html.
Scheuer, S. (ed.) (2005). *EU environmental policy handbook: A critical analysis of EU environmental legislation*. Bruxelles, Belgium: European Environmental Bureau.
Simonson, W. D. (1994). The genus linaria (scrophulariaceae) in the Western Algarve. *Boletim da Sociedade Broteriana*, 66(2): 343–359.
Sluka, R. D., Kaonga, M., Weatherley, J., et al. (2011). Christians, biodiversity conservation and poverty alleviation: A potential synergy? *Biodiversity*, 12(2): 108–115.
Society for Conservation Biology. (n.d.). *Religion and conservation biology* [website]. Available at http://conbio.org/groups/working-groups/religion-and-conservation-biology.
Spangenberg, J. H. (2007a). Biodiversity pressure and the driving forces behind. *Ecological Economics*, 61(1): 146–158.
Spangenberg, J. H. (2007b). Integrated scenarios for assessing biodiversity risks. *Sustainable Development*, 15(6): 343–356.
Spangenberg, J. H., Bondeau, A., Carter, T. R. et al. (2012). Scenarios for investigating risks to biodiversity. *Global Ecology and Biogeography*, 21(1): 5–18.
Spencer, N., and White, R. (2007). *Christianity, climate change and sustainable living*. London: SPCK.
Stuart, S. N., Archibald, G. W., Ball, J., et al. (2005). Conservation theology for conservation biologists: A reply to David Orr. *Conservation Biology*, 19(6): 1689–1692.
TEEB Report. (2009). *The economics of ecosystems and biodiversity for national and international policy makers, 2009*. www.teebweb.org.
The Gallup Organisation. (2010). EU barometer poll: Attitudes of Europeans towards the issue of biodiversity. *Flash Eurobarometer Report*, 290.
United Nations. (1997). *UN Conference on Environment and Development, 1992*. 23 May. Retrieved from www.un.org/geninfo/bp/enviro.html.
United Nations. (1992). *Convention on Biological Diversity. Rio de Janeiro*. 5 June.
Van Dyke, F. (2006). Cultural transformation and conservation: Growth, influence, and challenges for the Judeo-Christian stewardship environmental ethic. *Perspectives on Science and Christian Faith*, 58(1): 48–63.
Verschuuren, J. (2004). Effectiveness of nature protection legislation in the European Union and the United States: The Habitats Directive and the Endangered Species Act. In Dietrich, M. and van der Straaten, J. (eds), *Cultural landscapes and land use: The nature conservation-society interface* (pp. 39–67). Dordrecht, Netherlands: Kluwer.

World Council of Churches. (n.d.). Care for creation and climate justice. Retrieved from www.oikoumene.org/en/what-we-do/climate-change.

Vidal, J., and Kington, T. (2007). Protect God's creation: Vatican issues new green message for world's Catholics. *The Guardian*. 27 April. Retrieved from www.theguardian.com/world/2007/apr/27/catholicism.religion.

White, L. (1967). The historical roots of our ecologic crisis. *Science*, 155: 1203–1207.

13 A soul for European science
Exploring the new renaissance in the European Research Area

Diana Jane Beech

> Europe's rich spiritual and cultural history – combining elements of Antiquity, Judaism, Christianity, Islam, the Renaissance and the Enlightenment – has created an array of indisputable values, to which the European Union pays lip service, but which it often regards simply as pretty packaging for the things that really matter. But aren't these values what really matter, and are not they, on the contrary, what give direction to all the rest?
>
> Vaclav Havel, European Parliament (Havel 2009)

Introduction

Speaking in the European Parliament in 2009, former Czech President Vaclav Havel acknowledged the fundamental role that European values have played – and ought to continue to play – as key drivers of European policy. As Havel suggests, however, the importance of Europe's rich patchwork of customs and traditions for shaping the nature and direction of European policies has often become lost to seemingly more pressing, temporal demands to address fresh challenges and formulate new political and economic responses to both existing pressures and emergent threats. A brief glance over the historical development of the European project to date would seem to confirm Havel's thesis that Europe has lost sight of the values that "really matter". In spite of the fact that some of the major European treaties and charters from the twenty-first century pay homage to Europe's spiritual and religious foundations, Europe's institutions are, by and large, increasingly failing to integrate explicitly the practical lessons of social value that stem from them in their individual policies, strategies, and roadmaps.

This is nowhere more apparent than in the field of European Union (EU) research policy. Since the turn of the century in particular, a vacuum of values has opened up in the way in which science and research policy is discussed and implemented at the EU level. Despite a long history of employing science and research as a diplomatic tool to effect wider social cohesion and peaceable relations on the Continent, a neglect of the 'big questions' inherent to the scientific endeavour now, more than ever, threatens to distance the EU's contemporary knowledge policies from their original purpose of contributing to the common good and the fruitful flourishing of European civil society. Although explicit calls were issued to achieve a "new Renaissance" for European science in 2009 (ERAB, 2009) – the same year as Havel urged Europe's parliamentarians to reprioritise the values that "give direction" to the EU's policies and ambitions – EU science policy appears to have fallen victim to the dominance of a market-based politics. In the wake of the ongoing economic crisis and desperate attempts to overcome it, EU science policy has been brought into the direct service of the EU's economic ambitions – namely to help to secure Europe's global competitiveness and ultimately become the blueprint for what is now termed "smart, sustainable and inclusive growth" for the future (European Commission, 2010b).

This chapter focuses on the EU's apparent failure to effect a "new Renaissance" for its research. It seeks to draw attention back to spiritual and religious factors as core policy drivers in decision-making processes, building on the efforts of scholars such as Hitlin and Piliavin to revive the long "dormant concept" of investigating the influence of values in the wider political arena (Hitlin and Piliavin, 2004: 359). The chapter begins by examining the particular role that values have played in shaping the wider European project as well as the EU's peculiar strand of science and research policy as they have developed up to the present day.[1] The EU's roadmaps for research are perhaps not the first area of policy to come to mind in relation to religion, spirituality, or values and their importance as key drivers of contemporary policy debates. However, this chapter will demonstrate, through a predominantly discourse-analytical approach to the European research institute of CERN, not only how values have long formed the cornerstone of the EU's scientific enterprise, but also how its knowledge policies have been used over time as convenient vehicles to promote these values in a mutually reinforcing relationship. The chapter will go on to show that a failure to openly acknowledge the long-standing influence of values in the EU's science policy-making arena, together with the inability of earlier initiatives to equip the wider European project with a meaning – or a 'soul' – over and above market-based politics, has meant that a value-driven dimension appears to be lost in the formation and implementation of the EU's science and research agenda. As a result, the role and relevance of values in policy-making processes in the EU's recently established 'European Research Area' (ERA) today remain taboo. This problem is arguably exacerbated both by a reluctance to offend European citizens from particular faith (or non-faith) backgrounds and by current popular science and religion debates, which have done much to contribute to the perceived divorce of European science and research from any supposedly rational, moral, or value-based foundations.[2] The latter part of this chapter will, therefore, take the seeming vacuum of values in the EU's aptly named contemporary "knowledge-based economy" (European Commission, 2010c: 2) and attempt to account for the ongoing failure to integrate a values-based benchmarking system into policy-making structures

A soul for European science 253

in the ERA. The chapter will end by paying particular attention to the current state of affairs in the ERA under the new and predominantly market-driven 'Horizon 2020' framework programme. This came into force at the start of 2014 in an attempt to place the EU's knowledge policies firmly in the service of economic growth and wealth creation for the future. By exploring what exactly is driving the EU's 'Horizon 2020' funding juggernaut forwards, who stands to benefit from it, and to what end and purposes, the chapter will reflect on the larger normative question of whether it matters anymore if EU science and research policy is value-driven or not. To conclude, it will ask whether the proposed 'completion' of the ERA by 2020, as called for by the European Council, indeed represents a new horizon for the (re-)incorporation of spiritual values into the EU research agenda as an effective means of ensuring both the future success and sustainability of European science.

EU research policy: in the value-driven beginnings

The EU today is so clearly striving for competitive advantage over other major regions of the world and desiring to become a leading innovator on the global stage (European Commission, 2010b). It is thus easy to forget that this ambitious, modern-day Union of 28 nation states gradually arose out of the destruction and desolation left behind in the aftermath of the Second World War. As Gary Wilton's chapter has noted, European visionary Robert Schuman, desperate to avoid another calamitous continental conflict, proposed a pioneering economic plan in the form of the Schuman Declaration of 1950. This did not have as its central focus the pursuit of profit, but rather the goal of bringing about "the preservation of peace" in Europe through the pooling of natural resources (Schuman, 1950). The 'Schuman Plan' set out in the Declaration was intended both to neutralise competition between European nation states for scarce natural materials and to make the prospect of another war "not merely unthinkable, but materially impossible" (Schuman, 1950). It was Schuman's deep conviction that, by placing the Franco-German production of coal and steel under a common High Authority also shared by the Netherlands, Belgium, Luxembourg, and Italy, he could build sufficient trust in order ultimately to create "a wider and deeper community between countries long opposed to one another by sanguinary divisions" (Schuman, 1950). As Wilton puts it in his chapter in this volume, the Schuman design was intended to be "the political expression of the Christian values of forgiveness and reconciliation" and "the authentic expression of Christian political economy" (Chapter 1; see Appendix for full text of the Schuman Declaration).[3]

As Schuman's vision began to take shape in the form of the European Coal and Steel Community (ECSC), it was soon joined by two other similar organisations in 1957: the European Economic Community (EEC) and the European Atomic Energy Community (EAEC), the latter becoming known by the acronym 'EURATOM', named after its founding Treaty. Specifically, what the EURATOM Treaty (European Union, 1957) did was to establish a specialist market for the peaceable use of nuclear power in Europe, encouraging its six founding members to work together to develop nuclear energy and to distribute their outputs fairly amongst themselves, while also selling their surplus energy to non-EURATOM member states. By ensuring in its Preamble that the EAEC would associate external countries with its work and cooperate with other international organisations, the EURATOM Treaty can be seen to have been much more than a means of improving living conditions within its signatory states alone. Rather, it was also committed to the social development of both the wider European continent and the extended global community.

In keeping with Schuman's vision, the EURATOM Treaty was the first major supranational achievement of the early European project. It united formerly divided nations through a pledge to share knowledge, ideas, infrastructure, and resources. In doing so it created a unique community in which members began to support one another through a mutual dependence on energy production, not simply fostering prosperity exclusively for its own member states but also contributing to global prosperity and peace. Set against the immediate backdrop of the beginnings of the Cold War arms race, Schuman's EURATOM initiative became Europe's way of showing the world that non-proliferation was a realistic means to achieving peace by placing nuclear materials as well as the means to use them under genuine democratic control.

Of most significance for this chapter, at the heart of this courageous experiment in peace and reconciliation, was a new brand of post-war, pan-European science and research policy, which from then on became oriented not only towards a political end but also as the means by which this end could be achieved. Research – and specifically European atomic energy research – almost instantly became an output with the potential to enhance living standards across Europe on the one hand, as well as a vehicle by which to enhance closer cooperation and effect understanding and peace between different nation states on the other. In short, the EURATOM Treaty was the milestone that put European science and research policy firmly into the service of international diplomacy. In turn, the diplomatic achievements that Europe's research programmes eventually brought about also had the effect of strengthening its science and research base over the ensuing decades.

CERN: the EU's scientific disciple

To illustrate Europe's subsequent ventures in scientific diplomacy following the early successes of the EURATOM Treaty, we need only look to CERN – the European Organisation for Nuclear Research[4] – which following its establishment in 1954, began to serve as a complement to the work of the EAEC. Whereas the latter primarily concentrated on the production of atomic energy for domestic purposes, and thereby directly contributed to the economic restoration of post-war Europe, CERN was dedicated to the more abstract goal of furthering the understanding of fundamental physics, and has since developed into the world's leading organisation for research into complex particle physics. The name CERN has today become associated with some of the world's most significant scientific breakthroughs, such as the birth of the World Wide Web and, more recently, the discovery of the Higgs boson – an elementary particle that scientists claim could be responsible for all the mass in the universe. Yet very little attention has actually been paid to CERN's origins and founding principles.

In his personal contribution to a publication marking CERN's fiftieth anniversary in 2004,[5] Robert Eisenstein, a leading physicist who started work in CERN in the 1980s, wrote:

> It is important to remember back to the beginning. Fifty years ago, Europe was devastated. CERN was built with the goal of beginning to rebuild and reunify European science. . . . What CERN created after the Second World War is very subtle, with its complete openness at a time when that was desperately needed. Everybody was welcome – all they needed was a good idea. This principle still holds today.
> (Eisenstein, 2004)

CERN did indeed transform post-war European research into an arena of free and open inquiry – a truly remarkable feat after the early twentieth century had thoroughly exposed human cunning in applying science to torture, warfare, and other destructive, ideologically motivated aims, such as the development of chemical weapons and the atomic bomb, or the brutal application of Nazi eugenics. In short, the Second World War was the watershed at which, as Hudson puts it, "physicists lost their innocence" (Hudson, 2014: 21) or, as Oppenheimer more bluntly concluded, the seminal moment at which "the physicists have known sin," "a knowledge which they cannot lose."[6]

At a recent workshop in Brussels dedicated to exploring the values behind European science, Portuguese philosopher and Member of the European Parliament Maria do Céu Patrão Neves pointed out that "[w]e now know that all the research and knowledge we generate can be used somehow, somewhere." With the advent of the Second World War, she noted, "science stopped being an absolute value where all the means were justified by the ends, and was recognised as an instrument for achieving different goals."[7] What CERN successfully created was a fresh, 'clean' space in which scientists were free to carry out their research without fear of their outputs being misused or misconstrued for unethical and unintended purposes. This space not only allowed for freedom and creativity in the exercise of science but, more importantly, also created an atmosphere of openness, trust, and respect between scientific practitioners.

It is this latter dimension of CERN's operating structure that has long served to endow its research agenda with a much-needed conscience and that has kept it focused on universally accepted aims and ambitions. This is a blueprint for success that still governs CERN's mode of operation today. As CERN's own recruitment page puts it straightforwardly: "[r]espect isn't handed out automatically at CERN – it's earned. But, because of the nature of the work, people act with integrity. People are driven by scientific discovery. Their motivations are pure. They trust and are trusted" (Careers at CERN, Paragraph 3). In an interview with Spanish newspaper *El Mundo* in 2012, the Nobel prize-winning CERN scientist Peter Higgs revealed that, although he does not purport to be religious himself, many scientists in his field are religious believers. This may actually help CERN in its success at attracting a particularly virtuous and honest workforce, clean of 'impure' impulses and driven, by and large, by "feelings of awe."[8] A Wilton Park report has noted that these feelings are particularly "commonplace amongst physicists" (Wilton Park, 2012: 4). Moreover, according to Greek physicist and member of the European Parliament Ioannis Tsoukalas, "[w]e also have to think of the evolution of the scientist from a curiosity-driven human being [and . . .] from a man of virtue to a member of a community of professionals, functioning according to programmed or organised group morality."[9] This may also help account for CERN's exemplary success.

The deeply embedded sense of trust between Europe's citizens and CERN's scientists at the heart of CERN's organisational system is further enhanced by a sense of dependency and reliance created among its employees; as Tsoukalas puts it, this makes for a truly "collaborative world."[10] In CERN's scientific microcosm, "[s]eniors work with graduates. Physicists need engineers. Countries forget politics and collaborate to achieve. And knowledge – CERN's main commodity – is shared throughout CERN, its member states and the rest of the world" (Careers at CERN, Paragraph 4). By basing its pursuit of science on universal, human values and a robust system of collaboration, networking, and transparency that serves to keep its research in check, CERN has succeeded in transforming the simple act of research – the striving for knowledge for knowledge's sake – into something with remarkable power to enhance the lives of European citizens, not just through the results of its research but also through the very process of its scientific endeavour.

François de Rose – a French diplomat involved in CERN since the very beginning and the last of CERN's founding fathers to pass away (March 2014) – once referred to CERN as "such a noble cause" (De Rose, 2004). It was inspired by his own profound conviction that Europe's post-war reconstruction should be driven by the development of its fundamental research tools (O'Luanaigh, 2014). Now arguably the greatest example of scientific diplomacy in the world, CERN continues to work on the principle of fostering the common good and acting as a beacon for the successful use of science to achieve the original aims of Europe's founding fathers – namely to effect peaceable collaboration between the peoples and countries of Europe.

As the testimonies of those who have been involved in its development show, CERN is – and always has been – about much more than pure physics and particle collisions. John Wood, former Chair of the European Research and Innovation Area Board (ERIAB), has described CERN as "thousands of people from different backgrounds, working together on common problems. They have an assumption that they're going to collaborate, for the good – of science, society, their discipline or whatever their higher ideals may be" (Wood, 2014: 3). This sense of contributing to shared values has long been at the heart of the CERN enterprise, and those who work for CERN are, as Wood puts it, "indirect agents for peace" (Wood, 2014: 3). This is so not just within Europe but also for, and between, other major global knowledge economies that would traditionally be considered Europe's rivals, such as the USA, India, China, Japan, and Russia. In this sense CERN can be seen as Europe's scientific 'disciple', leading by example and spreading the values of its scientific message to the wider world.

It is also in the context of its scientific 'discipleship' that the strategic importance of CERN to developments in the wider international political arena must be assessed. Through its role as a significant site of cross-border cooperation, CERN has, over the years, not only helped Europe to overcome its own internal conflicts, but also eased tensions and facilitated peaceable collaborations between other global superpowers. As Robert Eisenstein once testified, "[t]he role CERN played in helping international relations, especially during the Cold War, is very substantive. It allowed communication in science between countries that were not talking to each other otherwise" (Eisenstein, 2004). By continuing to invest in its research and involve others in its scientific and technological endeavours without limitations, Europe was able to demonstrate through CERN that it was willing to pass on the fruits of its scientific diplomacy – overcoming political stalemate and preserving peace and stability – to the entire global community.

In an attempt to account for CERN's sustained successes over the past half a century, Egil Lillestol, a particle physicist from the University of Bergen, has looked to the nature and status of science itself as a force free from socio-political influences to explain its ability to act as an effective driver of social cohesion. In his view:

> The laws of nature are almost the only ingredient of human culture that are more or less safe from ideological differences, and people from all over the world work peacefully together at CERN, towards a common goal: a deeper understanding of the material world. This may be even more significant than the discoveries in physics, if such international co-operation helps, in the long run, to create better relations between nations, and to rid the world of the dangers threatening the existence of the civilisation that fosters our science.
>
> (Lillestol, 2008)

Lillestol's acknowledgement that CERN's societal achievements could even be more valuable than its scientific discoveries raises questions of how we ought to be measuring the success of the EU's research policies and whether we risk falling into a 'value trap', where an increasing tendency to 'econometrise' science gives undue priority to measureable economic returns on 'investment'. This anxiety over the threat to the 'real' value of European research motivated John Wood to host a workshop in Brussels to awaken public debate about the need for an ethical charter for future European science. His concern was to ensure that, "when the EU 'invests' in research and innovation, it does so not just for the economy, but for society more generally and for the future of European ideals" (Wood, 2014: 3).

The example of CERN shows that post-war European science and research policy has always been about more than the acquisition of knowledge, and certainly more than the direct pursuit of profit. From the start, European research policy has been imbued with unspoken, "hard-to-quantify dimensions" arising from its shared values of collaboration and openness (Wood, 2014: 3). Such values have also added to Europe's scientific excellence through the increased mobility of researchers and the heightened exchange of knowledge via new projects and scientific partnerships.

The wider search for Europe's values and 'soul'

A glimpse at the subsequent evolution of the EU – from the creation of a customs union to a political Union by the end of the twentieth century – shows that its early leaders were very aware of the importance of values within its overarching mission to contribute to global peace and prosperity. The Treaty establishing the European Community (EEC) of 1958, for example, recognised "the solidarity which binds Europe and the overseas countries" and the desire "to ensure the development of their prosperity" (European Union, 1958). The Single European Act (SEA) of 1986 similarly pointed to "the responsibility incumbent upon Europe ... to display the principles of democracy and compliance with the law and with human rights to which they are attached, so that together they may make their own contribution to the preservation of international peace and security" (European Union, 1986: 2). The Preamble to the Treaty on European Union (TEU) (2009) recognises that the EU draws inspiration from Europe's "cultural, religious and humanistic inheritance" (European Union, 2012: 13), and the Charter of Fundamental Rights (2000) identifies the importance of Europe's "spiritual and moral heritage" (European Union, 2010: 3).

Yet, already by the end of the Cold War, the then President of the European Commission, Jacques Delors, while keen to implement a European Single Market, began to claim that something was missing from the grand design of the European project as a result of ignoring the spiritual dimension. Anticipating Havel years later, Delors warned European parliamentarians that, "we need ... to reaffirm our values and fuse the sometimes contradictory aspirations of our new contemporaries into new constructs". While acknowledging that economic success was vital, he argued that "it will not be enough to create a large frontier-free market nor, as implied by the Single Act, an economic and social area. It is for us ... to put some flesh on the Community's bones and ... give it a little more soul" (Delors, 1989). In a similar appeal to Europe's churches only a few years later, Delors worried that, "[i]f in the next ten years we haven't managed to give a Soul to Europe, to give it spirituality and meaning, the game will be up" (Delors, 1992). As Williams puts it, Delors sought something that could "attract the greater loyalty and commitment of the people of Europe to this elusive polity constructed in their name" (Williams, 2010: 5–6). In his view, European institutions needed to start to incorporate in their policies and guidelines an explicit acknowledgement of Europe's cultural diversity and religious heritage, as well as the core values emanating from them. If the peoples of Europe were ever going to be able to identify with the highly complex evolving structure of the European Community, then it needed to ground itself clearly in common values and a shared heritage as its 'founding fathers' had once sought to do.

The outcome of this was the 'Soul for Europe' initiative, launched in 1994 (mentioned by Lucian Leustean in Chapter 9). Among other things, the initiative sought to encourage politicians and policy makers to reflect on the substance of European policies to ensure that they remained in line with the vision of Europe's 'founding fathers'. Yet the programme failed to take hold within EU institutions generally and, therefore, stopped short of permeating the EU's science and research agenda – the early bearer of its peaceable, diplomatic mission.

Towards a vacuum of values in European science

To many, it will be no surprise to discover the reluctance of present-day European officials to link Europe's science policy explicitly to moral and spiritual goals. First, a 2010 survey of public opinion in the EU revealed that, when asked to name the values that mattered most to them, European citizens ranked "religious values" the least important for them personally, scoring them at only 6 per cent as opposed to the 47 per cent for human rights – the highest-ranking set of values (European Commission, 2010a: 32). So it is understandable that EU policy makers prefer to cast science's inherent spiritual values in terms of supposedly more 'universal' aims and ambitions in order to ensure that EU taxpayers continue to view research as an endeavour worthy of their continued support. Second, the public relationship between science and religion has long been fraught and has been increasingly portrayed as a battle for supremacy in the public realm. This tension has been prompted in the main by the views of contemporary 'new atheist' science writers such as Richard Dawkins, who charges that religion "subverts science and saps the intellect" out of life (Dawkins, 2006: 282). Third, it must be borne in mind that, although scientific diplomacy has been a cornerstone of the pan-European project since the 1950s, EU member states maintain primary competence over the pursuit and use of science. Only with the introduction of the

SEA in 1987 was science and research deemed to be a 'Community responsibility', encouraging member states "to strengthen the scientific and technological bases of European industry and to encourage it to become more competitive at the international level".[11] By placing science and research firmly in the service of economic goals, it was always likely that the policy direction would soon harden into a more market-oriented course, leaving 'values-talk' completely out of the equation.

Yet faith and spirituality have always been crucial driving forces of scientific exploration and discovery. Many of Europe's most prominent scientists, from Galileo to Gell-Mann, have been driven by an intense sense of awe and wonder for nature and a deep curiosity to uncover the inner-workings of what for many was seen as a divinely created universe (Bersanelli and Gargantini, 2009). The scientific enterprise has long been preoccupied with 'big questions'. These encompass the essentially human characteristics of free will, creativity, intellect, and purpose, and many scientists have recognised a strong, complementary bond between spiritual drivers on the one hand and realities capable of scientific investigation on the other. As a Wilton Park report on the interfaces of human knowledge confirms, "[t]he passion for truth, depth for meaning and universality are shared by both science and religion. Both seek to reveal what is true, practical, compelling, and related to day-to-day life. For some the antithesis of science is not religion, but politics" (Wilton Park, 2014: 4).

Moreover, the influence of religion on science is not restricted to the theoretical dimension. In practical terms, too – as the short but successful story of post-war European science shows – an unspoken spiritual dimension has continued to inform Europe's research agenda ever since the early EURATOM years. Yet the EU's failure to equip its contemporary science policy with an identifiable 'soul' presents an opportunity for Europe's researchers, policy makers, and citizens alike to ask why Europe should be doing science at all and how the EU's science policies can begin to draw inspiration again from the original vision of its founders. In 2009, European scientific advisers and experts warned the Union's policy makers that a major reorientation was desperately needed with regard to the future of Europe's research agenda – "a paradigm shift in how we think, live and interact together, as well as a paradigm shift in what the role and place of science should be" (ERAB, 2009: 8–9). According to them, a "new, holistic way of thinking is required as technological answers alone are not the end-solution to a given problem" (ERAB, 2009: 9). We might hear this as including a call for the reintegration of spiritual and religious values into European science policy frameworks.

The 'Europe 2020' strategy and the dominance of market-based politics

The financial crisis of the present decade has, however, driven EU policy makers to concentrate even more efforts on reviving the EU's sluggish economy in the face of global recession. The EU's most recent push for prosperity was thus packaged in March 2010 as part of the 'Europe 2020' strategy, which set out a 10-year roadmap to help the EU meet ambitious targets in five of its fundamental policy areas. One such area includes research and development, in which it is hoped that all member states of the EU will achieve the target of investing 3 per cent of their GDP in science and research by the close of the present decade. Subsidiary aims are to improve the conditions for investment in science and research by the private sector and to develop an effective indicator to track innovation and provide a comparative assessment of the innovation performance of all EU member states.

As part of this wider Europe 2020 strategy, EU officials also established the 'Innovation Union', a flagship initiative which, for the first time in its history, places science and research at the heart of the EU's current drive for prosperity. The Innovation Union aims to transform Europe's best ideas into concrete products and services, with the express intention that these will, in turn, encourage Europe's economic growth, create more jobs, and boost wealth creation for the future. The Innovation Union has since become home to all policies, programmes, and action plans taking place within the 'European Research Area' (ERA), which is a relatively new conglomeration of European nation states committed to integrating their scientific and technological resources and effecting multinational cooperation in the fields of research, technology, and development (RTD).

Although the original members of today's EU have effectively cooperated in the fields of science and research since its early incarnation in the 1950s, the concept of creating an ERA was not formally proposed by the European Commission until the year 2000, in a move to strengthen Europe's scientific and technological capabilities (European Commission, 2000). Efforts to formalise the ERA were given an extra push in 2007 by a European Commission 'Green Paper' encouraging Europe to end the fragmentation of its science and research policies and to maximise the potentials of its skills, ideas, and resources (European Commission, 2007). As it stands today, then, the ERA comprises all 28 member states of the present-day EU as well as a further 11 associated countries that are equally entitled to EU-level funding and eligible to partake in EU-led scientific programmes, collaborations, and academic exchange schemes.[12] The ERA is, however, not yet complete, and by 2020 it is hoped that it will provide the necessary infrastructure to allow Europe's science to achieve maximum impact through, for example, optimised knowledge transfer systems – just one of the targets set by the European Council as part of the wider Europe 2020 goals. Founded on a shared commitment to capitalise on returns on research investment, the ERA can therefore essentially be seen as Europe's answer to a 'common market' for knowledge and RTD, where the best minds, ideas, and equipment can circulate freely in pursuit of marketable products and services.

Traditionally, scientific research programmes in Europe have been supported by the European 'Framework Programme for Research and Technological Development', which has been in existence since 1984 and implemented since then in a succession of distinct five-year phases. A proportion of money from this Framework Programme has, incidentally, been used to finance CERN over the years, as just one of Europe's scientific projects that maintains a 'free space' for serendipity and blue sky research. Specifically, from 2007 onwards, however, the European Framework Programme in its seventh incarnation has been used chiefly to fund more applied research projects taking place within the newly formed ERA for a period of seven years. The seventh Framework Programme, or 'FP7' as it commonly became known, was succeeded on 1st January 2014 by the eighth and most recent incarnation of the RTD Framework Programme. Rather than being referred to by the acronym 'FP8', however, the eighth Framework Programme has been named 'Horizon 2020' to signify a clear break with the patterns of the past and to acknowledge its specific role in promoting the wider Europe 2020 strategy through its new positioning within the Innovation Union.

Further setting the eighth phase of the European Framework Programme apart from its predecessors, the Horizon 2020 programme has been equipped with Europe's largest research budget to date. It promises to pump nearly €80 billion of public funding into research and innovation across the entire ERA for a seven year period until the end of 2020. The idea behind the inflated Horizon 2020 funding pot is that its generous resources will bring about more technological breakthroughs, scientific discoveries, and 'world-firsts' to Europe by facilitating the transition of great ideas from the lab or the library to the market and, thereby, creating guaranteed returns on public investment. The Horizon 2020 funding pot is intended to fund excellent ideas, and projects will be selected based on their potential to change lives and guarantee marketable outputs. This new approach appears, then, to be dominated in the main by short-term priorities, which enable Europe to successfully exit the economic crisis and to stake a claim to be a leader in the new, emerging global order. As Wood observes, "[w]hen politicians discuss research policy these days, it can sound more like economics than science" (Wood, 2014: 3).

New horizons for European research?

Impressive as the EU's new Horizon 2020 funding juggernaut may seem, however, its distinctly market-based criteria appears to signify a clear break from the principles of societal development that governed Europe's initial and long-running experiments in scientific diplomacy. Instead, dominating the present-day European research agenda is a more decidedly secular and materialist desire to boost competition between its member states and increase the efficiency and effectiveness of Europe's research systems to ensure maximum output – not simply in terms of products and services but also in terms of economic growth and jobs. The current state of Europe's science and research policy under Horizon 2020 thus fails to address the question of whether the newly formed ERA leaves any room to reintegrate the original moral and spiritual drivers of European science policy into its roadmaps and action plans. What scope will there be for the European research process in its new guise as a generator of revenue to recover its vocation as Europe's 'purest' disciple and to advance the EU's self-proclaimed role as a "contributor to peace", a "responsible neighbour", a "development partner", and a "human rights defender" (EEAS, n.d.)?

At least there may be hope that the current market-orientated focus of European science only dominates two of the three internal pillars propping up the new design for the present European research strategy.[13] A closer look at the complete roadmap for Horizon 2020 reveals that steps have indeed been taken 'behind the scenes' to make provision for a long-term strategy for European science that will endure long after the current economic crisis has passed, and that there is some recognition that the present preoccupation with visible impact metrics will risk restricting scientists' creativity and institutional offerings. The key to Horizon 2020's prospects for enduring success is hidden in the third pillar of its funding model, which sets its sights on longer-term and even global aims through the ambition to address the grand "societal challenges." These comprise climate change, food and energy shortages, pandemics, diseases and security threats, and are intended to be tackled by holistic research efforts that reach across borders, disciplines, and sectors.

By targeting the "grand challenges" in this way, the architects of Europe's scientific roadmap can clearly be seen to be reconnecting the economic value of European science with its 'real' value – namely its benefits to society. In short, the third pillar of Horizon 2020 can be interpreted as a political acknowledgement that in today's increasingly globalised and interconnected world, as much as Europe must safeguard its own economic interests, these cannot be detached from the flourishing of society at large, both within and beyond the EU's own borders. Through the presence of Horizon 2020's third pillar, then, EU science and research policy now displays a clear inconsistency between the market-driven workings of its policy roadmaps on the one hand, and its value-driven public façade on the other. As Anne Glover, former Chief Scientific Adviser to the President of the European Commission, emphasised to an audience of key stakeholders in the ERA, taxpayers are "paying for the research, and the accountability is [ultimately] to them".[14] Given this, the third pillar of Horizon 2020 can therefore be viewed as an implicit acceptance by EU policy makers of Delors' earlier warnings, as Williams put it, of the need to "attract the greater loyalty and commitment of the people of Europe" behind a science that is in the service of society, rather than, in the words of Hudson, simply producing "cannon-fodder to charge the guns of industry with products, services and ideas that we simply can't imagine yet".[15]

How the tension between the inner dynamics of Europe's market-driven research policy and its public value-driven façade will play out over the coming decade will be crucial in determining whether EU science policy can reclaim its original vision of contributing to peace and consolidation in Europe and beyond. Given the continuing pressures of the economic crisis and of competition from the impressive innovation outputs of other global knowledge economies, the EU will struggle to imbue its wider science policies with a much-needed *con*-science – such as that epitomised by CERN. Yet, an analysis of the current Horizon 2020 framework programme shows that EU science policy cannot any longer be separated from ethics. As Member of European Parliament Maria do Céu Patrão Neves puts it, "[i]f science is not an absolute value in itself, then the goals for scientific research have to be established elsewhere".[16] That must mean, at least, that the EU's research agenda needs to reconnect with the larger aspirations of its citizens. As the former European Commissioner for Research, Innovation, and Science recently said, "[r]esearch and innovation must [ultimately] respond to the needs and ambitions of society, reflect its values, and be responsible" (Geoghegan-Quinn, 2012). It is the task of the EU's citizens as well as its scientists to ensure that responsiveness. The values inspiring European science have never just been "pretty packaging" (as Havel put it), but are the constants that make it "really matter".

Notes

1 This chapter will use the terms 'science policy', 'research policy', and 'knowledge policy' interchangeably. This variation in terminology is purely in the interest of semantics and enhancing its readability. Thus, whenever the term 'science' appears, it is to be read and understood in the Germanic sense of the word *Wissenschaft*, meaning all academic pursuits, and not in the more conventional Anglophone sense of the physical or the natural sciences alone.
2 For example, Richard Dawkins has popularised the view that adhering to a religion or a specific moral code equates to "the total abdication of the responsibility to find an explanation". This, for him, stands in complete opposition to the concept of scientific discovery (Dawkins, 2006: 185).
3 In 1953, the then Italian Prime Minister Alcide De Gasperi even described the European project as "a divine gift for us" and one that "actually belongs to, and is addressed to, humanity as a whole". He continued: "how could we conceptualise a European construction without taking into account the Christian element, how could we ignore the lessons of fraternity, unity and social value that stem from it?" Quoted in Venneri and Ferrara (2010: 118).
4 The acronym CERN is derived from the French *Conseil Européen pour la Recherche Nucléaire* – a provisional body set up in 1952 principally to establish a centre to lead fundamental physics.
5 The publication is Hurter (ed.) (2004). All quotations from this publication have been taken from the edition of Hurter available on CERN's *People: In their own words...* website.
6 Oppenheimer (1947). Quoted in Hudson (2014: 21).
7 Maria do Céu Patrão Neves, quoted in Hudson (2014: 21).
8 Quoted in Jha (2012).
9 Quoted in Hudson (2014: 11).
10 Quoted in Hudson (2014: 11).
11 See Article 24, Title 130f, *Single European Act* (European Union, 1986).
12 As of 17th December 2014, Horizon 2020 Association Agreements have been concluded with: Iceland, Norway, Albania, Bosnia, and Herzegovina, the Former Yugoslav Republic of Macedonia, Montenegro, Serbia, Turkey, Israel, Moldova, Switzerland, and the Faroe Islands (European Commission, 2015).

13 The other two pillars comprise "excellent science" and "industrial leadership" – the former seeking to enhance Europe's competitiveness in research ideas and infrastructure and the latter to speed up the development of the innovations that will help European businesses to grow into world-leading companies (European Commission, 2010b).
14 Quoted in Hudson (2014: 19)
15 Quoted in Hudson (2014: 21)
16 Quoted in Hudson (2014: 21).

References

Bersanelli, M., and M. Gargantini. (2009). *From Galileo to Gell-Mann: The wonder that inspired the greatest scientists of all time in their own words.* West Conshohocken, PA: Templeton Press.
Careers at CERN website, *Why join us?* Retrieved from http://jobs.web.cern.ch/content/why-join-us.
Dawkins, R. (2006). *The God delusion.* London: Black Swan.
Delors, J. (1992). Speech to the churches. 4 February 1992. In *Newsletter of the Ecumenical Centre in Brussels.* Brussels: EECCS.
Delors, J. (1989). *Address given by Jacques Delors to the European Parliament No. Supplement 1/89.* (17 January). Brussels: Bulletin of the European Communities / Luxembourg: Office for official publications of the European Communities. Retrieved from www.cvce.eu/content/publication/2003/8/22/b9c06b95-db97-4774-a700-e8aea5172233/publishable_en.pdf.
De Rose, F. (2004). *A noble cause.* CERN. Retrieved from http://public-archive.web.cern.ch/public-archive/en/People/DeRose-en.html.
EEAS (European External Action Service). (n.d.). *The EU's many international roles.* Retrieved from http://eeas.europa.eu/what_we_do/index_en.htm.
ERAB. (2009). *Preparing Europe for a new renaissance: A strategic view of the European Research Area.* First Report of the European Research Area Board (ERAB). Brussels, Belgium: ERAB, European Commission. Retrieved from http://ec.europa.eu/research/erab/pdf/erab-first-annual-report-06102009_en.pdf.
Eisenstein, R. (2004). *Building bridges.* CERN. Retrieved from http://public-archive.web.cern.ch/public-archive/en/People/Eisenstein-en.html.
European Commission. (2015). *Associated countries* [to Horizon 2020]. Brussels, Belgium: European Commission. Retrieved from http://ec.europa.eu/research/participants/data/ref/h2020/grants_manual/hi/3cpart/h2020-hi-list-ac_en.pdf.
European Commission. (2010a). *Eurobarometer 74,* Autumn. Retrieved from http://ec.europa.eu/public_opinion/archives/eb/eb74/eb74_publ_en.pdf.
European Commission. (2010b). *EUROPE 2020 – A strategy for smart, sustainable and inclusive growth* (COM 2010, 2020). Brussels, Belgium: European Commission. Retrieved from http://ec.europa.eu/eu2020/pdf/COMPLET%20EN%20BARROSO%20%20%20007%20-%20Europe%202020%20-%20EN%20version.pdf.
European Commission. (2010c). *Lisbon strategy evaluation document* (SEC 2010 114 final). Brussels, Belgium: European Commission Staff Working Document. Retrieved from http://ec.europa.eu/europe2020/pdf/lisbon_strategy_evaluation_en.pdf.
European Commission. (2007). *The European Research Area: New perspectives.* Green Paper 04.04.2007. Brussels, Belgium: European Commission. Retrieved from http://

ec.europa.eu/research/era/docs/en/understanding-era-european-commission-eur2284 0-161-2007-en.pdf.

European Commission. (2000). Communication from the Commission to the Council, the European Parliament, the Economic and Social Committee and the Committee of the Regions of 4 October. *Making a reality of the European Research Area: Guidelines for EU research activities (2002–2006)* (COM 2000, 612 final – Not published in the Official Journal). Retrieved from http://eur-lex.europa.eu/legal-content/EN/TXT/?uri=CELEX:52000DC0612.

European Union. (2012). *Consolidated versions of the Treaty on European Union and the Treaty on the Functioning of the European Union. Official Journal C 326, 26/10/ 2012* P. 0001–0390. Retrieved from http://eur-lex.europa.eu/legal-content/EN/TXT/HTML/?uri=CELEX:12012E/TXT&from=en.

European Union. (2010). *Charter of Fundamental Rights of the European Union (2010/ C 83/02)*. Retrieved from http://eur-lex.europa.eu/LexUriServ/LexUriServ.do?uri=OJ:C:2010:083:0389:0403:en:PDF.

European Union. (1986). *The Single European Act*. Retrieved from www.eurotreaties.com/singleuropeanact.pdf.

European Union. (1958). *Treaty Establishing the European Economic Community, EEC Treaty*. Retrieved from http://eur-lex.europa.eu/legal-content/EN/TXT/?uri=URISERV:xy0023.

European Union. (1957). *Treaty Establishing the European Atomic Energy Community (EURATOM)*, Rome, 25th March, Retrieved from http://eur-lex.europa.eu/LexUriServ/LexUriServ.do?uri=OJ:C:2010:084:0001:0112:EN:PDF.

Havel, V. (2009). Speech of Vaclav Havel, European Parliament, Brussels. 11 November 2009. Retrieved from www.vaclavhavel.cz/showtrans.php?cat=projevy&val=1290_aj_projevy.html&typ=HTML.

Geoghegan-Quinn, M. (2012). Message delivered at the conference 'Science in Dialogue – Towards a European Model for Responsible Research and Innovation', Odense, Denmark. 23–25 April. In *Responsible Research and Innovation: Europe's ability to respond to societal challenges*, EU Publications Office, Retrieved from http://ec.europa.eu/research/science-society/document_library/pdf_06/responsible-research-and-innovation-leaflet_en.pdf.

Hitlin, S., and Piliavin, J. A. (2004). Values: Reviving a dormant concept. *Annual Review of Sociology*, (30): 359–393.

Hudson, R. (ed.) (2014). *The value(s) of science: An open inquiry into the ethics of Horizon 2020*. Brussels, Belgium: Science Business Publishing. Retrieved from www.sciencebusiness.net/OurReports/ReportDetail.aspx?ReportId=67.

Hurter, S. (ed.) (2004). *Infinitely CERN: Memories from 50 years of research*. Geneva, Switzerland: CERN et Editions. Retrieved from http://archive-public.web.cern.ch/archive-public/en/People/Personalaccounts-en.html.

Jha, A. (2012). Peter Higgs criticises Richard Dawkins over anti-religious 'fundamentalism'. In *The Guardian*, 26 December. Retrieved from www.theguardian.com/science/2012/dec/26/peter-higgs-richard-dawkins-fundamentalism.

Lillestol, E. (2008). *CERN: A unique experience*. Geneva, Switzerland: CERN. Retrieved from http://public-archive.web.cern.ch/public-archive/en/People/UniqueExperience-en.html.

O'Luanaigh, C. (2014). Last founding father of CERN passes away. Press release, 24 March. Retrieved from http://home.web.cern.ch/about/updates/2014/03/last-founding-father-cern-passes-away.

Oppenheimer, J. R. (1947). Physics in the contemporary world. *The Arthur D. Little Memorial Lecture*. Massachusetts Institute of Technology, 25 November.

Schuman, R. (1950). *The Schuman Declaration*, 9 May. Retrieved from www.eurotreaties.com/schuman.pdf.

Venneri, G., and P. O. Ferrara. (2010). Alcide De Gasperi and Antonio Messineo: A spiritual idea of politics and a pragmatic idea of religion. In Leustean, L. N. and Madeley, J. T. S. (eds), *Religion, politics and law in the European Union* (pp. 109–125). London: Routledge.

Williams, A. (2010). *The ethos of Europe: Values, law and justice in the EU*. Cambridge: Cambridge University Press.

Wilton Park. (2014). *The big bang and the interfaces of knowledge: Towards a common understanding of truth?* 23–25 June (WP1316). Retrieved from www.wiltonpark.org.uk/wp-content/uploads/WP1316-Report.pdf.

Wilton Park. (2012). *The big bang and the interfaces of knowledge: Towards a common language?* 15–17 October (WP1180). Retrieved from www.wiltonpark.org.uk/wp-content/uploads/wp1180-report.pdf.

Wood, J. (2014). A conscience for European science. In Hudson, R. (ed.), *The value(s) of science: An open inquiry into the ethics of Horizon 2020* (p. 3). Brussels, Belgium: Science Business Publishing.

14 Conclusion
Christianity and the 'souls' of Europe

Jonathan Chaplin

> If in the next ten years we haven't managed to give a Soul to Europe, to give it spirituality and meaning, the game will be up.
> (President Jacques Delors, 'Speech to the churches', Brussels, 4 February 1992)[1]

> [T]he absence of Christian values in the EU Treaty and Charter of Fundamental Rights is not to be interpreted as a thundering silence, but instead . . . as a positive affirmation of a secular approach that values diversity and cherishes all world-views while refraining from embracing any of them.
> (Zucca, 2012: 88)

This book has sought to illustrate how Christian political theology might contribute a critical, constructive voice to the common discourse of the EU. It has displayed a selection of the resources Christian political thinkers and actors might have available to them as they make such a contribution. This Conclusion will not comment in detail on the foregoing chapters nor seek to identify points of convergence and divergence among them. Instead, in the light of the varying foci of the chapters, it explores Christianity's potential contribution to an evolving EU which is *de facto* highly religiously, morally, and culturally diverse, while *de jure* religiously neutral.

Nearly a quarter of a century after Delors' passionate appeal for the creation of a European 'soul', hopes for the emergence of an identity-constituting Community-wide moral and spiritual vision look rather forlorn.[2] The 2004 enlargement, for example, evoked serious doubts (as Pabst notes) over whether a market-driven process of integration could produce the requisite "politically resilient solidarity" for enlargement to succeed. Today, the EU finds itself riven by its most disruptive financial and economic crises ever, wracked by persisting uncertainty about its future goals, priorities, and place in the world and confronted with an alarming crisis of legitimacy among its indifferent, alienated, or hostile populations. Ratifying its Charter of Fundamental Rights in 2002, the Union declared that it is "founded on the indivisible, universal values of human dignity, freedom, equality, and solidarity" (quoted in Casanova, 2006: 81). But as Casanova notes, the mere proclamation of such values "could hardly have the effect of grounding a common European political identity" (2006: 81).

A 'soul' or a forum of 'souls'?

In this Conclusion I explore one proposition: a political entity like the EU cannot possess, and should not seek, a single 'soul', but should be an open institutional forum in which a plurality of 'souls' can constructively cooperate and contest.[3]

In spite of the considerable expansion of its competences since the 1980s, the EU remains a 'thin' political structure as compared to the 'thicker', and more culturally embedded, political orders of its member states. It is likely to remain so in the foreseeable future, for at least three reasons. First, whatever short-term fixes are seized upon for the EU's current financial and economic crises, the EU will be dominated by the fall-out from these crises for years to come. As the chapters by Pabst on political economy; Hordern on place and identity; Weatherly, Branco, and Felgueiras on environmental policy; and Beech on science policy imply, getting and keeping questions of vision and values on the agenda of the EU will be an uphill struggle.[4]

Second, as Nelsen and Guth have argued, and as Loughlin's and Luitwieler's chapters indirectly confirm, the continuing force of the divide between the "confessional cultures" of a 'universalist' Catholicism and a 'nationalist' Protestantism has left the EU "unable to create a sense of community deep and broad enough to constitute a new European national identity" (Nelsen and Guth, 2015: 25). This divide is currently dramatized in the UK government's decision to put the country's very membership of the EU to a referendum by 2017, but Nelsen and Guth show that it is likely to remain a powerful factor in other historically Protestant settings as well (2015: Chs. 9–10).

Third, the more the EU expands through enlargement (and immigration), the harder it will be to nurture a thick sense of EU-wide identity. As Petkoff's account shows, the arrival of Orthodoxy has already presented both opportunities and challenges in this respect. Further enlargement will make such challenges more demanding; this will certainly be the case if Turkey – an officially 'secular' state superimposed upon a majority Muslim nation – accedes. Moreover, as Katzenstein observes, eastward expansion will not only disrupt the balance between Europe's confessional cultures but also between them and European secularism. By bringing within the EU significant numbers of new, often traditional religious believers, eastward enlargement may have the effect of "chipping away at [Europe's] exceptional secularism" and thus may "demand new terms of coexistence with secularism" (Katzenstein, 2006: 2).

Given these (and other) obstacles, we should not expect thick, Community-wide cultural, still less 'spiritual', values to emerge any time soon. I want to propose that it is manifestly preferable for the EU to settle for a more limited agreement on a set of specific constitutional norms and precisely definable political objectives (certainly more definable than 'ever closer union'). To adapt Hordern's terms (for my own purposes), the "adequate identity" we should seek for the EU as an emerging political community consists just in a commitment to these norms and objectives, and the "sufficient agreement" we should strive for need only be that minimally required for a workable political consensus on them. In 2003 Pope John Paul II lamented the "loss of Europe's Christian memory and heritage;" Europeans were, he charged, living like "heirs who have squandered a patrimony entrusted to them by history."[5] Now it might, perhaps, be argued that a *civilizational entity* such as 'Europe' (assuming we can define it) needssomething like a 'soul' if it is to retain its identity and dynamism. But that is a different question from whether a *political structure*, like the EU, needs a 'soul'. I suggest that a culturally 'thin' entity like the EU with restricted purposes does not need an *officially recognized* 'soul' but should rather strive to be an open forum enabling many 'souls' to engage in vigorous dialogue over the EU's norms and objectives. The larger debate about visions, values, and 'souls' that might be needed as the basis of a putative European identity should be left to free debate in the realm of civil society (in which, of course, the EU's political leaders themselves should play an active role).

One retort may be that, in the absence of such a 'soul', the EU will not even be able to agree on its minimal constitutional norms and political objectives and that the EU will thus fail to engage the deep attachment of its citizens (even its officials). But the history of the EU, however fractious and turbulent, offers a degree of mitigation against such scepticism. While there is clearly no consensus on the EU's underlying moral foundations or overarching spiritual purpose (*finalité*), there is already a tolerably wide, albeit often patchy and fragile, area of consensus on the content of some of the EU's minimal constitutional norms and political objectives. For example, the Charter enshrines many such norms, and various EU decisions are incrementally extending the range of such norms (such as, for example, the 2013 'Guidelines' on religious freedom considered in Chapter 8). Wilton's chapter shows how the contemporary EU continues to pursue (if not always coherently) many of the original political objectives of its founders. (How it negotiates its way out of the euro crisis will be a critical test of its capacity to snatch workable consensus out of the jaws of policy defeat.) What is more, these norms and objectives are only 'thin' in the sense that they are not *explicitly or officially* tethered to deeper cultural or religious commitments. In the minds and motivations of EU citizens and actors they certainly need to be (a task, I am suggesting, falling primarily to European civil society). Such norms and objectives have nonetheless often proved sufficient guides to political action, even if they admittedly carry limited symbolic or affective heft.

Such norms and objectives, however, must remain contestable and revisable. Indeed it is precisely the role of traditions of normative critique such as political theology to ensure that such norms and objectives are rigorously and continually interrogated. Foret implicitly confirms this possibility in suggesting that religion in the contemporary EU "appears … as a potent symptom or marker of the underlying resistances of identity and the normative dimensions of politics summoned up by the functionalist steamroller of European integration" (2010: 32).

I offer three observations on the contribution of political theology to this role of 'resistance'. First, political theology should engage with the full range of the Union's substantive policy concerns. It is often assumed that the principal concerns of religious lobbies in the EU are either issues of self-interest (defending religious freedoms, or protecting access – perhaps privileged – to public fora) or a specific set of 'lifeworld' issues such as family, gender, and sexual ethics or medical and bio-ethics. Undoubtedly, these have been and will remain a significant focus of religious mobilisation in the EU (and not only for the Catholic church). But Leustean documents how, from their earliest interactions with European institutions, religious actors have demonstrated a concern for a very wide range of public policy issues. Indeed, in one way or another, all the chapters demonstrate that the concerns of Christian political theology, and the likely targets of its normative critiques, can range across economic, environmental, educational, territorial, constitutional, global, and other questions. A suitably resourced political theology should aspire to address every area of current EU concern while also being ready to press onto EU agenda issues its leaders and institutions would rather ignore or have not yet even recognised.

Second, this suggests the need for an important qualification to Philpott and Shah's prediction that, in an enlarged EU, European religions "are more likely to be engaged in clashes with European secularism than with each other" (2006: 62). On environmental questions, for example, Christian political theology will find many allies among secularists. The Christian environmental ethic outlined by Weatherley, Branco, and Felgueiras will only clash radically with secularists committed to the pursuit of unlimited economic growth at the expense of (e.g.) the 'intrinsic value of nature'. It might find itself ranged equally against fellow believers who endorse such a pursuit. The Social Market Economy model shown by Lachmann to be consonant with Protestant ethics will only be fundamentally at odds with secularists who endorse either libertarianism or state socialism; indeed the same could be said of Pabst's model drawing from Catholic Social Teaching (notwithstanding the evident difference of emphasis between it and Lachmann's). Both could find many secular allies in the spaces between those two ideological positions. Add to this the continuing disagreements between diverse strands of Christian political theology, and we can likely expect, not a straightforward clash between Christianity (or religions generally) and 'secularism' but a series of shifting contestations and coalitions depending on the issue concerned and the protagonists addressing it.

Third, such normative critique will need to be mounted from many sites, both those located in the wide spaces of the EU's civil society (including political parties, and not only Christian democratic ones), and those in the

European Parliament and national parliaments. If so, part of the task of political theology will be to urge that all such fora are maintained in good health and kept fully free for the cultivation of such critique, and not, as Pabst warns, marginalized or eviscerated either by bureaucratic or commercial imperatives. Such faith-based civil society actors could include anything from a localised evangelical grassroots environmental organisation documented by Weatherley, Branco, and Felgueiras, to the lay Orthodox poverty-relief initiatives in Greece described by Petkoff, to the Catholic or Protestant political movements and parties cited by Loughlin and Luitwieler, to the Brussels-based religious representatives surveyed by Leustean. That, of course, is only to mention Christian ones.

There is a further reason for restraining aspirations towards a unifying EU 'soul', argued for in Chapter 8: 'soulcraft' is not the proper task of political institutions at all. Political authorities, especially 'thin' ones like the EU, should refrain from *officially* promoting any particular religion or belief and treat all as even-handedly as possible. The ill-tempered arguments over whether 'God' or religion (or humanism) should be cited in the proposed EU Constitution, narrated by Milton in Chapter 9, confirms in my view the unsuitability of seeking such recognition within a document that must be the product of interest-driven bargaining.

Christianity, secular humanism and other minorities

The proposal that the EU should serve as an open forum of many 'souls' has important implications for how Christianity should comport itself in relation both to European secular humanism and to other (minority) faiths within the pluralistic public spaces of the EU.

Secular humanism's claim to comparable pride of place in the shaping of the EU is worthy of respect. I would submit that secular humanism is now by far the dominant 'soul' of Europe, but whether or not that claim is accepted it is clear that maintaining a mutually respectful relationship between these preeminent European traditions remains a major challenge. The EU has adopted neither the model of the confessional state exemplified by some of its member states (e.g. Italy, the UK, Greece, Ireland, Finland), nor the model of strict separationism that would keep religion out of the public sphere (as in French *laïcité*). As is noted in Chapter 8, the EU's *de facto* stance towards religion is now approximating the cooperationist model seen in member states such as Germany, Belgium, and the Netherlands.[6] In such a model, official state neutrality and extensive religious freedom are combined with openness to religious expressions in the public square and constructive partnerships with religious organisations in the delivery of public services such as education, welfare, and health, or in the media.[7]

Such a direction of travel should be essentially congenial to Christian political theology. The implication of such a cooperationist model, however, is that Christian churches and organisations should not seek privileged status for Christianity in official EU settings. They might work via civil society initiatives and public argument to move the EU *de facto* closer what Pabst terms a Christian "civic commonwealth" (just as others may seek to shape the EU according their own visions) but they will not seek any official EU recognition of Christianity beyond, perhaps, an acknowledgement of its unique historical role. Nor, for example, will they seek anything more (or less) than a level playing field with secularists or other faith communities when they participate in various ways in the public sector.

Equally, alongside others who value an open EU public square, they should resist attempts to bend the EU in the direction of strict secularism. This will not be easy, since even religion-friendly cooperationist regimes in some member states (notably the Netherlands and Belgium) are under pressure to adopt more secularist postures. Cooperationism must be a mutually respectful partnership and not merely a cloak for a creeping, bureaucratically imposed secularism. It would resemble what Willaime calls a *"laïcité of recognition"* (Willaime, 2010: 25).[8] Along similar lines, Zucca rejects an "aggressive secularism" and commends an "inclusive secularism," a constitutional framework allowing maximal pluralism (2012: xx).[9] As he notes in the epigraph to this chapter, the absence of reference to Christianity in the EU's constitutional documents should be read not as a "thundering silence" but rather as a "positive affirmation" of an inclusive secularism. But French *laïcité* falls short because it "creates an asymmetry between religious and non-religious people to the detriment of the former" (2012: xix). Indeed as he cautions, "because Europe is already biased in favour of secularism ... we should be particularly careful when we strike the balance between secular law and religion" (2012: 36). The problem, he holds, "is not religion but the secular state's inability to cope with diversity" (2012: 30). If 'secularism' is understood not as a worldview but as a constitutional norm permitting public space for a plurality of worldviews, then "to assert a *secular* Europe is not to deny a Christian Europe or a humanist Europe" (2012: 68).[10] Pollock, however, implausibly charges that the EU is biased *towards religion*. The Lisbon Treaty's provision in paragraph 3 of Article 17 for "dialogue" with churches and religious associations is itself a form of unjustified privilege, he claims, disadvantaging "weaker" humanist organisations such as his own European Humanist Federation. He asserts this in spite of the fact that the Article's mention of "organisations" specifically includes the "philosophical and non-confessional" ones mentioned in paragraph 2 (Pollock, 2013).

Here McCrea's comprehensive analysis of the "public order" of the EU (2010) is very important. His argument is that the EU is committed to seeking a "proper balance" between the religious, humanist and cultural legacies underlying its public order (2010: 2–8). First, religion is recognized by the EU not as a source of truth claims but as one type of many plural cultural identities it is willing to acknowledge; religious claims to a public monopoly on truth are resisted. Second, religious identity is recognized both as an individual choice and as a collective choice, such as in the autonomy of religious institutions and public morality reflected in national laws. Third, these collective manifestations will, however, be limited by the EU's respect for a humanist insistence on individual freedom. Fourth, religious claims that reject one or other element of this balance will struggle to gain acceptance. Given Christianity's cultural rootedness and general tolerance of pluralism, its public claims will often be accommodated, while those of faiths that are hostile to the notion of balance, especially if they are outsider religions (those not seen as 'European'), will be resisted.

While the aspiration towards a "proper balance" between Christianity and secular humanism is essentially congenial to the argument proposed here, McCrea's case requires an important qualification and evokes an unresolved question. The qualification applies to his suggestion that a commitment to individual freedom derives largely from the secular humanist legacy of Europe. Siedentop (2014), however, argues that the very notion of 'the individual' was itself largely the creation of Christianity; and Chapter 8 in this book shows how the idea of individual religious freedom first emerged from radical Protestantism. McCrea's assumption that the European tradition of "questioning religion, of imposing a degree of separation between the religious and political realms, and of respecting individual autonomy" come mainly from humanism *rather than* Christianity (2010: 13) is historically questionable.

Where precisely the "proper balance" between the public claims of Christianity and secular humanism should be struck will be a matter of ongoing contestation. But the struggle for such a balance is equally relevant to 'outsider' minority religions. McCrea's account leaves unresolved whether, and if so how, the EU's public order might need to be significantly restructured to accommodate the legitimate claims of such minorities. Historically dominant religions represented in EU member states will, he suggests, "inevitably" exercise greater influence over EU law than more marginal faiths, not least because of the EU's traditional deference to member states' national traditions in which some traditional religions still enjoy a certain pre-eminence. Thus an EU-wide "levelling down" of the religious influence of majority faiths to that of minority ones would be problematic (2010: 264). But a "levelling up", whereby outsider religions are allowed public influence comparable to that of insiders would, he declares, be "inconsistent with the overall notion of balance between religious and humanist influences" (2010: 263).

This problem is accentuated by the fact (noted in Chapter 8) that the EU, and the ECtHR, tend to construe 'religion' and religious 'manifestation' in essentially 'Christian' (even 'Protestant') terms, namely as interior individual beliefs with only limited implications for communal or public expression. But as non-Christian faiths increasingly bring unfamiliar and unsettling claims to the public realm, the scope afforded, for example, to reasonable accommodation will need to be re-examined and, perhaps, expanded. Christians seeking to expand that scope for themselves are then obliged to countenance the same for other minority faiths (Chaplin, 2011). Such claims should be examined on a case-by-case basis; it should not simply be assumed that new accommodations would disturb the "proper balance" of the EU's public order. While it is clear that some fundamental EU norms (not least its commitment to religious neutrality and religious freedom) could not be renegotiated without imperilling the very identify of the EU as an open forum or risking unleashing a destructive process of communal balkanization, beyond those, many complex debates between Christianity, humanism, and other faiths lie, the outcomes of which should not be prejudged. A Christian political theology eschewing a desire for primacy, ready to offer robust normative critiques across a wide range of public issues, and open to ad hoc collaborations with a range of coalition partners, would be well placed to make an important contribution to defining the terms of a *properly pluralistic balance* in the public order of the EU.

Notes

1 Delors (1992). Quoted in Leustean and Madeley (2010: 4).
2 For an assessment of the EU's 'identity construction policy' see Nelsen and Guth (2015: 324–344). This was also the concern prompting Romano Prodi's initiative in 2002 to form the 'Reflection Group on the Spiritual and Cultural Dimension of Europe' (Biedenkopf, Geremek and Michalski, 2004).
3 I do not assume that all contributors will agree with this proposal.
4 Scharpf's analysis suggests that there are now deep structural pressures arising from the legal integration of member-state economies which work to undermine the operation of the Social Market Economy where it currently exists in the EU and prevent it from being extended elsewhere (Scharpf, 2010).
5 *Ecclesia in Europa* (2003). Quoted in Hehir (2006: 107).
6 The UK is a mixed model, combining 'weak' establishment with elements of cooperationism.
7 These allow for a fuller presence of faith-based institutions, and arguments, in the political sphere than would be permitted by Habermas's more restrictive 'constitutional patriotism' (discussed by Hordern).
8 Willaime wants to detach *laïcité* from its typical association with France and claim it as a truly European ideal.
9 For parallel proposals, see Modood's account of a "moderate secularism" (Modood, 2009: 180), and William's notion of a "procedural secularism" (Williams, 2012: 27).
10 For his critique of Joseph Weiler's proposal for a 'Christian Europe', see Zucca (2012: Ch. 4).

References

Biedenkopf, K., Geremek, B., and Michalski, K. (2004). *The spiritual and cultural dimension of Europe: Concluding remarks*. Vienna, Austria: Institute for Human Sciences / Brussels: European Commission.
Casanova, J. (2006). Religion, European secular identities, and European integration. In Byrnes, T. A. and Katzenstein, P. J. (eds), *Religion in an expanding Europe* (pp. 65–92). Cambridge: Cambridge University Press.
Chaplin, J. (2011). *Multiculturalism: A Christian retrieval*. London: Theos.

Delors, J. (1992). Speech to the churches. 4 February. In *Newsletter of the Ecumenical Centre in Brussels*. Brussels, Belgium: EECCS.
Foret, F. (2010). Religion: A solution or a problem for the legitimation of the European Union? In Leustean, L. N., and Madeley, J. T. S. (eds), *Religion, politics and law in the European Union: An introduction* (pp. 31–44). London: Routledge.
Hehir, J. B. (2006). The old Church and the new Europe: Charting the changes. In Byrnes, T. A. and Katzenstein, P. J. (eds), *Religion in an expanding Europe* (pp. 93–116). Cambridge: Cambridge University Press.
Katzenstein, P. J. (2006). Multiple modernities as limits to secular Europeanization? In Byrnes, T. A. and Katzenstein, P. J. (eds), *Religion in an expanding Europe* (pp. 1–33). Cambridge: Cambridge University Press.
Leustean, L. N., and Madeley, J. T. S. (2010). Religion, politics and law in the European Union: An introduction. In Leustean, L. N. and Madeley, J. T. S. (eds), *Religion, politics and law in the European Union: An introduction* (pp. 1–16). London: Routledge.
McCrea, R. (2010). *Religion and the public order of the European Union*. Oxford: Oxford University Press.
Modood, T. (2009). Muslims, religious equality and secularism. In Levey, G. B. and Modood, T. (eds), *Secularism, religion and multicultural citizenship* (pp. 164–185). Cambridge: Cambridge University Press.
Nelsen, B. F., and Guth, J. L. (2015). *Religion and the struggle for European Union: Confessional cultures and the limits of integration*. Washington, DC: Georgetown University Press.
Philpott, D., and Shah, T. S. (2006). Faith, freedom and federation: The role of religious ideas and institutions in European political convergence. In Byrnes, T. A. and Katzenstein, P. J. (eds), *Religion in an expanding Europe* (pp. 34–64). Cambridge: Cambridge University Press.
Pollock, D. (2013). Article 17: Reasons for concern. In Leustean, L. N. (ed.), *Representing religion in the European Union: Does God matter?* (pp. 122–135) London: Routledge.
Scharpf, F. W. (2010). The asymmetry of European integration, or why the EU cannot be a 'social market economy'. *Socio-Economic Review*, 8: 211–250.
Siedentop, L. (2014). *Inventing the individual: The origins of western liberalism*. London: Allen Lane.
Willaime, J.-P. (2010). European integration, laïcité and religion. In Leustean, L. N. and Madeley, J. T. S. (eds), *Religion, politics and law in the European Union: An introduction* (pp. 17–29). London: Routledge.
Williams, R. (2012). *Faith in the public square*. London: Bloomsbury.
Zucca, L. (2012). *A secular Europe: Law and religion in the European constitutional landscape*. Oxford: Oxford University Press.

Index

Acts of the Apostles, Book of 143
Adenauer, Konrad 14, 28, 33, 40, 41, 48n4, 50, 54, 99
Agamben, G. 119
Ahdar, R. and Leigh, I. 151, 168n4, 169n17
American Revolution (1765–83) 36
Amsterdam Treaty (1997): biodiversity and EU nature legislation 234; Declaration on status of churches and non-confessional organisations 162, 163, 164; EU Constitution, religion and 194
'Anglo-Saxon" federalism 39
Annan, Kofi 16
Anthroposophical Society 160
Anti-Revolutionary Party (ARP) 56–7
Aron, Robert 38
association 3, 76, 109, 114, 119, 126, 131, 134,139, 143, 162, 164; free association 111, 118, 119; political association 18; voluntary association 5, 110, 120, 121, 122, 126, 155
Augsburg, Peace of (1555) 35
Auriol, Vincent 41
Austria-Hungarian Empire 41

Barre, Raymond 100
Barroso, Juan-Manuel 185
Bauman, Z. 119
Beech, Diana Jane xi, 7, 251–67, 269
Belgian Parliamentary Commission on Cults 160
Bell, George 58
Benedict XV 37
Benedict XVI 46, 47, 48n3, 118, 126, 204, 239; Catholicism and evolution of EU 44–5
Berdyaev, N. 86n1

Berger, P., Davie, G. and Fokas, E. 188n14
Berger, Peter 175
Berlaymont Building, Brussels 13
Berlin, Isaiah 122
Berlin Wall, fall of (1989): Catholicism and evolution of EU 45; Orthodoxy and EU 71
Beza, Theodor 169n13
bicameralism 120–21
Biedenkopf, K., Geremek, B. and Michalski, K. 118, 120, 275n2
Biggar, Nigel 143, 146n12
biodiversity and EU nature legislation 7, 230–46; Biodiversity Strategy 234–5, 236, 245; Camphor Thyme *(thymus camphoratus)* 242; Christian environmental ethic 231–2; Christian perspective on biodiversity protection 238–41; European Ecological Footprint 231; intrinsic value, notion of 231, 232, 235–6, 237–8, 239–40, 241, 245–6; Natura 2000 network 233, 242; Portugal, case study on nature legislation in 230, 241-4, 245–6; Sustainable Development Strategy (2001) 234; utilitarian ethical framework 240; World Summit on Sustainable Development (UN, 2002) 234–5
Bismarck, Otto von 41, 89
The Bloudy Tenent of Persecution (Williams, R.) 153
Bobbitt, P. 110
Bonhoeffer, Dietrich 105n5
Boulgakov, S. 86n1
Brague, Rémi 50, 51, 65, 66n3, 119
Branco, Tiago xi, 7, 230–50, 269, 271, 272

278 *Index*

Brandt, Willy 43
Britain: accession to Common Market 50; Brexit 116; Britain in Europe 23–4; British churches' Peace Aims Group 58–9; Common Market, British campaign for membership 59; European integration and 57–60; Glorious Revolution (1688) 36
Broadcasting Directive (2007) 163
Brok, Elmar 201
Bruening, Heinrich 14
Brunner, E. 105n14
Bruton, John 201
Buchanan, James 106n23
Buchman, Frank 54
Bundesbank 100, 101
Bureau of European Policy Advisors (BEPA) 180
Burke, E. 122
Burleigh, M. 36
Busher, Leonard 153
Byrnes, T.A. 52, 54
Byrnes, T.A. and Katzenstein, P.J. 188n14
Byzantine Orthodox Commonwealth 5, 35, 70–71

Caesar, Augustus 146n15
Caesaro-papism 76
Calhoun, C., Juergensmeyer, M. and Van Antwerpen, J. 3
Calvin, John 153, 169n13, 169n19
Cameron, David 146n15
Casanova, J. 3, 159, 268
Castellio, Sebastian 153, 169n13
Catholic Church: history of relationship with Europe 34–7; influence of 193–4; international reach of 26–7; post-1945 European integration and 40–44; 20th century perspective on Europe and 37–8; universalism of 53, 57; *see also* Catholicism and evolution of EU
Catholic European Study Information Centre (OCIPE) 178, 182
Catholic Pastoral Information Service 198
Catholic Social Teaching 271
Catholicism and evolution of EU 1, 4, 33–48; Benedict XVI 44–5; Byzantine Empire 35; Catholic Church and Europe: history of relationship between 34–8; Catholic Church and post-1945 European integration 40–44; *Esprit* 39–40, 42; European Constitutional Convention and Catholic Church 45–7; European flag, inspiration for 33–4; Fascism in Italy 37; *fédéralisme intégral* movement 39, 41; Intergovernmental Conferences (IGCs) 45; Ireland, Catholicism and nation in 37; John Paul II 44–5; 'modernity,' Catholic responses to 37; National Socialism in Germany 37; *nouvelle théologie* 42, 43; *Ordre Nouveau* 38–40; Ostpolitik 42–3; *Pan-Europa* (Coudenhove-Kalergi, R. von) 38; *Pastoral Constitution on the Church in the Modern World (Gaudium et Spes)* 42–3; patriarchal Sees 34–5; personalism, philosophy of 38, 39–40; Poland, Catholicism and nation in 37; Popes, Europe and the world 38–40; preferential option for the poor 46–7; Protestant Reformation, modern nation-state and 35–6; Second Vatican Council 42–3; secularist tradition in France 33; secularization of European mind 36; Soviet Bloc 44–5; state and nation, creation of link between 36; ultramontanism 37; unification, Catholicism and project of 33–4; Wars of Religion 36
Cavanaugh, W.T. 36, 132, 145n2, 169n9
CERN (Conseil Européen pour la Recherche Nucléaire) 7, 252, 254–8, 262, 264; societal achievements 257–8; strategic importance of 257
Chalcedonian Eastern Orthodoxy 71
Chaplin, Jonathan xi, 1–10, 63, 64, 66n1, 66n6, 151–74, 268–76
Charbonneau, Bernard 39, 40
Charles V 152
Charter of Fundamental Rights of the European Union (CFREU, 2000): EU Constitution, religion and 193; identity, place and EU citizens 144; Protestantism and EU 63; ratification of 268–9, 270; religious freedom, place in EU 163
Chenu, Marie-Dominique 42
Chevalley, Claude 38
Chişinău, Bishop of 43
Christian churches, European consciousness and 143–4
Christian Democratic Appeal (CDA) 57

Christian Democrats 1–2, 14, 33, 40–41, 71, 83, 121, 193; Protestants and EU 54, 55, 56–7, 60, 66n5
Christian heritage, European Union and 118–19
Christian political parties 43–4
Christian political theology 2, 7, 27, 268, 271, 272–3, 275
Christian polity: renewal of 122–5; secular polity and 125
Christian pro-European movement 58–9
Christian Responsibility for European Cooperation' (CCREC) 177
Christian Socialism 94–5
Christian Study Group on European Unity (CSGEU) 175–6, 177
Christianity in EU of today 7, 268–75; Christian memory and heritage 270; civil society 270, 271–2; need for critique from 271–3; constitutional norms 269–70, 270–71; cooperationism 272–3; environmental questions 271; ethics 271; European identity 270; European 'soul,' Delors' appeal for 268–9; even-handedness, need for 272; evolution of EU, potential for Christian contribution to 268; expansion (enlargement and immigration) 269; founding objectives 270; humanism 272, 273–4, 275; inclusive secularism, call for 273; minorities 272–5; national identity, divide on 269; pluralism 272, 273–4, 275; political objectives, definition of 269–70, 270–71; politically resilient solidarity 268–9; public order 273–4; public policy issues, concerns for 271; religious identity, recognition for 273–4; resistance to integration, political theology and 271; secular humanism 272, 274; spiritual purpose 270
Churches Commission for Migrants in Europe (CCME) 24
Churchill, Winston 25, 38
civic commonwealth, vision of 117–22
Climate Action Directorate-General 230
Club de Moulin 38–9
Colbert, Jean Baptiste 89
Cold War 6, 41–2, 86n1, 114, 177, 184, 186, 188n16, 254, 257, 258
Cologne European Council (1999) 192–3
Colossians I, Book of (15–19) 246n3
Commission of Bishops' Conferences of the European Community (COMECE): Catholicism and evolution of EU 43; EU Constitution, religion and 198, 199, 204; representation of religion in EU 178, 182, 183, 185; Schuman legacy 17
Committee of the Representatives of the Orthodox Churches at the European Union (CROCEU) 82–3, 84; human rights, education strategies and rule of law, calls on 83
Common Agricultural Policy (CAP) 21
Common Fisheries Policy 142
Common High Authority 20
Conference of European Churches (CEC): EU Constitution, religion and 198–9; Orthodoxy and EU 72, 82, 83, 84; Protestantism and EU 56, 59; representation of religion in EU 182–3, 185
Conference of International Catholic Organizations 181
Confessional Church (Bekennende Kirche) 94–5
confessional cultures 1–2
Congar, Yves 42
Congregation for the Doctrine of the Faith (CDF) 44
consent 3, 19, 113, 153
Conservation Biology, Society of 239
Constantine, Emperor 34
Constantinople, fall of 73
Constitutional Convention 191–2; drafting process 200–201, 201–2; evaluation of 204–6; negotiations within 199–202; outcome of negotiations 202–4; participants in 196–9; process of 194–6
constitutional norms 269–70, 270–71
constitutional patriotism 140
Consultative Committee of Churches for the European Communities 177, 187n4
Contonou Agreement with the African, Caribbean, and Pacific (ACP) countries 23
Convention on Biological Diversity (UN, 1993) 234
Convention on the Future of Europe (2001) 180
cooperationism 168, 272–3, 275n6
Corinthians II, Book of 97, 105n12
Coudenhove-Kalergi, Count Richard von 38, 49, 56
Council of Chalcedon (451) 79–80

Index

Council of Europe: legitimacy crisis for EU 120–21; Orthodoxy and EU 85; religious freedom, place in EU 157, 160, 161, 170n47; representation of religion in EU 177–8; Schuman legacy 14–15; science and research policy 261
Coupland, P.M. 54, 56, 58, 59, 60, 187n6
cultural diversity or plurality 63, 122
cultural identity 5, 51, 109, 133
Cyprus, accession of 18

Dandieu, Arnaud 38
Daniel, biblical figure 105n13
Daniel-Rops, Henri 38
das Neves, Jorge César 179, 180
Davie, G. 1, 187n1
Dawkins, Richard 259, 264n2
De Gasperi, Alcide 14, 28, 33, 40, 41, 48n4, 50, 264n3
de Gaulle, Charles 99
de Lubac, Henri 42, 44
de Rose, François 256
de Rougemont, Denis 38, 39, 40, 187n3
de Vigo, Inigo Mendez 201
Declaration of the Rights of Man and Citizen (1789) 154
Delors, Jacques 7, 39, 45, 48n5, 86, 179, 180, 184, 258, 259, 263, 268, 275n1
Delors Report (1988) 101
Denmark: accession to Common Market: Protestantism and EU 50; *X v Denmark* (ECtHR, 1976) 158
d'Estaing, Valéry Giscard 45, 194, 195, 196, 199, 200, 201, 202, 205, 206
Deuteronomy, Book of 97
Dibelius, Otto 94
Dimas, Stavros 231
Dissenters 153–4, 156
Doe, N. 162, 163, 164, 168n5, 170n50, 170n51
Dooyeweerd, H. 63
Duchrow, Ulrich 105n11
Dutch Catholic People's Party (KVP) 55, 56–7

Ecclesia in Europa (Apostolic Exhortation, John Paul II, 2003) 202
Ecumenical Commission on European Cooperation (ECEC) 176–7, 184
Ecumenical Patriarchate 179, 182
Eisenstein, Robert 255, 257
Ellul, Jacques 39, 40
English Revolution 153

enlargement 16, 45–6, 61, 71, 100, 268–9; Constitution, religion and 193; legitimacy crisis and 109, 113, 114–15, 117–18, 121; Schuman legacy 18–19
Enlightenment 2, 3; Enlightenment philosophy 36; nation-state and 35–6; religious freedom, place in EU 152, 154, 156–7
Environment, Food and Rural Affairs, Department for (DEFRA) 237–8
Environment Directorate-General 230, 231, 232–3
environmental and biodiversity policy 232–5; environmental protection work 231, 232, 234, 237, 240, 244, 245; nature legislation and 230–32, 234, 235, 240–41, 243, 245; values influencing 235–8
equality 2, 3, 21, 26, 40, 47, 98, 111, 118, 122, 123–4, 210, 268; gender equality 82
Erhard, Ludwig 5, 93, 94, 99, 105n8
Esprit 39–40, 42
ethics: Christianity in EU of today 271; ethics-driven approaches 76; freedom, ethical argument for 154–5
ethnocentrism 129–31; threat to peace 131–8
EU Constitution, religion and 6, 191–206; Catholic Church, influence of 193–4; Christian Democratic political movement 193; Constitutional Convention 191–2, 194–6, 196–9, 199–202, 202–4; constitutional tradition of France 196–7; enlargement 193; established state religions 197; 'ever closer union' 192; *invocatio dei*, issue of 191–2; Irish Constitution 197; party affiliations 198; Pius XI 194; political identity, nature of 193; religion, discreet nature of 194; religion, recognition of role of 194; rights and freedoms of others, protection for 196; solidarity 193; subsidiarity, appropriation of principle of 193–4; transfer of power from national to EU level 192; Turkey as candidate country 193
Eucken, Walter 91, 94, 103, 105, 106n27
EURATOM 253–4, 260
euro area crisis 109, 112–14, 115, 116; roots of 211–13
Europe 2020 strategy 260–62
Europe and EU, Orthodox world and idea of: Orthodoxy and EU 70–71
Europe as Christendom, notion of 65–6

Index   281

European Atomic Energy Community (EAEC) 253–4
European Central Bank (ECB) 212, 225–6, 227n2
European Christian Political Movement (ECPM) 66
European Coal and Steel Community (ECSC): EU Constitution, religion and 192; Protestantism and EU 54; representation of religion in EU 177–8, 181, 186; founders of 187n3; science and research policy 253
European Committee for Catholic Education 178
European Communities (EC): churches' involvement with 175–6; Constitution, religion and 192
European Constitution, preamble to 191, 192
European Constitutional Convention, Catholic Church and 45–7
European Convention on Human Rights (Council of Europe, 1950) 6; Constitution, religion and 196; religious freedom, place in EU 151–2, 157, 160, 162–3, 165
European Court of Human Rights (ECtHR): Christianity in EU of today 274–5; identity, place and EU citizens 144, 146n16; religious freedom, place in EU 151–2, 156, 157, 158, 159, 160–62, 163, 164, 167–8; Schuman legacy 20
European Court of Justice (ECJ): biodiversity and EU nature legislation 243; identity, place and EU citizens 144, 146n16; legitimacy crisis for EU 116; religious freedom, place in EU 163, 168
European Ecological Footprint 231
European Economic and Monetary Union (EEMU) 101
European Economic Community (EEC): EU Constitution, religion and 192; science and research policy 253, 258
European Ecumenical Commission on Development (EECOD) 179
European Environmental Agency 235–6
European Evangelical Alliance 183
European External Action Service (EEAS): religious freedom, place in EU 165, 166; Schuman legacy 22–3, 25; science and research policy 262–3
European flag, inspiration for 33–4

European integration 1, 4, 25, 71, 72–3, 140, 193, 205, 208, 224, 271; Christian heritage and future of European polity 109, 111, 113, 121; German Social Market, role in 89, 98, 99, 100, 101; Protestantism and 50–51, 52, 54, 55–60, 61, 62, 64–5, 66; recent history of 111–12; religion, representation in EU of 175, 176–7, 178, 181, 182–3, 184, 186, 188n16; see also Catholicism and evolution of EU
European Jewish Congress 179
European Monetary and Economic Union (EMU) 100–101, 208, 209, 211, 212–13, 216, 218, 220
European Monetary Institute (EMI): financial crisis, Christian economic ethics and 211; German Social Market Economy (SME) 101
European Monetary Systems (EMS) 101
European Neighbourhood projects 18
European Parliament: activity on religious freedom 166; direct elections to 192; elections to, participation in 18–19; European values, Havel's speech to European Parliament on (2009) 251; John Paul II's address to (1988) 33; Working Group on Freedom of Religion or Belief (EPWG on FoRB) 166
European Research and Innovation Area Board (ERIAB) 257
European Research Area Board (ERAB) 252, 260
European Research Area (ERA) 7, 252–3, 261–2, 263
European 'soul,' Delors' appeal for 268–9
European Union (EU) 1–2, 3, 4–7; Orthodox Churches, EU and political theology 70, 75–7, 78, 79, 81; political theology and 2–3, 5–7, 27, 129, 268, 270–73, 275; religious freedom and 162–6
European Union of Christian Democrats (EUCD) 55
European Union of Jewish Students 179
European Year for Development (2015) 23
European Young Christian Workers 181
euroscepticism 3, 60
Evangelical Church of Germany (EKD) 182, 188n15
Evans-Pritchard, A. 47n1

Index

'ever closer union' 130, 270; challenge of 19; Constitution, religion and 192
exit from eurozone: advantages of 219; disadvantages of 219–20

Federal Cartels Office 99
federalism 3, 58, 177; choice between two types of 116, 117–18; *fédéralisme intégral* movement 39, 41
Felgueiras, Marcial xi, 7, 230–50, 267, 271, 272
Ferrari, Alessandro 168
Ferrari, S. and Pastorelli, S. 168n5, 170n31, 170n37
Ferrari, Silvio 162, 168, 170n46
financial crisis, Christian economic ethics and 6–7, 208–27; Christian values 209–11; current account divergencies 211; devaluation 219; economic developments within eurozone 214–15; euro crisis, roots of 211–13; eurozone integration, option of further development of 216, 220; evaluation 223–6; free currency exchange system, advantage of 224; inflation rate differences 212–13; labour costs 211, 212–13; Lehman Brothers collapse (2008) 208; national currencies, option of return to 216, 222; Optimal Currency Area (OCA) theory 217–18, 220, 221–2, 225, 227n3; policy options 213–17; political heterogeneity 225; productivity growth 211–12; prosperity, harm of decline in 223; real estate bubble 212; real interest rates, downward pressures on 212; reconfiguration, transition costs for 218; several countries leaving eurozone, option of 216, 220–21; splitting euro into neuro and zeuro, option of 216, 221; structural differences 213; subsidiarity, principle of 210–11, 225; trade imbalances 212; *see also* exit from eurozone
Fini, Gianfranco 201
Finland, accession to EU 50
Finnis, J. 79, 145n6
Fogarty, M. 55
Foret, F. 1, 2, 170n48, 188n12
Foret, F. and Schlesinger, P. 188n12
Forward Studies Unit (FSU) 179–80, 187n10
Fountain, J. 14, 54
Fourth Crusade (1202–04) 35
Framework Directive (2000) 163–4

Framework Programme for Research and Technological Development 261–2
France: constitutional tradition o 196–7; French-German compromise, need for 100; French Revolution (1789–93) 36, 57
Francis 46, 239
Frank, S. 78, 86n1
Freiburg Circle 93–4, 95, 99, 105n7
Freiburg School 91–2, 105n3

Galatians, Book of 52, 97, 209
Galileo 260
Gamble, A. 110
Garcia-Solanes, J. and Torrejon-Flores, F. 227n5
Gell-Mann, Murray 260
General Synod of Church of England 59–60
Genesis, Book of 97, 98, 155; Genesis (2.15) 246n3
Geneva Circle 54, 55
Geoghegan-Quinn, M. 264
George, R. 79
German Social Market Economy (SME) 5, 89–106, 271; brotherly assistance (*Nächstenliebe*) 93; Bundesbank 100, 101; Christian Socialism 94–5; common currency 100, 101; competition in efficiency (*Leistungswettbewerb*) 91; competitive order 92; constitutive principles for economic success 103–4; core principles, origins of 89; economic justice 94; economic liberalism 94–5, 96; economic order and system, Rich's perspective on 95; economic policy implications of SME 90–91; economic policy success, principles for 103–5; European crisis and future prospects 101–3; French-German compromise, need for 100; Great Depression, memories of effects of 94; international competition 102–3; leading ideas of, theological appreciation of 96–8; market outcomes 91, 92; minimal state (*Nachtwächterstaat*) 90; neoclassical economics 92; ORDO-liberalism (Freiburg School) 90, 91–2, 93, 94, 99, 102, 103, 105n3, 106n17; orienting concept (*Stilgedanke*) 91; Planned Economy and Market Economy (Müller-Armack, A.) 94; potential additional principles for economic success 103, 104; regulative principles for economic success

103, 104–5; SME thinking, Eucken's principles of 91–2, 94; social question *(Soziale Frage)* 90; 'socialists of the chair' *(Kathedersozialisten)* 90; truthfulness 98
Gibson, M. 161, 164
Glover, Anne 263
Gollwitzer, Helmut 95, 105n11
Goudzwaard, B. 63, 64, 66n7
Graafland, J.J. and Blok, M. 210
Graafland, Johan xi–xii, 6–7, 22, 62, 208–29
Gratian, Emperor 34
Great Depression, memories of effects of 94
Great Schism (1054) 35
Greco-Roman tradition 110, 118, 121
Greece 6–7; Constitution of 197; Cyprus and, economic meltdown of 72; Grexit 216, 220–21, 226; *Kokkinakis v Greece* (ECtHR, 1993) 158, 160
Group of Political Advisors to the European Commission (GOPA) 180
Grubb, Kenneth 187n3
Guidelines on the promotion and protection of freedom of religion or belief (European Council, 2013) 165–6
Gutiérrez, G. 43

Habermas, J. and Ratzinger, J. 7n4
Habermas, J. 124, 139, 141, 144, 145n2, 275n7
Habitats Directive 233–4, 235, 236, 237, 239, 241, 242, 243, 244, 245, 246n8
Hanseatic League 35
Havel, Vaclav 251, 258, 264
Hayek, F.A. 91, 93
Heinemann, Gustav 177, 187n3
Heitz, Arsène 34
Helsinki European Council (1999) 193
Higgs, Peter 256
Hobbes, Thomas 36, 111
Holy Roman Empire: Catholicism and evolution of EU 35, 36; religious freedom, place in EU 152
Hordern, Joshua xii, 5, 129–48, 243, 269, 270, 275n7
Horizon 2020 Programme 7
House of Bishops' Europe Panel 59–60
Hudson, R. 255, 263, 264n6, 264n7, 264n9, 264n10, 265n14, 265n15, 265n16
human dignity 14, 40, 46, 82, 94, 97, 124, 156, 208–9, 211, 223, 268

human freedom 95, 97–8, 114–5, 151
human rights 3, 18, 19, 20, 22, 25, 46, 73, 79, 82–4, 118, 209, 258, 259, 263; discourse on 156–7; international law and, engagement with 79; religious freedom and 162, 165, 167–8, 169n23
humanism 272, 273–4, 275
Hume, David 36
Hurter, S. 264n5

identity: European sense of 51; lack of discussion concerning 205–6; shared values and 192–3
identity, place and EU citizens 5–6, 129–46; allegiances, theological interplay of 138; Christian churches, European consciousness and 143–4; church and nation, distinction between 144–5; constitutional patriotism 140; cultural adaptability 136–7; ecology 141–3; European Christian wisdom 132; financial affairs, reduction of politics to 129–30; goods, agreement about 132–3, 135–8; home, good of place called 137–8; identification: conceptualisation of 130; people, place and 129–31; identity and agreement, tasks of 138; justice 144, 146n16; knowledge 137; marriage 137, 138; national identity 134; oikophilia 138, 140–41, 142–3; political and religious identity, interplay of 132–3; political identity, adequacy of 133–4; social communication 131; space, liveability of 131; theological perspective, sufficiency of agreement on 138
Inter-Governmental Conference (IGC, 2004) 194, 195, 202–3
International Centre for Reconciliation at Coventry Cathedral 17
International Co-operation for Development and Solidarity (CIDSE) 178
invocatio dei, issue of 191–2
Ireland: Catholicism and nation in 37; Constitution of 197
Islam, challenge of integration of 123
Italy: Fascism in 37; *Lautsi v Italy* (ECtHR, 2011) 159

Jansen, Thomas 180, 188n13
Jardin, Jean 38
Jeremiah, Book of 138
Jewish Contribution to an Inclusive Europe (CEJI) 179

Joachim III 74
John Paul II 33, 44, 45, 46, 47, 179, 202, 239, 270; Catholicism and evolution of EU 44–5
John XXII 42
John XXIII 42, 43, 44
Johnson, Boris 146n15, 147n16
Joint Protestant-Catholic Working Group 178–9
Judeo-Christian tradition 119, 121
Juncker, Jean-Claude 180
justice: German Social Market Economy (SME) 97; identity, place and EU citizens 144, 146n16; judicial impartiality 3; principle of 210
Justinian I, Emperor 48n3

Kaiser, W. 1, 41, 55, 57, 111, 187n8
Kant, Immanuel 38, 111
Katzenstein, P.J. 1, 4, 7n1, 167, 269
Keohane, R.O. and Hoffmann, S.H. 63
Keynesianism 99
Kohnstamm, Max 177, 187n3
Kuiper, Roel 66n2
Küng, Fr. Hans 44

labour costs 211, 212–13
Lachmann, Werner xii, 5, 89–108, 271
Lacroix, Jean-Louis 179
Ladele, Lillian 161
Laplace, Comte de 36
Launay, M. 38, 40, 41
Lausanne Conference and World Evangelical Alliance 239
League of Nations 121
legitimacy crisis for EU 5, 109–26; alienation from European project 113–14; banking union, proposal for 115; bureaucratic collectivisation 109–10; Christian heritage 118–19; civic commonwealth, alternative vision of 117–22; commercial commodification 109–10; crisis in EU, perspective on 112–14; cultural bonds 118; cultural diversity, assumption of incompatibility in 122; emerging shape of Europe 114–17; euro area crisis 109, 112–14, 115, 116; federalism, choice between two types of 116; fiscal union, decision-making and 115–16; global resurgence of religion in political life 122–3; interpersonal relationships 109, 110–11; legitimacy, crisis resolution and failures of 116–17; legitimate rule, transcendence of 113; moral relativism 118; multispeed EU, multipolar polity and 109–10; negative liberty 122, 123–4; neo-functionalism 112–13; political extremism 113–14; reciprocal balance, economic arrangements of 111; secular law, primacy over religious principles 123; secular liberalism, crisis of 124; secular 'market-states' of Europe 109–10, 110–12; social contract theory 110–11; social imaginary 113–14; supranational institutions 120; transcendent finalities, recognition of 124–5; universal principles, need for recognition of 118–19; voluntary association of states 120
Lehman Brothers collapse (2008) 208
Leigh, I. 158, 160, 168n1, 168n5, 169n28
Lenders, Rev. Marc 187n5
Leo XIII 37, 39, 42, 206
Letter Concerning Toleration (Locke, J.) 154
Leustean, L.N. xii, 2, 6, 56, 70, 168n5, 175–90, 187, 187n2, 187n7, 187n11, 188n12, 259, 271, 272, 275n1
Leustean, L.N. and Madeley, J.T.S. 2, 188n14
Leviticus, Book of 106n16
liberalism 2, 3, 19, 37, 38, 90, 118, 122, 123, 132; classical liberalism 89; economic liberalism 94, 96; secular liberalism 124; *see also* ORDO-liberalism
Lijphart, A. 63
Lillestol, Egil 257
Lisbon Treaty (2009): Catholicism and evolution of EU 45–6; dialogue with churches, undertaking on 2, 273; institutionalisation and 185, 186, 188n18; Orthodoxy and EU 72, 79, 82, 83–4
Locke, John 36, 111, 154
Lossky, V. 78, 86n1
Loughlin, John xii, 1, 4, 26, 33–49, 62, 121, 269, 272
Luitwieler, Sander xii–xiii, 1, 4, 34, 50–69, 269, 272
Luke, Book of 143, 210
Luther, Martin 152, 155
Lutheranism 35–6, 54, 60, 76, 93, 95, 96, 152
Luyckx, Marc 179, 180

Maastricht Treaty (1992): Catholicism and evolution of EU 45; deficit criteria in 102; financial crisis, Christian

economic ethics and 211; legitimacy crisis for EU 114; representation of religion in EU 180, 181, 182; Schuman legacy 21
McCrea, R. 158–60, 162–5, 167–8, 168n5, 169n17, 169n22, 170n35, 170n36, 170n38, 170n41, 170n45, 170n50, 188n14, 273, 274
McIntyre, A. 7n4
Madeley, J.T.S. 1, 151, 188n14, 275n1
Madeley, J.T.S. and Sitter, N. 55, 60
Mahillon, Pierre 187n3
Mann, Thomas 38
Marc, Alexandre 38, 39
Maritain, Jacques 3, 38
marriage 137, 138
Marshall Plan 14
Martin, D. 187n1
Matthew, Book of 52, 210; Matthew 6.28–29 246n3
Mayer, René 33
Mazyek, Aiman 205
Merger Treaty of European Community (1966) 181
Merkel, Angela 204
Milbank, J. 7n4, 119
militant secularism, rise of 72–3
Mill, John Stuart 89
Millennium Development Goals (UN) 23
Millennium Ecosystem Assessment report (2005) 236
Milton, Guy xiii, 2, 6, 26, 45, 191–207, 272
minorities: Christianity and 272–5; religious freedom under ECtHR and 157–62, 164
Mit Brennende Sorge (Pius XI, 1937) 37–8
Mitrany, D. 112
'modernity': Catholic responses to 37; Schuman legacy for Europe 27
Modood, T. and Levey, G.B. 124
Monnet, Jean 13, 14, 28, 33
Montfort, Elizabeth 203
Moral Re-Armament (MRA) 54, 58
moral relativism 118
Morel, Jean-Claude 179
Moslem women's right to manifest 161–2
Mounier, Emmanuel 39, 40, 42
Mouw, R.J. and Griffoen, S. 62
Muller, J.-W. 139, 140
Müller-Armack, Alfred 94, 105, 105n6
multiculturalism 62, 67, 114, 123, 125

Nantes, Edict of (1598) 152–3
Napoleon Bonaparte 38
national identity: concern at loss of 19; divide on 269; place, citizenship and 134
National Socialism in Germany 37
Natura 2000, Portugal 7, 233, 242
Nehemiah, Book of 105n13
Nelsen, B.F. and Guth, J.L. 1, 50, 52, 53, 54, 188n12, 269, 275n2
Nelsen, B.F., Guth, J.L. and Fraser, C.R. 33, 41, 50, 61, 188n14
Nelsen, B.F., Guth, J.L. and Highsmith, B. 55, 60, 61
neo-functionalism 112–13
neoclassical economics 92
Netherlands and European integration 56–7
Nice Treaty (2001) 192
Nietzsche, Friedrich 38
Nobel Peace Prize 17
Noël, Émile 179
Nordic countries and European integration 60
North Atlantic Treaty 14–15, 16
nouvelle théologie 42, 43
Nouvelles Equipes Internationales (NEI) 54, 55, 58, 66
Novak, M. 96
Novosseloff, Alexandra 16
Nye J.S. 74

O'Donovan, O. 2, 131, 145n4, 145n6
O'Donovan, O. and O'Donovan, J.L. 2, 145
Open Access knowledge 137
Oppenheimer, J.R. 264n6
Optimal Currency Area (OCA) theory 217–18, 220, 221–2, 225, 227n3
Order of Malta 182
ORDO-liberalism (Freiburg School) 90, 91–2, 93, 94, 99, 102, 103, 105n3, 106n17
Ordre Nouveau 38–40
Orthodoxy and EU 1, 4–5, 70–86; Byzantine Orthodox Commonwealth 70–71; soft power potential of 74–5; Caesaro-papism 76; Chalcedonian Eastern Orthodoxy 71; dogma, commitment to unity of 70, 75–6; dogmatics-driven approaches 76–7; economic crisis and engagement of Orthodox churches 72; Europe and EU, Orthodox world and idea of 70–71; extra-territorial ecclesiastical

jurisdiction 71–2, 73; hierarchical institutionalism, decline in 79–80; human rights 73; institutional internationalization 77; international law and human rights, engagement with 79; levels and forms of engagement in EU context 81–6; militant secularism, rise of 72–3; natural law, questions of compliance with positive law 79; Orthodox approaches to EU, multiciplicity of 74; Orthodox diasporas 70; Orthodox engagement with EU, theological underpinning of 75–7; Orthodox Eucharistic theology, power of 78; Orthodox faith-based organisations (FBOs), coalitions with 85; political institutions, calibrated approach to 85–6; powers, symphony of 75, 77–81; pragmatism 76; priesthood of all believers 80; prospects for engagement, EU legal order and 77–81; regional and international institutions, engagement with 84; relativism, rise of 72–3; religious nationalism, Babylonian captivity of 77–8; Second Coming 76; *sobornost,* concept of 77–8; social doctrine 73; social engineering 76–7; sociality, concept of 77–8; spirituality, commitment to unity of 70, 75–6; states and Orthodox churches, relationship between 76; technology, development of 78–9; temporal powers, prayer for 75–6; tensions between Orthodox churches 73–4; theological perspective 76–7
Ostpolitik 42–3

Pabst, Adrian xiii, 5, 62, 109–28, 167, 268, 272
Pacelli, Eugenio 38
Pacem in Terris (John XXIII) 42
Paisley, Rev. Ian 33, 41
Pan-Europa (Coudenhove-Kalergi, R. von) 38
Pastoral Constitution on the Church in the Modern World (*Gaudium et Spes*) 42–3
Patijn, Connie L. 187n3
Paton, William 56
Patrão Neves, Maria do Céu 255, 264, 264n7
Patriarchates of Constantinople and Moscow 34–5, 72, 73–4, 86n2
Paul VI 42, 43, 44

Peace beyond Borders, European legacy of 16–17
Peace-Building Partnerships 17
Pentarchy of the Ancient Patriarchates 70–71
Pentecostal European Fellowship 183
People of God, roles of 80
personalism, philosophy of 38, 39–40
Petkoff, Peter xiii, 1, 4–5, 70–88, 269, 272
Philip, André 33, 187n3
Philpott, D. and Shah, T.S. 1, 52, 53
Pius IX 15, 37
Pius XI 37, 146n10, 194, 226n1; EU Constitution, religion and 194
Pius XII 33, 38, 40, 41, 42, 71
places: identification with 130; importance of 130–31; places to live 139–43
Planned Economy and Market Economy (Müller-Armack, A.) 94
Platz, Heinrich 14
Pleven, René 33
pluralism 26, 27, 109, 125, 156, 158, 161–2, 168, 272, 273–4, 275
Poland: Catholicism and nation in 37; Constitution of 197
Polanyi, Karl 109, 110, 111
political extremism 113–14
Pollock, D. 273
Popes, Europe and the world 38–40
Portugal: case study on nature legislation in 230, 241–4, 245–6; Ria de Alvor, Algarve 241–2, 244, 245; A Rocha in 241–2, 243–4, 246n11
Potočnik, J. 233, 235
Praesidium 200–201, 206n7
Prodi, Romano 180, 275n2
Programme of Action (European Commission, 1962) 100
Protestant Christian-Historical Union (CHU) 56–7
Protestant Reformation: emancipatory dynamics of 51–2; modern nation-state and 35–6; Reformation and Counter-Reformation 71
Protestant Reformed Political Party (SGP) 57
Protestantism and EU 1, 4, 50–66; Catholic universalism 53, 57; Christian pro-European movement 58–9; contemporary Protestant view on EU 61–5; cultural identity, expression of 51; cultural plurality 63; ecclesiastical structure 53–4; election, doctrine of 53; Europe as Christendom, notion of

Index 287

65–6; identity, European sense of 51; institutional change, Protestantism and 53–4; multiculturalism 62; ordinary life, affirmation of 51–2; political parties, emergence of 54; political parties, support for integration by 56; political parties, transnational agenda and 66; Protestant followers and European integration 60–61; Protestant rejection of universal empire 53–4; Protestantism and European identity 51–2; Protestantism and unity in Europe, ideas and institutions 52–5; public justice, notion of 62–5, 65–6; religion in shaping attitudes to EU, decline in 61; Roman Catholic perspectives, dominance of 51; societal plurality, types of 62–3; spiritual and temporal authority 53; state, civil society and market 62–3; structural plurality 62; transnational ecumenical channels 59–60; universality of the *invisible* church 52–3
Psalms, Book of (24.1) 246n3
Putnam R.D. 119

Quadragesimo Anno (Pius XI, 1931) 210

Ramadan, T. 188n17
Ratzinger, Josef 44, 45
Rawls, John 122, 152
Reflection Group on the Spiritual and Cultural Dimension of Europe 119–20
Reformed Political Federation (RPF) 57
Reformed Political Union (GPV) 57
Regulatory Fitness and Performance Programme (REFIT) 234, 237
religious freedom, place in EU 6, 151–70; accommodation entitlements 164; *The Bloudy Tenent of Persecution* (Williams, R.) 153; competence, religious freedom and 151; curtailments of freedom 161–2; divinely conferred universal right to freedom 156; Framework Directive (2000) 163–4; *Guidelines on the promotion and protection of freedom of religion or belief* (European Council, 2013) 165–6; historical perspective 152–4; human rights discourse 156–7; illiberal tendencies 160; indirect discrimination 158–9, 163; individual and institutional freedom, distinction between 158; *Letter Concerning Toleration* (Locke, J.) 154; "modus vivendi" on religious freedom 152–3; public secularism 159; religious devotion, symbols of 161; religious freedom, challenges on 166–8; religiously-fuelled wars 152–3; right to believe and right to manifest, distinction between 157, 160–61; secularism, pluralism oriented nature of 162; state neutrality towards religion 151; state-religion relationships, traditions of 158–9, 160–61; theological arguments for religious freedom 154–7; toleration, theories of 153–4
representation of religion in EU 6, 175–88; census of religious organisations 179; Conference of International Catholic Organizations 181; Consultative Committee of Churches for the European Communities 177, 187n4; Convention on the Future of Europe (2001) 180; diplomatic representations 181–2; Ecumenical Patriarchate 179, 182; European Committee for Catholic Education 178; European Communities (EC), churches' involvement with 175–6; European Evangelical Alliance 183; functional breakdown of representations 181–3; institutionalisation of religious relations 180; inter-church or convictional organisations/networks 182–3; International Co-operation for Development and Solidarity (CIDSE) 178; official representations of churches 182; Pentecostal European Fellowship 183; policy considerations on 'religion' and 'faith' 183–6; private-public nature of religion 178; religious and ethical issues, Delors' interest in 179, 184; religious dialogue with Commission, Luyckx's drive for 179–80, 184–5; religious dialogue with European institutions 175–80; religious orders 183; Roehampton Conference (1974) 178, 184; Schuman Declaration (1950) 175, 176; Second Vatican Council 181; single-issue organisations 183; Spirituality, Culture and Society in Europe (ESPACES) 183; transnational reflection groups 176
Rerum Novarum (Leo XIII, 1891) 37, 39, 42
research *see* science and research policy

Rey, Jean 177
Rich, Arthur 95
Rio Summit (1992) 234, 239
Robbers, G. 168n4, 188n14
Robert Schuman Foundation 15
Robert-Schuman.com 47n1
Rocha, A. 241–244, 246, 246n11, 246n12, 249
Rodenburg, P. and Zuidhof, P.W. 211, 212, 213
Roehampton Conference (1974) 178, 184
Roman Empire 34–5, 144; Romanised law 27
Romans, Book of 57, 156
Roncalli, Angelo 42
Röpke, Wilhelm 98, 106n17
Rose, A.K. 227n4
Roudometof, V. and Makrides, V. 72
Rousseau, Jean-Jacques 36, 111
Roy, Christian 38, 39, 40
Roy, O. 188n17
Rueff, Jacques 100
rule of law 3, 17, 18, 19, 20, 25, 83–3, 90, 118, 121, 122
Russian diaspora 71
Russian expansionism 16
Russian Orthodox Church (ROC) 72–3, 81–2, 84
Russian Revolution (1917) 73

Sajó, András 160
Salter, Noël 59
Sandel, M.J. 64
Scheler, Max 39
Schengen agreement 136
Scheuer, S. 232, 233, 237
Schiller, Karl 99
Schirrmacher, Thomas xiii, 6, 151–74
Schmoller, Gustav von 90
Schuman, Robert 4, 40, 41, 48n4, 50, 54, 192, 224, 253, 254; Christian statesman and father of Europe 14–15
Schuman Declaration (1950) 4, 6, 175, 176, 192, 253; EU Constitution, religion and 192; representation of religion in EU 175, 176; Schuman legacy 13, 15–16, 19, 23, 25; transcript of 28–30
Schuman legacy 1, 4, 13–30; Berlaymont Building, Brussels 13; Catholic Church, international reach of 26–7; Christian statesman and father of Europe, Schuman as 14–15; Christianity and European democracy 25–8; church presence and participation, state and 27–8; Common Agricultural Policy (CAP) 21; Common High Authority 20; Cotonou Agreement with the African, Caribbean, and Pacific (ACP) countries 23; Council of Europe 14–15; Cyprus, accession of 18; division of Europe, complex nature of 18; enlargement of EU 18–19; ever closer union, challenge of 19; forgiveness and reconciliation, Christian values of 13–14; free movement of labour 16; inequalities 22; International Centre for Reconciliation at Coventry Cathedral 17; Marshall Plan 14; 'modernity' in Europe 27; national identity, concern at loss of 19; North Atlantic Treaty 14–15, 16; rebuilding of Europe, dedication to 14; Robert Schuman Foundation 15; Schuman Declaration (1950) 13, 15–16, 19, 23, 25; content and significance of 15–25; sharing of sovereignty 19–20; solidarity with wider world 22–4; solidarity within Europe 20–22; sovereignty 20–22; state power, Church and 27; supranational organisation, nation state and 20; unity in Europe 17–19; war and dreams of freedom from 13–14; working with United Nations (UN) 24–5; World Peace 15–17
science and research policy 7, 251–65; Europe 2020 strategy 260–62; European values, Havel's speech to European Parliament on (2009) 251; Framework Programme for Research and Technological Development 261–2; holistic thinking, need for 260; human knowledge, interfaces of 260; knowledge-based economy 252–3; market-based politics, dominance of 252, 260–62; Renaissance for research 252; research, spiritual dimension in 260; research policy, vacuum of value in 251–2; research policy, value-driven beginnings 253–4; science, competence over pursuit and use of 259–60; scientific exploration, faith, spirituality and 260; Single European Act (SEA, 1986) 258–9, 260; Soul for Europe initiative (1994) 259; Treaty on European Union (TEU, 2009) 258; vacuum of values in European science 259–60; values and 'soul' in European mission 258–9; *see also* CERN; EURATOM

Scientology 159–60
Scruton, Roger 138, 140, 141, 142, 145, 146n13, 146n14
Second Vatican Council: Catholicism and evolution of EU 42–3; representation of religion in EU 181
secular humanism 272, 274
secular liberalism, crisis of 124
secular 'market-states' of Europe 109–10, 110–12
secularism 3–4; pluralism oriented nature of 162
secularization 1, 3; of European mind 36
Siedentop, Larry 3, 113, 274
Silvestri, S. 161, 166, 170n31, 188n17
Simonson, W.D. 243
Single European Act (1986): biodiversity and EU nature legislation 232; identity, place and EU citizens 135–6; representation of religion in EU 179, 181, 183; science and research policy 258–9, 260
Smith, Adam 89, 91, 95
social contract theory 110–11
social justice 43, 46, 85, 91, 94, 95, 96, 194
Social Market Economy (SME) *see* German Social Market Economy (SME)
sociality, concept of 77–8
societal plurality, types of 62–3
Society for Social Policy *(Verein für Socialpolitik)* 90
solidarity 22–4; Constitution, religion and 193; within Europe, Schuman legacy and 20–22; principle of 109, 112–13, 116, 118, 125–6, 210; value of 224–5
Soul for Europe initiative (1994) 259
sovereignty 19, 20–22, 35, 56–7, 123, 224; political sovereignty 110; pooling of 120, 126; sovereignty-driven legislation 73
Soviet Bloc 44–5; breakdown of relations with Russia 15
Spaak, Paul-Henri 33
Special Areas of Conservation (SACs) 233
Special Protection Areas (SPAs) 233
Speyer, Diet of (1526) 152
Spirituality, Culture and Society in Europe (ESPACES) 183
Spruyt, H. 35
Spurgeon, Charles 238

St. Ethelburga's Centre for Peace and Reconciliation in London 17
Stark, Jürgen 225
state, civil society and market 62–3
state and nation, creation of link between 36
state neutrality towards religion 151
state power, Church and 27
state-religion relationships, traditions of 158–9, 160–61
Stefani, Umberto 179
stewardship 231, 232, 238–9, 246
Structural and Cohesion policy 21
subsidiarity: appropriation of principle of 193–4; engagement with principle of 84–5; principle of: financial crisis, Christian economic ethics and 210–11, 225; German Social Market Economy (SME) 103; legitimacy crisis for EU 109, 112–13, 116, 118, 125–6
supranational institutions 120
supranational organisation, nation state and 20
Sustainable Development, 2012 UN Conference on (Rio+20) 237
Sustainable Development Strategy (2001) 234
Sweden: accession to EU 50; religiosity and EU in 61
Syllabus of Errors (Pius IX) 37

Tawney, R.H. 112
Taylor, Charles 37, 51, 113, 114, 124
Temple, William 58
Theodosius, Emperor 34
Thielicke, Helmut 95, 105n14
Thorn, Gaston 179
Thucydides 200
Tibi, B. 170n31, 188n17
Tiebout, Charles 106n23
Timmermans, Frans 180
Tocqueville, Alexis de 122
Toleration, Act of (1689) 153
toleration, theories of 153–4
Treaty Establishing a Constitution for Europe (2004) 199–200
Treaty of Rome (1957) 5; Catholicism and evolution of EU 33–4, 42; conflicts and compromises leading to 98–101; drafting of 191–2; original preamble to 204; representation of religion in EU 175; Schuman legacy 21, 22; technocratic text of 192

Treaty on European Union (TEU, 2009) 258
Trichet, Jean-Claude 116
Troeltsch, E. 169n12
Tsoukalas, Ioannis 256
Turkey 3; as candidate country 193; *Refah Partisi v. Turkey* (ECtHR, 2003) 167, 168n2

ultramontanism 37
unemployment: harm of persistence in 223–4; trends in, insights from 222–3
United States Declaration of Independence (1776) 191
unity in Europe 17–19, 52, 54, 56, 58, 66, 112, 115, 118
Universal Declaration of Human Rights (UN, 1948) 154, 157
universality of the *invisible* church 52–3

Van Dyke, F. 231, 239, 246n5
Vignon, Jérôme 179
Visser 't Hooft, Willem 56
Volksnation 131–2, 139
Vollaard, Hans 56, 57, 66n1
Voltaire 36
von Balthasar, Hans Urs 44
von Schnurbein, Katharin 180

Waldron, J. 3, 9, 155
Walz, Hans Hermann 175, 176
Walzer, M.L. 63
Ware, K.T. 80
Wars of Religion 36, 152–3
Weatherley-Singh, J., Branco, T. and Felgueiras, M. 7, 269, 271, 272
Weatherley-Singh, Janice xiv, 7, 230–50
Weigel, G. 45
Weiler, Joseph 275n10
Weninger, Michael 180, 188n13

Werner, Pierre 100
Werner Report (1969) 100
Wesley, John 238
Westphalia, Peace of (1648): Catholicism and evolution of EU 35; religious freedom, place in EU 153
White, L. 250
Wilberforce, William 238
Willaime, J.-P. 273, 275n8
William of Orange 56
Williams, A. 259, 263
Williams, Roger 153, 275n9
Williams, Rowan 1, 3, 7n6, 19, 26, 27, 122, 132, 143, 146n15
Wilton, Gary xiv, 1–10, 13–32, 33, 66, 121, 224, 253
Wilton Park 256, 260
Witte, J. 3, 168n8, 169n11, 169n19
Witte, J. and Alexander, F. 7n5, 7n6
Wojtyla, Karol Jozef (John Paul II) 44
Wolterstorff, N. 8n6, 156
Wood, John 257, 258, 262
World Council of Churches (WCC): biodiversity and EU nature legislation 239; Protestantism and EU 56, 58; representation of religion in EU 176–7, 182–3
World Peace, Schuman legacy and 15–17
World Summit on Sustainable Development (UN, 2002) 234–5
Worms, Edict of (1521) 152

Yannaras, Christos 78, 79, 85, 86n1, 86n9

Zagorin, P. 152, 153, 155, 156, 168n7, 169n11, 169n14, 169n19, 169n20
Zizioulas, J. 78, 86n9
Zucca, L. 160, 170n47, 268, 273, 275n10

CPSIA information can be obtained
at www.ICGtesting.com
Printed in the USA
LVHW080408151021
700456LV00002B/103